"Colón Man a Come"

Caribbean Studies

Series Editors
Shona N. Jackson, Stanford University, Program in Modern Thought & Literature, and Anton Allahar, University of Western Ontario

Editorial Board
Edna Acosta-Belen, SUNY–Albany; Holger Henke, CUNY; Brian Meeks, University of the West Indies; Velma Pollard, University of the West Indies; John Rickford, Stanford University; Sylvia Wynter, Stanford University

Lexington Books' Caribbean Studies Series is committed to publishing scholarship that either rethinks or imagines anew all aspects of Caribbean history, culture, politics, literature, and social organization. The Series will be interested in publishing studies and monographs that deal either with the Caribbean as a discrete geographical region or that treat the Caribbean and its diaspora collectively. Ever since it was brought into the orbit of Europe, the Caribbean has been defined by overlapping cultures of difference and similarity that are always in contest and conversation. This is the idea of creolization and syncretism that defines the Caribbean and its people, and that cannot be ignored in any attempt to understand the region and its diasporas. The Series' editors recognize the great insular and regional diversity that characterize the Caribbean and its diasporas and are most keen to highlight the multiplicity of theoretical and intellectual approaches needed to capture this most complex region, both historically and in contemporary times. To this extent they welcome manuscripts written from structuralist, poststructuralist, modernist, postmodernist, and even micro-interactionist perspectives. The latter speaks in part to the question of psychology. For while there are many macro studies of the Caribbean from historical, sociological, political, economic, and literary points of view, there is precious little that has been done on a "Caribbean psychology" or something that seeks to capture the essence of the "Caribbean mind or psyche." In all of this one thing remains clear: the Caribbean cannot be subsumed beneath the banner of any one school or perspective. Nor can it be studied (a) independently of each state's own cultural and political situation and contemporary relationship to international capital, or (b) without taking into account the interrelationships among other Caribbean states. In other words, the Series seeks to promote a cross-disciplinary appreciation of the Caribbean that is just as intellectually robust as the Caribbean itself.

Titles in the Series

"Colón Man a Come": Mythographies of Panamá Canal Migration
by Rhonda D. Frederick

Negotiating Caribbean Freedom: Peasants and the State in Development
by Michaeline A. Crichlow

"Colón Man a Come"

Mythographies of Panamá Canal Migration

Rhonda D. Frederick

LEXINGTON BOOKS
Lanham • Boulder • New York • Toronto • Oxford

LEXINGTON BOOKS

Published in the United States of America
by Lexington Books
An imprint of The Rowman & Littlefield Publishing Group, Inc.
4501 Forbes Boulevard, Suite 200, Lanham, Maryland 20706

PO Box 317
Oxford
OX2 9RU, UK

Copyright © 2005 by Lexington Books

All rights reserved. No part of this publication may be reproduced, stored in a retrieval system, or transmitted in any form or by any means, electronic, mechanical, photocopying, recording, or otherwise, without the prior permission of the publisher.

British Library Cataloguing in Publication Information Available

Library of Congress Cataloging-in-Publication Data

Frederick, Rhonda D., 1965–
  "Colón man a come" : mythographies of Panama Canal migration / Rhonda D. Frederick.
    p. cm. — (Caribbean studies)
  Includes bibliographical references and index.
  ISBN 0-7391-0889-1 (cloth : alk. paper) — ISBN 0-7391-0891-3 (pbk. : alk. paper)
  1. West Indian literature—20th century—History and criticism. 2. Alien labor in literature. 3. West Indians in literature. 4. Panama—In literature. 5. Alien labor, West Indian—Panama—History. 6. West Indians—Panama—History. 7. Aliens—Panama—History. 8. Panama Railroad Co.—History. 9. Panama Canal (Panama)—History. I. Title. II. Series: Caribbean studies (Lanham, Md.)

PN849.C3F75 2004
809'.9327287—dc22   2004018804

Printed in the United States of America

∞™ The paper used in this publication meets the minimum requirements of American National Standard for Information Sciences—Permanence of Paper for Printed Library Materials, ANSI/NISO Z39.48-1992.

Contents

Series Editor's Introduction   vii

Preface   ix

Acknowledgments   xxiii

Introduction   1

1   History/Histories/Stories: Narrating the Panamá Canal and Colón Men   19

2   "The Money Was Paid Small, but We Live Big": Epistolary Narratives of the Panamá Canal   59

3   "Colón Man a Come": Isthmian Migrants in *The Harder They Come* and *In the Castle of My Skin*   91

4   "With him watch chain/a knock him belly": Migration, Masculinity, and the Colón Man in *Banana Bottom*, "Window," and *Tropic Death*   125

5   Out of One, Many People: Disorderly Narrations and the Colón Man in Maryse Condé's *Tree of Life: A Novel of the Caribbean*   169

Conclusion: Panamá Woman a Come   197

Bibliography	215
Index	229
About the Author	237

Series Editor's Introduction

The first in the Caribbean Studies Series, Rhonda Frederick's *"Colón Man a Come": Mythographies of Panamá Canal Migration* is a highly imaginative work that uses literary and other theoretical models to think about the complex relationship between labor migration, history, and identity. Using work like Maryse Conde's *I, Tituba, Black Witch of Salem*, Audre Lorde's *Zami: A New Spelling of My Name*, and Joan Dayan's *Haiti, History, and the Gods* collectively as cross-disciplinary models for her own method, Frederick is able to read images of Colón Men in George Lamming's *In the Castle of My Skin*, Claude McKay's *Banana Bottom*, Olive Senior's "Window," Maryse Conde's *Tree of Life*, and Herbert de Lisser's *Susan Proudleigh*. Frederick reconciles the fictive narratives of Colón Men's lives with historical material in order to uncover a dimension of these "resistant realities" that are often obfuscated by traditional modes of analysis. In doing so, Frederick herself "re-creates" their stories, using creative and critical approaches that give us a new way of viewing both literature and history. In her reading of Lamming's character Pa in *Castle*, for example, Frederick reveals the way in which this character imbues the Canal Zone project with significance; the significance it has for his own life and what he has accomplished in it. She foregrounds the historical, intellectual, and cultural crosscurrents which inform the "layering" of Colón Men's experience, within and across time, allowing Lamming to depict what she refers to throughout the book as the imaginative and imaginable truths of these men's lives. Frederick is able to shed light on the kind of knowledge Colón Men like Pa bring to the Barbadian society of Lamming's novel and more broadly to Caribbean society and anticolonial discourse. Frederick does not read Lamming's or other work as simply fiction, but as key documents in the "mythography" of Panamá migration, something that performs both a narrative and historic function. Frederick argues that "mythographies" are needed to understand the complex motives of these migrants who traveled to the Canal Zone despite the imminent possibility of death. Like the stories she considers, Frederick's narrative emerges from the meeting of mythography and history, posing a crucial and critical resistance and literary intervention, in order to reveal the complex forces that shaped the lives of men whose actions have defied traditional modes of representation and articulation.

S. Jackson, coeditor

Preface

> That is all as it should be . . . truth is only to be had by laying together many varieties of error.
>
> —Virginia Woolf, *A Room of One's Own*[1]

I

A conversation I had with a historian friend started me on the path that has led to this book. This friend and I completed our dissertations at about the same time and were chatting about our processes. When we discussed the number of endnotes in our respective treatises (he had almost twice the number I had), he jokingly stated that number of notes I had was a direct reflection of the amount of research I conducted. At that time, I was uncertain about what he meant, but over the years I have come to a conclusion. I, after all, spent innumerable hours reading about Caribbean and Panamanian histories, labor histories, Caribbean migrations and masculinities, literature, and literary criticism (among other things). The only way that this work could not "count" as "research" would be because it deviated from *his* historical research methods. When I understood the reasoning behind my friend's comment (at least my take on his reasoning), I also understood that the "rumors" about the differences between literary and historical scholarship were in fact true.

Perhaps because I completed my degree in *Caribbean* literature, an emergent literature that—since its inception—embraced history,

"Postage stamp commemorating West Indian labor in the construction of the Panama Canal from 1904–1914." Courtesy of Photographs and Prints Division, Schomburg Center for Research in Black Culture, The New York Public Library, Astor, Lenox, and Tilden Foundations.

sociology, politics, and the imagination, it never occurred to me that these disciplines were rigidly bounded.[2] I maintained this position despite debates about what was then described as Caribbean History (capital "H" and/or singular) and histories (lowercase "h" and/or plural). Colonialism, oppression/victimization, and white/black binaries define the former and plural and oppositional definitions of "history" (oral, creative, "disorderly," etc.) define the latter. Colonial History thus locked Caribbean peoples into the roles of victimage and mimicry, while Caribbean histories recast colonialism, slavery, and indenture in the region as truths to be imaginatively refigured as more than sites of victimization. If I have been successful, *"Colón Man a Come": Mythographies of Panamá Canal Migration* will persuade readers, through its "migrations" between genres and disciplines, of the possibilities that accrue when history is creatively engaged.

Taking its cue from "imaginable truths" that informed Caribbean workers' migrations to the isthmus of Panamá, *"Colón Man a Come"* uses recurrent depictions of Caribbean isthmian workers to build on conclusions available in existing narratives about the construction of the United States' canal. Such truths reflect workers' readily *and* less-readily quantifiable historical, cultural, and individual migration experiences. To mark the contours of these imaginable truths, I sample several contemporaneous (late nineteenth and early twentieth century) and more recent canal histories, geographies of Colón Men from Barbados and Jamaica, Caribbean migration narratives, and letters written by former workers. Literary sources from the circum-Caribbean region are especially important, specifically novels, poems, and short stories by Louise Bennett, Maryse Condé, George Lamming, Claude McKay, Olive Senior, Michael Thelwell, and Eric Walrond. This sampling marks a disjunction between common historical renditions of this worker (alien, homogeneously "West Indian" or "black," poor, poorly trained, and exploited labor in contemporaneous histories; recuperated and locally situated in recent historical narratives) and fictive ones (Pan-Caribbean, steadfast and committed workers, affluent, ancestral figures, lovers, exemplary models of manhood, and more or less willing participants in modern capitalist projects). The "mythographies" that result from this genre/disciplinary migration speak directly to central features of the "quarrel with history," namely the refiguring work achieved by "migrations" between consciousness and ego, as Wilson Harris describes, and physical and disciplinary migrations that Gayatri Spivak explores.

"Colón Man a Come" resists the "either/or" binary that often attends this debate, a binary that poses historical *or* imaginative analysis as the most constructive means of "destroying Euro-Caribbean hegemony through the delegitimating of their colonial projects."[3] Instead, by exploring creative representations of Caribbean Panamá Canal workers, I re-place (because

"fictions" were always present and vital to migrants' migration decisions) and then demonstrate the interpretative value of creative imaginings of isthmian migration.[4] What *"Colón Man a Come"* does not do is offer an "imaginative" history of Panamá Canal migrations or "correct" historical narratives about this movement. To do so would both devalue the truths revealed in the various construction histories as well as consign creative depictions of this important migration into a wholly supplementary role. A complementary relationship between disciplines and their findings—or a layering of Virginia Woolf's "errors"—best represents "truths" about the Caribbean's Panamá migration.

II

Many acknowledge that the problem of theorizing Caribbean colonial histories might be addressed through the region's multi- and interdisciplinary cultural and intellectual traditions. Yet when scholars attempt to draw on such traditions, the difficulty in using these cultural and intellectual "tools" immediately becomes clear. The methodological problem that ensues hinders the intellectual projects such scholars undertake. Paget Henry, for example, states: "We find a tradition of [Caribbean] philosophy so indelibly marked by forces of an imperial history, and by its intertextual relations with neighboring discourses, that it is necessary to begin with a general characterization of philosophy that is more appropriate to its pattern of development" (Henry 1). He also recognizes that, "there is a consistently significant philosophical substratum to be found in the works of physicists, sociologists, biologists, creative writers, and other knowledge producers" (3) and that Caribbean philosophy is a cultural and an art form (8). Henry positions Wilson Harris and Sylvia Wynter within the poeticist school of Caribbean philosophy, both of whom are disciplinary *and* genre bordercrossers because they "philosophize" in fiction, nonfiction, literature, history, and philosophy. Nevertheless, I do not find the interdisciplinarity/ intergenre movements that Henry recognizes evident in his analysis of the poeticist tradition, at least not in his discussion of Harris's oeuvre.

Instead of making use of Caribbean philosophy's existing "disciplinarities," Henry comments that, "the tendency [among Caribbean philosophers] has been toward particularization and fragmentation within [poeticist and historicist] schools" (6). I would argue that *Caliban's Reason* is subject to this critique with regard to Henry's use of the imaginative *and* critical works that are central to Wilson Harris's thinking. To support his interpretation of Harris's poeticism, Henry only *makes reference to* Harris's creative/literary works to clarify arguments made in Harris's nonfictional/philosophical ones, and then only briefly (one in-chapter reference to *Palace of the Peacock* and two of thirty-six endnote references to one page of *The Guyana Quartet*). Henry, therefore, establishes disciplinary and genre boundaries that he is at pains to deconstruct. More efficient use of Harris's literature would, I believe, better articulate the diversity of themes and influences in Caribbean philosophy. Henry's inability to capitalize on the *body* of Harris's work might result from Caribbean philosophy's inefficient creolization (it is "the least creolized of [Afro-Caribbean cultural forms]") and its orientation toward "its European heritage and underidentified with its African inheritance" (8). Still, I would argue that Henry's emphasis on nonfictional sources is a most pressing problem, one that explains the absence of women among the region's philosophers. Broader consideration of Caribbean literature—in which a "consistent philosophical substratum" is found—would certainly swell the ranks of female philosophers beyond Sylvia Wynter.

To return to an earlier point, this difficulty might lie in how *critics* use the imaginative arts, for Henry cites several *writers* who "with varying degrees of success have been able to forge some measure of unity between these historicist and poeticist traditions that have been so basic to thought in the region" (113). "[C. L. R.] James, [Frantz] Fanon, Aime Cesaire, Edward Kamau Brathwaite, George Lamming, Orlando Patterson, Rex Nettleford, and V. S. Naipaul" are the writers who have been able to bridge the poeticist/historicist philosophical divide (ibid).[5] Henry describes these men as "writers" (where I would describe them [with a caveat about Fanon] as "creative writers"), a move that affirms his characterization of Caribbean philosophy as both "cultural" and "art" forms. I believe Henry's terminology is import here because, methodologically speaking, his critical underuse of literature suggests a disciplinary and genre separation belied by his depiction of Caribbean philosophy.

In that Henry's "writers" achieve what Henry-as-critic does not, there must be "something" in the creative process that facilitates the border crossings that Henry describes. It is true that the histories of Indian and African descended Caribbean people were disrupted by indenture and slavery. It might also be argued that Europeans in the region were likewise and increasingly removed from their ancient histories. But if migration into the region (existing along a voluntary/involuntary continuum) demands a shift in historical consciousness, a concomitant shift in historical method—at least at the level of the individual—must also occur. Caribbean people of different races and ethnicities live "history" in ways that critically engage and redefine the term; creative writers have been relatively successful in putting this process into words. Thus, critics can similarly devise methodologies that evolve from these lived realities. By starting with Colón Men's creative representations, informed as they are by workers' imaginable truths, this book attempts to enact this practice.

Derek Walcott's thoughts on the creative appropriation of history support this critical movement, for he claims:

> the truly tough aesthetic of the New World neither explains nor forgives history. It refuses to recognize it as a creative or culpable force. This shame and awe of history possess poets of the Third World who think of language as enslavement and who, in a rage for identity, respect only incoherence or nostalgia. . . . The great poets of the New World . . . reject this sense of history. Their vision of man in the New World is Adamic.[6]

Walcott argues that being a victim of history—that is, succumbing to its events, definitions, and traditions—is "uncreative." The "truly tough aesthetic" demands that New World writers skillfully deploy history. For such people, Walcott continues, "history is fiction, subject to a fitful muse, memory. Their philosophy, based on a contempt for historic time, is revolutionary, for what they repeat to the New World is its simultaneity with the Old" (111). If old and new worlds exist simultaneously, the duration or uninterrupted aspect of a history cannot be a controlling factor in defining the "worth" of a country or its inhabitants. The Old World has its stories to tell, as does the New, and they must do so by acknowledging each other (since they exist simultaneously). I do not see this kind of acknowledgement as the work of a sycophant; instead, Walcott casts it as a step in the process of creatively remaking the future. However, where Walcott proposes that a Caribbean or New World historical aesthetic be "Adamic" (a reproduction of Adam's prelapsarian role in Eden, as the patriarch given the power to name), I believe there are models that migrate among and between multiple influences rather than ones like Walcott's that chart only the affect of the namer (Adam) on the named (New World).

Walcott shares his critique of a limiting notion of history with Wilson Harris, yet the latter proposes an imaginative way to negotiate the dissonance created by the conflict between Caribbean peoples' lived and learned histories. In posing as objective truth, learned histories mask their biases and, importantly, efface other kinds of meaningful realities. This kind of history eschews undercurrents that, according to Harris, characterize the Caribbean experience. He clarifies this position in *History, Fable, and Myth in the Caribbean and Guianas* where he critiques a "comedy of manners" history. Using James Anthony Froude (the author of *The English in the West Indies* [1888]) as an example, Harris claims that Froude suffers from "historical stasis" characterized by a "distrust of change since . . . everything was so dicey, so fortuitously consolidated that change . . . was likely to rob [English West Indian society] of any conservative historical shape it already possessed" (Harris 1995: 15). Arguing for Jamaica's continued dependence on England, and responding to the fear of unchecked African "savagery" exemplified by the Haitian Revolution, Froude's history is rife with descriptions of Afro-Jamaicans' backwardness (if not savagery) and Anglo-Jamaicans' political naïveté. Yet Froude, according to Harris, invokes "the mantle of history" to mask these concerns. *The English in the West Indies* purports to be a historical examination of Jamaica; instead, Harris interprets it as a tract designed for an English audience and to solidify specifically English colonial authority in the region.

Harris too finds that anticolonial challenges to Froude's kind of history, evinced by J. J. Thomas's *Froudacity* (1889), continue within the frame set by the 1888 text. C. L. R. James, writing in his 1969 introduction to *Froudacity*, celebrates Thomas's promulgation of history as a "controlling LAW" against Froude's (mis)use of history to defend property and privilege. However, Harris equates Thomas and Froude's methods, finding that both fall into the trap of history-as-stasis. Harris continues:

> it is my view . . . that Thomas does not really overwhelm Froude. The duel which they fought is nevertheless a very instructive one in pointing up the historical stasis which afflicts the West Indian sensibility and which may only be breached in complex creative perspectives for which the historical convention would appear to possess no criteria. (Harris 1995: 17)

In other words, Thomas merely exchanges Froude's ideological leanings with his own.[7] Harris argues that other tools—more complex and creative ones—are necessary, an assertion that, at the time (Harris delivered this lecture in February 1970), seemed particularly contentious.

I want to make use of Henry's *Palace of the Peacock* example to highlight how Harris's philosophy informs my thinking. Harris argues that the "arts of the imagination," one of the ways that "consciousness" becomes visible, realigns a Caribbean ego that is too deeply steeped in processes that result in history-as-stasis.[8] In the end, this inauthentic ego resituates itself by willfully acknowledging its complementary relationship to consciousness, and thus different ways of seeing occur. As Henry documents, "in Harris's fiction, inauthentic characters are constantly having intrusive experiences in which they see the world from the perspective of the universal consciousness" (100). This idea can be seen through the narrator in Harris's novel, *Palace of the Peacock*. A vision allows the narrator to see the world differently, through "an eye" he only shares with what he describes as "the soul" or "mother of the universe" (ibid). The "eye" allows the narrator to see trees move and wave their "arms," sight that re-places the man the narrator once was in a way that would have been impossible without his soul-eye. Rather than fear and thus hide from this novel vision, the narrator tremblingly embraces it, overcoming his impulse to protect against consciousness. This response marks *Palace's* narrator as authentic, one who must "clearly recognize that its tendencies to flee or withdraw from consciousness are misguided and inappropriate responses. Much more appropriate would be the building of a relationship of trust. In this relationship, the ego must learn to live in the void 'with hope'" (Henry 102).

Harris's fiction thus portrays an embrace of "another," imaginable vision, a different way of seeing that leads to a different way of being in the world. Fear, for Harris, rather than a disabling or consolidating emotion, is a creative and transformative one. The fear of change that he interprets in Froude's history, and by extension in Thomas's, reifies and extends colonial offenses well into the postcolonial moment. But imagination affects the kind of change that transforms peoples locked within colonial legacies. Harris's interpretation of the imagination explains why Caribbean men and women continued to migrate to Panamá when word of the dangers to be found in the Canal Zone permeated the region. The financial draw of canal work does not provide sufficient explanation because it neglects migrants' "internal migrations," their personal negotiation of communal/class, cultural, and familial realities. Where Harris might value these negotiations over migrants' compromises with their external world, the conversations between the two reveal much more than either can do alone. The complexity that results from physical and metaphorical migrations, for me, revives details that have fallen out of existing canal narratives. Put to critical use, retrieved stories can have extra-literary value.

III

If "literature is not an occasion for discourse among critics but is necessary nourishment for [the writer's] people and one way by which [these people] come to understand their lives better," then the task of better representing Caribbeanness has important and practical implications.[9] Speaking explicitly about the Caribbean, Edouard Glissant furthers Christian's assertion, arguing that Caribbean intellectuals are:

> capable of carrying forward [their] people to self-renewal and of providing them with renewed ambition, by making them possess their world and their lived experience (wherein a Caribbean identity is present) and by making them fall into step with those who also share the same space.[10]

Caribbean writers/intellectuals incorporate the region's imaginable truths into texts that proclaim a broader experience, one more able to initiate radical shifts in thinking. These scholars communicate an intricate view of their communities and reflect that view back onto its source. In seeing themselves represented in the full potential of their dreams and capabilities, individuals might experience a transformation of consciousness, toward Caribbeanness and away from a learned history of dependence.

In "Caribbean Man in Space and Time," Kamau Brathwaite observes that the field of Caribbean Studies lacks scholarly methods that can comprehend histories whose traces resist traditional historical perspectives.[11] To reveal and articulate these kinds of narratives, he argues, one would need interpretive methods derived from a number of disciplines; he specifically cites the fields of the creative arts, history, social science, sociolinguistics, ethnomusicology, and religion (Brathwaite 1975: 9). The resulting interdisciplinary approach can register narratives that have become obscure over time and reintroduce complexity into examinations of Caribbeanness. Paget Henry's study of Caribbean philosophies offers a recent example of the scholarly move in this direction. The utility of critical transformations of this kind is equally relevant to social, economic, and political transformations of the kind examined by comparativists in global literatures.

Overlapping concerns put Wilson Harris and Gayatri Chakravorty Spivak in conversation. Both invoke "an imaginative making" (Spivak 31) as a means through which one might "go from our high serious certainties when we undertake the imaginative task of moving out of ourselves" (109–10n5). I find Spivak most useful here for what she advocates is an intellectual migration enabled, in large part, by global migrations (Spivak 1–9). Where Harris draws on internal migrations (between consciousness and ego) to theorize a renewed Caribbean subject, Spivak deploys metaphorical and physical migrations to transform the discipline of Comparative Literature. The effect of their projects approaches a similar end. Spivak uses the term "teleopoeisis" to describe not only the process through which the creative arts (specifically literature) can affect disciplinary change, but also change on the level of individual teachers and students (future comparativists). Teleopoeisis might offer "protection from self-destructive competition" among national literatures through acknowledgement of "a definitive future anteriority, a 'to come'-ness, a 'will have happened' quality" (6). In other words, Spivak suggests that attention to the future (unhinging the desire to know—definitively—in the present) can be a disciplinary/individual goal in itself. She holds that Comparative Literature, its teachers, and students strive "to affect the distant in a *poeisis*—an imaginative making—without guarantees" (31). For individuals, this requires "imagining yourself, really letting yourself be imagined (experience that impossibility) without guarantees, by and in another culture, perhaps. Teleopoeisis" (52). "Real interdisciplinarity" brings about the disciplinary equivalent to this personal, intellectual migration.

To counter what she sees as a move in Comparative Literature to consolidate itself against the growth and influence of Ethnic and Cultural Studies, as well as the deliberate "bypassing" of "the literary and the linguistic" (4) in current reevaluations of Area Studies, Spivak proposes a real interdisciplinarity (7), one defined by the appropriate union of the best of multiple disciplines—and genres. The strength of Comparative Literature is its "care for language and idiom" (5); Area Studies can contribute its "built-in, restricted, but real interdisciplinarity" (7). Such a merger could potentially:

> go beyond this acknowledgment and this competition. It would work to make the traditional linguistic sophistication of Comparative Literature supplement Area Studies (and History, Anthropology, Political Theory, and Sociology) by approaching the language of the other not only as a "field" language.... We must take the languages of the Southern Hemisphere as active cultural media rather than as objects of cultural study by the sanctioned ignorance of the metropolitan migrant. (9)

Spivak's belief in the need for individual and disciplinary migrations matches what she describes as changing global movements and relations. Yet what is imperfectly represented by globalization's superficial contacts ("virtual" ones enabled by the internet and visual medias) can be more richly achieved through the interdisciplinary opening up of global literatures.

Spivak provides a wonderful explication of these ideas through her analysis of Maryse Condé's novel *Heremakhonon*. Reading the original French version against the later English version, and interpreting both through an Area Studies frame, Spivak exposes several erasures revealed in a conversation between the novel's protagonist (Veronica Mercier) and an unnamed West African woman. When the woman lists "Toucouleur" among Fulani and other African language groups, Veronica misses the implications of Fulani and Toucouleur appearing together. "Nineteenth century French ethnographers" divided the Fulbe people into two groups: peuls (non-Muslim pastoralists) and toucouleur (Muslim agriculturalists); "English travelers to the Sokoto Palisades (in present day Nigeria) adopted the Hausa word for the Fulbe there—Fulani." Perhaps it goes without saying that these peoples referred to themselves differently, as "Haalpulaar'en (singular Haalpulaar, speaker of pulaar)" (Spivak 18). "The New Comparative Literature," unlike the "old-fashioned" one:

> makes visible the import of the translator's choice. In the translation from *French* to *English* lies the disappeared history of distinctions in another space—made by the French and withdrawn by the English—full of the movement of languages and peoples still in historical sedimentation at the bottom, waiting for the real virtuality of our imagination. (18)

Spivak's interpretation of Condé's English *and* French texts, read through a West African regional history and geography, foregrounds these erasures. Spivak's use of *Heremakhonon* also implicates Condé's black, Guadeloupean protagonist in this factual glossing, a move that Spivak does not explore but that I find provocative. Spivak's reading of Condé's novel locates it squarely within intellectual debates among Caribbeanists that occur in several nonfictional genres, as Henry's *Caliban's Reason* affirms, but additionally within literary texts that straddle Anglo- and Francophone colonial traditions. Maryse Condé's literature is in direct dialogue with the works of prominent Francophone Caribbean writers;[12] Spivak's reading of *Heremakhonon's* translations represents an unexpected invocation of this dialogue that results in complexities that Condé may not have imagined. The conflicts resulting from Veronica Mercier's physical return to the African motherland challenge Négritude's simplistic diasporic consciousness; the protagonist's many lovers challenge the desexualized role to which Caribbean women have been consigned. Spivak's analysis reveals that Mercier's narcissism (she's flattered that the unnamed woman finds her beautiful) mirrors that of colonial authorities who rename with abandon, and scholars who ignore genre and disciplinary truths with impunity.

Neither Spivak nor Harris, I believe, advocates the idea that imagination exists as "a blueprint to be followed in unmediated social action" (Spivak 23). Instead, it can be the means through which a revolutionary kind of learning can occur; the possibilities that can result from this learning are what I believe each finds suggestive. Spivak describes this process as the "training of the imagination" (12), that is, training it not to transcode (as with metaphor), but rather to draw a response (13). To put it another way, a "trained" imagination can be open to another cultural reality without folding it into an established way of knowing. Thus literature:

> may give us entry to the performativity of cultures as instantiated in narrative. Here we stand outside, but not as anthropologist; we stand rather as reader with imagination ready for the effort of othering, however imperfectly, as an end in itself. (13)

The state of mind that the imagination fosters is best realized when complemented by the work of other disciplines. Such a broadened perspective can also been seen as triggering revelations that run across a variety of fields. Reading through the disciplinary "errors" that surround a particular topic, such as the "Africa" revealed in Spivak's critique of Condé's novel, exposes truths that escape the bounds of the creative text. This process can also reach back into the past to foreground realities that have become obscured over time.

IV

Because some aspects of isthmian migration remain elusive, and existing methodologies have not thus far made them known, interpretive strategies based on imaginable truths are useful. Panamá Canal mythographies respond to the call for more productive critical and socially engaged methods. The meanings and methods of historical and fictive isthmian narratives target a historically denigrated group, namely the African-descended Caribbean workforce, bringing its narratives into conversation with histories in which it has been ignored or misrepresented. Drawing on vernacular histories and stories, and putting them in conversation with contemporaneous canal narratives, mythographies worry the boundary between "fact" and "fiction." Imaginable possibilities proceed from these transgressions.

RDF
New England
Summer 2004

NOTES

1. As quoted in Gayatri Chakravorty Spivak, *Death of a Discipline* (New York: Columbia University Press, 2003): 42.
2. Creative disruption of colonial histories has long been a concern in Caribbean literature. In the novel *Abeng* (Trumansburg, NY: Crossing Press, 1984), for example, Michelle Cliff writes of the Jamaican town of Runaway Bay where, months before the official end to slavery, a slave owner burns one hundred enslaved people alive. Cliff's narrator says:

> the bones of dead slaves made the land at Runaway Bay rich and green. Tall royal palms lined the avenue leading to the houses of the development. Breadfruit trees, branches fat with their deep green lobed leaves, created shade around the stucco bungalows. The breeze from the sea came through the windows of the houses and made the walls taste of salt. (Cliff 1984: 40)

Cliff's narrator attributes the landscape's fertility to the bodies of formerly enslaved people and thus aggressively brings to the fore the simultaneity of the past (Jamaica's brutal history of slavery) and the present (the current fertility of the landscape) in order to affirm Afro-Jamaicans' stake in the country. The author fictionally reintroduces links between this population and the land, remembering their heritage of enslavement, a history effaced in a colonial system of education and forgotten by those convinced of their racial inferiority. Cliff's history differs from and, significantly, adds to accounts of Jamaican slavery that dehumanize enslaved *people* by transforming them into their circumstances, remaking them into *slaves* and *victims*. *Abeng*'s story recalls another story; these enslaved people's contribution to the land's bounty, indistinguishable from the tortures they lived (and that some survived), cannot be denied. The visceral response to Cliff's "story" goes beyond the mere reestablishment of an Afro-Jamaican relationship to the land; she palpably represents the experience for all Jamaicans by making the bodies of enslaved people, hence their reality, accessible through the landscape's lushness. At the same time, this alternative vision denies the slave owner's complete authority: his human sacrifice to "the way things should be" cannot erase the continued "presence" of these Jamaicans. What might at first seem to be another rendition of Afro-Jamaican brutalization at the hands of whites has been recast as the recognition of enslaved peoples' sacrifice and an insistence on the present it bought. Cliff revalues the Jamaican self—that is, she challenges the "self-lessness" prescribed by colonial discourse and assumed by the presently unaware—by drawing on a vernacular story. Her creative process undercuts the authority of the official record.

3. Paget Henry, *Caliban's Reason: Introducing Afro-Caribbean Philosophy* (New York: Routledge, 2000): 3.

4. Bonham Richardson's study of migrations of people from St. Kitts and Nevis implicitly speaks to the role of the imagination:

> since successfully coping with the many hazards facing extraisland migrants requires them to display a variety of talents and to overcome formidable obstacles, returning men are understandably proud of their achievements. "So when men gather together in rum shops or beneath the palm trees on the beach much of their conversation is taken up with stories of their exploits—mostly those that occurred abroad."

Caribbean Migrants: Environment and Human Survival on St. Kitts and Nevis (Knoxville: University of Tennessee Press, 1983): 25.

5. Although he does not discuss why Fanon appears among this list of creative writers, Henry describes the psychiatrist's "overall philosophy" as "multidimensional, interdiscursively embedded and indelibly marked by the peripheral dynamics of Caribbean cultural systems" (89). This description jibes with the cross-disciplinarity practiced by the above-mentioned creative writers.

6. Derek Walcott, "The Muse of History," *Carifesta Forum: An Anthology of Twenty Caribbean Voices*, edited by John Hearne (Kingston: Institute of Jamaica/ *Jamaica Journal*, 1976): 112.

7. Faith Smith makes a compelling argument that Harris's critique does not consider the social and cultural forces that inform Thomas's text, considerations of which Thomas was certainly aware. As a financially insecure, self-schooled child of formerly enslaved parents, Thomas's survival depended upon the "generosity" of local white and brown elites. Faith Smith, *Creole Recitations: John Jacob Thomas and Colonial Formations in the Late 19th Century Caribbean* (Charlottesville: University of Virginia Press, 2002).

8. I cannot efficiently summarize Harris's thinking through his creative works here, so I offer the following summary derived from two of his lectures as well as Paget Henry's critique of them. Some might say that this convicts me of undertheorizing Harris's fiction, the same charge I make against Henry, but I hope that the manuscript addresses this critique.

Harris suggests that history must be informed by "the authentic," a state represented by "the founding capabilities of consciousness" (Henry 95). In Harris's thinking, "consciousness" is "a universal dimension that embraces all existence, but remains an absent or unconscious presence for most [human and natural] life forms." He argues that, "there can be no final or total grasping of [it]" (ibid) but its traces can be seen in "dreams, visions, visits from one's fictional characters, states of possession, or moments of ego collapse" (100). Harris gives this definition decidedly local tones when he states, "the native and phenomenal environment of the West Indies is broken into many stages in the way in which one surveys an existing river in its present bed while plotting at the same time ancient and abandoned, indeterminate courses the river once followed" (Harris 1973: 30; see also Henry 100). Understanding the region's past requires an interpretation of the "now," the present riverbed (or the Caribbean ego), in relation to consciousness or the river's ancient and indeterminate courses. Harris's geographically oriented method involves reconstruction and negotiation, the "plotting [of] ancient and abandoned, indeterminate courses the river once followed" while "[surveying] an existing" course. He can only mark the present riverway *as* present because it was once somewhere else; meaningfully, where that "somewhere else" was may not be factual—documentable—but merely imaginable. Because Harris's consciousness disturbs most familiar forms of the "now," and thus produces unexpectedly creative responses to "real" problems, he "is uncomfortable with [historicist] discourses that recognize only the passive shaping of consciousness by material forces" (Henry 100).

9. Barbara Christian, "The Race for Theory," *Culture Critique* 6 (Spring 1987): 53.

10. Edouard Glissant, *Caribbean Discourse: Selected Essays*, translated by J. Michael Dash (Charlottesville: University of Virginia Press, 1989): 223–24.

11. Edward Kamau Brathwaite, "Caribbean Man in Space and Time," *Savacou* 11/12 (September 1975): 9. Wilson Harris concurs with Brathwaite on the need for alternative historical methods for the study of the Caribbean. Rather than one that consolidates into stasis, Harris argues for the possibility for another kind, one that can apprehend "a figurative meaning beyond an apparently real world or prison of history" (Harris 1995: 18). Harris finds such possibility in the Caribbean's "arts of the imagination" (he references limbo and Haitian *vodun*) that carry the weight of Caribbean realities and, therefore, histories. What makes Harris's arts paradigmatic, however, are their emergences out of, and continued evolution from, uniquely New World experiences (ibid).

12. Chapter 5 contains a detailed examination of Condé's conversation with Francophone Caribbean writers.

Acknowledgments

The list of folks to thank is long and my skill at adequately expressing my gratitude is short. As a consequence, what follows can only be an approximation of my heartfelt appreciation. I hope I'll soon have the opportunity to express myself better.

Robert Carley, my Lexington Books editor, I meant it when I said that my mother is the only person more excited about this book than you. Your encouragement and support came at a time when I was most uncertain. You renewed my passion for this manuscript and for this I am in your debt. I believe I also have you to thank for my wonderful readers. Without their insights and powerfully decisive comments, this book would not be what it is.

Perhaps because I started these acknowledgements at the end, with those who helped to bring the finished manuscript into the world, I should now turn to the people instrumental in its inception. Jim English, Professor of English at the University of Pennsylvania, chaired my dissertation committee and took what I thought was a good idea to places I could not have imagined. Jim, your careful reading and pointed questions terrified me, but forced me rise to the challenge. If I could go through the process again, with all its twists and drama, I'd pick you to captain the ship. To Herman Beavers and Farah Jasmine Griffin, and especially Sandra Pouchet Paquet who kept me on when she moved on, it was joyous working with each of you. A week rarely goes by when I don't give thanks to the "dissertation gods" for bringing us together.

The next stage of my intellectual development began in 1998 when I joined the English faculty at Boston College. Since then, several people were directly or tangentially involved in bringing this project to fruition. Professors Robin Lydenberg, Andy Von Hendy, and Chris Wilson read drafts of the manuscript well before I could legitimately call it one. Robin, Andy, and Chris, you've seen me at my scholarly "worst" and continued to greet me in the hallways; I could not ask for better. Professors Mary Crane, Alan Richardson, Amy Boesky, and Carlo Rotella read drafts (upon drafts) of individual chapters as well as the book proposal. Each of you taught me some aspect the (alien) genres of "Introduction" and "proposal" writing. Before I began, I had no idea that such beasts would be so hard to master, but each of you gave willingly of your time and attention, teaching me what I needed to know to reign them in. Associate Vice President for Research Mick Smyer and Arts and Sciences Dean Joe Quinn approved the funds that allowed me to devote my mental energies to this book. Dean Smyer, thank you especially for supporting me at the final hour. I must extend a special thanks to my senior colleague, Professor Henry Blackwell, for his unceasing moral support and guidance. Thank you, Henry, sincerely. The long departed Patrice Scott, the recently departed Melissa Coté, and the present and accounted for Jackie Skolnik, Judy Plank, and Dee Speros always gave me administrative and moral support. To you goddesses all blessings are due!

Without taking away from the above mentioned people, I have to say—without one bit of hyperbole—that the Schomburg Center for Research in Black Culture Scholars-in-Residence/NEH Program (2001–2002), and the individual scholars, informed every line and idea in this book. Directors Miriam Jimenez-Roman and Colin Palmer, SIRs Kim Butler, Lisa Gail Collins, Chouki El Hamel, Michelle Mitchell, Thomas Reinhardt, Jeffrey O. G. Ogbar, Samuel Kelton Roberts, Jeffrey Sammons, and Barbara Dianne Savage, each one of you helped my poor literary self develop into a historian-at-large (I'm still not "grown" enough to be a full fledged "historian"!). The staff of the Schomburg Center's Rare Books and Manuscripts, Main Reading Room, and Photographs and Prints Divisions made researching a pleasure. I am especially pleased to thank Mary Yearwood (Director, Photographs and Prints Division) for guiding me through the George W. Westerman photographic collection, and Janice Quinter (curator) for sharing the Westerman papers with me before anyone had access. Two people at the Schomburg stand out even among these stellar individuals: Shobana Shankar, who helped me because she wanted to, and Peter Hobbs, whose research and humor is most evident in chapter 2. Peter, my friend, you still amaze me; *buena suerte*.

I used several collections over the years, housed in libraries from Boston to Barbados. Boston College's Burns Library, particularly the

Nicholas M. Williams/Caribbeana Collection; the library of the Afro-Antillian Museum (Panamá City, Panamá); the West Indies Collection and the Elsa Goveia Reading Room staff (especially Mrs. Vanciana) at the University of the West Indies, Mona (Jamaica); and the West Indies Collection, University of the West Indies, Cave Hill (Barbados), provided me with materials that shocked and delighted me.

To my friends, sister Caribbeanists, and collaborators who kept me afloat through the writing, revising, and securing-a-publisher processes, each of you are my strength and my blessing. Rhonda Y. Williams (Case Western Reserve University), you gave my first and second chapters the "Rhonda treatment" and I could not be more grateful. A friend like you is rare, but an editor/critic like you is priceless! Thanks for your time and care. Patricia J. Saunders (University of Miami), you continually teach me what it means to be "incommunity." All good things in the preface I attribute to your diligence. I love ya like cooked food! Michelle Rowley (University of Cincinnati), you taught me much of what I needed to know about Caribbean masculinities. You've also given me a model for the "grown lady" scholar I look forward to being . . . one day . . . soon . . . if I'm lucky. Giselle Liza Anatol (University of Kansas), how many times did I read my convoluted sentences to you over the phone? How many times did you help me out? Innumerable and always. We grew into Caribbeanists together and I know I am much better for it. Winnifred Brown-Glaude (Rutgers University), you had this uncanny knack for writing me just when I was about to give up the ghost. Your faith in me and your encouraging words were most useful when I was least productive; I couldn't have gotten through the final draft without you! And, Faith Smith (Brandeis University), I leave you for last because I owe you my best thanks. No matter how busy you were, you gave me a bit of your precious time. For this I am particularly grateful. *Abrazos* to you all!

I learned, through this process, that support comes in myriad forms. My friend Darquetta Dennis, you made me feel like I was an intellectual when I was feeling most unscholarly. Ian Strachan, your recent life-experiences taught me to value what's really important. Kali Gross, for me you can do no wrong. You tackle the things you care about with a conviction that makes me know many things are possible. Julie Crawford and Liza Yukins, you two live the life that I want to lead when I grow up (i.e., after this book is out of my hands!). This truth has spurred me on; thanks grown-ladies. Kiran Asher, you stepped in at the final hour and gave me your best. Frederick Gates, your advice and wisdom have been my lifesavers. Finally, for sustenance of the more physical kind, *gracias* to the wonderful staff at Emack and Bolio's (Roslindale Village, MA)—first and foremost Miguel, Ben, and Mark—for the coffee, tea, egg-and-cheese-on-a-sesame-bagel, and pineapple sorbet that supported me through the final revision. Stephen Babcock, scholar-at-large, I'll always appreciate your conversation, sentence-level revisions, and moral support during the final stretch.

My first, best, and last thanks go to My Colón People: *mi madre*, Monica Frederick (my number-one cheerleader), *y mi padre* William G. Frederick, Jr.; *hermano* Wayne, *primos* Earl and Dominga Watson, *y la raza*: *las familias* Acham, Buval, Davis, Eaves, Hudson, Mayers, Prescott, Quinlan, Russell, *y* Small. *Te amo siempre y mucho.* I would not have had my "dissertation epiphany" if it weren't for you; neither would I have had the stamina to stick with this project. This book is the reason why I missed so many BBQs, birthdays, and holiday celebrations, but I hope you find in it the love and respect that I would have shown each of you if I were there.

Introduction

> Any attempt to reconstruct [Jean-Jacques] Dessalines historically involves ambiguities, obscurity, and details that do not cohere. But perhaps that is how gods are born. . . . The popular and oral canonization of Dessalines, unlike the public and written, is quite comfortable with a Dessalines apotheosized but not purged of incoherence.
>
> —Joan Dayan, *Haiti, History, and the Gods*

> One, two, three, four
> Colon Man a come
> with him watch chain
> a knock him belly
> Bam Bam Bam
>
> Ask him what's the time
> and he look upon the sun
> with him watch chain
> a knock him belly
> Bam Bam Bam
>
> —Olive Senior's "The Colon People"[1]

I

Armed only with a reference to an enslaved West Indian woman and a brief transcript of her witch trial "confession," Maryse Condé gives

"Six West Indian employees before a smelting furnace at the mechanical division in Balboa after their retirement in 1949. From left to right: Ethelbert A. Corbin (Barbados), John Brewster (Barbados), Charles A. Winner (Antigua), Donald Braithwaire (Barbados), John Dunbar (Jamaica), Victor Emmanuel (St. Lucia). Panama Canal Zone." Photographer unknown. Courtesy of Photographs and Prints Division, Schomburg Center for Research in Black Culture, The New York Public Library, Astor, Lenox, and Tilden Foundations.

the protagonist of *I, Tituba, Black Witch of Salem* a family, culture, and spiritual life that exposes the paucity of the official record.[2] Condé thus imagines and inserts Tituba's story into the history of the Salem Witch Trials as well as that of slavery in the Americas. In doing so, the author foregrounds the diverse but effaced *histories* and *stories* that coexist with the history that has been commonly told. In piecing together Tituba's fictionalized narrative, Condé does not merely celebrate a self that has been excluded from mainstream versions of history; instead she identifies the simultaneity of different, sometimes divergent, and always multiple stories.

Literature, songs, histories, and memoirs about the twentieth-century migration of Caribbean people to the isthmus of Panamá mirror the trajectory set by Condé in *I, Tituba*. With railroad and canal construction occurring soon after the end of slavery in the Anglophone Caribbean (1838), Panamá migration and the singular nature of canal work (nonagricultural, labor-intensive, and modern) distinguished Colón Men from other intra- and extraregional migrants, thus giving them the space and tools to construct a new vision of themselves.[3] In spite of this, contemporaneous canal histories typically cast Caribbean workers as minor players within the drama of the construction—that is, if they reference them at all. When depicted in this context, migrants' denigration within the Caribbean because of race, slavery, poverty, and (for some) lack of education are featured. While living on the isthmus, Colón Men were additionally subjected to exploitation, color/race prejudices, and antiforeign propaganda. While these characterizations of Caribbean laborers are accurate, Colón Men who appear in more recent narratives, as well as in popular and creative genres, are rendered more diversely.[4] Given the groundbreaking nature of the canal project and the chaos that distinguished its execution, Colón Men portrayed in early histories were lost among the compelling details of engineering achievements. These laborers were obscured, as well, by the political force of U.S. concern with its foreign policy and position among world powers. However, since "bottom up" histories and creative genres render a range of Colón Men's experiences, it is clear that they draw on workers' realities that resist standard explication. The Colón Man has therefore come to embody diverse responses to foreign powers, migration, and modernity, and to express multiple and complex Caribbean identities.

The verses used as this chapter's second epigraph are one example of the many lyrical depictions of Caribbean Panamá Canal workers. Songs about this figure mark his ubiquity in the circum-Caribbean region,[5] perhaps arising out of the recollections of people from "almost every community in the West Indies" who could recall men who left for the isthmus with nothing and returned with "savings enough to set them up for life" (Lewis 1980: 34, see also Haskins 1913: 157). "Colón Man a Come" is a Jamaican song that represents the Colón Man in his most common lyrical incarnation: one who's "Panamá Money" allows him to buy things he is more interested in sporting than using.[6] Though humorous, the verses reflect an ambivalent relationship to modernity. The watch chain's symbolic function (the wearer earns cultural capital by wearing it) is more meaningful than its practical one (securing a watch, a device the wearer probably does not own). The song also recalls isthmian migration, construction, financial possibilities, death and illness, and possibilities for success and failure. The meanings of the Colón Man's exploits, recorded in the Caribbean's lyrical imagination, accrue when the figure migrates into other genres.[7]

II

Contemporaneous histories of the Panamá Canal are largely silent on the contributions of Caribbean workers, despite their overwhelming numbers. Men from the Caribbean worked on the U.S.-backed Panamá Railroad (1850–1855), the canal enterprise initiated by French financier Ferdinand de Lesseps (1881–1898), and the successfully completed U.S. canal (1904–1914). Yet despite the close relationship between Caribbean laborers and each venture, "top down" canal histories typically emphasized U.S. interests in the project and highlighted the contributions of its planners and engineers. When such narratives depict Caribbean workers, they appear as foils that highlight North American ingenuity.[8]

The representation of Colón Men in mainstream histories was constructed through sources that served U.S. canal and/or ideological purposes. Consider, for example, that in reconstructing the story of the successful U.S. canal, historians writing at the time of the construction have made claims based on sources that document the amount of soil removed from the construction site, workers' contracts, canal authorities' work-related and personal correspondence, newspaper articles and editorials about canal policies, material requisition orders, budgets, and other similarly "factual" items.[9] But because much of what characterized canal construction *could not* be documented—such as an accurate number of work-related deaths—these kinds of materials can tell only part of the wide-ranging story of the canal.[10] Records on Colón Men, for example, were particularly thin since such workers were made indistinguishable from other African-descended employees by the practice of describing all black workers as "West Indians." Because many Caribbean laborers also worked without contracts or changed their names and/or jobs to avoid undesirable work or to secure higher pay, the "official" record is further distorted.[11]

Isthmian workers from the Caribbean have recently been recuperated in historical and geographical studies of Panamá Canal migration. Examining the canal project from Colón Men's perspectives—culled from oral histories, recollections of descendants, and demographic information from Caribbean parishes—oppositional Panamá narratives uncover the vital role these migrants played at most levels of the project as well as their positions in isthmian and Caribbean societies. These more broadly informed canal stories elaborate on earlier ones by providing insight into workers' views on their migration and labor, the type of worker who elected to migrate, the kinds of jobs they held, their social and economic impact on the Caribbean, and the regard in which their communities held them. Notwithstanding these important interventions, marked differences between historical and fictive narratives remain.[12]

Canal workers from the Caribbean who appear in various histories differ from, but nonetheless inform, characters that appear in Herbert de Lisser's *Susan Proudleigh* (1915), Eric Walrond's *Tropic Death* (1926), Claude McKay's *Banana Bottom* (1933), George Lamming's *In the Castle of My Skin* (1953), Michael Thelwell's *The Harder They Come* (1980), Maryse Condé's *Tree of Life* (1992), and Olive Senior's "Window" (1995).[13] As previously noted, the historical persona is often recognized in songs collected by Louise Cramer in "Songs of West Indian Negroes in the Canal Zone" (1946) and by Trevor Marshall (et al.) in *Folk Songs of Barbados* (1981).[14] The Colón Man figure is more richly depicted in the memories of "old timers" who, despite the hazards inherent to the project, poignantly remember their contributions to the canal, as can be seen in the Isthmian Historical Society's *Letters from Isthmian Canal Construction Workers* (1963). Whereas contemporary canal histories oversimplify or underrepresent Caribbean people, Colón Men's creatively rendered experiences communicate subsumed stories about Panamá migration, laborers, and work. Literary, lyrical, and epistolary accounts mark significant ruptures between the United States' opportunistic use of African-descended Caribbean laborers, on the one hand, and the desires of these workers on the other. The fictive Colón Man can be identified by his migration-forged masculinity, cocky attitude, material possessions, broadened worldview, and sometimes his work-related illnesses. Largely because of the cultural and social significance of these features, he has come to embody one of the Caribbean's largest internal migrations and one of the twentieth century's seminal engineering achievements. "*Colón Man a Come*" foregrounds the meanings revealed in fictive canal narratives as they enter into conversation with histories about the U.S.-built Panamá Canal.[15]

Still, the differences between historical and creative Colón Men raise an important question: what enables the transformation of the canal project, described in early histories as unexceptional in its exploitation of black workers, into something more complicated for Caribbean prose and song writers who appropriate the figure, for Caribbean people for whom the figure is expressively remembered, and for Colón Men themselves? This book, though historically grounded, takes a decidedly literary approach in considering the "imaginable truths"—real though not realized, possible though unprecedented—that affect fictive depictions of isthmian migration and Caribbean workers. Like some oppositional histories, fictive narratives communicate Colón Men's experiences from a Caribbean perspective, but these imaginative stories are able to articulate workers' less-easily "quantifiable" truths.

The significance of imaginable truths to the study of the Caribbean's isthmian migration can readily be seen in interpretations of "Panamá songs." These songs are signs of the Colón Man's regional ubiquity but, falling within the Caribbean tradition of lyrical documentation of events, they also "reflect the moods, ideas, and feelings that people have about the things that concern them at any period."[16] Offering an analysis of lyrics to identify the range and evolution of socially recognized masculine behaviors, Patricia Mohammed holds that the study of popular Trinidadian song lyrics, "this crucial vehicle of popular message-carrying, [reveals] what ideas about gender were being debated and thus imprinted on the minds of listeners" (38). Panamá songs, then, reflect but also prescribe listeners' migration behaviors. If the "popularity of a song is itself the extent to which it captures the fantasy of the listener and can enter the popular imagination" (34), then Panamá songs are "icons of [this] period"; they have "captured the popular imagination and . . . speak to the universal rather than to the particular, thus coming into being as folk culture" (40). Attention to this genre, therefore, reveals how lyrics identify and shape the climate surrounding isthmian migration, an atmosphere characterized by individual and communities' "moods, ideas, and feelings" about this particular movement. The more these songs' lyrics reflected this climate, the more popular they became; once popular, they nurtured the climate, establishing both acceptable and unacceptable views of the migration, for lyricists and singers, but importantly for potential migrants. To put it simply, Panamá migration songs capture, reflect, and prescribe the imaginable (possible) and imagined (hopeful) truths that reveal why workers' migrated and what they expected from it. In doing this, analyses of this genre reveal what Caribbean people thought of the migration at the time and which sources most influenced their perceptions.

Critical use of Panamá migration songs demonstrates what genre critiques of Panamá Canal narratives can reveal about the migration and about migrants' imaginable truths, truths that arise from the parts of Colón Men's experiences that could be imagined but that escaped conventional methods of documentation. George Lamming picks up on this abstraction when he asserts that "at a deeper level of intention than literal accuracy, [the novelist] seeks to construct a world that might have been; to show the possible as a felt and living reality."[17] Lamming's novelist does not simply duplicate in fiction an idea or experience that can be documented historically; instead, the writer elevates experience to the level of symbol and then puts it in service of another, possible truth that can convey complex Caribbean lived realities. *"Colón Man a Come"* creates and recreates Colón Men's stories through examinations of their literary (public and written) and mythic (popular and oral) constructions, through their memoirs, and through songs about them. The Colón Man figure that emerges in these varied sources are cosmopolitan, ladies' men, Pan-Africanist, rich, and above all, full of contradictions. Creative narratives refigure representations of Colón Men as tools that enable the portrayal of the North American worker as "rugged individual." In arguing that fictive isthmian narratives make "undocumentable" aspects of the canal enterprise accessible, this book puts forward the idea that multiple stories told in multiple genres productively communicate the chaos and disorder of the canal project. In doing so, unexpected Caribbean subjectivities emerge.

Traditionally told canal histories have not shed light on why Caribbean men continued to migrate when death was almost certain and when financial success was atypical. Neither has this type of account addressed why returned Panamá migrants continued to foster the belief in personal success afforded by Panamá migration nor why their communities seemed to require it. Mainstream historical approaches have also failed to address the Colón Man's desire to migrate in order "to become a man" or so that he might partake of the "freedom" legislated but denied in the Anglophone Caribbean after Emancipation. Fictive narratives conjure migrants' hopes and dreams, factors that weighed significantly in their decisions to move to Panamá and determined the quality of their lives there. The imagined *possibilities* of isthmian migration allowed Colón Men, those who bore witness to their deeds, and the region's cultural producers to perceive and experience something that differed from the documented experiences of isthmian life and labor. In the hands of creative writers of the literary or lyrical variety, the figure of the Colón Man embodies and stages migrants' imaginable truths. Such truths evoke the more conflicted experiences of migrants' lives and work on the canal, their sense of themselves as men, their relationships to their island communities, and the less easily quantifiable "value" of their Panamá Money. Such truths speak to the *potentialities* afforded by canal work—even if they were belied by other truths. Finally, when authoritative sources do not exist—whether they have been lost in time, never existed, or were deemed meaningless—imaginable truths offer the only version of the construction project. For those considering migration, imaginable truths speak to the possibility for a different reality, notwithstanding past oppressions and the likelihood of ruin and death in Panamá. Creative writers capture the intangible desires that motivated Colón Men's migration, a movement that—if truths about the hazards of isthmian work were the only measure—cannot otherwise be explained. Thus the fictional Colón Man highlights imaginative constructions that represent isthmian life as it might look if unbounded by disciplinary categories.

From the perspective of imaginable truths, one can see that relationships within the enterprise were not as one-sided as some historical accounts suggest. Migrants came to Panamá to profit from their U.S. employers, but Colón Men also traveled with desires that had little to do with the United States or canal construction. Traditional historical narratives have not featured the motivations of Caribbean workers, but "mythographies" analyze these motives, identify intersecting historical realities that affected them (Caribbean slavery/Emancipation, colorism/racism, migration, colonialism/imperialism), and bring into play imaginable truths that were inextricably tied to their migration and labor.

III

"Colón Man a Come" brings imaginable and historical narratives of Colón Men's experiences into productive dialogue. In this, the book has affinities with certain contemporary hybrid genres such as Audre Lorde's "biomythography," *Zami*.[18] Lorde's deliberate intermingling of myth, autobiography, biography, and storytelling to present her protagonist's life provides a model for the ways that myriad isthmian narratives can coexist. In *Zami*, Lorde produces a text that conveys the simultaneity of various aspects of her protagonist's persona. Through her narrative machinations, Lorde achieves a persona that resists the conventionally distinct categories of "black," "woman," and "lesbian."

However because Lorde's project is decidedly an individual one, it is difficult to read her narrative process as archetypal for the escape of limiting categories. In addition, Lorde arguably proposes a unified self that is made up of "parts" in opposition to a more simply constructed identity. Instead of reducing literary, lyrical, epistolary, and historical truths into a seamless Colón Man persona, this book examines and retains contradictions inherent in representations of the figure that compete across genres and that serve varied narrative goals. Mythographies of Panamá migrants are based upon histories, yet are animated by imaginable truths and thus uncover tales overwhelmed by orderly narrations of isthmian migration and construction.

In "Tradition and the West Indian Novel," Wilson Harris argues that West Indian literature should aspire to depict a *"fulfilment* of character" instead of "the consolidation of character."[19] The former allows for the continued influence and—significantly—the maintenance of "the series of subtle and nebulous links which are latent within [the West Indian], the latent ground of old and new possibilities" (Harris 1973: 28). The distinction Harris makes between "fulfilment" and "consolidation" is pertinent to this study. Instead of a unified or consolidated figure that depicts the mythographic Colón Man as *the* Caribbean subject, *"Colón Man a Come"* re-composes a persona that is reviled, celebrated, envied, emulated, free, and exploited. In other words, by analyzing canal migrants' mythographies, this book offers a vision that is more meaningful than any one of its constitutive parts. Instead of merely excavating the figure or offering an imaginative version of Colón Men's histories, my emphasis is on the preservation of the complexities of isthmian migration for the Caribbean and the productive and nonproductive aspects of work on and return from the isthmus.

"Colón Man a Come" draws on several genres to produce intricate portraits of Colón Men and describes their participation in the construction project as a whole. The resultant ensemble is indebted to Joan Dayan's *Haiti, History, and the Gods*, specifically the author's investment in the ability of popular, spiritually based narratives to articulate Haiti's subsumed stories. Dayan depicts the country as a product of "strange bedfellows, spiritual connections that had as much to do with domination as resistance, with reinterpretations of laws laid down, tortures enacted, and the barbarous customs of a brute white world" (xvii–xviii). Thus she creates a "complex and perplexing" Haiti by bringing to light stories sustained in the myths, religious beliefs, and the so-called unofficial histories maintained by the country's "unlettered," majority population. Her goal is to narrate a Haiti necessarily born out of violence *and* expectation, hope *and* hopelessness; her book thus responds to silences in the country's official record.[20]

Dayan's book succeeds because of her critical use of *vodou*. As a critical tool, one rendered from and reflecting the lived realities of Haiti's black majority, *vodou* illuminates the complexities of Haiti and its majority population. As the above epigraph suggests, popular and oral accounts of Dessalines—the man and the *lwa*—illustrate a comfort with complexity (contradiction, ambivalence, nonsense) that is absent from written accounts of the revolution, the revolutionary, and country. Dessalines' deification recognizes his role in liberating Haiti from France, the ruthless violence of his short regime, his investment in Haiti as a black republic, the brutality of his assassination, and the obscurity surrounding his burial. Through a more indeterminate Dessalines, one can access the man's vexed historical moment; this characterization allows interpretation of the politics of his violent death, but also, and in a more contemporary context, the possibilities of his vision. One could argue that his deification captures Jean-Jacques Dessalines' moment in time, his physical self, and his symbolic function, but also the fulfilled and unfulfilled potential in each.

Mythographic Colón Men offer a similar corrective to critical models that privilege margin/center analyses and global north/south dichotomies. The latter perspectives often produce binaristic accounts that cast canal authorities as powerful oppressors and Colón Men as powerless and oppressed. Accounts of canal construction written from the perspective of a margin/center opposition and hierarchy tend to emphasize quantifiable—often economic—reasons for migration; fictive depictions of the enterprise present a more diverse picture, one that is not hemmed in by this binary but also one that opposes boundaries between fact and fiction, powerful and powerless, oppressor and oppressed. Mythographic Colón Men are shaped not only by a history of shifting labor needs, but also by oppositional and vernacular histories, in addition to shifting Caribbean, U.S., and Panamanian cultural and social realities.

While neither denying nor rejecting the fact and impact of exploitation, Panamá Canal mythographies stress the imaginable aspects of the Colón Man's experience. The shift that this perspective affords allows those who employ the mythographic figure to identify the ideological baggage of more univocal canal narratives. Creative writers then use oppositional/imaginable accounts to challenge various oppressions and, importantly, offer strategies through which Caribbean peoples can be sustained by recognizable realities; this investment in multiple and competing versions of Colón Men's stories thus inaugurate psychic, economic, and political shifts in consciousness.

In identifying spaces where official and oppositional, creative and historical narratives interact, this book exposes the ideological motivations behind simplified characterizations of early isthmian workers. In addressing this kind of simplification, *"Colón Man a Come"* does not merely collect and remember Colón Men's narratives, but brings creative and imaginable possibilities to the surface of discourses about canal construction and puts them in service of discourses of Caribbeanness.

IV

Although *"Colón Man a Come"* attempts to depict Caribbean canal laborers complexly, the necessity of portraying their stories coherently risks producing a figure that resembles a mosaic, its identifiably different features cohering into a discernable whole. I address the problem of how to maintain *and* explicate the figure's unruliness by attending to differences in genre, and by interrogating the contributions and limits of each type of narrative. Tracking the same story through many genres, and uncovering the differences each narrative introduces, can maintain the complexity of the men, their experiences, and the canal project itself. Understanding these narratives not as autonomous and separate, but as facets refracted through the others, reveals a panorama of complex relationships, contexts, and—ultimately—the ideologies each serves. By presenting Colón Men's isthmian experiences through these shifting narrative "scraps," mythographies of Panamá Canal migration encourage readers to rethink that which consigns Colón Men to predetermined relationships to history, labor migration, and power.

The mythographic Colón Man-as-trope, as a model through which colonialism, modernity, and subjectivity in the Caribbean can be examined, excludes women's realities. Second, one must acknowledge the disruptions that resulted from the sense of fulfillment and financial achievement inspired by isthmian work; many Caribbean people—from every class—rued the Panamá Money that allowed some returnees to breach class and color lines. But even these as yet underexamined concerns contribute to mythographies of the migration. They constitute two of the many possible "unruly disruptions" that typify canal workers' narratives and that allow for more complex readings of Caribbean histories, cultures, and subjectivities.

Critics who interpret Caribbean literature as beginning with modernity argue that documenting it in a linear fashion offers little insight into its concerns.[21] It follows, then, that analyzing it in terms of oppression and exploitation is similarly inadequate. It is here that *"Colón Man a Come"* intervenes in the field of Caribbean Studies. The agency, achievement, and status that Colón Men make manifest are diminished if they are merely viewed as exploited labor or if their behavior is merely understood in terms of economic deprivations or reactions to oppression. Keeping this in mind while pursuing Colón Men through several genres will make it more difficult to reduce the figure to a static relationship to canal authorities and labor migration.

V

The preface critically positions *"Colón Man a Come"* within the field of Caribbean Studies by invoking debates about history and literature and then applying its analyses to Colón Men's mythographies. This chapter then proceeds more suggestively by identifying how this volume might usefully engage postcolonial critical and disciplinary concerns with imaginative culture, generally, and literary culture in particular.

Chapter 1 composes a historical narrative about the building of the Panamá Canal, the recruitment of workers, and the conditions under which they worked using contemporaneous historical narratives and song verses that elaborate on this perspective. The chapter then turns to a historiography of canal workers that explores French and U.S. canal authorities' perceptions of Caribbean laborers and the exploitative conditions under which they worked. It continues to investigate more recent narratives that reclaim the Colón Man from his infamous place in early-twentieth-century accounts. Drawing on features of intra- and extra-Caribbean migrations, this chapter finally remarks on the kinds of stories that historical investigations of the canal project tell, particularly with regard to explanations of why Caribbean workers continued to migrate despite proliferating stories of death, disease, and financial ruin.

Chapter 2 acts as a vehicle through which former canal workers tell their stories in their own words. It analyzes a transcription of handwritten letters collected from former canal workers as part of a contest for the best tales told by non-U.S. citizens. Here I emphasize how Afro-Caribbean workers represent and remember their tenure on the isthmus, focusing on their quantifiable and less-quantifiable reasons for migration, and how they remembered themselves as workers. The Caribbean viewpoint represented in these canal workers' first person accounts is developed further in the creative narratives of cultural workers, from professional writers to popular song lyricists.

In chapter 3, I examine Colón Men in George Lamming's *In the Castle of My Skin* and Michael Thelwell's *The Harder They Come*. Both writers enliven historical representations with myths about returned migrants, and expand traditional historical concerns to include examinations of cosmopolitanism, postcoloniality, and Caribbean subjectivities. Drawing on song lyrics that describe Barbadian laborers' activism and willingness to migrate, this chapter weds historical and creative versions of the canal worker to present Colón Men who are more than—as depicted in one history of the project—"very expensive freight."

Chapter 4 examines masculinity, class, and modernity in a Caribbean context, all significantly informed by isthmian labor. Featuring analyses of Claude McKay's *Banana Bottom*, Eric Walrond's short story collection, *Tropic Death*, and lyrics that describe Colón Men as lovers and as men made by their Panamá Money, this chapter considers how money, property, and women-as-property function as signs of Panamá-influenced masculinity and class mobility. At the same time, the Colón Man as worker and as financial success signifies the problems of modernity and anxieties surrounding interclass movement. Olive Senior's short story, "Window," further complicates issues of class and modernity by introducing race/color and gender into the analysis.

Chapter 5 focuses on Maryse Condé's *Tree of Life: A Novel of the Caribbean*, a novel in which all of the previously mentioned tensions are articulated through a single character. The sexual and spiritual exploitation that motivate Colón Men's migration is traced through protagonist Albert Louis's characterization and legacy throughout this "novel of the Caribbean." Condé's canal worker uses his migration as an act of resistance, but his time in Colón amplifies his most contradictory characteristics: he is victimizer and victimized; poor and rich; antiwhite, problack, and antiblack; nationalist and colonial. Colón Man Albert, therefore, embodies Condé's notion of "disorder" and suggests the fundamental importance in Caribbean culture of multiple and disruptive stories.

The conclusion examines Herbert de Lisser's *Susan Proudleigh* and develops a vision of isthmian migration obscured in previous depictions of mythographic Colón Men. Since the novel portrays one woman's class aspirations and desire to travel to the isthmus to achieve them (but only under the auspices of a male lover), it appropriately pushes the limits of interpretations revealed in previous chapters, particularly through its emphasis on Caribbean social, gender, and class concerns. In concluding this study with a creative narrative, I affirm the value of imaginable truths in constructing interpretations of Panamá Canal mythographies.

NOTES

1. Joan Dayan, *Haiti, History, and the Gods* (Berkeley: University of California Press, 1995); Olive Senior, "The Colon People," *Jamaica Journal* 11.3/12.4 (1978): 62–71, 87–103.

2. Maryse Condé, *I Tituba, Black Witch of Salem*, foreword by Angela Y. Davis, translated by Richard Philcox (Charlottesville: University of Virginia Press, 1992).

3. "Colón Man" and "Panamá Man" are the names given to Caribbean laborers who traveled to work on Panamá's railroad and canal. The names derive from the country's largest, northeastern city and the country itself. This worker has also been called a "Silver Man," denoting the currency in which he was paid and the euphemism for "black" and "unskilled worker" used by North American railroad and canal authorities. In addition to canal migration being mainly comprised of men, it was largely a phenomenon of the Afro-Caribbean. Although East Indian (1845–1917) and Chinese (1853–1879) peoples were moving into the region, very few migrated to Panamá. Additionally, while a small number of men from China were conscripted to work on the canal, for a number of reasons, they died in large numbers. Many of the Chinese workers who survived were then sent to Jamaica. "The Chinese in the English-Speaking Caribbean," *Encyclopedia of World Cultures, Volume 3: Middle America and the Caribbean*, volume edited by James W. Dow (Boston: G. K. Hall & Co., 1995): 56; Olive Senior's "The Chinese Who Came from Panama," *Jamaica Journal* 14 (1980): 78–79. Patrice C. Brown's "The Panama Canal: The African American Experience," *Prologue: Quarterly of the National Archives and Records Administration* 29.2 (Summer 1997) references East Indians in Panamá.

4. I use variations of the phrases "top down history(ies)," "mainstream history(ies)," "traditionally told history(ies)," "contemporaneous history(ies)," or "traditional approaches to history(ies)" to describe narratives about the Panamá Canal written near the time of the construction and/or told from the perspective of the United States and French governments and canal companies. I use the modifiers "oppositional," "more recent," or "bottom up" to represent histories told from a Caribbean perspective and that complicate or elaborate on the former histories. The latter type of history draws significantly from Caribbean workers' oral histories and popular stories about them. I draw from five of the most cited mainstream histories of the Panamá Canal to offer insight into the most common depictions of Colón Men in addition to the U.S. involvement in canal construction. They are John Major's *Prize Possession: The United States and the Panama Canal, 1903–1979* (New York: Cambridge University Press, 1993), Walter LaFeber's *The Panama Canal: The Crisis in Historical Perspective* (New York: Oxford University Press, 1989), David McCullough's *Path Between the Seas: The Creation of the Panama Canal, 1870–1914* (New York: Simon and Schuster, 1977), Willis J. Abbot's *Panama and the Canal in Picture and Prose* (London: Syndicate Publishing Company, 1913), and Frederic J. Haskin's *The Panama Canal* (Garden City, NY: Doubleday, Page & Company, 1913). Similarly I invoke frequently cited oppositional narratives to represent a vision of Caribbean workers that extends the version offered in other construction histories. These kinds of narratives include: Michael L. Conniff's *Black Labor on a White Canal: Panama, 1904–1981* (Pittsburgh: University of Pittsburgh Press, 1985); Bonham C. Richardson's geography of Barbadian canal workers, *Panama Money in Barbados, 1900–1920* (Knoxville: University of Tennessee Press, 1985); Velma Newton's *The Silver Men: West Indian Labour Migration to Panama, 1850–1914* (Mona, Jamaica: Institute of Social and Economic Research of the University of the West Indies, 1984); Lancelot Lewis's *The West Indian in Panama: Black Labor in Panama, 1850–1914* (Washington, DC: University Press of America, 1980); and Olive Senior's previously cited "The Colon People" as well as "The Panama Railway," *Jamaica Journal* 14 (1980): 66–77. George Westerman's articles and unpublished manuscripts on Caribbean people in Panamá, in addition to Roy Bryce-Laporte's studies of Caribbean migrations, balance the above; I reference these specific sources in subsequent chapters. While I detail the use of and employ these historical categories in chapter 1, generally speaking this categorization allows me to identify differences in the kinds of stories told in historical isthmian narratives and thus set the stage for the kinds of stories told in literature, songs, and memoirs. I do not want to imply, however, that the boundaries between the varied historical *and* creative narratives are fixed.

5. Throughout this book, I use the terms "West Indian" and "West Indies" specifically to refer to people from the English-speaking part of the region or the region itself. I use the term "Caribbean" to refer to the entire geographical area and to suggest a unity of its diverse geographies, languages, politics, economies, and cultures deriving from similar experiences of slavery, the plantation, European colonialism, and U.S. imperialism. When speaking generally about the canal's majority workforce, I use "Caribbean" to recall the nationally diverse workers who migrated from the area; yet island-specific references are necessary when my analyses are island-specific.

6. "Panama Man," a song popular in Barbados, offers a slightly different depiction of this popular figure. The Bajan song expresses the disappointment of a woman whose lover returns from the isthmus without any Panamá Money. *Folk Songs of Barbados*, researched and compiled by Trevor Marshall, Peggy McGeary, and Grace Thompson (Kingston, Jamaica: Ian Randle Publishers, 1996): 61–62. Although the returned Bajan laborer does not have his Jamaican peer's money, their respective communities mock them. See chapter 4 for a detailed discussion of "Panama Man."

7. Olive Senior indicates that myths about Colón and the life to be had there were embodied in the image of the successful Colón Man (Senior 1978: 64). Colón Men demonstrated how much they were influenced by the myth when they performed it and thus encouraged those who witnessed the transubstantiation (from myth to reality) to emulate their migration. Bonham Richardson concurs: "An assessment of the variety of stereotypes and characteristics of the returning Panama veterans . . . helps to delineate the variety of impressions they made on friends and relatives who greeted them upon their return" (Richardson 1985: 148–49).

8. In a late-twentieth-century context, little has changed with regard to representations of laborers from the Caribbean. Despite the plethora of newspaper and magazine articles emanating from the 31 December 1999 transfer of the Panamá Canal, there has been little mention of the presence and impact of Caribbean workers. This recent erasure is not surprising, however, since it follows a trend that consigned Colón Men to less than supporting roles in isthmian work and life. This erasure also reflects how their Panamanian hosts treated these laborers and their families. They were perceived of as *extranjeros* (foreigners) during and after each isthmian construction project. After the completion of the Panamá Canal, the continued presence of Caribbean workers troubled Panamanian officials so much that it became an issue in U.S./Panamá treaty negotiations in the 1970s. Bonham Richardson's *The Caribbean in the Wider World 1492–1992: A Regional Geography* (Cambridge: Cambridge University Press, 1992): 139. Despite the fact that many Caribbean people elected to remain on the isthmus, the Panamanian government continued to view these people and their descendants as aliens and the responsibility of the United States authorities that brought them. This thinking extended well into the twentieth century where Panamá-born children of Caribbean parents had to apply for Panamanian citizenship. Panamá's ill treatment of its Afro-Caribbean population can be understood in terms not only of a Panamá/U.S. conflict, but also in terms of racist attitudes evinced by McCullough's observation that Panamanians were particularly color-conscious (McCullough 1977: 576). To address problems experienced by this country's Afro-Caribbean descended population, and in recognition of this group's contribution to Panamá, Mr. and Mrs. Claral Richards founded "La Día de la Etnia Negra," first celebrated on 30 May 2001 (see http://diadelaetnia.homestead.com/home.html).

9. For example, David McCullough makes claims about John Stevens' commitment to the eradication of yellow fever and malaria in the Canal Zone by noting how much window screening the engineer requisitioned during his tenure (McCullough 1977: 466). Frederic Haskin debunks a popular tale that linked the number of deaths during the construction of the Panamá Railroad to the number of railroad ties by citing records that indicated that a total of 6,000 employees built the railroad using 150,000 total railroad ties (Haskins 1913: 103).

10. McCullough, speaking in terms of how the Canal Zone existed in the imaginations of the U.S. people, acknowledges, "The popular mental picture of what life was like in the Canal Zone, and popular pride in the kind of society that had been created there, were founded on a very limited and *erroneous* view of reality. The measure of Utopia achieved through American know-how and largess was again relative. . . . And as a consequence of such *distortion*, most all of what would be written in the way of a social history of these [canal construction] years contains but part of the story" (575–56, emphasis added). What McCullough describes as "erroneous" and "distortion" might more usefully be understood as one ideologically motivated story about the building of the canal, one with its own emphases and concerns.

11. Velma Newton states that authorities of the U.S. canal commission commonly referred to all "dark-skinned employees" as "West Indians" no matter their country of origin (Newton 1984: 132). In support of the common practice of name changing, Trinidadian Helon I. Allick stated that he "was then fancy by my Boss that he asked me to change my name and take me on as a new man at 13 cent, it was so done for I was then Henry Thomas." *Letters from Isthmian Canal Construction Workers (LICCW)*, transcribed by Ruth C. Stuhl (The Isthmian Historical Society, 1963): Allick, page 1 of 1.

12. The word "fictive" describes fictional Panamá narratives as well as those constructed through imagination, memory, and myth. The term describes literary, lyrical, and epistolary narratives that portray the migration of Caribbean laborers to the isthmus of Panamá, the migrants themselves, and the work they performed.

13. Herbert de Lisser, *Susan Proudleigh* (London: Metheun & Co., 1915); Eric Walrond, *Tropic Death* (1926. New York: Collier Books, 1954); Claude McKay, *Banana Bottom* (1933. San Diego: Harvest Books/Harcourt, Brace, and Company, 1961); George Lamming, *In the Castle of My Skin* (1953. New York: Schocken Books, 1983); Michael Thelwell, *The Harder They Come* (1980. New York: Grove Press, 1988); Maryse Condé, *Tree of Life: A Novel of the Caribbean*, translated by Victoria Reiter (New York: Ballantine Books, 1992); Olive Senior, "Window," *Discerner of Hearts and Other Stories* (Toronto: McClelland & Stewart, 1995): 57–74.

14. Louise Cramer, "Songs of West Indian Negroes in the Canal Zone" (*California Folklore Quarterly* 5 [1946]: 243–72).

15. While Colón Men who worked on the U.S. canal are this book's primary focus, I will discuss and draw on depictions of laborers on the Panamá Railroad and the canal attempted by the two French companies (*Compagnie Universelle du Canal Interoceanique* [1881–1888] and *Compagnie Nouvelle du Canal de Panama* [1894–1898]) when illustrative.

16. Patricia Mohammed, "Refining Gender Methodology: Studying Masculinity through Popular Song Lyrics," *Caribbean Masculinities: Working Papers*, edited by Rafael L. Ramírez, Víctor I. García-Toro, Ineke Cunningham (San Juan, Puerto Rico: HIV/AIDS Research and Education Center/University of Puerto Rico, 2002): 39.

17. George Lamming, introduction, *In the Castle of My Skin*, foreword by Sandra Pouchet Paquet (New York: Ann Arbor Paperbacks—University of Michigan Press, 1991): xl.

18. Audre Lorde, *Zami: A New Spelling of My Name: A Biomythography* (Freedom, CA: The Crossing Press, 1982).

19. Wilson Harris, "Tradition and the West Indian Novel," *Tradition, the Writer, and Society: Critical Essays* (1967. London: New Beacon Press, 1973): 28–29.

20. The "Haiti" that develops over the course of the book responds to a mythologized, post-revolutionary image of the country. In identifying the existence of multiple "Haitis," in effect Dayan's book asks readers to consider for whom and for what purpose Haiti simply represents "Liberté, Egalité, Fraternité." Using *vodou* as an interpretive device, specifically its ability to embrace contradiction, the author highlights an extraliterary Haiti recognizable to those ill served by "the standard 'drum and trumpet' histories of empire" (xvii). For this population, the author argues, "the very suppressions, inarticulateness, and ruptures in ritual might say something about the ambivalences of the revolution: it was not so liberating as mythologizers or ideologues make it out to be, and the dispossessed, who continue to suffer and remember, know this" (29).

21. J. Michael Dash expressed this idea in "Theory and the Caribbean," a course in the Caribbean Writers Summer Institute (CWSI) at the University of Miami, July 1994. This is an elaboration on an idea that he earlier expressed in "Haitian Literature—A Search for Identity," *Savacou* 5 (June 1971): 81–94.

1

History/Histories/Stories: Narrating the Panamá Canal and Colón Men

> Panama was a crossroads of global trade, the keystone of the great Spanish Empire, a century before the first white settlers struggled ashore at Massachusetts Bay. From its beginnings, the Isthmus was destined to be "the center of the universe," to use the later phrase of the Latin American liberator, Simón Bolívar. The prize has been neither easily seized nor cheaply held.
>
> —Walter LaFeber, *The Panama Canal: The Crisis in Historical Perspective*

> Matty oh, Matty oh
> Gone a Colon[1]

I

Because of its unique topography and geography, the country now known as Panamá has long been used as a crossroads.[2] It observed the comings and goings of several populations but its inhospitable climate at first discouraged European settlement. The country soon cohered around Spain's use of it, for across its narrow expanse Spaniards transported riches extracted from its western colonies (Major 1993: 9).[3] Attracted by these treasures, the up-and-coming English nation usurped Spanish authority on the isthmus. The Central American territory was also shaped by the rise of the United States as a world power, and came to symbolize U.S. foreign policy in Latin America and the Caribbean. In the end, Western

19

"Panama Canal builders at work, ca. 1908." Photographer unknown. Courtesy of Photographs and Prints Division, Schomburg Center for Research in Black Culture, The New York Public Library, Astor, Lenox, and Tilden Foundations.

claims on Panamá directly influenced its population, its economic and political growth, and, as I will argue, conditions under which Caribbean people lived and worked within its borders.

The construction of Panamá's railroad and canal reflect its early, tumultuous history; the country's chaotic past also anticipates the significance that fictive narratives have in communicating isthmian realities. Histories of both constructions are punctuated by inexplicable events that made some aspects of these projects all but inaccessible. For example, the unexpected turns that characterized canal construction, the misuse and abuse of black workers, and the prevalence of undocumented workers seriously hindered attempts to record features of the enterprise accurately. As a consequence, narratives that make use of the "undocumentable" aspects of the canal enterprise not only offer insight into the less available features of canal construction, but also extend the meanings that can be found in existing scholarship about the building of Panamá's canal.

This chapter presents historical narratives about Panamá, the Panamá Railroad and Canal, and isthmian workers from the Caribbean. These first sections prepare the way for the historiography of Colón Men that, in turn, sets the stage for the appearance and use of creative narratives about the figure.

II

Charles V (then king of Spain) quickly recognized the benefit that traffic across the isthmus afforded Spain, and sought to preserve and expand it. As early as 1534, the king commissioned surveys designed to improve transportation across the isthmus and to ascertain whether its geography was suitable for a canal (LaFeber 1989: 4; Senior 1978: 88). The recommendations from this first appraisal were ultimately rejected, after thirty years of consideration, because King Charles concluded, "if God wanted the oceans to meet he would have built the canal Himself" (LaFeber 1989: 5).

By 1572, this Spanish territory was rich and largely unprotected, two factors that caught the attention of English government officials. Pirate Francis Drake made his name by raiding Spanish fleets and capturing rich isthmian trading areas. His successful incursions, in addition to those of his successors, helped finance the British Empire (ibid). Spain fought with England to maintain control over the lucrative route, but English assaults on Spain's financial resources hampered the latter's ability to defend its colony.

British/Spanish battles over the isthmian throughway foretold its contentious future. After the decline of Spanish authority, the imperial struggle continued with the United States challenging Britain for control of the territory. By seizing control of the isthmus, the United States plotted to take command of burgeoning international trade routes and thus affirm its position as a world power. Although North American government officials recognized how beneficial such a route could be, they were also aware of England's naval and commercial superiority (Major 1993: 10–11). The burgeoning superpower, therefore, only sought to prevent England from monopolizing any means of transportation through Central America and negotiated with England for multinational control of such a route, should it ever come to fruition. U.S. government officials soon came to reconsider this position.

In 1844, England established settlements in Nicaragua to facilitate building a canal there. The United States countered by quickly ratifying a treaty with nearby New Granada over its isthmian province. The Bidlack Treaty guaranteed the U.S. "the right of way or transit across the Isthmus of Panama, upon any modes of communication that now exist, or that may be, hereafter, constructed." This treaty did not abrogate New Granada's sovereignty over the isthmus, but gave the United States the right to ensure safe transit across it (Major 1993: 12; LaFeber 1989: 8–9; McCullough 1977: 32–33). Bidlack, ratified in June of 1848, put England and the United States at odds over which country would control a Central American, trans-isthmian canal. Reluctant to go to war over this issue, both countries agreed to the Clayton-Bulwer Treaty of 1850: they would cooperate in building any Central American, trans-isthmian canal and neither country would seek to control it exclusively (LaFeber 1989: 9; Major 1993: 14).

However, by 1890 several factors contributed to the renegotiation of the 1850 agreement. U.S. officials cited intranational economic reasons (LaFeber 1989: 12–13), but its military and nationalist aspirations appeared to be more significant. In addition to benefits derived from canal-related employment and economic stimuli, a U.S.-controlled canal would serve defensive purposes by giving the emerging superpower speedy access to western territories annexed in 1845 (Texas) and 1846 (parts of the Pacific Northwest), and later won from Mexico (New Mexico and "Upper" California) (Major 1993: 13). The annexation of the Hawaiian Islands (1893–1894) and territories won in the Spanish-Cuban-American War (1898) greatly contributed to the United States' desire to control a trans-isthmian canal.[4] Invoking Manifest Destiny and the Monroe Doctrine, in addition to the authority afforded them through the Panamá Railroad, the North American country bullied its way into exclusive control of the canal in New Granada and, consequently, dominance of global trade and naval routes (Major 1993: 24). The belligerence suggested by the word "bullied" could be seen in comparison to how French authorities described their attempt to build the canal. When the French attempted to build a canal across Panamá, investors promoted the venture as something of value to the world—but necessarily brought to fruition by a glorious France. For the United States, particularly as expressed by President Theodore Roosevelt, the canal was "first, last, and always ... the vital—the *indispensable*—path to [the United States'] global destiny" (McCullough 1977: 250).

The U.S. began its challenge of the 1850 Clayton-Bulwer Treaty by calling for renewed negotiations with England. England's preoccupation with the rising German threat in Europe and the Boer War in South Africa influenced these renegotiations. Being so distracted, the European country was willing to reconsider its position as outlined in the 1850 convention and government officials in the United States were more than ready to exploit this advantage. The path to these revisions began in 1881 when Secretary of State James Blaine was instructed to revise the article that prevented either country from exclusively controlling and fortifying a canal (Major 1993: 21). North Americans wanted the right not only to build a canal, but also to ensure that it be used to its benefit—and against that of its enemies—in times of war (McCullough 1977: 257). In 1898, John Hay, then secretary of state, successfully continued Blaine's efforts. Ultimately named after principal negotiators John Hay (U.S.) and Sir Julian Pauncefote (England), the Hay-Pauncefote Treaty passed in 1901, giving the U.S. exclusive rights to construct and secure a Central American canal (Major 1993: 26–31; McCullough 1977: 259).

After a volatile debate over possible locations for the canal (Major 1993: 14–15, 24), the scale was tipped toward Panamá, where two French companies had already begun work on an inland waterway. Subsequent negotiations between the U.S. and New Granada/Colombia, dubbed the 1903 Hay-Herrán Convention, called for an initial $10,000,000 disbursement and then $250,000 in annual installments paid by the U.S. government to its Colombian counterpart. The South American country was also supposed to share judicial and military influence in the six-mile Canal Zone (an area extending three miles on either side of the canal). This convention, however, did not include the $40 million deal between the United States and the second French company, *Compagnie Nouvelle du Canal de Panama*, in which the U.S. agreed to purchase the latter's rights and equipment. The Colombian legislature quickly rejected the convention; they received the same annual payments from the less-profitable Panamá Railroad and resented their exclusion from the multimillion-dollar deal with the French company. President Roosevelt responded to the rejection with thinly veiled threats of invasion.

U.S. military action proved to be unnecessary, however, because the disagreement between the North and South American governments seemed to facilitate separatist feelings of individuals living on the isthmus. Some have argued that Roosevelt's displeasure with the Colombian government *created* the isthmus's revolutionary sentiment since it did not take shape until insurrectionists secured U.S. support (McCullough 1977: 341–45).[5] Phillipe Bunau-Varilla, mediator between Panamanian separatists and

U.S. Assistant Secretary of State Francis Loomis (and also a major stockholder in *Compagnie Nouvelle*), was instrumental in having the USS *Nashville* stationed off the shores of Colón. Charles Darling, the ship's captain, was ordered not to allow "ANY ARMED FORCE WITH HOSTILE INTENT, EITHER GOVERNMENT OR INSURGENT" (367) to land on the isthmus; in effect, the captain was ordered to prevent Colombia from landing troops to quell the revolution. In 1903, Panamá declared its independence, a declaration quickly recognized by the United States.

It soon became evident that Panamanian sovereignty facilitated the interests of the United States. The North American country claimed moral and, importantly, legal justification for building a canal in Panamá by loosely interpreting the 1848 Bidlack Treaty it made with Colombia. The treaty, specifically Article XXXV, ensured Colombian sovereignty over the province but also gave the United States exclusive "right of transit" across the isthmus via existing or future technologies (Major 1993: 35–36). Authorities of the U.S. government chose to respect Article XXXV, but rejected other aspects of the convention to allow them to build the canal. Adherence to the spirit of the Bidlack Treaty, therefore, was ultimately rejected in favor of the propitious Panamanian revolution.[6]

When the dust had settled, the United States and the Republic of Panamá ratified the Hay/Bunau-Varilla Treaty, but under terms that denied Panamá the sovereignty promised to Colombia in 1848. Through Bunau-Varilla's machinations, the six-mile Canal Zone was expanded to ten, the land lease was extended from the 999 years outlined in Bidlack to an ambiguous "in perpetuity," and Panamá was denied judicial and military influence in the Canal Zone. In addition, no land previously leased to railroad or canal companies would revert to the new republic, it had no role in the defense of the canal, and U.S. authorities could seize isthmian land that might assist in the construction and defense of the canal—as the North American country saw fit (LaFeber 1989: 30; Major 1993: 43–44).[7]

Now that the treaty was negotiated and ratified—and not likely to be more suitably renegotiated in Panamá's favor (Major 1993: 109)—canal work soon began.

III

United States, English, and Spanish interests in the Panamanian isthmus largely determined the course of Panamá's early history. The expressed ideological intentions of the English government, but particularly those of the United States, provided the frame for the above narrative; U.S. agents were cast as mavericks, English and Colombian "characters" provided dramatic tension, and Panamanians were written in as dupes and foils. As the story of the founding of Panamá and the building of the canal unfolded, North Americans came off as the victors and, in some renditions, the heroes. The canal drama continued in a similar vein once the railroad and canal construction projects began. The concerns of French and U.S. authorities not only overshadowed those of the new Panamanian republic, but also those of each project's black and majority labor force.

The presence of Caribbean recruits in Panamá corresponded to three labor-intensive construction ventures. Traveling to work on the railroad (1850–1855) and the French (1881–1894) and the U.S. canals (1904–1914), Colón Men made isthmian migration one of the largest in the circum-Caribbean region. Because French and U.S. agents were most concerned with successfully completing their projects, the impact of this migration on Panamá and the Caribbean was incidental. To complete the canal successfully, construction authorities needed a sizeable labor force; the composition of this force did not matter as much. They believed that the proximity of the Caribbean, not to mention regional underemployment and low wages, made this area a rich and likely source of labor; however, the prevalence of stereotypes about lazy black workers put officials in search of other candidates—specifically Chinese ones—for their manual labor needs (see McCullough 1977: 474). After Chinese and other sources of labor failed (because of resistance from segments of the U.S. and Panamanian populations as well as high death rates among Chinese recruits), Caribbean workers were once again sought after, though no less stereotyped.

Colón Men almost exclusively functioned as manual laborers on the French and U.S. canal projects. In the latter building era, they also worked as artisans, machinists, and white-collar workers. No matter the type of employment, the view of Colón Men as unskilled laborers prevailed, particularly because this image affirmed entrenched racial stereotypes and stood in contrast to the rugged individualist persona of the North American worker. The ambivalent representation of Colón Men—they were cast as lazy, lethargic, unskilled, and plentiful workers—nevertheless produced a more nuanced characterization. Consider that John Stevens, the first chief engineer of the U.S. Isthmian Canal Commission (ICC), stated that the quality of West Indian labor was not solely determined by "nature" even though he believed that "the efficiency of the average West Indian was about one-third that of an American laborer, white or black" (McCullough 1977: 474). Stevens alleged that West Indians could learn, if given the chance, and that their traditional high starch diet might explain their apparent "lassitude." These observations proved to be correct since these workers became "increasingly proficient with tools and at working in unison and in association with heavy machinery" (477). Stereotypical portrayals nonetheless remained constant and plagued Colón Men throughout their tenure on the isthmus.

Accounts written soon after the canal was completed either failed to mention the army of Caribbean workers involved in its construction, for example, W. Leon Pepperman's 1915 *Who Built the Panama Canal?*, or depicted these workers as poorly skilled hindrances to canal authorities, for example, Willis J. Abbot's *Panama and the Canal in Picture and Prose* and Frederic J. Haskin's *The Panama Canal*, both published in 1913.[8] These last two narratives used the image of the incompetent Colón Man to promote North American canal planners and workers as mavericks committed to the completion of the canal. In response to a tourist who opined that his job did not appear to be difficult, J. A. Loulan (an engineer at a rock crushing plant at Ancon) responded anecdotally that "A Jamaican Negro hostler" caused an engine to be mired in the mud. Loulan called together a crew at 2 a.m. to free it, a task that took about four hours. The engineer was motivated by the desire to maintain his schedule, as was his crew; therefore after this sleepless night, not one member of the ad hoc crew "was late getting back to work after four hours of strenuous extra night duty" (Haskin 1913: 148). The unnamed Jamaican made these Americans' work all the more difficult; his portrayal simultaneously permitted Loulan—and Haskin—to illustrate the dedication of U.S. laborers.

Abbot, Haskin, and Pepperman were particularly interested in U.S. citizens who were involved in the canal venture and the implications of their involvement. To serve these interests, they drew largely from sources sanctioned by the ICC. The title page of Abbot's book, for example, declares it as "a complete story of Panama, as well as the history, purpose, and promise of its world-famous canal—the most gigantic engineering undertaking since the dawn of time" (Abbot 1913: i). He continues by stating that his book was "approved by leading officials connected with the great enterprise" (ibid). Taken collectively, these contemporaneous studies usefully examine the canal construction project, adding insight into the republic's independence, engineering innovations that enabled the completion of the railroad and canal, U.S. foreign policy in Central America and the Caribbean, and the North American country's status as an emergent world power. Thus Haskin, Pepperman, and Abbot's narratives reveal much about U.S. actors involved in both isthmian projects and less about the lived realities of railroad and canal laborers from the Caribbean. This said, one cannot overlook how the work of these writers (and, to a lesser extent, that of McCullough, Major, and LaFeber) define the narrative uses to which the Colón Man figure was put in historically oriented accounts of Panamá's canal. Interestingly enough, representations of Caribbean canal workers have a pedigree; they build upon images that appear in descriptions of the trans-isthmian railroad.

Many events contributed to the desire for quick passage across the isthmus, but none more influential than the 1849 discovery of gold in California. To meet the demand for expeditious access to the North American West, representatives of the Panamá Railroad Company required inexpensive and available labor. Isthmian natives appeared to be the most obvious choice but, for a number of reasons, they were not employed in large numbers.[9] Railroad administrators then turned to Jamaica as the closest labor source, ultimately drawing the majority of its approximately 5,000 workers from this island (Haskin 1913: 103; Conniff 1985: 3–4; Senior 1980: 67).

Jamaican railroad recruits worked for wages ranging from about 40 cents to $1.00 per day and were engaged in clearing land and laying ties and trestles.[10] The former task, made all the more difficult because of Panamá's dense forests and long rainy season, required diligent labor. Manual laborers also experienced the highest risk of disease and death since their work obliged them to be in contact with deadly insects and reptiles. As can be imagined, the safest and highest paying positions on the railroad were reserved for white North Americans (McCullough 1977: 147). After the railroad's 1855 completion, many Jamaican laborers paid for their return passage or continued to migrate. Those who remained in Panamá settled in Colón and Panamá City, the railroad's terminal cities.

The next wave of Caribbean labor migration began in 1881 when French entrepreneurs attempted to construct the canal. These officials, with much moral and financial support from small investors, attempted to build a sea-level canal across the Colombian-controlled isthmus. Riding the wave of his successful promotion of the Suez Canal, Ferdinand de Lesseps sought similar success in Central America. Although commissioned studies indicated that a lock-type canal would be cheaper and easier to construct (McCullough 1977: 78–79), de Lesseps—apparently by force of personality alone—was able to push through plans for a sea-level canal.[11] One supporter claimed that "the bankers and the public would not give a cent to any route that was not patronized by M. de Lesseps. . . . So that to abandon that route was to abandon entirely for France the glory of cutting the interoceanic canal, and that was not to be thought of for a moment" (77).

De Lesseps' *Compagnie Universelle du Canal Interoceanique* managed the canal from 1881 to 1888. His effort failed because of the impracticality of a sea-level canal and poor management among canal authorities; however, unexpectedly high rates of death and disease among laborers also thwarted the canal's successful completion. The *Compagnie Nouvelle du Canal de Panama* continued excavation in 1894, but—being equally unsuccessful despite implementing construction of a lock-type canal—agreed to sell its rights to the United States government in 1898 (Newton 1984: 30–31).

About 50,000 Jamaicans comprised the majority of the labor force for the French canal, but each French company also heavily recruited in Barbados, St. Lucia, and Martinique (Newton 1984: 39, 44–45; see also McCullough

1977: 147; Lewis 1980: 17; Senior 1978: 62; Conniff 1985: 4). Officials of the *Compagnie Universelle* did recruit workers from China, Ireland, Colombia, and India when they were no longer happy with the "nomadic" nature of Jamaican laborers (it was said that these workers did not stay put, instead opting to travel along the canal line in search of better paying and/or less strenuous jobs). However, ill health and suicide detracted from purportedly more stable foreign replacement workers. Colón Men in this stage of construction worked with "pick and shovel, and wheelbarrow" (McCullough 1977: 158). They were also put to work digging ditches, cutting brush, carrying lumber, and unloading boxcars of dynamite (476) regardless of previous training as teachers, carpenters, etc. (476–77). Nonetheless, artisan or white-collar Colón Men were present: "The Compagnie Universelle and its contractors employed them . . . as work supervisors, office assistants, as carpenters who helped build the docks, warehouses, and other buildings at the French port of [Cristobal], and helped erect quarters for company employees, and as machine shop assistants at Emperador and other centers along the canal line" (Newton 1984: 116).

Unfortunately, Colón Men's diligence did not persuade French canal officials to value them, as exemplified by authorities' poor responses to the astoundingly high death rate among this population. Regardless of the number of deaths, French officials did not consider a high mortality rate a problem because replacements could easily be recruited from the circum-Caribbean region (Lewis 1980: 22). Additionally, French executives saw Colón Men as "inconsistent" employees, ones not sufficiently committed to the completion of the canal. However, what was reported by French authorities to be a lack of commitment might have been differently represented if observed from the perspective of the workers themselves. Considering that they were not contracted for a specified period of time (Newton 1984: 116–17) and some "black workers were leaving faster than they were being replaced, going home to spend their money 'before they [were] killed by the climate'" (McCullough 1977: 181), Jamaican Colón Men seemed to have acted in accordance with their interpretations of loosely worded contracts and their own sense of self-preservation.

Though failing to complete the canal, the work of each French company greatly contributed to the success of the U.S. project. Yet the French debacle adversely impacted the ICC's ability to recruit in Jamaica as well as in other parts of the Caribbean (McCullough 1977: 471–72).[12] Repatriating Caribbean workers left destitute after the *Compagnie Nouvelle*'s collapse strained Jamaica's treasury and thus turned this and other Caribbean governments against canal recruiters. Officials in the Jamaican government ultimately "refused to allow any recruiting on the island and imposed a tax on anyone desiring to leave for the isthmus" (ibid; see also Haskin

1913: 218). Finally, Jamaican Governor Alexander Swettenham forbade the migration of the island's citizens because then U.S. Secretary of State William Taft refused to include a free repatriation clause in its labor contracts (Major 1993: 81).

Nonetheless, the lengths to which Jamaica's government went to prevent the migration of its citizens did not stem the tide of potential laborers from the island. Jamaicans who continued to travel to the isthmus did so without contracts and at their own risk. This group, greatly inspired by countrymen who returned with sizable amounts of Panamá Money (Haskin 1913: 156), made officially sanctioned canal recruitment almost unnecessary. In addition, the tax imposed by Caribbean governments changed the composition, but did not prevent the migration, of Colón Men. The tax increased the migration of skilled artisans and others who could afford to pay it. These relatively well-to-do Caribbean migrants increased the number of white-collar and skilled workers on the isthmus as well as those providing services for canal employees.

Despite—or perhaps because of—recruitment obstacles, in gathering men for canal work the ICC was more thorough than its predecessors. The Commission followed previous authorities in seeking workers from the Caribbean because of its proximity, but contracted the majority of its "unskilled pick-and-shovel workers" in "Barbados, rather than Jamaica" because of problems stemming from the French company's bankruptcy (McCullough 1977: 472). While Barbados was the official labor source, the U.S. project drew workers from all parts of the Caribbean and "by November 1905 more than 14,000 men were carried on the [payroll] of the Commission and the Railroad, almost all of them from the Caribbean" (Major 1993: 82). Over the entire U.S. construction period, laborers from the Caribbean comprised an average of 60 percent of "the brawn required to build the Panama Canal" (Haskin 1913: 154).

While Jamaican, Barbadian, and other Caribbean men comprised the majority of the canal's unskilled labor pool, they also held a variety of other positions and earned varying rates of pay. Like Colón Men on the railroad and the French canal, on the U.S. canal Caribbean men were unskilled blue-collar workers (such as diggers, and water and messenger boys) to be sure, but also skilled and white-collar workers (waiters, artisans, machinists, subforemen, clerks, typists, and timekeepers) (Conniff 1985: 31). In addition, Jamaican farmers, professionals, speculators, and entrepreneurs composed part of the isthmian workforce (Senior 1978: 63). Yet while these facts demonstrate some diversity in skills of and employment for Caribbean workers, all Colón Men working during the U.S. period shared with their predecessors similar experiences of hardship.

During the building of the U.S. canal, the ICC provided room and board for its black workers, but lodgings were little more than poorly built shacks inadequately equipped to withstand the weather (particularly during the rainy season) and located in the unhealthiest areas—that is, locations closest to work sites.[13] These quarters were located in places specifically designated by the ICC: "La Boca, located in the Balboa area on the Pacific Side, Red Tank and Paraiso near Pedro Miguel; and Santa Cruz. . . . On the Atlantic Side are located Chagres, Camp Bierd, Silver City, and Camp Coiner."[14] Yet the Commission had trouble securing funds to maintain these residences; from 1916 until the 1940s, the U.S. Congress failed to approve such appropriations (Westerman 1951: 7, 8). Without adequate funding, these accommodations were often neglected and ill equipped for the climate. Although all barracks for black workers were far from adequate, single men fared better in ICC quarters than married workers: the Commission provided "only a few crude quarters" for married black workers and only for those who were legally married (McCullough 1977: 577).

Residence in Colón and Panamá City, where most unmarried black couples chose to live, was often dismal. These cities did not have proper sewage systems, paved streets, or sidewalks; in addition, available apartments were often crowded and overpriced. Colón Men living in these cities also fell victim to corrupt landlords charging exorbitant rents (Westerman 1951: 8). Still other Colón Men, single and partnered, chose to squat on land held by railroad or canal companies (Haskin 1913: 154–55). There they built their own homes, lived with their families, and grew some of their own food.

U.S. canal authorities tried to counteract the isthmus's high cost of living by providing for many of their workers' needs.[15] The Commission built cafeterias where workers could purchase three meals per day for about 10 cents per meal; unfortunately, this rate forced low-ranking laborers to spend over a third of their daily earnings on food. Still, as John Butcher recalled, this ICC benefit was hardly beneficial. This Colón Man remembered "cooked rice which was hard enough to shoot deer; sauce spread all over the rice; and a slab of meat which many men either spent an hour trying to chew or eventually threw away."[16] The poor services that the ICC provided its black laborers forced some Jamaicans to strike (Lewis 1980: 47; Major 1993: 88, 89), though most chose to make do on their own.

But there was something insidious in the ICC's provision of housing and board for workers. Through these services the Commission could wield an inordinate amount of control over its workforce and thereby could prevent workers from lodging work-related complaints. In this light, black workers who avoided ICC benefits, presumably because of their poor quality, may have also been resisting official attempts at controlling their private lives. Squatting, then, allowed Caribbean workers to slip the ICC's yoke, at least while they were off the company clock.

The uncertainties of Panamá's climate, specifically the difficulties involved in toiling in it, rendered official attempts at control on the isthmus illusory. The hot and wet climate made the most strenuous kinds of canal work all the more hazardous and probably contributed to many work-related deaths. Panamá's weather also nurtured poisonous insects and reptiles that killed workers or caused them to be chronically ill. Central America and the Caribbean might have had similar types of weather, but the length of the isthmian rainy season and the vermin that thrived in it were enough to put Colón Men off balance. And while they were familiar with agricultural work in the hot environments of their home countries, Caribbean laborers could not be completely prepared for the degree of physical exertion required by railroad and canal construction.

While such environmental issues did not greatly figure into the ICC's official policies toward Caribbean workers, the Commission exhibited some concern because the environment's effect on workers could adversely affect the canal's timely and successful completion. Panamá's climate supported mosquitoes, a strain of which soon came to be known to carry viruses for yellow fever and malaria. Before this means of transmission was discovered, most believed these diseases were caused by "bad air." This ignorance, not to mention Caribbean workers' poorly protected houses and occupations, overexposed them to these sicknesses.

The high death rate of the U.S. canal's black, foreign workforce conflicted with reports that suggested that these men were immune to disease. The nature of the confusion can be seen in the fact that "the only two [mortality estimates] actually based on the *Compagnie Universelle*'s records were reports made by the *Compagnie Nouvelle*'s Technical Commission in 1898, and by Colonel W. C. Gorgas of the ICC in 1904. "Unfortunately, both computations are of deaths which occurred in hospitals only, and, since many workers died outside these institutions, are not an accurate guide to the number of deaths which actually occurred" (Newton 1984: 125). Of course, the fact that Caribbean men represented the majority of canal workers also accounts for their overrepresentation in even these statistics, although their seeming physical superiority could also be attributed to the number of illness among Caribbean workers that went unreported (127). Yet even when adjusted for Colón Men's numerical superiority, statistics based on hospital admission and treatment showed that "Panama was still four times more deadly for the black man than it was for the white" (McCullough 1977: 582). Given that many black canal workers avoided hospitals as well as white doctors and nurses, this figure would greatly increase if unreported deaths could be included (Newton 1984: 127). In the final analysis, no one can accurately say how Colón Men responded to Panamá's diseases in comparison to their coworkers.

Ignorance and/or lack of interest might explain the prevalence of the myth of Colón Men's physical superiority, despite contradictory evidence: Haskin asserts that West Indian "Negroes" were "unusually susceptible to disease" (154) but McCullough posits that Colón Men might have increased their chances of surviving subsequent exposure to yellow fever if they had been previously exposed to it (McCullough 1977: 140–41). Despite the myth, Colón Men by the "hundreds succumbed to, or were permanently weakened by malaria and yellow fever . . . pneumonia, black fever and all the other diseases which were prevalent on the Isthmus" (Newton 1984: 127).

Notwithstanding the threat that worker incapacity posed to the canal project, the ICC considered a successfully completed throughway an engineering rather than medical matter, so much so that officials did not deem doctors—or individuals experienced in sanitation—essential members of the Commission (McCullough 1977: 407). This remained the official position despite the fact that death from disease was a key factor in the French failures. Thus the health and welfare of workers—particularly black and foreign ones—were considered less important than any engineering concern.[17] In this context, it cannot be surprising that black labor on the isthmus was "figured like freight, very expensive freight" (111).

The problems of climate and nature of work on the isthmus were compounded by complications brought by local Panamanians as well as officials of each engineering project.[18] Colón Men were at odds with Panamanians, European and Euro-American laborers, as well as French and North American supervisors whose racial prejudices resulted from xenophobia, racism, religious and language differences, and/or economic competition. Racially motivated conflicts between black workers and white supervisors existed at each stage of railroad and canal construction and under each administration; however, North Americans generally, and ICC officials specifically, brought a new component to the Panamanian landscape—segregation so entrenched that it "cut through every facet of daily life in the Zone, and it was as clearly drawn and as closely observed as anywhere in the Deep South or the most rigid colonial enclaves in Africa" (McCullough 1977: 576). Reflecting U.S. ideology of the time, Panamá's color line was alleged to be "kindly but firmly drawn," the dependability of which was evinced by signs posted all along the canal line (Haskin 1913: 159–60). Colón Men could avoid conflicts with their white employers if they were "polite" and observed "their place" (157).

Perhaps the most obvious manifestation of the Canal Zone's color line regarded the ICC's method of remuneration. Having roots in procedures instituted by the Panamá Railroad Company, the ICC made "gold" and "silver" employee classifications official policy. Originally signifying the currency in which each group was paid, U.S. citizens in gold and all others in silver, these designations came to mean more (Westerman 1951: 12).[19] Gold roll employees received benefits denied silver men including paid vacations, sick leave, and furnished quarters (Major 1993: 79). These proved to be added benefits for gold employees since, in 1909, gold was twice the value of silver. Further, the ICC spent about $750 per year in U.S. dollars on entertainment for "the average skilled (white) . . . married" gold roll employee; the expenditure for "the average unskilled (black) . . . married" silver roll worker was $50 (McCullough 1977: 578).

Yet gold/silver classifications did not refer exclusively to race until 1908; before this, black American and a few exemplary Afro-Caribbean workers could be found on the gold roll and white workers could also be found on the silver. However, because this was said to have "[complicated] bookkeeping and violated the color line," this oversight was soon corrected.[20] Though the U.S. canal commission and government hotly denied accusations of racism in the Canal Zone, racial segregation was clearly coded as gold and silver. These labels appeared on—and determined the quality of—hospitals, dining halls, housing, and recreational facilities. Silver facilities were further segregated to provide European workers living, eating, and leisure quarters separate from people of African descent (Newton 1984: 132). The gold/silver policy touched every aspect of life in the Canal Zone but existed largely without official documentation (McCullough 1977: 576). Much of what did appear in print misrepresented the ICC's de facto racial guidelines by characterizing Caribbean workers as "knowing their place" (Haskin 1913: 157) and, in effect, choosing to self-segregate.[21]

Although the Commission's gold and silver policy codified racial separation on the isthmus, officials of the railroad and each canal venture had other racially informed beliefs that determined how they treated the Caribbean workforce. When railroad officials first recruited Jamaican laborers, they generally described them as strong and "naturally" suited for work in Panamá. These authorities maintained this "positive" characterization throughout most of the construction, "for in 1854 the directors are reported to have spoken favourably of [Colón Men]" (Newton 1984: 116). Unlike their predecessor, French and ICC officials' estimations of Caribbean laborers progressed from positive to negative. Sources detailing French attitudes toward Caribbean labor do not offer much insight into their motivations; however, the U.S. company's attitude likely resulted from racial ideologies in the United States' as well as its extreme self-interest with regard to the Panamá Canal and its subsequent role in the Americas. U.S. needs and perspectives far outweighed those of any other American nation.[22]

Insignificant in terms of the needs of the ICC and the government of the United States, discounted because of their foreignness, and denigrated because of their race, Colón Men were nonetheless, and perhaps counterintuitively, valued because of race-based stereotypes. Their "brawn" was said to have conquered the most difficult part of canal excavation, the Culebra Cut (Haskin 1913: 163). Colón Men were also described as being amenable to guidance by a firm U.S. hand (162–63). In the words of Secretary of State Taft, the Colón Man "has his faults; he is lazy, and he does loaf about a good deal, but he is amenable to law, and it does not take a large police force to keep him in order" (Major 1993: 82). The Colón Man's "hardy physique, surprising capacity to endure the sultry tropical weather, as well as his strong resistance to local diseases, [proved] that he was the fittest type of worker to cope with the Isthmian environment" (Westerman, "Glimpses," 2).

Official perspectives on Caribbean workers, then, largely presented the concerns of the ICC and U.S. government. Alternative views can be seen, however, if one shifts perspective. The implications of such a shift are visible if one reconsiders the ICC's housing and food policies. Typically, U.S. officials viewed Colón Men who eschewed ICC's services as backward (they did not know how good they could live) and immoral (because they opted to live with their partners, though unmarried) (Haskin 1913: 154–55). From these workers' perspective, however, these same acts take on a revolutionary tone: Colón Men who secured their own room and board could reject the ICC's authority over their personal, and to a lesser extent, their public lives. Both points of view provide feasible renditions of life in the ten-mile Canal Zone; yet taken together, the interpretive possibilities proliferate.

IV

Taken solely from the perspective of histories that feature the perspectives of Western canal authorities and governments, it is clear that the work performed by Caribbean workers made it possible for U.S. visionaries to bring the canal to fruition. However, these laborers were given little credit for the completion of Panamá's railroad or canal. What becomes clear through historiographical examination of isthmian narratives is that adding "bottom up" histories to "top down" accounts exposes Colón Men's own views on their migration, jobs, and lives on the isthmus. Importantly, a historiography of the Colón Man stresses the uncertainties that inhered in each isthmian construction project, particularly as the tumultuous environment impacted on laborers from the Caribbean. Building the canal was not, as Abbot optimistically put it, "an act of unselfish bounty" that corrected "the long record of international perfidy, piracy, and plunder which is the history of Panama" (Abbot 1913: 6). Attempts at so organizing Panamá's story effaced the complexities of the construction period and it certainly influenced how the struggles of Colón Men were represented in the historical, social, and cultural imagination of the Americas.

Haskin's *The Panama Canal* describes the American segment of the canal's workforce as committed to the completion of the project, no matter how long it took or how difficult the task (Haskin 1913: 148). This attitude apparently extended to every U.S. citizen in the Canal Zone, for "the man who has 'nerves' would never stick it out on a job like [building the canal].... The result is that a process of elimination has gone on until the men who have 'nerves' have all left and their places filled with those who are stoical enough to take things as they come" (148–49). The difficulties they faced "temper[ed] the steel in their make-up" (145). This representation surely cemented local U.S. support for the project, and the prevalence of such rugged individualist narratives made it more difficult for alternative narrations of suffering and resistance to emerge. As David McCullough suggests, the sanguine view of white American life in the Canal Zone was largely rhetorical; in addition, "and as a consequence of such distortion, most all of what would be written in the way of a social history of these [canal construction] years contains but part of the story" (McCullough 576). McCullough's characterization of popular representations of the Zone as "erroneous . . . distortion" suggest some malicious intent on the part of contemporaneous and official researchers, which might be the case, but this image of the Canal Zone as an American utopia is merely one of many descriptions. And as this representation shaped the popular image of the North Americans in Panamá, it had a coincidental effect on Colón Men narratives, particularly with regard to portrayals of their contribution to isthmian work and life. One can begin with officially sanctioned accounts of the Canal Zone to access Caribbean workers stories, but the former can only produce glimpses of Colón Men's realities. It is necessary, therefore, to draw on sources and perspectives that embrace the experiences of Caribbean isthmian laborers. Interestingly, what "top down" histories have done—through their emphases on North Americans' role in canal construction—is define spaces where oppositional Panamá narratives can take root. Traditional approaches become more valuable as they dialogue with other types of isthmian narratives. Such a conversation broadens the view of the canal project and the contributions of all its participants.[23]

Although characterized as occupying the most insignificant places in isthmian society, Colón Men were the most ubiquitous *and* invisible people throughout the U.S.-controlled Canal Zone and Panamanian-controlled cities. These workers made every aspect of canal life run efficiently. Clearing land and laying ties during construction of the railroad, participating on sanitation teams charged with eliminating yellow fever-carrying mosquitoes, preparing the way for the ninety-five-ton Bucyrus shovel used to excavate the Culebra Cut, or performing all manner of domestic services, Caribbean isthmian workers facilitated the realization of Panamá's railroad and canal.

Because of the number of undocumented workers secured by the ICC, the "circular migrants" who frequently traveled between the isthmus and their home countries when their Panamá Money ran low, and the inordinate number of undocumented deaths, it is impossible to determine the actual number of Colón Men who worked in Panamá. Some have, however, sought to fill in this "hole" by tendering more or less useful estimates. Consider, for example, Michael Conniff's calculation of Caribbean laborers:

> Officially, canal authorities brought over 31,000 West Indian men and a few women. But in fact, between 150,000 and 200,000 men and women must have migrated during the construction era, for in most years some 20,000 West Indians were on the canal payroll, and turnover was high. Contemporaries estimated that only about a third of the West Indian community worked for the canal at any moment. The rest were dependents or had jobs and businesses in Panama's terminal cities. These figures are staggering when we recall that in 1896 Panama City had only 24,000 inhabitants and the country as a whole 400,000. The West Indian migration to Panama constituted a demographic tidal wave, the largest yet in Caribbean history. (Conniff 1985: 29)

Attempting to offer proof of how many Colón Men migrated to the isthmus, Conniff's approximations more effectively illustrate how *elusive* their numbers are. This passage persuasively suggests that the total number of Caribbean workers on the U.S.-built canal was larger than most official accounts indicated; it also alludes to the tremendous size of the migration. However, it simultaneously reveals that ICC payroll records and ship manifests alone were inadequate measures of these migrants' presence. Since these sources can only imprecisely record the number of Caribbean workers, similar types of records must be similarly inadequate. Still, Caribbean demographic surveys, social scientific data, and oral histories complement evidence that is more easily reproducible.

Colón Men migrated to Panamá in droves and they comprised the largest segment of railroad and canal workforces, bringing each enterprise to completion. It is their willingness to migrate that is interesting here. Historical accounts demonstrate that these workers were exploited, discriminated against, that their work was not valued, and Panamanians resented their presence. Additionally, few Colón Men made money or remained healthy in the Canal Zone; in fact, hundreds of thousands died, and died poor. Of those who lived, many never returned to the Caribbean, opting to remain in Panamá or to migrate to other locales. Neither did migration to Panamá offer a respite from hardship, because the difficulties Afro-Caribbean workers faced in Panamá were very similar to those they confronted at home.[24] It appears, then, that the substantial features of isthmian migration and work could not sustain the hopeful swell of Caribbean migrants.

A brief examination of Caribbean migration—its motivations, conclusions, effects, and migrants' connections to "home"—is useful here, but the most valuable material is found in the particular anecdotal and recollected imaginings of Panamá migrations.[25] Both the general study of Caribbean migration and the specific investigation of Panamá migration taken up here reveal the central importance of a mythology built on imaginable truths.

Traditional migration studies have recently begun to analyze this phenomenon in the context of the Caribbean, a change initiated by Caribbeanists in search of alternate means of analyzing the facts and fictions about these movements. Migration has long been seen as integral to "the mythologies of citizenship and mobility, of heroism, exploitation and conquest" and as an "aberrant event" bringing poor, black workers into colonial or imperial centers (Chamberlain 1998: 5, 6). While each of these perspectives resonates in European contexts, neither captures the subtleties of Caribbean migrations. With regard to this dissonance, Elizabeth Thomas-Hope posits that:

> the extent to which Caribbean migration has evolved its own dynamic, rooted in social institutions and consciousness, has been omitted from the concept of migration in most of the academic literature. The paradigms which have dominated thinking in relation to international migration present a conceptualization of a movement at all times responding to negative conditions. As a result, analyses frequently have confused explanation of migration in general with causation of one movement or type of movement in particular. (Thomas-Hope 1992: 15)[26]

Glossing economic, political, and societal systems approaches, she identifies blind spots that make analyses from these distinct perspectives insufficient measures of migration in the circum-Caribbean region.[27] Such models merely explain when and how many people migrate but do not address migrants' motivations or migration as a social, historical, and cultural construct (Chamberlain 1997: 6). To adjust for deficiencies in these approaches, and to embrace cultural, social, and otherwise "positive" characteristics that figure into Caribbean people's decisions to migrate, Thomas-Hope suggests that a multidimensional theoretical frame, composed from aspects of each of the above methods, would best serve the study of Caribbean migration (Thomas-Hope 1992: 22).[28] To this end, the geographer proffers a model that intends to explain "the tendency for migration, and not solely the volume and timing" of it (15). She states:

> environments at all levels of scale reflect historical-structural factors manifest in global inequalities, societal tensions between and within societies and political tensions between individuals and the state, as well as between source and destination countries. These structural factors are significant in the decision-making processes relating to migration *through their impact on the nature of the images which are formed in the minds of potential migrants.* (22, emphasis added)

Thus potential migrants recognize many types of "environmental influences" that inform their migration behavior, but they sift them through their own vision of migration, in its potential *and* active forms. Their images of migration are made up of elements that are deemed personally and communally relevant (Thomas-Hope 1992: 22–23). In other words, the perception of a particular migration can reflect many factual features (economics, immigration laws, etc.), but "family stories and memories" are equally significant (Chamberlain 1997: 9; Richardson 1983: 174). One must then consider that a potential migrant's image of his/her migration may not reflect the factual reality of the movement. If this is the case, then "the model appropriate for analysis of the migration process must include the existence of the two separate, but closely connected, planes of reality—that of the actual or objective reality and that of the perceived reality of the image. The decision-maker lies at the interface of these two planes" (Thomas-Hope 1992: 24; Richardson 1983: 176). But identifying an individual's perceived reality about a migration has proven to be challenging for traditional migration studies methodologies.

Economic pushes and pulls, movements of global labor, and histories of global North and South relations are all factors of Caribbean isthmian migration, but aspects that are harder to measure—migrants hopes and dreams, family stories, social norms and pressures, and the possibilities that inhere in each—have proven to be as, if not more, important than these factors. Piecing together these motivations, the imagined (hopes) and imaginable (possibilities) truths that shape migrants' behaviors, uncovers items significant to the field of migrations studies, but particularly for this study of isthmian mythographies. Imaginable possibilities are central to fictive isthmian narratives in that they enable the inclusion of quantifiable as well as more elusive Caribbean perspectives in U.S.-oriented canal histories. The same can be said about the decision to migrate to Panamá and the belief in the success to be had there, both of which withstood factual influences to the contrary.

Facts about Colón Men's financial realities, victimization, poverty, illness, and death imperfectly explain their continued migration. For less documentable reasons, "they had . . . been able to adapt to life in the Spanish-American tropics, where Europeans and Americans had failed often" (Conniff 1985: 22). Colón Men, despite being denigrated as people and as workers, believe that their labor was valuable and that they were superior to most other canal workers. These workers complimented North Americans for their ingenuity in conceiving the canal; they nevertheless celebrated their own physical superiority and stamina. Canal histories written by scholars of the Caribbean seem to begin from this imaginable position.

This difference in perspective can be put to the test with regard to the ambivalent representation of Colón Men's susceptibility to illness. If traditional narratives do not offer satisfying conclusions about Caribbean workers' immunity to isthmian diseases, the following verse at least attests to these men's knowledge of and concern with such dangers. This "incidental" song indicates that they were not only susceptible to disease, but they were very aware that death was possible.[29] The song, allegedly passed down by Panamá returnees, includes the following lyrics:

> Fever and ague all day long
> At Panama, at Panama
> Wish you were dead before very long
> At Panama, at Panama (Richardson 1985: 121)

"Ague" is a malarial fever or a shivering fit, consequently its use in the opening line is deliberately repetitious. The repetition can indicate the severity of the illness as well as the degree of workers' concern with it. Because popular song, as a genre, can potentially reach a wide range of individuals—literate and illiterate—Caribbean people were likely more aware of their vulnerability to isthmian diseases than ICC officials and historians allowed.[30]

Because the above verse was sung on board a Colón-bound ship, even soon-to-be Colón Men were aware of malaria, its symptoms, and likely result. Rumors about the prevalence of death on the isthmus began during railroad construction and supports the way the song's meaning was disseminated. For instance, a popular railroad era anecdote asserted that there was one worker death for each railroad tie (Lewis 1980: 19). According to a couple of interpretations, however, if one accounted for the actual number of ties requisitioned for this project (around 150,000) and compared this to the number of documented employees (between 5,000 and 6,000), the story does not hold up (Haskin 1913: 103; McCullough 1977: 36–37). This "factual" analysis discounts another possibility. Another story in circulation when the United States took on canal production alleged that "black workers were sometimes disposed of in the dumping grounds—simply rolled down an embankment, then buried beneath several tons of spoil—appears in several accounts and is undoubtedly based on fact" (McCullough 1977: 173). In the absence of certificates or other forms of documentation, the deaths of these unnamed workers can only be recalled anecdotally and through repeated tellings. But the accuracy of either song or story is less important than the image of extreme human sacrifice each invokes. The anecdote and song would have been particularly meaningful for Colón Men whose lives—and deaths—lay outside certain documentable realities. Furthermore, the popularity of both popular narratives suggest "the extent to which [they capture] the fantasy of the listener and can enter the popular imagination, despite the class, culture or age group of the listener" (Mohammed 34).

Even with direct knowledge of death and disease on the isthmus, Colón Men continued to migrate in droves. This has typically been explained by the powerful financial lure that Panamá symbolized. Undoubtedly Panamá Money pulled—and economic need at home pushed—Caribbean workers to the isthmus; however, their attraction extends beyond facile materialism. Lancelot Lewis remarks that:

> almost every community in the West Indies had its own men who had gone to Panamá with only the clothes on their backs, a small tin trunk, a dollar canvas steamer chair, and a few chickens; and who had come back with savings enough to set them up for life. So determined were these men to save their money that many fell ill because of malnutrition. (Lewis 1980: 34)

Richardson confirms the lengths Colón Men were willing to go to succeed financially in Panamá:

> some Barbadians in Panama, inspired by dreams of taking money home, seem, literally, to have worked themselves to death. In late 1905 a Barbadian man known only as Prince was familiar to many persons around the Colón dockyard. Prince . . . was reported by returnees to Barbados "to have stiffened out and died after thirty days and thirty nights of uninterrupted labour." (Richardson 1985: 148)

Both Lewis and Richardson imply that underemployment and low wages played significantly in Caribbean men's desire to work on the isthmus. The decision to seek employment abroad was additionally inspired by overpopulation on some islands (Conniff 1985: 20; Richardson 1985: 84; Lewis 1980: 30; Newton 1984: 18). But the deprivations to which workers subjected themselves in the Canal Zone speak of more than the wish—even the need—to earn money and buy things. Apparently they were willing to make sacrifices on the isthmus to achieve a higher standard of living—but so that they could take their Panamá Money home.

The act of migration, then, could provide migrants with *cultural* capital. For Caribbean men, migration was an outward manifestation of their masculinity and ambition, qualities that they could parlay into "commodities": reputation/status, goods, land, or even an eligible mate. Money and material goods reflected migrants' personalities, but less tangible signs—such as a cosmopolitan air, an assumed accent, and knowledge about other people and lands—also shaped their identities. Returning migrants reaped the benefits of their travels, and so did their families. Still these benefits were only tangentially important; what was most significant was whether or not the migrant's home community *believed* that he was successful while abroad. Failure to return with some sign of their travels would be a source of shame for both migrants and their families.[31] Since the number of Caribbean people involved, the potentially large amounts of money to be made, and "modern" skills to be learned distinguished isthmian migration, this particular movement was attended by an impressive amount of cultural capital.

So determined were isthmian laborers to return to the Caribbean with bulging pockets, and so expected was this result, that some remained in Panamá because they "were ashamed to return without money, because they had left home hoping to better their condition" (Newton 1984: 158; Mohammed 49). Accomplished returnees personified Panamá success; they became known for their spending, flashy clothes, and assertive demeanor. In this guise, returnees soon passed into myth; this mythic Colón Man, by contrast, then gave birth to—and made life difficult for—his less successful counterpart.

Successfully returning from Panamá—not to mention the pluck necessary to go there in the first place—manifested in some migrants as cockiness or bravado (Richardson 1992: 152). "Older Barbadians," for example, "recall with amusement the images conveyed by 'Panama men' who returned from the Canal Zone with a strutting self-consciousness, bedecked with the latest fashions from Colón" (151). Colón Men therefore embodied myriad Caribbean realities, particularly ones that defined "men" by their reputations and masculine performances.[32] Local residents might have enviously derided isthmian returnees, but this response reflects a couple of social issues. The economic and status gains of Panamá migration sometimes translated into Colón Men's challenges to local class structures. Though isthmian migration and work might have provided emigrants the money and cultural capital to win the acclaim of their peers, tensions erupted whenever they moved too far "out of place": the ease of Colón Men's social movements was marred by their lack of upper class pedigree, color, and/or education.

A different kind of tension resulted when returned peasant and/or working class migrants strutted back home. "Capitals" afforded them by isthmian migration let Colón Men claim some features of "hegemonic masculinity," though their inclusion in the paradigm was blocked because only white, upper class men were granted full access.[33] Black and brown men of the upper classes were allowed limited access, but buying into the paradigm meant preventing "lower class" men from entering the ranks since hegemonic masculinity had a distinctly upper class bias.[34] Because of this "gate keeping" dynamic, under the hegemonic masculinity model, men unified more around class than race (though, perversely, race and skin color still militated against black men's full entrance into the ranks of hegemonic masculinity) (Downes, "Boys of Empire," 30, 31). Nevertheless, because the entire social structure in the Anglophone Caribbean[35] was shaped around the hegemonic masculine norm, even unschooled and poor men were intimately aware of it through sports (particularly cricket), war (and the rhetoric of war), muscular Christianity (Downes, "Boys of Empire," 4, 8, 10, 11), and (for the literate) "penny dreadfuls" (ibid, 18–19). Economic decline among all blacks mitigated the impact of the educational system as a means of transmission (few, even the brown-skinned elite, could afford school fees) (Downes 2003: 319–20); more emphasis on the above-mentioned alternative means of transmission and, thus, this dominant notion of masculinity still reigned.[36]

Migration, and isthmian migration in particular, can be placed among these alternate means of masculine indoctrination since canal work could readily be recast in terms of physicality/athleticism and soldiering: confronting *and* surviving physical, natural, and human dangers and returning with capitals identifies men of the peasant and working classes as "men."[37] Migration also served as an option for poor and black-skinned men (and possibly for lighter and more affluent others) when other means of access to the masculine ideal were denied them (Downes 2003: 312; Newton 1984: 170). Emigrants therefore carried this Caribbean social reality with them to the isthmus; it necessarily evolved in response to the uniquely North American and white brand of masculinity (characterized by the mythologized "rugged individual") that dominated the isthmus. Colón Men's concept of a masculine identity continued to develop when they confronted the powerful and ubiquitous myth of the Panamá Canal worker. The myth, maintained by both migrants and their communities, compelled returnees to live up to its mythic proportions by wearing costumes identified with Panamá, affecting an "American" accent and behavior, and using Panamá Money to buy a home or land, or to support a woman (or women).

In light of the social and cultural experiences that shaped most Caribbean migrants, official claims of these workers' inferiority took a backseat to what Colón Men could take from their Panamá experiences. Although the most positive description that isthmian authorities attributed to Caribbean laborers was that they worked cheaply and were plentiful, Caribbeanists cite instances where Colón Men thought differently. Many of them believed in their importance to the canal enterprise, a belief that could be seen in the ways they applied the skills learned through canal work when they returned home. They often used their isthmian experiences to improve their families' lives and those of their neighbors. Colón Men participated in an exploitative project, but they learned more than victimization: they used their work experiences to revise the ways exploitation defined them.

Caribbean men traveled to the isthmus to better their fortunes, in search of adventure, or to learn something about the world. These truths, when considered with economic reasons for the movement, stand as signs of a "social existence" beyond "the immediate control of the dominant."[38] Colón Men, therefore, were not limited by the views of their supervisors; they possessed their own agendas, ones that contested their officially denigrated bodies and labor. This reclamation manifested as their revised vision of themselves.[39] Examples of Colón Men's social existence complicate the view of these men as slaves to economic trends or passive victims of railroad and canal officials.

Historians and geographers of the Caribbean locate Colón Men not only within regional traditions of work and migration, but also within the Caribbean's history of slavery and emancipation. Emancipation in the Anglophone Caribbean left most of the formerly enslaved population with a strong desire to partake of all the benefits of freedom; unfortunately, most planters refused to recognize this desire (Senior 1978: 65, 67).[40] When former plantation owners resolutely exploited the labor of formerly enslaved peoples, the latter actively resisted by refusing to work or by migrating. Dissatisfaction with unfavorable economic and/or social conditions made isthmian migration an option, even if not always the most desirable one; only in the absence of an acceptable quality of life at home did Caribbean people chose to go in search of it (Senior 1978: 65). This idea is confirmed by the following verse, recollected by Douglas Gay of Miles Corner, Christ Church, Barbados:

> We want more wages, we want it now
> And if we don't get it, we going to Panama
> Yankees say they want we down there,
> We want more wages, we want it now. (Richardson 1985: 132)

This threat seldom brought wage increases; therefore, Panamá migration remained a practical alternative.

Some workers resisted undesirable labor and wage practices in their home countries by moving, much to the chagrin of local planters who often lost their best workers to the isthmian project. Barbadian planters sought to stem this tide by encouraging the government to reinstate defunct anti-emigration laws. As proof of the need to curtail Panamá migration, one member of the Barbadian Legislative Council claimed to have overheard an "incident" where a young Panamá-bound man yelled to "a gang of sugar estate workers being supervised by the plantation manager . . . 'why you don't hit de manager in de head, and come along wid we!'" (Richardson 1985: 106). This Panamá-inspired attitude, the councilman feared, might spark a working-class revolution on the island; therefore, the Barbadian government felt it had the moral and political obligation to thwart black workers' migration. Members of Barbados' upper classes knew, perhaps intuitively, that isthmian emigration meant not only the loss of a surplus labor force, but also changes in the country's social makeup: Panamá might enable a revolution in class—and possibly racial—hierarchies.

The Caribbean's restrictive social environment might have prevented returned Panamá migrants from producing significant social or economic change back home (Newton 1984: 108), but there is evidence that disputes this claim. Colón Men may have played an integral part in the formation of labor unions in Jamaica, judging from the acknowledged behavior of other returned migrants.[41] Speaking generally of agricultural migrants returning from the circum-Caribbean, Richardson notes, "colonial officials [in the Lesser Antilles] dreaded the men's return . . . because, for the next few months, unemployment always became a problem on the local sugarcane plantations, incipient labor protest and disturbances surfaced, and burglary rates rose" (Richardson 1992: 140). He continues by describing a revolutionary organization called the Caribbean League, formed by West Indian soldiers who served in World War I. These men were "fed up with the racism they had suffered during the war" and through their association "vowed that blacks should govern themselves upon their return to the British Caribbean, using force if necessary" (Richardson 1992: 179).

Finally, speaking of the impact of Panamá Money in Barbados, Richardson maintains that:

> the loss of many people and the gain of unprecedented amounts of cash by the black working class on Barbados set significant social and economic forces in motion. The workers' exodus undermined an antiquated sugar cane industry and inspired its modernization. Barbadian planter-worker relations then changed. . . . A decline in planter paternalism was accompanied by heightened class consciousness and incipient political activity on the parts of black Barbadians. (Richardson 1985: 3)

If a migrant's home-island would not support this level of activism, at minimum returned isthmian workers could make choices about the kinds of work they would perform. Rather than go back to estate work, Jamaican returnees "would emigrate again, even repeatedly, and ultimately stay permanently abroad" (Thomas-Hope 1978: 76). Ideally, returnees sought employment other than plantation work, sometimes opting for entrepreneurial ventures. These examples suggest strongly that returning migrants likely used their migration experiences to respond differently to, if not to transform, social conditions and to address racial discrimination once on their home islands.

Caribbean migration to Panamá must be measured in these social and cultural terms, but the material economic gains remain crucial. In other words, in the case of isthmian migration, the sociocultural and the economic are inextricably tied (and the same can be said of the relationship between the various Panamá narratives). The lure of Panamá Money appeared to outweigh the possibility of illness and/or death as a result of canal work (McCullough 1977: 181). Depending on social and economic/land conditions on their home islands, money could translate into a manner of class mobility for Colón Men or permit them to purchase property and consumer goods, set up small farms, build or improve upon homes, and open small shops (Newton 1984: 106; Richardson 1985: 153).[42] Money distributed in the region profited Colón Men, their families, and, by extension, various Caribbean social/public institutions. Because workers in Panamá sent money and goods to friends and family through the mail, postal systems in Jamaica and Barbados had to improve to accommodate the increased activity (Senior 1978: 64; Richardson 1985: 161). Lastly, one cannot overlook Jamaican farmers who, growing food staples and exporting them to the isthmus, got their piece of Panamá's bounty without leaving home (Senior 1978: 92, 101–3).

Still, the value of Panamá Money extended beyond the material. The degree to which Colón Men and their families felt exploited by white plantation owners is evinced by the following verse:

> Mass Charley say wan' kiss Matty
> Kiss him with a willing mind
> Me ra-ra boom oh
> Colon money done (Senior 1978: 89)

Migrants used Panamá Money to free themselves from familiar financial dependence as well as other forms of coercion practiced by the powerful. Returning with money addressed certain types of exploitation, and the Colón Man's self-possession, and his family's security, thrived.

Though not as measurable as cash, Panamá workers brought back skills, learned through railroad and canal work, that they would not have otherwise acquired. These skills frequently translated into improved farming and building techniques in Jamaica (103). It has been demonstrated that in Barbados:

> [Panama men] made subtle but important contributions around their houses and tenantry yards, such as improving drainage in their house plots or screening windows, . . . thereby improving local health conditions by implementing what they had learned in Panama. Their presence, moreover, added to the local reservoir of wisdom and knowledge about the world outside, and . . . they became the village elders, older and experienced men and women to whom everyone else in the community would take their problems as well as appeals for advice. (Richardson 1985: 153)

Panamá Money was certainly a significant "pull" factor in isthmian migration, but one cannot underestimate the psychic benefit that the promise of unprecedented amounts of cash afforded Colón Men and their families. It allowed a small measure of autonomy from plantation owners who previously had a major claim on their lives and livelihood. More difficult to quantify were the skills Colón Men learned in the Canal Zone and practiced at home. Isthmian migration, then, linked financial and material, quantifiable and undocumentable, lasting and ephemeral experiences for Colón Men and their communities.

Notwithstanding the strength of these factors, it is clear that potential migrants considered that they had some say in their fate. A migrant's "luck," more than tales of death, disease, and racist bosses, determined how he would succeed—or not succeed—on the isthmus (Newton 1984: 172). For example, one's "bad luck" in having a low-paying job in the Caribbean could be changed, thus bringing "good luck," by migrating to Panamá. Some soon-to-be migrants even deemed isthmian migration educationally profitable, because of the potential exposure to other peoples, languages, and customs (Newton 1984: 170; Senior 1978: 70).

Although Colón Men helped build the routes that gave the United States access to its western shore and bolstered its global standing, their contribution to Panamá's throughways and development has not been adequately recognized.[43] At the end of the U.S. canal period, the ICC unceremoniously shipped most Caribbean laborers out. The Commission planned to phase out thousands of canal jobs and, between 1913 and 1916, discharged almost 30,000 workers. The U.S. government repatriated almost 13,400 more workers by 1921 (Newton 1984: 157–58). The Commission had finished with its Caribbean workforce. Nevertheless, some Colón Men continued to negotiate a space for themselves on the isthmus (Lewis 1980: 97). Those who were unwilling to deal with the long-tense relationship with Panamanians signed on to farm labor projects in Latin America and the Caribbean.

V

By drawing on social and cultural dimensions of canal workers' experiences, in addition to their material realities, Caribbean creative writers do more than supplement historical Panamá Canal narratives. These writers challenge the notion that any one account can productively depict the breadth of Colón Men's realities. Mythographies of Panamá Canal migration and Colón Men embody a more cumulative, a more creatively nuanced approach to the study of the canal and the experiences of its workers. Yet fictive manifestations of the Colón Man cannot be dismissed as mere examples of artistic license any more than historical records can be seen as the entire truth of his experiences. Rather, I see the relation between these genres as a complex negotiation that reveals much about the lived experience of Caribbean people, one that binds together literary, cultural, and social truths with the realities of economics, geography, and migration. The creative dimension of Caribbean isthmian realities is not simply derived from the history of the canal; it also contributes to the shaping of that history. This is why it is important to reimagine Caribbean history and identity in terms other than those determined by exploitation and oppression.

In fictionalizing workers' narratives, writers draw from the words of the migrants themselves, as they have been recorded in memory and letters. While there was a strong possibility that Panamá-bound migrants would be unsuccessful, they continued to migrate *and* to believe that they would prosper on the isthmus. This belief, then, motivated Panamá migration more than the proliferating "stories" of death and disease on the isthmus deterred them. In the hands of Caribbean writers, the Colón Man is this belief incarnate. The figure is made "real" through and because of these imaginable motivations.

NOTES

1. These lyrics appear in Louise Cramer's "Songs of West Indian Negroes in the Canal Zone." Of the two versions of the song, Cramer notes the "first version was one learned in Jamaica by [Mr. Charles] Barton, while the second . . . was contributed by Clemente Ara of La Boca [Panamá]" (252). Lancelot Lewis's study of Caribbean canal laborers references a letter by George H. Martin that mentions this song, though Martin's song features "Nattie" rather than "Matty" (Lewis 1980: 124; *LICCW*, George H. Martin Letter, page 4 of 7).

2. From the sixteenth century until 1821, what is now Panamá (a "Cueva Indian word [for] a place where many fishes are taken" [McCullough 1977: 112; LaFeber 1989: 4]), was a Spanish territory. In 1821, it was declared independent from Spain

and became part of Gran Colombia. The country became the Province of New Granada in 1830. Thirty-three years later, the province was absorbed into Colombia proper, but was largely ignored. Finally, in 1903, the Republic of Panamá won its independence from Colombia, mainly through U.S. governmental and military involvement.

3. The name *Castilla del Oro*, by which the land was known in 1519 (McCullough 1977: 111–12), reflects the quantity of Spanish treasure passing through the territory.

4. There were some in the United States, namely investors in the transcontinental railroad, who opposed the construction of a canal. These businessmen correctly believed that their financial interests would not be served by the construction of the faster canal route and actively—though unsuccessfully—campaigned against it.

5. See Richard Collin's *Theodore Roosevelt's Caribbean: The Panama Canal, the Monroe Doctrine, and the Latin American Context* (Baton Rouge: Louisiana State University Press, 1990): 132, for a discussion of Panamá's independence movements. Although the United States claimed not to be directly involved in the revolution, officials suggested that they would not interfere in the internal affairs of another country, effectively signaling its support (LaFeber 1989: 24). According to McCullough, "without the military presence of the United States—had there been no American gunboats standing off shore at Colón and Panama City—the Republic of Panama probably would not have lasted a week" (McCullough 1977: 379). Major continues in this vein by citing President Roosevelt who "spoke of the possibility of a Panamanian revolt which could bring about 'a condition of things that will warrant the action we desire [the building of the canal] being taken openly, honestly, and in good faith'" (Major 1993: 37). Also, the leaders of Panamá's revolution had one thing in common: they were all affiliated with the U.S.-controlled Panamá Railroad Company. Dr. Manuel Amador Guerrero was the Railroad's doctor; José Arango, its attorney; James Shaler, the superintendent of the Railroad; and James Beers, the freight agent. These men and their descendants dominated Panamá's government for the next sixty years (LaFeber 1989: 25).

6. Appearing to be an attempt to correct its inappropriate support of Panamá's revolution, in 1921 the United States government authorized "an indemnity of $25,000,000 [to Colombia] . . . for the loss of Panama" (McCullough 1977: 617).

7. The Panamanian government nominated Bunau-Varilla as "envoy extraordinary and minister plenipotentiary to Washington" to negotiate the canal treaty. As previously mentioned, Bunau-Varilla was affiliated with *Compagnie Nouvelle* and, acting in this capacity, he was invested in negotiating a profitable deal with the U.S. government. He, therefore, largely ignored the concessions outlined by Panamá's new government. The Republic demanded the reversion of all lands previously leased to railroad and canal companies; a share of all proceeds from the sale of Panamanian assets; leave to charge duties on imported consumer goods; shared judicial and law enforcement duties in the Canal Zone; and, finally, "$2 million of the canal indemnity should be given to Panama, leaving $8 million to be invested by the U.S. government so as to produce an annual income of $240,000 in addition to the $250,000 annuity" (Major 1993: 43).

8. W. Leon Pepperman, *Who Built the Panama Canal?* (London: J. M. Dent and Sons, 1915).

9. At this time, and throughout the building of each project, the isthmus was an unhealthy place, particularly its coastal towns. Knowing the climate, native peoples refused to work there (Senior 1980: 67; Lewis 1980: 15). Additionally, as locals were native to the country, they could easily disappear when the required labor became onerous. Lastly, as far as authorities were concerned, there were not enough native workers to suit them, communication was a problem between English-speaking bosses and Spanish-speaking workers, and the latter were said to be weak and lazy (McCullough 1977: 111; Major 1993: 81; Newton 1984: 36, 38).

10. Although it is difficult to determine the exact wage for agricultural workers in the Caribbean from 1850 to 1855, Elizabeth Petras indicates that it was low and dropping. *Jamaican Labor Migration: White Capital and Black Labor, 1850–1930* (Boulder: Westview Press, 1988): 93. However, wages during the construction of the U.S. canal might provide a useful perspective. Manual laborers on the United States' canal could earn ten cents an hour while agricultural workers in Barbados made twenty cents a day—but only during harvesting season (McCullough 1977: 475); in Jamaica during the same period, "the [Isthmian Canal] commission was able to exploit such a vast number of imported workers at such depressed rates precisely because of the extremely low wage threshold [workers] obtained in their labor market of origin" (Petras 1988: 175).

11. A sea-level canal would require a trans-isthmian cut of relatively equal depth. This type was impractical, but not impossible, at the time because Atlantic and Pacific tides were significantly different; a sea-level canal, therefore, likely would not accommodate the higher and rougher Pacific-side tides. A lock-type canal gradually raises ships entering on the Atlantic side up to a median point and then lowers them to the Pacific level, through which the roughness of the latter would be ameliorated. However impractical for the time, de Lesseps' desire for a sea-level canal was germane. Looking toward the future, and imagining it marked by a physical sign of his glory, the financier knew that a sea-level canal would (almost) never become obsolete. Unlike a lock-type canal that could only accommodate vessels that fit within its dimensions, a sea-level canal could more easily be made to receive ships of many sizes. See Jonathan Bolt's *To Culebra: A Play in Two Acts* (Salt Lake City: Gibbs Smith Publisher/Peregrine Smith Books, 1989) for a fictionalized account of de Lesseps and his aspirations. See also McCullough's third chapter, "Consensus of One" (70–86) for a detailed discussion of the French financier and the failure of the first French canal company.

12. George W. Westerman, "Glimpses of West Indian Life on the Isthmus and the Role of the Isthmian Negro Press," Writings Unpublished D-N, Box 4, "Glimpses of West Indian Life . . . " Folder (George W. Westerman Collection, Rare Books and Manuscripts Division, Schomburg Center for Research in Black Culture, New York Public Library): 2.

13. McCullough offers a conflicting view of black laborers' housing during the French canal period. He says that "barracks for black workers were set on high concrete footings, a precaution against floods and rats. The buildings were large

enough for fifty bunks each. Well-seasoned lumber was used, and the design was sensible for the climate, with long verandas and plenty of windows" (McCullough 1977: 133). These buildings probably deteriorated by the time of the U.S. canal attempt and were replaced by quarters the author described as "deplorable" due to poor construction, location, and institutional racism (576, 585). I do, however, find it hard to believe that there was such a drastic difference between accommodations for blacks provided by French and U.S. authorities. This is borne out by a photograph that Willis Abbot describes as "a typical scene in the negro quarters of Colon during the period of French activity in Panama." The caption proclaims: "FILTH THAT WOULD DRIVE A BERKSHIRE FROM HIS STY" (Abbot 1913: 121). Contrary to McCullough's characterization, Abbot references paving and sanitary improvements in the "negro quarters" under the U.S. regime (Abbot 1913: 120). Nevertheless, testaments of former Colón Men, documented in *LICCW*, indicate across-the-board dissatisfaction with ICC-provided housing. Rufus Edward Forde, a Colón Man from Trinidad, elected to rent a room rather than take advantage of free ICC housing (Forde, page 1 of 5). Barbadian John F. Prescod remembered a dynamite-box shantytown that workers built and inhabited (Prescod, page 2 of 2). As James Ashby notes, the existence of the shantytown could have signaled resistance to ICC authority of another kind. He remarks that workers "still had to report on the job and work for if one did not work they could not sleep in the camp at night. Police officer would take them to jail" (page 1 of 1). Other contestants stated that their actual accommodations failed to meet those described in their work contracts (see Gard, page 1 of 2), possibly because Caribbean workers were sometimes housed in boxcars or tents (see Martin, page 1 of 7, and Belgrave, page 1 of 3; see also Allick, page 1 of 1, and Beckford, page 4 of 11). Finally Jacob Joseph writes that often men were housed six per room, requiring some to sleep on the floor (Joseph, page 1 of 1). It goes without saying that some were satisfied with their accommodations, which suggests that the location of their accommodations determined its quality: Ange Julienne Lunche is certain that housing in Empire was best (Lunche, page 1 of 1). Philip McDonald, a migrant from Grenada, similarly determined that he was appropriately quartered because he lived in rooms set aside for "colored Americans" (McDonald, page 3 of 9).

14. George Westerman, *The West Indian Worker on the Canal Zone* (National Civic League, 1951): 7.

15. The ICC provided for the material needs of their workers to encourage a stable workforce; they attempted to provide for men's conjugal and domestic needs as well, by importing women from Martinique (McCullough 1977: 577). Of course, the latter practice was stopped as soon as people in the States got wind of what they interpreted as government-sponsored prostitution.

16. *LICCW*, John Butcher letter, page 4 of 6.

17. This attitude changed—dramatically, but largely for the canal's white employees—when John Stevens was named chief engineer of the canal project in June 1905. "The digging is the least thing of all, [Stevens] declared. Starting at once, Dr. Gorgas was to have whatever men and supplies he needed" (McCullough 1977: 465). Under the former chief engineer, Dr. Gorgas was expected to address the isthmus's sanitary and health concerns with an annual budget of $50,000; under Stevens, Gorgas was able to requisition $90,000 worth of wire win-

dow screen, not to mention a significant amount of medical supplies and manpower (466).

18. Described as "the proud, allegedly racist, white population of Panama," locals were not pleased to entertain the railroad or canal's black, Caribbean, Protestant, and English-speaking workers, particularly when they did not leave at the end of construction (Newton 1984: 112). See McCullough 1977: 585–87 on U.S./Panamanian tensions, particularly with regard to Caribbean workers.

19. George Westerman, "Gold Men and Silver Men," Writings Unpublished D-N, Box 4, "Gold Men and Silver Men" Folder (George W. Westerman Collection, Rare Books and Manuscripts Division, Schomburg Center for Research in Black Culture, New York Public Library): 1. North American blacks proved to be an anathema to the Canal Zone's gold/silver system. As blacks, they were supposed to appear only on the silver roll, but as U.S. citizens they were entitled to be on the gold. Haskin notes "very few of the Negroes ever made any protest against [gold/silver segregation, although] once in awhile an American negro would go to the post office and be told that he must call at the 'silver' window. He would protest for awhile, but finding it useless, would acquiesce" (160). Patrice Brown concurs, but draws attention to the pressure faced by black Americans to "use common sense and follow the course of least resistance" and "transact [their] business on the side where others of [their] race transact their business" (P. Brown 1997: 124, 125). Brown also notes that, as a body, black Americans sought to secure rights afforded them as U.S. citizens (126); unfortunately, their complaints were most often met with "piecemeal concessions [that] were granted only as requested and only when canal authorities thought it necessary" (125). Under John Stevens, North American blacks were allowed to remain on the gold roll, but only as policemen, postmasters, and teachers (Major 1993: 79; see also McCullough 1977: 576).

20. An internal letter between commission officials reveals the nature of this complication. Writing to Gaillard, Slifer notes "I have been endeavoring to transfer all Negroes from the Gold to the Silver roll. . . . The situation, however, is getting to be somewhat awkward, as we have divided the Gold from the Silver employees in our commissary. . . . It is the policy of the Commission to keep employees who are undoubtedly black or belong to mixed races on the Silver rolls" (from Slifer to Gaillard, 12 and 15 February 1908, in Panamá Canal Commission 2-F-14, quoted in Conniff 1985: 32; P. Brown 1997: 123). Major shows that canal authorities also took steps to move "Silver whites" to "the Gold rolls as fast as possible" (Major 1993: 79). ICC authorities tried to address the similar though thornier problem of black Americans on the gold roll by "ceasing to hire American Negroes for the gold roll, although they allowed the few still carried on [it] to remain there. From early 1907 on, 'special' contracts were devised that put African Americans on the 'silver' roll but granted them some privileges given to American citizens on the 'gold' roll" (P. Brown 1997: 123, see also 124).

21. McCullough further complicates the issue of racial injustice in Panamá by identifying economically and politically motivated reasons for it. He says that "simple problems of supply and demand also [influenced racial disparities on the isthmus], [as] experienced technicians . . ., doctors, and competent clerical people were always in short supply and had to be kept satisfied if the canal was to be built; common unskilled laborers from the impoverished islands of the Caribbean

were always available in abundance and expected no better than what they got, which for the most part was better than what they had known at home. And besides, there was the political factor: the labor force was not merely black, it was foreign; these were not United States citizens and in Washington therefore they represented no constituency" (578–79). These contributing factors, though persuasive, do not explain why equally foreign and similarly poor European laborers were afforded privileges denied black Caribbean workers.

22. One can get a sense of this attitude from the following. In 1915, Secretary of State Robert Lansing spoke of the need for the U.S. to fortify the Panamá Canal diligently. Speaking specifically with regard to Panamá's interests in the completed trans-isthmian canal, "Lansing wrote with brutal candour that the Monroe Doctrine was 'founded . . . upon a fact, namely the superior power of the United States to compel submission to its will. . . . In its advocacy of the Monroe Doctrine, the United States considers its own interests. The integrity of other American nations is an incident, not an end'" (Major 1993: 5).

23. Abbot's *The Panama Canal in Picture and Prose*, Haskin's *The Panama Canal*, and Pepperman's *Who Built the Panama Canal?* are contemporaneous accounts that celebrate North American achievements in the Canal Zone and downplay problems with construction and the rigid social system perfected by the ICC. McCullough's *The Path Between the Seas*, LaFeber's *The Panama Canal: The Crisis in Historical Perspective*, and Major's *Prize Possession* take a broader approach than do the older narratives, yet their U.S. orientation leaves little space for sustained and critical discussions of the Commission's Caribbean workforce.

24. Olive Senior draws parallels between the experiences of Jamaicans in Jamaica and in Panamá, arguing that "while the horrors of Colon may have exposed the majority of Jamaicans to experiences of a new and different *character*, in its particulars the *quality* of life in Colon differed little from what the masses of people migrating had been accustomed to in their homeland" (Senior 1978: 63). Bonham Richardson invokes a similar sentiment in locating "the Panama Canal experiences for black Barbadians was imbedded in the cumulative and complex history of Caribbean colonialism" (Richardson 1985: 5). Irma Watkins-Owens describes Caribbean peoples' isthmian migration as the movement that facilitated Caribbean/U.S. migrations, and that offered these migrants their first experience "with American-style Jim Crow." *Blood Relations: Caribbean Immigrants and the Harlem Community, 1900–1930* (Bloomington: Indiana University Press, 1996): 14.

25. Velma Newton defines migration as "a permanent, or semi-permanent change of residence, irrespective of distance, and [of] the voluntary or involuntary nature of the act" (Newton 1984: 3). Additionally, Elizabeth M. Thomas-Hope identifies the political connections to the home country that migrants maintain as significant features of Caribbean migration. *Explanation in Caribbean Migration: Perception and the Image: Jamaica, Barbados, St. Vincent* (London: MacMillan Press/ Warwick University Caribbean Studies, 1992): 19. Watkins-Owens makes a similar claim about migrants' continued personal connections (Watkins-Owens 1996: 11). By pointing out that Caribbean governments rely on foreign capital remitted by citizens who have migrated, Mary Chamberlain also affirms that migrants maintain relationships to their home countries. *Caribbean Migration: Globalised Identities* (New York: Routledge, 1998): 5.

26. In her study of Caribbean immigrants in England, Chamberlain concurs by identifying "a Caribbean *migratory* culture which not only functions as an explanatory factor in migration itself, but continues to function as a cohesive and distinctive force within the host society." *Narratives of Exile and Return* (London: MacMillan Press/Warwick University Caribbean Studies, 1997): 3. In their thinking on uniquely Caribbean migration traditions, these scholars evoke Bonham Richardson who, in his study of migration patterns among the people of St. Kitts and Nevis, comes to the same conclusions (Richardson 1983: 175–76).

27. Thomas-Hope identifies two types of economic approaches, functionalist and historical-structuralist interpretations. Functionalist interpretations suggest that migrant behavior is driven by a rational evaluation of the costs and benefits of moving from a negative environment (low wages, underemployment, overpopulation, etc., known as "pushes") to a positive one (high wages, etc., known as "pulls") (Thomas-Hope 1992: 16; see also Chamberlain 1997: 5). Economic approaches fail, according to Thomas-Hope, because "people do not evaluate the environment and its opportunities or constraints simply on the basis of their impressions of the 'here and now'" (Thomas-Hope 1992: 18). Chamberlain argues that economic models do not account for the impact of culture, history, and/or individual preference (Chamberlain 1997: 5). Historical-structuralist interpretations, based on center-periphery models, posit that workers enter the global marketplace via migration to contribute their labor to "the international exchange and transfer of value" (Thomas-Hope 1992: 18). Yet some migrants defy the inference that their labor is their only commodity. Some are "petty capitalists, using their own migration to further their objective of capital formation"; others are part of the middle classes of their own countries and not the typical "exploited proletarian class" (ibid). Finally, migration is not always aligned to need; people continue to migrate to colonial centers even when centers experience job shortages (ibid). Political approaches can only explain migrations that result from local political crises, as in the case of refugees and others seeking political asylum. These kinds of approaches also presume that refugees sever ties, political ones mostly, with their home countries (19). Finally, a societal systems approach incorporates social, psychological, and economic perspectives and is most often used to explain Caribbean migration. However, this perspective often lacks a theoretical foundation (20) but contributes a discussion of culture "defined as the symbols of power and prestige" to the discourse of Caribbean migration (21). Richardson draws similar conclusions from his survey of models of international migrations (Richardson 1983: 175).

28. Thomas-Hope is not alone in arguing for a multipronged approach to the study of Caribbean migration. Richardson (1983, 1985) concurs with Petras (1988), Senior (1978), McCullough (1977), and Newton (1984) in attributing migration to low wages at home. They, as well as Conniff (1985), also see the potential for high wages on the isthmus—despite rumors of death and disease there—to be another contributing factor. Yet each of these scholars considers the migrant's personal desire to change his situation as significant to his decision to move. Chamberlain argues for the importance of migrants' families in their migration decisions (Chamberlain 1997: 8), and suggests that an approach that combines social and behavioral sciences models can tap into the importance of these features of Caribbean migratory culture (9).

29. These lyrics fit the definition of an "'incidental' song because they deal with some real 'incident'" (Cramer 1946: 249).

30. Other genres support the wide circulation of oral tales about work in Panamá. Since literacy in the Caribbean was generally low, potential migrants were made aware of increased opportunity in, as well as the dangers of, Panamá through song, word-of-mouth, or personal contact with friends/acquaintances who returned with money and in fair health (Newton 1984: 23, 24). Those who could read were subjected to ICC recruiters' dramatic inducements. Readers were bombarded with (sometimes misleading) advertisements extolling the advantages of canal work (Newton 1984: 6–7, 24, 78–85; Lewis 1980: 29–33). Newton offers a prime example: "A trip to Colón?/ Wanted immediately!/ 10,000 labourers/ for the/ Panamá Canal Company./ No indenture. Passengers returning when they like./ Both passage and food given./ $1.50 to $3.00 per day./ Medical care given when sick./ Apply to Charles Gadpaille/ Hincks Street/ Agent, Panamá Canal Company" (80).

31. Velma Pollard, "Imagination and Reality: The Profile of the Colon-man in Jamaican lore and literature" (paper presented at the Twenty-Sixth Annual Conference of the Caribbean Studies Association, St. Maarten, 27 May–2 June 2001).

32. Although a relatively new field in Caribbean Studies, the topic of "Caribbean masculinities" has recently been taken up by scholars in several disciplines, evinced by the following anthologies: *Confronting Power, Theorizing Gender: Interdisciplinary Perspectives in the Caribbean*, edited by Eudine Barriteau (Kingston, Jamaica: University of the West Indies Press, 2003); *Caribbean Portraits: Essays on Gender Ideologies and Identities*, edited by Christine Barrow (Kingston, Jamaica: Ian Randle Publishers/Centre for Gender and Development Studies, University of the West Indies, 1998); and *Caribbean Masculinities: Working Papers*, edited by Rafael Ramírez, Víctor García-Toro, and Ineke Cunningham (San Juan, Puerto Rico: HIV/AIDS Research and Education Center/University of Puerto Rico, 2002).

33. Historian Aviston Downes defines the term as "a discursive construct of masculinity that gains and maintains preeminence through its ideological linkages with socially dominant men." "Gender and the Elementary Teaching Service in Barbados, 1880–1960: A Re-examination of the Feminization and Marginalization of the Black Male Theses," *Confronting Power, Theorizing Gender* (Mona, Jamaica: University of the West Indies Press, 2003): 319. He continues by identifying its prominent features (economic dominance and "headship of the nuclear family unit" to name two), but most relevant to this study is Downes's contention that "only elite men had full access to masculinity so constructed, but subordinate men were allowed to share, albeit as 'secondary patriarchs,' in the spoils of male dominance" (ibid). Other scholars have similarly identified hegemonic masculinity as a paradigm that informs Caribbean masculinities. See *Caribbean Masculinities: Working Papers*: vii, and the following chapter in the same collection: Rhoda Reddock's "'Man Gone, Man Stay!': Masculinity, Ethnicity and Identity in the Contemporary Sociopolitical Context of Trinidad and Tobago," 158; and Hilary McD. Beckles's "Centreing Woman: The Political Economy of Gender in West African and Caribbean Slavery," *Caribbean Portraits* (Kingston, Jamaica: Ian Randle Publishers/Centre for Gender and Development Studies, University of the West Indies, 1998): 99, 103.

34. In order "for any representation of masculinity to become hegemonic, cooptation or complicity of 'lesser masculinities' is necessary." Aviston Downes's "Boys of the Empire: Elite Education and the Socio-Cultural Construction of Hegemonic Masculinity in Barbados, 1875–1920" (e-mail version of an unpublished conference paper): 3. Thus the indoctrination of a select few began through the organization of elite schools for mulatto and black boys, thus inaugurating the use of educational institutions to reshape Bajan and other Caribbean societies. Ironically, women both participated in and resisted dominant masculinities, but for the most part the overarching patriarchal system remained stable (Beckles 1998: 94).

35. Although Barbados and Jamaica, the two Anglophone islands of interest here, were English colonies, the differences between their systems of government (the former locally governed and the latter a Crown colony) make it harder to generalize their experiences of dominant masculinity to each other or to the entire Anglophone Caribbean. As Aviston Downes contents with regard to his study of the elementary teaching service in Barbados, "the imposition of Crown colony government in Jamaica after 1865 provided the imperial centre with greater influence over colonial education policy than in the case of Barbados, with its almost unbridled assembly controlled by merchants and planters," thus making a comparative history troublesome (Downes 2003: 305). However, the similarities evident in Bajan and Jamaican masculine identities render the generalizations advanced here useful. With regard to the didactic influence of English juvenile literature, for example, "the experience of [C. L. R.] James in Trinidad had its resonance in the boyhood of Frank Collymore, a coloured Barbadian, also from a lower middle class background" (Downes, "Boys of the Empire," 19).

36. Christine Barrow, "Introduction and Overview: Caribbean Gender Ideologies," *Caribbean Portraits: Essays on Gender Ideologies and Identities*: xvii, xx.

37. Hegemonic masculinity is the dominant, and dominating, model in the English-speaking Caribbean, but it is not the only one. Caribbean men modified it (introducing unique class/status/color inflections; using it to achieve social advancement; rejecting the most unobtainable conventions) and also subscribed to West African gender traditions. Hilary Beckles has argued persuasively that Barbadian masculine identities—and generally Anglophone Caribbean ones—evolved out of "an early modern encounter and clash [between] two formally contradictory gender orders—one European and one West African" (Beckles 1998: 99, see also 93, 98). Beckles's encounter/clash construct allows for the recognition of parallels between West African and European masculinities (subordinate women's roles within patriarchal authority for example) while simultaneously acknowledging English notions of manhood as dominant (99). Following a similar process, and adding Hindu-derived gender traditions, Rhoda Reddock makes an analogous observation about Indo-Trinidadian masculinity (Reddock 2002: 151–52). To the extent that blacks deviated from this hegemonic norm, local and Crown authorities implemented strategies to bring them in line. These correctives were intended not only to curb the perceived threat that black women's authority might bring (Downes 2003: 306), or to bring blacks in line with the English ideal, but also—perhaps most importantly—to forge additional supports for the ideal itself (322).

38. James C. Scott, *Domination and the Arts of Resistance: Hidden Transcripts* (New Haven, CT: Yale University Press, 1990): xi.

39. Paule Marshall provides a relevant example of Barbadian women who migrated to the United States. "The Making of a Writer: From the Poets in the Kitchen," *Reena and Other Stories* (New York: Feminist Press/CUNY, 1983): 1–12. These women maintained a vision/version of themselves that contradicted definitions made by others. In describing her muses (her mother and her Bajan immigrant women-friends), Marshall attributes their strength to their control of language. She says:

> my mother and her friends were after all the female counterpart of Ralph Ellison's invisible man. Indeed, you might say they suffered a triple invisibility, being black, female and foreigners. They really didn't count in American society except as a source of cheap labor. But given the kind of women they were, they couldn't tolerate the fact of their invisibility, their powerlessness. And they fought back, using the only weapon at their command: the spoken word. (7)

40. Elizabeth Thomas-Hope, "The Establishment of a Migration Tradition: British West Indian Movements to the Hispanic Caribbean in the Century after Emancipation," *Caribbean Social Relations*, edited by Colin G. Clarke (London: University of Liverpool/Centre for Latin American Studies, 1978): 66. Senior and Thomas-Hope define "freedom" as the ability to possess one's self and time, to demand and get a decent wage for one's labor, and to be free to pursue avenues of self-improvement—as defined by the individual. Caribbean-oriented Panamá narratives include descriptions of workers, defined as "property" while enslaved, whose migration provides them a vehicle through which they could enact their freedom. With the post-Emancipation timing of railroad and canal construction, Panamá migration and the nonagricultural nature of canal work gave Colón Men the space and tools to re-vision themselves. These attitudes mirror those of Jamaicans enslaved on plantations in the parish of St. Thomas in 1832. Mary Turner shows that through relationships with members of "the free coloured and black population," enslaved people had intimate knowledge of sociopolitical forces that they then deployed to revise their workloads or obtain other compensation. "Chattel Slaves into Wage Slaves: A Jamaican Case Study," *Labour in the Caribbean: From Emancipation to Independence*, edited by Malcolm Cross and Gad Heuman (London: MacMillan Press/Warwick University Caribbean Studies Series, 1988): 20–21. Turner also documents what can only be called a tradition of labor activism practiced by enslaved people (16–17). Chattel slaves engaged in work stoppages and slow-downs to protest ill treatment by sadistic overseers. These types of actions demonstrated that enslaved Jamaicans were aware of the value of their labor (26).

41. George Lamming, personal interview, July 1994.

42. There is a wide range of estimates of Panamá Money alleged to have circulated in Barbados—and an even wider speculation about the money circulating in other Caribbean countries. Newton places the amount between £355,000 and 1,122,000 in the years 1861–1920 (Newton 1984: 105) while Richardson more confidently places it closer to £1,000,000 by 1920 (Richardson 1985: 160). Since money sent through the mail and brought back with emigrants could not be included

with calculations of postal money orders, neither figure can accurately express the total amount of Panamá Money in the circum-Caribbean region. An anecdote from George Lamming's childhood is appropriate here. He says that he remembers writing "Thank You" notes to his grandmother (who was then living in Panamá) who sent him "American dollars" in the mail (Lamming, personal interview, July 1996). Another story speaks not only to the popularity of money orders, but also suggests ways that Colón Men and other isthmian workers supplemented their incomes. Philip McDonald, resident of St. Georges, Grenada, and Canal Zone worker in 1908, indicated that "Mr. Spright P.O. Master they used to have a very big business every Sunday morning after pay day, i.e. in issuing money orders to the West Indies because every man is working Monday to Saturdays no time to go to the Post" (*LICCW*, McDonald, page 1 of 2).

43. Jamaica's *Daily Gleaner* cites Colonel Goethals's understanding that West Indians played a vital role in the construction of the Canal. Goethals says that "as a class, they improved steadily in efficiency, and have been a cheerful, obedient, and orderly body of workers . . . it can be said truthfully that by furnishing close at hand an ample labour supply, they made the task easier of accomplishment than would have been possible without them" (Newton 1984: 159). Unfortunately, this acknowledgement did not improve working conditions, improve relations with Panamanians, or sufficiently compensate workers in their retirement. Panamanians similarly devalued Colón Men's contributions and made those who remained after the opening of the canal bear the brunt of their animosity toward the United States (see Westerman 1951: 15).

2

"The Money Was Paid Small, but We Live Big": Epistolary Narratives of the Panamá Canal

Some of the costs of the canal are here [in Colón hospitals],—sturdy black men in a sort of bed-tick pajamas sitting on the verandas or in wheel chairs, some with one leg gone, some with both. One could not but wonder how it feels to be hopelessly ruined in body early in life for helping to dig a ditch for a foreign power that, however well it may treat you materially, cares not a whistle-blast more for you than for its old worn-out locomotives rusting away in the jungle.

—Harry A. Franck, *Zone Policeman 88*[1]

But the workers' particular islands of origin meant little, if anything, to American supervisors. "We need more niggers," was a common request by . . . John Stevens, to his labor recruiters in the islands at the height of the blasting and earth moving. . . . The black workers themselves, of course, made finer distinctions about their own insular identities and those of fellow laborers than did their American supervisors. Black men from Jamaica, Barbados, drought-prone Antigua, the volcanic Windwards, and all the other British islands worked alongside one another.

—Bonham Richardson, *Panama Money in Barbados*

Indeed to some degree life was some sort of semi slavery, and there was none to appeal to, for we were strangers and actually compelled to accept what we got, for in any case of an argument we would have to shut up, right or wrong. . . .

—Harrigan Austin, *LICCW*[2]

"Letters to the Editor: Panama Canal (Contest Call, Isthmian Historical Society)." © The Daily Gleaner, The Gleaner Company Limited 1963.

I

The following anecdote has been widely attributed to John Stevens, Chief Engineer for the ICC from 1905 to 1907. The engineer was said to have used it to re-create for those removed from the Zone a sense of the difficulties he encountered in attempting to build the Panamá Canal. Stevens allegedly "watched three West Indians at work with a wheelbarrow. When the wheelbarrow was full, two of them hoisted it onto the head of the third man who carried it away" (McCullough 1977: 477). Willis J. Abbot tells a very similar story in a very different tone:

> in Panama an engineer told me of ordering a group of Jamaicans to load a wheelbarrow with stones and take it to a certain spot.
> "Would you believe it," he said, "when they had filled that wheelbarrow, two of the niggers lifted it to their companion's head, balanced it and he walked off with it as contented as you please." (Abbot 1913: 19)

David McCullough recounts the story as an example of a peculiar construction problem (that of poorly trained workers), while Abbot includes it as one of numerous "characteristics of the native Jamaican." These two tellings—McCullough's historical account appearing more than sixty years after Abbot's first person version—speak to the story's accessibility and utility. The power of the anecdotal form—evident in the story's durability, the impact of the racialized images it brings into play, and the multiple meanings the images project—can be seen when the tale is reproduced in another genre.

Likely taking his cue from Chief Engineer Stevens, "a writer for the popular *Outlook* magazine declared that in all his weeks on the Isthmus he had never once seen a West Indian swing a pick properly." This same reporter also said that if one was to "watch them work for but a single day [one would puzzle] over the worst problem that faces our engineers. The only labor they can find in the Western Hemisphere for building the canal has less than one-third the efficiency of our labor of the North" (McCullough 1977: 474). Thus the wheelbarrow story travels well (operating in social history, personal narrative, and print journalism), gains authority because it was attributed to the ICC's chief engineer, and because the writer for a popular magazine and another "insider" attest to it—and because it triggers familiar images for U.S. readers. The story's tractability and adaptability, then, make its accuracy almost immaterial.

For audiences lacking direct experience with the ins and outs of canal building, this particular anecdote might have provided them access to Stevens's "problem" through familiar stereotypes of blacks' incompetence. The familiar tone of—and racial ideology suggested by—the oft-repeated account likely pulled readers in and shaped them into "Stevens supporters" and advocates of the canal project itself. Contemporary readers of the wheelbarrow story obviously were not the only ones influenced by its ideological baggage, since McCullough claims "reporters were told of the West Indian's 'childish irresponsibility,' that he was 'wasteful . . . stupid . . . possessed with unutterable hatred of exertion other than conversation.'" He continues: "Reporters from their own observations reached much the same conclusion" (ibid). ICC officials appeared determined to shape public opinion about Caribbean workers, not only by inviting reporters to the Canal Zone, but also by creating situations in which they would reproduce the official storyline, putatively from their own observations. In this way anecdotal information formed the most prevalent, pernicious images of the Caribbean workforce and allowed bystanders to participate in the construction of Colón Men as incompetent workers and as unique problems for canal authorities. In the imagined context that the wheelbarrow story creates, Colón Men are not only ignorant but, perhaps more importantly, possible threats to the successful completion of the canal. Still, while ICC officials acted in their own self-interest—and represented the Caribbean labor force in ways that best served this interest—official depictions of these workers were not uncomplicated.

The Commission's 1906 annual report stated that Barbadians' "disposition to labor . . . seems to be as frail as their bodily strength" (Major 1993: 82), an assertion synecdochically reinforced by Secretary of War William Taft, who argued that "the West Indian . . . '[had] his faults; he is lazy, and he does loaf about a good deal, but he is amenable to law, and it does not take a large police force to keep him in order'" (ibid). Ironically, John Stevens and others eventually came to believe that the quality of Caribbean men's labor was not solely determined by "nature." They recognized that some of the characteristics that they found most troublesome could be attributed to Colón Men's lack of training and their traditional high starch/low protein diets (McCullough 1977: 474). These "faults" notwithstanding, most "could not help but be amazed . . . at the degree to which the entire [canal] system . . . depended on black labor" (575). Although authorities were aware of Colón Men's overwhelming presence and factors that militated against their work performance, this knowledge did not translate into policy changes, increased responsibility, or improved housing and pay for the majority of Colón Men. In fact, ICC officials put policies in place that implicitly discouraged them from improving their skills (Conniff 1985: 31).

Racist ideologies defined Caribbean men as "bad" workers (lazy, incompetent) while equally racist ones defined them as "good" (passive, respectful of authority). Thus prevalent racial ideologies formed the basis of ICC policies and, via official authorization, informed popular opinion about this alien (though racially familiar) group of workers. Significantly, these machinations (good/bad worker; familiar race/unfamiliar nationalities) played themselves out through an anecdote, a distinctly creative genre.

Yet despite being (over)burdened by others' meanings, John Stevens' wheelbarrow story nevertheless reveals uncommon truths. Colón Men were not merely empty vessels existing at the (dis)pleasure of canal officials. They came to the isthmus with their own experiences—specifically work experiences—derived from the antiquated process of sugar cultivation. As descendants of those who survived the Middle Passage, African Caribbean workers retained African cultural traditions and practiced them throughout the circum-Caribbean region, including the Canal Zone. Taken in this context, Caribbean workers' method of carrying heavy loads was one manifestation of such diasporic memories, a culturally specific and work-related skill. It stands to reason that Colón Men also traveled to the isthmus with myriad non-work-related desires. Interpreted from these perspectives, the wheelbarrow legend does not merely represent Colón Men's incompetence; it denotes their unique agriculture-related expertise as well as their inexperience with modern technology.[3]

Although the wheelbarrow tale has been evocatively portrayed from a U.S. perspective, its flexibility is manifest in the way it lends itself to a Caribbean perspective and then reveals a new set of interpretations. The variations of this single story show how valuable telling and retelling stories about canal construction can be in providing a more complex narration of workers' lived experience as well as the construction process.

Exchanges about Colón Men circulated within formal and informal segments of Canal Zone society, which might suggest a certain level of complexity, yet these laborers were almost always stereotyped in the ICC's official record. Consider that, "in [the] official journal of Zone life, the *Canal Record*—a reliable, admirable publication in most other respects—the black employee went unrecognized, except in death, and then only in a line or two, his tag number invariably appended, as if he were not quite human" (McCullough 1977: 575). This peculiarity suggests that there were de facto restrictions on what could be told in particular kinds of narratives and brings to light a distinction between genres. Thus creative means of rendering canal construction narratives are crucial, for without them—and the meanings they contain—certain facts and possibilities about the project, workers, and isthmian life would never be known. Thus it is not only important to tell the *same* stories in different genres, but also to tell *different* ones in creative genres. The telling/retelling process demonstrates how permeable boundaries between narratives are and how the resulting mythographic hybrid can disclose unexpected meanings.

The Richardson epigraph reflects how ICC officials commonly viewed and treated Caribbean workers and Harry Franck's first-person account demonstrates his empathy with the physical costs paid by the canal's foreign workers. Yet neither the official position nor other demonstrable truths about the Panamá Man's victimization, illness, death, and inhospitable reception can fully explain his seemingly unflagging desire to work in the Canal Zone or the place the figure holds in Caribbean literature and culture. Because former canal employees fondly (and cynically) remember the days of construction, alternative truths play significantly in their remembered (and, ultimately, fictive and mythographic) experiences, an idea confirmed by the stories they tell. When given the opportunity to chronicle their experiences, they reveal perspectives that, for the most part, existed outside of the purview of the ICC.

As part of events commemorating the fiftieth anniversary of the 1914 opening of the Panamá Canal, the Isthmian Historical Society (IHS) planned a contest to elicit "stories of personal experiences of non-U.S. citizens during the Construction Days."[4] Through an advertisement that appeared in newspapers in Antigua, Barbados, British Honduras, Grenada, Jamaica, St. Lucia, and St. Vincent, as well as in food packages provided for non-U.S. citizens who retired from canal service (known as Disability Relief recipients), the Society asked for "the best true stories of life and work on the Isthmus of Panama [by] West Indians and other non-U.S. citizens who were on the Isthmus prior to 1915." Specifically, contestants were asked to include their names, addresses, the year they arrived in Panamá, where they were employed, and describe the types of work they performed; many respondents also noted their countries of origin. The IHS compiled and published 112 submissions under the title *Letters From Isthmian Canal Construction Workers*. Although contest organizers do not describe their criteria or selection process in the compilation, three letters won IHS approval; the Society awarded $50 (U.S.) to the first-place account (Bahamian Albert Peters), $30 to the second (Barbadian George H. Martin), and $20 to the third (Honduran Alfonso Suazo). Two contestants composed their letters from journals they kept while employed by the ICC,[5] but the others seemed to have put their memories to paper for the first time with the hope of winning the contest's first prize.[6] Since it seems that the monetary prize was the primary motivation for most of the men (many of them confessed to having some financial difficulty in their retirement years), it is not clear whether they would have otherwise recorded their stories.

The narratives included in this collection were written and arranged fifty years after the official opening of the canal and as much as fifty-nine years after some respondents first arrived on the isthmus. They have, therefore, been mediated by time, but also by the contest requirements and Ruth Stuhl's transcriptions and interpretations. Stuhl claimed that "although an effort was made to reproduce the letters exactly as they were written, it is probable that there are errors." In addition, participants' stories have been subjected to the vagaries of each writer's memory and their desire to win a contest, raising questions about whether what has been documented has been embellished or if it occurred at all. Despite these potential limits, these stories remain important evidence of how imaginable (possible and creatively nuanced) truths begin to reframe Colón Men's historical representations into mythographies of their migration to and labor in the Canal Zone.[7]

Taken as reflections of workers' imaginable truths, these entries contain descriptions that reenact the most common narratives about the building of the Panamá Canal, but from the perspective of its majority labor force. As one of the few venues available to them, the collection reflects workers' experiences as they remembered them, perhaps as they wanted them to be. Some respondents took the contest requirements literally and submitted letters consisting of a few lines. Others filled as many as eleven single-spaced pages. No matter the amount of detail, these letters express ideas that supported and challenged contemporary canal histories, asserted truths about Canal Zone life and work that differ from other renditions, and contained stories that cast isthmian life from a uniquely Caribbean perspective. To put it succinctly, the collected letters function as creative nonfictions through which workers revealed the possibilities of their migrations to, and continued employment and lives in, the Canal Zone.

Unlike other genres, epistolary narratives offer readers the most direct insight into Colón Men's personalities. Their transcribed voices conjure up images of how they saw themselves as individuals, as members of families and communities, and as workers. The *LICCW* collection also allows readers to attach names to men fictionally reconstructed in creative narratives or simply reduced to "West Indians" in historical ones. Where most historical accounts detail Barbados and Jamaica's human contribution to the isthmian enterprise, epistolary narratives include contributions of workers from the Bahamas, St. Lucia, Trinidad, Antigua, Grenada, Dominica, and St. Vincent (not to mention others from Panamá, Honduras, and Colombia). Even as they expand knowledge of the national scope of Caribbean isthmian migration, the letters reformulate and recast the most common descriptions of the construction enterprise, including the oft-cited financial motivation for Caribbean migration. The *LICCW* collection additionally reveals particulars about workers' daily lives in the Canal Zone and their concern with diseases and retirement compensation.

II

Historical narratives often understood isthmian workers as men lured from the "impoverished" Caribbean islands by the promise of unprecedented amounts of money. While the *LICCW* letters affirm this financial attraction, they simultaneously show that money formed only a small part of contestants' motivations. The range of contestants' economic and migratory goals complicate simple push/pull analyses, invoking their premigration imaginable truths as well as their Canal Zone lived realities. The resulting dialogue, occurring across genres, reveals a fuller picture of what it meant for Colón Men to leave islands in the circum-Caribbean region to work in the Canal Zone.

Bahamian Albert Peters avowed that he moved to Panamá because he was "eager for some adventure and experience," so much so that he ignored his parents' warnings about "the Yellow Fever, Malaria and Small pox that infested the place." Despite having previous knowledge of these dangers, Peters wrote, "I and my pals are just going to see for ourselves" (Albert Peters, 1 of 4). In this desire for adventure and to satisfy his curiosity, Peters was not alone. Joseph Brewster set sail from Barbados in 1906 "urged with the desire to travel and to earn a living" (Brewster, page 1 of 2). John Altyman Richards, formerly of Jamaica, "was intrigued by the Canal Construction done in this beautiful tropical country" and after he "discussed the possibilities of working in a different country and of learning a strange language with my relatives; . . . I partook for Panama in 1914" (Richards, page 1 of 2).

A thirst for adventure seemed to be a lure for the above participants, but Alfred Mitchell rode into Panamá on the wave of his mother's will. He stated, "I was brought from Jamaica at the age of 14 years old in the year of 1904, with my mother. . . . Mother was working and fortunately I got a job as water-boy on the Panama Rail Road docks, and same year Mother took me on the lines, to a place called Bas-Obispo Canal Zone. I worked there carrying water for a drilling gang" (Mitchell, page 1 of 2). Little is known about women from the Caribbean who traveled at the height of the U.S. construction, and Mitchell does not discuss his mother's motivations.[8] Still, Ms. Mitchell's resolve can be seen in the fact of her migration, and also because she traveled with her young son. Perhaps the best measure of her will was the fact that she got her son hired at all: he was seven years younger than the minimum age for employment by the ICC. Officially speaking, authorities could not hire anyone under the age of twenty-one, but even though this rule was largely ignored, Alfred was uncommonly young. Ms. Mitchell's fortitude might possibly reflect the strength of her premigration imaginings of the Canal Zone—a correlation suggested by the words of Peters, Richards, and in other contest entries. These suggestive inferences, then, help provide insight into why Panamá had such considerable allure for Caribbean migrants.

Prince George Green (who did not identify his country of origin) migrated for reasons comparable to those above, but also for more epic ones.

"You see," he said, "most of us came here with the Same spirit as a Soldier going to war, don't dodge from work or we will never finish it" (Green, page 1 of 1). Former workers who described their premigration motivations carried and recalled images of their migrations that were uniquely personal (family conferences, mother's motivations) and yet they reflect familiar "migration images" in the region.[9] These vignettes also reveal attitudes about self—determination to succeed and see the job through to conclusion—not prominently featured in other types of isthmian narratives.

The pride evident in Green's quotation is mirrored in the following description. George H. Martin framed his decision to migrate as a response to an invitation extended by the people of the United States. Martin's mood and felling almost radiate from his words:

> I were only 18 years a school boy, with a thinking ability, a voice from a great people saying "Hearken ye, people of a different tribe, Let not your heart be troubled, and so we were invited; at this age with the others I accepted, for this people, no other than the American people
> promised strong protection, and so I leave father and mother, brothers, and relatives, away in the land of the Indies, in the west, and came to this strange land now 54 years ago, still with a great heart for the same people I served before. (Martin, page 6 of 7)

Accepting that Martin documented these thoughts some years after the fact, his metaphorical invitation is provocative. It suggests that Martin was a sought-after and desirable worker, and not just one who was most cheap and mobile. Rather than a beast of burden, this Colón Man was a thinker ("a *school* boy, with a *thinking* ability") whose well-selected phrases simultaneously infused the work he performed—and his *self*—with biblical resonance. From this perspective, Martin and his peers worked "cheerfully, and faithfully; thus giving the American people their hearts desire" (page 2 of 7). As he told it, Martin's willful and decisive efforts complemented those of the North Americans. Grenadian emigrant E. W. Martineau was similarly active in his remembrances of his migration to and work in the Canal Zone. At twenty-one, Martineau was an "old" man when he traveled to Panamá in 1912; also unlike most emigrants from the Caribbean, he did not work for the ICC but sold "airated water" along the canal line. Martineau's entrepreneurial venture freed him from the most arduous kinds of labor, thus allowing him to act informally as a journalist/historian of Colón Men in the Canal Zone (Martineau, page 1 of 6).[10] He remarked that by the time of his arrival recruitment was no longer necessary in the Caribbean; sufficient numbers of workers came to Panamá without it. The end of recruitment brought different kinds of migrants: "Professional men and women [who] were allowed to practice their profession in order to releave pressure on the government agencies in this interprize"(Martineau, page 2 of 6). While Martin was invited and Martineau was "self-propelled," both recollections suggest that their motives jibed with—and were not subsumed by—those of ICC officials. Emigrants in the above recollections actively pursued work on the isthmus, complicating push/pull economic constructs that lock them in on the passive "pull" side. The sense of adventure, active participation, and personal ambition unveil workers' imagined selves as agents working in concert with seemingly dominant forces.

Investigations of migrants' financial motivations have been productive, but attention to their nonmonetary motives reveals migration images that distinguish this isthmian movement from other migrations.[11] This adjustment also begins to address why Colón Men continued to migrate when stories about illness, death, exploitation, and probable financial ruin pervaded the region. These attitudes stand as testaments to migration images that survived despite the animosity and disregard demonstrated by U.S. authorities from the time laborers' were recruited until the canal was completed.

For most Colón Men who contributed to the *LICCW* collection, image and reality collided when they arrived in the Canal Zone and set about working. Interestingly, their entries allude to the permanence as well as the evolution of their migration images, as the following recollections of certain isthmian realities suggest. Many IHS respondents worked as manual laborers, jobs that required little or no training. Others identified some form of carpentry as their primary occupation. The number of workers who identified as carpenters, as well as references to other occupations, indicate that there were significant exceptions to the general "rule" that Colón Men were wholly unskilled workers. Luther McEnnis "started to work in Panama in 1904, with the Fumigating Gang" (McEnnis, page 1 of 1). Workers like McEnnis were thus trained to perform one of the most important jobs in the Canal Zone: he was part of the so-called "Sanitation Team" charged with controlling malaria- and yellow fever–carrying mosquitoes. Enrique Plummer (born in Gorgona, Panamá)[12] worked as a messenger (Central Division, Affairs office), but nicely described the eradication procedures performed by McEnnis and others. Plummer stated:

> Sanitation in those days were terible, some of the U.S. citicens got sick with yellow fever, and some of them died. Col. Gorgas took charge of the Sanitary Division, and finally clean up things. The system used was to have men go from house to house sealing up all seams with paste and paper, place a pot of sulfer in each house, light it and leave it to burn killing any-thing alive. Before doing so the people had to take out all their clothes ect. to avoid them getting discoloured. Then he would have men go through all the swampy land, digging drains to which they would hang cans of mosquito oil dripping and spredding all through the area. (Plummer, pages 1–2 of 5)

The successful prevention and treatment of the isthmus's most deadly diseases was one of the most celebrated features of the construction. Members of Sanitation Teams learned and performed very specialized tasks, and they were engaged in important work, thus these truths beg the question: What did it mean to be "skilled" and "unskilled" in the Canal Zone? Sanitation workers obviously did not have the same skills as carpenters or engineers, but they were nonetheless skilled, credit for which they rarely received.

This failure to recognize skilled Colón Men was clearly on the mind of John Oswald Butcher since he dedicated much of his letter to identifying Caribbean artisans and skilled workers. Butcher "landed in Colon on January 12, 1906 from the island of Barbados." He listed by name seven exemplary West Indians and the positions they held: "the names of those men who wee rated Foreman Carpenters were: Johnny Haynes, B. C. Quimby, J. B. Fields, father of our present Rev. J. S. Fields, Ed Gallagher, Jerry Kirby, William Murtaugh, Ernest Harrod, and others" (Butcher, page 5 of 5). "Naturally," he said, "there were other crafts represented—plumbers, painters, roofers, electricians, etc." (ibid). By acknowledging that Colón Men performed a range of skilled work, Butcher challenges the ICC's public record and the assumption that black workers were incapable of holding such jobs.[13] Implicitly responding to the assessment of Caribbean workers evident in Stevens's wheelbarrow story, Butcher's letter—and numerous others—also suggest that some Colón Men arrived with skills. Peters applied his Bahamian carpentry training to railroad work in the Canal Zone (Albert Peters, page 1 of 4); George Martin was a carpenter's apprentice in Barbados (Martin, page 3 of 7). Other contestants claimed to have become acquainted with unfamiliar tools and acquired valuable skills through their employment with the Commission. Bajan John Garner "worked along with men who had done this work [servicing railroad track] before so I did not take very long to break in" (Garner, page 1 of 3; see also LeCurrieux page 7 of 7). St. Lucian Charles Moses (page 1 of 1), and Alfred E. Dottin (page 1 of 2) worked with jack hammers and star drills and thus became technologically sophisticated through their isthmian labors. That some men applied their skills and others quickly learned more demonstrates their potential to learn and work—and to do both successfully.

Canal histories include Colón Men among those performing the most dangerous work on the isthmus, yet contestants only recalled observing—rather than carrying out—these jobs. They did, though, express dissatisfaction at being forced into unappealing (poorly paid and supervised) jobs. The IHS collection prominently features descriptions of Colón Men whose imagined and lived realities collided around salaries. This conflict remained a problem although some entrants devised ways to negotiate this bad situation.

Promising to pay ten cents an hour for a ten-hour workday and a six-day workweek, the ICC offered most Colón Men more than they could have earned in the Caribbean. In Barbados at the time of canal construction, for instance, agricultural workers made about twenty cents a day, but only during harvesting season (McCullough 1977: 475). The isthmus's financial draw was obviously appealing, but the expressed conflict between what Colón Men thought they would earn and what they actually earned—and had to spend—informs how they valued their Panamá Money. Judging from the *LICCW* collection, there was no change in these workers' hourly rate from 1905, when Harrigan Austin arrived on the isthmus, through 1913, when Trinidadian Helon Allick landed. Second, of respondents who mentioned wages, most described them as low, regardless of the hourly rate. Instead of celebrating the hourly rate, contest participants emphasized the low cost of living in the Canal Zone and their ability to supplement their incomes creatively.

While some were happy with their take-home pay, citing plentiful overtime (Martin, page 2 of 7) and timely payment (Albert Banister, page 2 of 5), most respondents complained about inadequate hourly rates and overall negligible salaries. George H. Martin, Harrigan Austin, and Albert Peters noted their daily wages without much critique,[14] but others expressed their frustration. Wesley Beckles, who "arrived here in Panama in the year 1913 January 9th" and worked for the ICC's Municipal Division at "10 cents an hour," maintained that salaries were just plain low: "Living conditions weren't so good at that time. Due to the fact of the small salary. Many of the Days I've gone to work with hunger" (Beckles, page 1 of 1). Jamaican Nehemiah E. Douglas reached Panamá in January 1911. He prepared explosives on the highly dangerous "Pow[d]er Gang" and earned more than Beckles. He nonetheless considered his pay insufficient, when declaring that he "only" earned thirteen cents an hour (Douglas, page 1 of 2). Hired as a skilled carpenter in November 1909, Alfred E. Dottin earned even more than Beckles, but even he argued that "Salaries were fantastically low $0.16 to $0.20 was the going rate for hourly employees with $0.25 for the sub-foreman" (Dottin, page 1 of 2).

Starting as a waterboy, perhaps the most junior of ICC positions, G. Mitchell Berisford (formerly of Barbados) shared a story that casts this discussion in a most distressing light. Listing his rates of pay over his tenure in the Canal Zone, Berisford said "at that time I was only working for small wages 7 cents 10, 13¢ 16¢ an so on many days I had to take lunch from the other men who was getting more than me" (Berisford, page 3 of 3). While it remains unclear whether coworkers gave Berisford food or whether he stole it from them, his desperation is particularly palpable: as a full-time ICC employee, he could not afford to feed himself. St. Lucian Banister uses a metaphor that invokes the sentiment of Berisford's account, but does so with a flare that reveals much about his own personality: "ten cents per hour was just like a flie into one of those big American mule nosstrill" (Banister, page 4 of 5).

LICCW entrants allegedly earned "plenty money," yet they remained dissatisfied with their ICC salaries. Significantly, those who expressed some pleasure with their pay highlighted the creative ways they and their coworkers supplemented their incomes.[15] Banister remembered that "we had colored time keeper they know their stunt they would time dead man get plenty money pay-day" (Banister, page 5 of 5). If submitting hours for dead men was one way Colón Men made money, simply collecting money without working was another. Plummer knew of men who were hired by but never worked for a subcontractor. He noted:

> the locks were build by a contracting firm name The macklintic Marshal Co. If they did not luse money doing it, I am sure they did not make all they should, because I know their timekeepers carried a lot of men to whom they would issue metal checks who would only come around on pay days to collect without working. One of the boys who worked with me as messenger quit his job and went to work for them as timekeeper to do likewise. (Plummer, page 2 of 5)

These examples indicate that factors other than the ICC's famed hourly wage determined how Colón Men "valued" their pay. As Plummer and Banister's quotations demonstrate, their peers' willingness to work and make money in Panamá revealed more about their personal determination than the Isthmian Canal Commission's "generous" wages. Faced with extremely exploitative circumstances, these workers found ways not only to resist the exploitation but also to resist the ways it defined them.

At least one ICC staffer seemed to have participated in this kind of "wage adjusting." For example, Trinidadian Helon I. Allick arrived on the isthmus on 12 July 1913 and was put to work "cleaning or mucking" in "Balboa around the Shops" two days later. Mr. Allick earned ten cents an hour, but forces soon conspired to change this situation. According to his letter, he "was then fancy by my Boss that he asked me to change my name and take me on as a new man at 13 cent, it was so done for I was then Henry Thomas" (Allick, page 1 of 1). In this way, Allick's boss circumvented starting wage guidelines intended for Caribbean workers. The absence of references to ICC staff members in the following examples suggests that workers took it upon themselves to change their names. Henry Paily, who arrived on the isthmus in 1905, claimed he used the name Henry Macarie while working for the Sanitary Department in Culebra. Around 1911 he met a woman and "at this times I got married on my good and real name witsh is Henry Paily. My name was then canges from Henry Macarie to Henry Paily wich is my right name" (Paily, page 1 of 1).

Frederick James indicated, by means of a postscript, that he was "better known in Antigua [as] Mr. James Frederick" (James, page 2 of 2). Finally, Lessep O. Brown said that while "dispatching trains from various Tracks," his "name was changed from Joseph Brown to Lessep O. Brown which is my correct name" (L. O. Brown, page 1 of 2). Apparently this practice was so common that legislation had to be enacted to stop it. Wesley D. Clarke reported that he "worked from [7 August 1911] on with that name as Joseph Graham until 1929 when the Governor had all who were not working with their right name change to the correct one" (W. Clarke, page 1 of 1).

Most workers seem to have taken it upon themselves to change their names, one of many strategies they used to secure better jobs and pay—and avoid punishments meted out by officials.[16] Several contestants mentioned another, more dangerous tactic that allowed some workers' to accumulate substantial caches of money. Banister, a 1914 arrivee, recalled:

> plenty men trying to save some money to go home   I also every man you will find him with a leather belt round his waste on his skin those that want to care themself   eat good and tidy themself   was compell to spend what they have round their person   Hundreads of men lying down in Colon streets dead some   pick up on arrival dead some 2 days after dead   all the report from the Doctor was stavation kill him man hungry till he drop. (Banister, page 3 of 5)[17]

These men were so determined to save money that they elected not to spend it on food. Even if, previous to arriving on the isthmus, money drew Colón Men, the economic realities of the Canal Zone soon taught them that only inspired schemes could allow them to achieve their financial goals, particularly if they worked at the bottom end of the scale. Respondents' diligence in maintaining their sanguine, premigration images allude to the evolution—rather than eradiation—of those images. Nevertheless, and despite this obvious determination, realities in the Canal Zone often thwarted Colón Men's best efforts.

Manassah Maynard's entry suggests that the cost of living in the Canal Zone played a significant part in determining how contestants viewed their Panamá Money. "Living conditions in those days was much better than now," Maynard wrote, "everything was much cheaper, i.e. Steak @ .12 Lb., Codfish @ .08 Lb., Salad Oil .08 per qt., Onions @ .02 Lb., Red Salmon @ .12 tin and a large tin of Ham cost $1.20 ea." He reiterated "everything was much cheaper, even though the rate of pay was small, so there were no complaints" (Maynard, page 1 of 1; Mitchell, page 2 of 2). Maynard's grocery list suggests that he prepared his own meals (or had someone to cook for him), an option that would have further reduced his living expenses—if descriptions of ICC services were any indication. Men who availed themselves of meals prepared by the ICC complained bitterly about the cost and quality of this benefit. Leonard A. Chase's letter included the following breakdown of his take-home pay. He "arrived March 22, 1906 at Gorgona . . . loading cars with stones, and working on track line, moving rails, pushing cars . . . at this the rate was 10¢ per hour, we had to take meal tickets to get your meals, 30¢, leaving us .50 proper a day" (Chase, page 1 of 1). Chase's take-home pay was a mere $.30/day more than he could have made harvesting sugarcane in Barbados, not the $.80/day difference promised by the ICC. The well-documented financial draw of isthmian work was a mere stepping-off point for contestants who were determined to manage their money, an attitude developed well before Panamá Men arrived in Panamá. These more elaborate representations of Panamá Money not only complicate simplistic descriptions of this motive, but they also provide access to workers' practically inaccessible work ethic and determination.

The letters in the *LICCW* collection contain signs that imaginable truths about Panamá's financial bounty, and the quality of life that Panamá Money could purchase, survived the completion of the canal. Bajan emigrant George Martin's entry references his Panamá Money, but his descriptions of the food he bought took up more space. For the most part, Martin fondly remembered his days as an ICC employee; in fact, one might describe the tone of his letter as exceedingly happy. Working on a pick and shovel team, he remembered that "the boss, Johnson . . . did not order or compelled, he only plead, so we obeyed." This attitude, but also his lengthy conversation about how he earned—and spent—his Panamá Money, distinguishes his letter. Describing a time when he double-ordered a commissary book,[18] he said:

> if we order a $5.00 book, and in a day or two and that book does not show up, you are told to order again   Sometimes both orders would meet, and we would have two $5.00 book, $10.00   what to do with $10.00 in those days? Here is a story, it caught me once. I bought some of everything, shoes also, to do away with it, $10.00 would not finish. I bought a ham, at that time it look as big as I were, I paid $2.21, talking about ham, real lean, I took ham to work every day in order to have it finish, my associate and I ate ham for days. I don't think about ham these days   its too high in price, now it is for the other fellow. (Martin, page 2 of 7)

This description is one of few that consist of wholly positive memories of ICC provisions. But since a number of respondents frankly declared the food to be inedible *and* expensive (stories of this kind rarely distinguished between home-cooked and Commissary-prepared meals), some have read Martin's recollections as hyperbole.[19] But rather than merely dismiss his reminiscences as wishful embellishments, other possibilities present themselves. Offering readers insight into the cost of living in the Canal Zone, Martin's emphasis on food—specifically on ham—can also be interpreted as support for Chief Engineer Stevens's comments about Caribbean workers' traditional high starch/low protein diets. Martin so jubilantly remembered his ham because he so rarely ate it, thus making it an exotic delicacy for him. Finally, his emphasis on food reflects *his* imagined isthmian reality. At another point in his recollections, Martin described his lunch in this way: "lunch mostly in those days were bread, sardine, and ice cream, and at times for a change, we would have bread, corn-beef-hash, and never forget our ice-cream, I am saying here it was refreshing" (page 1 of 7). For Martin, then, food—in as much variety as he could find—was important and it therefore informed the way he remembered his time as a Panamá Man. This interpretation is supported by his more impoverished circumstances at the time of his letter's writing (he stated "on account of high cost of living I am not in a position of a little money to perchase writing paper to write all that I remember" [page 3 of 5]). But whether or not Martin's memories are "true" is not as important as what the possibility of the meals meant for him, both when he first consumed them as well as when he summoned his memories of them. Martin's memories link his pay to food (purchased and consumed) and his quality of life, a connection that exposes this man's hopes and dreams; that is, his imaginable truths.

The above entries represent realities that survived beneath ICC surveillance, realities that offer insight into some Colón Men's migration images as well as their unique personalities. Whether contest participants discussed approaches to supplementing their incomes or negotiating the Zone's high cost of living, they fought for every advantage; in other words, they did not simply accept whatever the ICC offered. This attitude, then, offers important insight into what Panamá Money and working in the Zone meant to these Caribbean migrants. It also serves as a tool to interpret respondents' descriptions of other features of isthmian life, particularly working conditions, labor policies, and other ICC employees.

Allan C. Belgrave "arrived in Panama a Sunday at 3:30 p.m. the 12th of September 1905" (page 1 of 3). He witnessed, but did not benefit from, a group of skilled workers' successful fight to improve their working conditions. Still his quotation illustrates that he was aware of his own inadequate pay as well as the steps dissatisfied workers might take to change their conditions. Belgrave complained:

> living and working conditions (personal) was not favorable, (reason) The boiler-makers and shipfitters fought for shorter working hours, and an increase in pay, they won, ten hours was changed to eight hour per day, from 7 o'clock in the morning to 11 o'clock, and from mid-day 12 o'clock to 4 o'-

clock in the evening, with the understanding that, any time worked after 8 hours will be overtime (time and a half). The helpers had to worked 8 hours, but whenever called to work after 8 hours, had to work straight 10 hours before getting overtime. So, when there was no overtime which was seldom, I found living conditions difficult, even when commodities were at reasonable prices, because of inadequate salary, I was unable to support my family properly. (Belgrave, page 3 of 3)

Belgrave's critique takes the form of a side-by-side comparison of overtime (and length of workday) for shipfitters/boilermakers and that of their helpers (a job he held). Set up in this way, he makes the inequality clear; what this Colón Man also makes clear is the link between this injustice and the strength of workers' desire to transform their working conditions.

Though Belgrave merely witnessed other workers' labor action, other *LICCW* respondents described their own protests over poor wages and working conditions.[20] Jules LeCurrieux, from French Guiana by way of Barbados, entered the Canal Zone on 14 January 1906. His letter described what occurred after a gang of manual workers elected him spokesman. Moving through several jobs, LeCurrieux's:

shop moved to Mech Div [Mechanical Division] where I was employed for years until one day we were all sent to work in an oil tanker and we could not take it on account of the scent of gas from the oil, and we all decided to get on deck and make our complaint, and boys to talk for them, and the boss to them, if you men want to work get back down in the hole, but you [LeCurrieux] get up in the office for your clearance, Sir. (LeCurrieux, pages 1–2 of 7)

When a worker was cleared, or fired, from his job, he had to produce a letter describing the reason for his clearance upon demand, therefore hindering future employment in the Zone. In light of this familiar policy (several participants described this), the decision to protest working conditions could have lasting effects. But as LeCurrieux represents this scene, he seemed unconcerned with the repercussions and he decided to complain, a position apparently shared by all those in the tanker that day.

LeCurrieux's quotation also represents his boss's arbitrary and binding decision. Later in his letter, this Colón Man noted other supervisors' capricious decisions, ones that worked in—and against—his favor. LeCurrieux "met one of my old foremen who questioned me and told me to call on him the next morning when he employed me and turned me on to work right away, and continued in same employment until my employer was leaving on retirement, and just as the new boss took over I was laid off" (ibid). Another entrant's story refines decisions that read like individual idiosyncrasies in LeCurrieux's letter. Jamaican Rufus Lucas, who arrived in Panamá in 1913, claimed to have "worked with the Dredging Division for a short period as an oiler . . . with a man by the name of Mr. Wright. He looked at me one day and said 'you are fired right now.' It was for no just cause but I couldn't talk back because in those days every white man thought he was GOD down here" (Lucas, page 1 of 3). That he was subjected to his boss's whims was bad enough, but the tone of his letter suggests that he was particularly bitter about being subordinated to "every white man" in the Zone.

The influence whites wielded over Colón Men was a topic tackled by many entrants, but this situation seemed to bother participants more acutely when white bosses were not qualified to supervise. To add insult to the injury of his insufficient salary, Harrigan Austin claimed his supervisor was not trained to perform his job: his "foreman was a white man, he appointed one of the most experienced men to be sub foreman as really the only thing he knew to do was to watch us but really very little about handling or directing a Carpenters gang" (Austin, 1 of 5; see Watkins-Owens 1996: 17). Neither did Austin limit his critique to whites directly involved in hiring and firing Colón Men; he also critiqued supervisors who failed to keep their charges safe on the job. He asserted, "some of those in authority were untrained for their positions, causing many accidents." Even medical professionals were subject to critique: "poorly trained doctors and nurses indeed many went to an early grave because of the lack of proper care and trained attendants who had any understanding of handling a sick human being" (Austin, page 2 of 5).[21]

Panamá Men's frequent references to whites' preferential treatment suggest that this practice amounted to a de facto ICC policy. Lancelot Kavanagh, writing from Manchester, Jamaica, told the following story:

> I got a job as cook at Washington Hotel   then Americans started up a hospital on the beach   I took a job there as Steward   had to go in the market early mornings to buy meat & vegetables   that was the Colon market Manager of the hospital was a Gentleman named Dr Kerr but after the hospital began to Improve more were coming in   I lost the job to a white man at that time. (Kavanagh, page 1 of 3)

Working at a hospital on the beach, and performing relatively light duties, Kavanagh held an enviable position. White privilege, if Kavanagh's words and tone (evident in the pause suggested by the space before his last sentence) are any indication, trumped his experience in the kitchen and tenure on the job. Philip McDonald remembered that he, too, lost his job to a white worker. He "got a job at Gamboa Signal station [after resigning from an unsatisfying storeman's position] lasted one month   Laid of in preference to a retired U.S. salior" (McDonald, page 8 of 9). In these instances, race (white) and nationality (U.S.) seem to decide who could fill some jobs. In stories told by other *LICCW* participants, race and nationality also determined which jobs were filled and at what pay, though blackness and Caribbeanness were the defining categories in these cases.

Antiblack racism dogged contestants during their tenure in the Canal Zone, but they were likewise affected by a lack of political representation, both in the Zone and the United States (where many ICC policies originated). Judging from the contents of some *LICCW* letters, participants were well aware of how these factors combined to affect their quality of life. This awareness is best reflected in Colón Men's descriptions of jobs and pay that were reserved for people of different races and nationalities. Amos E. Clarke was an artisan and seaman who described himself as a "native and citizen of the Republic of Panama."[22] He wrote, "wages in those days were not very high. The highest pay for White and Colored American was from $65.00 to $75.00 per month (U.S. cu.). West Indians were paid 10¢ per hour (U.S. C.), Italians, Greeks and Spaniards 20¢ per hr. (U.S. Cy). Limited time of work in those days was 10 hours" (Amos E. Clarke, pages 1–2 of 3). Barbadian Thomas Gittens affirmed A. E. Clarke's memory: "my first job [after his 26 August 1905 arrival] was on the track ling I work there for some time then for health department then at the ending of 1906 and 1907 I started to work with the railroad with the sivel engineers work as rodman for $30.00 a mounth in those days a rodman from the states was paid $83.33" (Gittens, page 1 of 1). Although McCullough argues that "simple problems of supply and demand [influenced racial disparities on the isthmus], [as] experienced technicians . . . doctors, and competent clerical people were always in short supply" and "common unskilled laborers from the impoverished islands of the Caribbean were always available in abundance," these descriptions cannot explain why North American and Caribbean workers performing the same job received different pay (McCullough 1977: 578–79). The historian is more persuasive when he states, "there was the political factor: the labor force was not merely black, it was foreign; these were not United States citizens and in Washington therefore they represented no constituency" (579); on this point, Clarke and Gittens' remembrances seem to concur.

While workers specifically complained about depressed wages, job insecurity, white privilege, and nationality bias, their critiques more broadly challenged ICC policies. Official positions on jobs and pay seriously affected the degree to which Colón Men could enact their migration images. Nonetheless, the *LICCW* letters persistently reveal images of Caribbean men-as-workers that belie the difficulties evinced by their complaints.

III

The "imaginable Colón Man" portrayed in the above quotations proposes this worker's superiority, for if he could survive the worst conditions, then no other worker—black American, Panamanian, or white American— could compare. At least, this was how respondents remembered it.

Contestants used their recollections of North American and Panamanian workers to highlight the efficiency and diligence of workers from the Caribbean. The image of Colón Men in epistolary narratives thus counters stereotypical portrayals that appear in stories disseminated by ICC officials. Albert Banister's reference to black American workers sets up this comparison. He attributed the relative absence of black American canal workers to the large presence of West Indian ones. He also demonstrated some insight into relations between black and white North Americans. He commented:

> we had Colored Americans working   good men skillful men but they can't pull with the White Americans   always a fight and trouble   if not West Indians could never be hear because Uncle Sam have plenty Colored Americans to do his work   also they don't like down hear   to get away they make plenty trouble   at that rate West Indians get a break if not so when we had arived from our native land to Cristobal Dock No. 2 we would have to take the next boat back home   it would be too many dogs for the pice of bone. (Banister, pages 1–2 of 5)

Supporting this contention, Plummer (in his reporter's guise), wrote "during the construction men was imported from Jamaica, Barbados, Spain, and some coloured U.S. citizens. The coloured Americans did not stay very long however, they were shipped back home because they were making trouble" (Plummer, page 1 of 5). Both accounts allude to "trouble" between black and white North Americans, but Plummer merely confirms the presence and removal of black American workers while Banister acknowledges how the racialized U.S. conflict provided opportunities for the Caribbean workforce.[23] Additionally, imbedded in Banister's recollection is the assessment of who could better "pull with the White Americans." Since black Americans did not remain on the isthmus in significant numbers, Colón Men believed themselves better able to manage their relationships with their white bosses and thus remain integral to the canal enterprise.[24]

The skill that allowed Panamá Men to better "pull with" whites in the Canal Zone not only established them as the best *black* workers, but apparently it made them the *best* workers—period. Even Harrigan Austin who, judging from the tone of his letter, cynically viewed his tenure on the isthmus, demonstrated a pride in Colón Men's contribution to the construction. Perhaps characteristically, he reveals this pride through a harsh evaluation of Panamanian ICC employees. He said: "but few of the natives of Panama were interested to work in the canal in those days—the few who ever did was unreliable. Most of them, as soon as they got the first pay, they'd go drinking and may show up some future time. The men who stuck to the job, as with a purpose were the West indians and the Europeans" (Austin, page 4 of 5). Entrepreneur Martineau compared Panamanian workers and Caribbean ones and found that, while the latter worked well and steadily, "our Latin brothers were bringing up the rear to the best of their ability" (Martineau, page 2 of 6). Arriving in 1907, John Thomas Mark claimed to have never seen "a native of this country working on the Canal" (Mark, page 2 of 2). Amos Parks migrated to the isthmus from Barbados near the end of the construction (and had trouble finding work), but made the strongest statement against Panamanian canal workers. After working at two ICC jobs, Parks said "all these times no Panamanians was round much only bare West Indians was going too and fro, from home to work daily." From this, he concluded, "that's why of today when I hear the Spaniards talk that they want the Canal, I ask them on many occasion how many Panamanians ever worked during construction days, and how many lost their lives. None of them could answer" (Parks, page 1 of 1). He does not take his argument to its logical conclusion—that those who worked on and died during construction, namely Caribbean workers, had a larger claim to the U.S.-built canal—but the inference is there. Parks' statement best characterizes the imaginable Panamá Man that evolves over the course of the *LICCW* collection. His observation likely represents the pre- and postconstruction tensions that existed between Caribbean workers and their Panamanian hosts; it might also reflect the Commission's official evaluation of the isthmus's natives. Still, it is clear that Parks and his peers believed that their dedication and commitment made them central to the canal effort, a characterization that was common in epistolary narratives.

Yet these Colón Men did not base this image of themselves solely on their ability to outperform black Americans and Panamanians. Respondents imagined themselves better than *all* other workers, even white American ones, because of *who they were*. Banister introduces this idea with a discussion of the isthmus's rampant diseases but ends on an altogether different note. He said:

> Malaria was raging   yellow fever   was raging   another fever was call tyfod fever rageing in matachin section. United States Citensin and West Indian lives and blood was taken to put through this Canal   Uncle Sam had to run through the door   left it open and get   foreners to do his wark. (Banister, page 1 of 5)

Banister's words not only communicate a pride based in Colón Men's sacrifice to get the job done ("West Indian lives and blood was taken to put through this Canal"), but he takes his evaluation a step further. Colón Men not only came amidst rumors of disease, death, and injustice, they remained under exceedingly difficult conditions—and did so when "Uncle Sam *had to run* through the door." Obviously, Banister did not consider himself "cheap," "ignorant," "unskilled," or "lazy," adjectives often used to describe the canal's Caribbean workforce. Barbadian emigrant Fitz Thomas concurred when he described taking:

> residence in Culebra and began to work on the track line. I soon helped to build Culebra jail as a carpenter; my gen. foreman was Mr. Greir, my foreman was a black man, John ____ of Jamaica, and the work we performed was so good Mr. Greir transferred us to the white quarters, and removed the white gangs as they failed in finish work. (Fitz Thomas, page 1 of 1)

Thomas's example highlighted the fact that his boss recognized the quality of his work at the time it was performed. It is also important to note that he yoked this memory to an example of white workers' poor skills and/or work habits. The connection reinforces the collection's representation of Colón Men as the best men for the job. They were not only skillful (when freed from myriad injustices), but also committed, loyal, and determined.

The following examples of workers' commendations support this image of Colón Men as superior workers and, thus, integral to the construction project. Joseph Brewster (page 2 of 2) made brief reference to a promotion he earned, but his peers used quite a few lines to detail incidents when their supervisors recognized and rewarded their good work. John Oswald Butcher believed that he would benefit from a job well done. "Mr. Walter D. Smith, assistant quartermaster," Butcher wrote, "was a real pusher. He always promised permanent work to the better workmen. Hearing this, I tried my best to work harder and more than anyone else." He said that many rose to this challenge "but of course, as far as plumbers were concerned there were none better than the Nolan-Butcher team" (Butcher, page 1 of 6). One of Rufus Forde's supervisors gave him a promotion after noting how quickly he learned; as Forde remembered it, his *boss* attributed this perspicacity to his training in Trinidad. Conducting some initial work on one set of the canal's locks, Forde "catch on to the job" quickly and his boss said to him "you have a quick head, you dint spend too years in the [Trinidadian] foundary for nothing, I better make you my straw boss" (Forde, 3 of 5; see also Berisford, page 1 of 3, Rouse, page 1 of 2). Bajan John Garner purported to live by the motto "Perform the fullest measure of work first and expect reward after" and it seemed to have paid off for him (Garner, page 3 of 3). Trained in preparing the terrain for steam shovels, Garner transferred into a new gang and had "to be broken in to this type of work as I knew nothing about sounding with leadline. . . . I got along with these men very well and after a year working I was promoted to Foreman" (page 2 of 3). George Hodges gained from his on-the-job training and saved his coworkers' lives. Working with different types of detonating powders taught him that Trojan, rather than "key-stone & du-pont," worked best. Hodges learned that when "Trojan powder gets into the hole . . . it boils like a pot because you can naturally hear it" giving laborers a chance to escape before the dynamite detonated. Hodges's bosses accepted his advice and many lives were saved when the bubbling Trojan powder signaled a premature explosion. He was financially rewarded (his coworkers took up a collection for him) and applauded for his know-how.

The "Colón Man image" that develops over the course of the IHS collection is composed of participants' recollections of "inferior" non-Caribbean workers as well as memories of Caribbean workers' skill. This image is also rhetorically constructed, as can be seen in the way some entrants positioned themselves in the stories they tell. Jamaican Daniel T. Lawson remembered his participation in the unofficial end to canal construction, the destruction of the dike at Gamboa, as follows:

> my boss, learning that a special train was to have ran on the occasion for the white Americans entreat me to board the train with tool bag and other pieces of tools. It was a packed train, I had was to stand between two coaches on the platform. I was not opposed. The great Governor Goethals was on the scene, thousands of spectators with wrist watches and cameras were all alert watching and waiting for the final minute, the specified time was less than two minutes, then the blast, water and dirt were hurled into the air, coming down spraying everybody in its wake. (Lawson, page 4 of 5)

Lawson's telling is all the more dramatic when compared to another version of the same occasion. Wesley Clarke also "experienced the day they blew the dyke. [He] stood up and watched the water coming down looking for it to come with plenty power but it didn't. It took its own time and came down gradually" (W. Clarke, page 1 of 1). The men probably watched the event from different points along the canal line, but this likelihood does not take away from the portentous tone of Lawson's version. He inserted himself into the drama of the occasion, rhetorically linking the awesome opening to his presence and person. Note that this Panamá Man made particular reference to his tools. As Lawson remembered it, his boss entreated him to board with them, but for no discernable reason; the trip was for entertainment purposes, a short ride with little threat of mechanical difficulty. Lawson was, therefore, on the scene as a *worker* and thus integral to the project so demonstrably completed. He also commented that the explosion caused a spray to cover *everybody*, even him as he rode between cars. This scene conjures an image of exclusion (Lawson stood outside on the platform), yet Lawson writes himself in as an equal—perhaps as better because of his status as "worker." Other workers were even more explicit in describing themselves as integral to the canal enterprise.

Prince Green worked as a janitor for his first year in Panamá. On 1 May 1910, he transferred to "work for Governor Goethels on his inspection motor car" until he retired in 1954. While chauffeuring the governor, he observed events all along the canal line and offered a most articulate statement about why Caribbean men elected to work for the ICC. Green wrote:

> the construction worker gave everything he possessed to the U.S. Government; in regards of work, we worked in rain, Sun, fire, Gun powder, explosions from dynamite; in house and out Side, we had to be hiding for our lives, Yellow fever, Bad water, long hours, in some jobs, no overtime, ten cents an hour, but our interest was to see the Canal finish cause we came here to build it . . . and it was done not in six days, but our part was completed, thank God, I live to See the foundation we have laid down. (Green, page 1 of 1)

This fuller representation of an earlier reference (Martin's "Hearken ye, people of a different tribe") provides evidence for Green's rhetorical manipulation of the image of the Caribbean worker. Invoking the Bible as metaphor (the canal, unlike the world, was not built in six days) to contextualize the enormousness of the enterprise and strength of its Caribbean workforce (it is hard to ignore the link between God's work and Colón Men's work), Green couched workers' motivations, sacrifice, and expertise in monumental terms. Six years did not appear to diminish this sentiment, though a marked change in the form of veneration occurred. E. W. Martineau made elaborative use of military metaphors to describe Caribbeans working at Gatun. He averred: "I saw the work men cautiously creeping up the ridges with their drills as soldiers going up Majuba hill in Mesopotamia in battle array. With great dexterity they pressed forward in blasting and drilling, while others with water hose washing down the soft earth to make way for the gallant men who were storming the rocks with gallantry" (Martineau, page 3 of 6).[25] Martineau's use of military metaphors reflects his rhetorical flair and, perhaps, the effect of revisiting the construction period from the perspective of the successfully completed canal. It is also possible that Green, Martineau, and (previously) Martin appropriated the symbolic vehicle best suited to his memory of his experience. One cannot know whether these men, while in the midst of the construction, thought of themselves in biblical or warrior terms. Still the frequency of these and similar characterizations implies that writers of *LICCW* letters believed themselves and their labor to be equal to a momentous adventure.

The magnitude of the "Colón Man image" is also visible in contrast to others' depictions of them. The subsequent clash between the two images forces us to recognize the Colón Men indeed had their own image of themselves, one that did not necessarily jibe with the one held by U.S. and canal authorities. This conflict between workers' sense of themselves and officials' sense of them is best revealed in letters that describe the surprising end to canal construction. Despite what participants described as years of dedication and sacrifice, ICC authorities unceremoniously cast them aside. Most were stunned by the absence of veneration (and remuneration) worthy of their centrality to the successfully completed canal.

Martin (page 5 of 7) and Austin (pages 4–5 of 5) considered it a joke whenever they heard talk about the completion. Apparently this "joke" was a familiar one because when the work was done, many Colón Men described being taken by surprise. Bajan John F. Prescod portrayed the event in this way:

> Big boss Mr. Hagon say who the hell tell you to put that machine up there take it down   Canal his finish. I say what the hell I am going to do now no money   only the pay check that coming   now one man in the gang eating flour dumplin drop out of his mouth   what sir!   the canal finish I have no money. (Prescod, page 1 of 2)

The unexpected end to the work obviously shocked Prescod and his companion. Z. H. McKenzie was more expressive in his description when he wrote that:

> the Completion of the water way Brought great Desolation on the W.I. Employees. Some of us were Transferred to other Places. others were Sent Home to different Islands. The wage Scall during the Canal Conscrution was So Small that we could not put by any Saving in the Bank. Hence the mejority of ous left Empty handed. to lived or die. Of which many died from a weak heart. (McKenzie, page 1 of 2)

Prescod and McKenzie appropriately translated the end of the construction as the end of their income, preventing them from returning home as they—and their Caribbean communities—expected. Being stranded in this way also put them at the mercy of canal and Panamanian authorities.

When wages, inadequate though they were, stopped so abruptly, most workers stubbornly continued to search for work in Panamá. Aaron Clarke described a scene where men "wandered here and there in search of work; and very often was arrested by policemen for loitering and when placed before the magistrate who never used reason in those day, they were sent to prison" (Aaron Clarke, page 4 of 4). Whether destitute, repatriated, or subjected to harsh justice, Colón Men's postconstruction lives were exceedingly difficult.[26]

Respondents expressly linked descriptions of their mistreatment at the hands of canal officials (inadequate salaries/savings) and Panamanian authorities (confrontations with police) to their health and financial problems that extended well into their retirement years. Yet these Colón Men did not call on the sympathy of canal authorities; they framed their appeals by recounting examples of their investment in Panamá and the canal. Clifford Hunt's complaint about his pension seems to embrace the sentiment of most who used the contest as an opportunity to plead their cases. Hunt argued:

> I work with ever thing that come to put thrue the Canal   Men in my gang tell the Boss I am going out to ease my bowels and they die in the bush and nobody look for you   I cry sometimes to see how I work to put this Canal through   up to know they don't pay us no mine today men are walking in and have everything sweet   I am one up to the time they retire me in 1950 and the little small pension we are dying for Starvation. but I ask God to open you all hearts and have mercy on us (Hunt, page 1 of 1; see also Parks, page 1 of 1, LeCurrieux, page 2, 7 of 7, McKenzie, page 1 of 2, John Morgan, page 1 of 1)

These "old timers" did not seem to want charity, but instead they merely wanted their due.

IV

These epistolary Panamá stories shed light on experiences that are not fully realized in other genres. The import (and implications) of these multiple and intersecting epistolary narrations can be seen in this chapter's title. Taken from George H. Martin's entry, the words evoke the contrasts that typify migration to and work in the Canal Zone, Colón Men's hopes for canal work, and also the ways their labor defined them. They simultaneously evoke, and extend, accounts of the canal that merely focus on the contributions of the United States. Martin's remembrance of "small" money and "big" living complicates canal authorities, historians, and some creative writers' representations of high wages on the isthmus and instead focuses on the "bigness" of Colón Men's tenacity and unwillingness to take what little ICC officials were willing to offer. Martin's use of the passive voice directly speaks to this unwillingness. He wrote that while the money *was paid* small—suggesting that what *employers* offered was meager—what workers were *able to take* was another matter altogether.

Peter Hermon wrote "my memory can't aford me thru old age to give more details" (Hermon, page 1 of 1), but his letter and those of the others demonstrate that the meanings of these narratives lie in more than the details. This idea is best expressed in George Hodges's entry. By way of invitation, he said, "should there be any slight doubt on these [facts as he represents them], please refer to records; for I am certainly sure that they are recorded. *Maybe, not as I explain*, but they are there along with many many more" (Hodges, page 5 of 5, emphasis added). Hodges indicated that his version of events have been officially recorded (and can therefore be verified) but as he "explains" it, his remembrances are "true" since they best represent *his* image of Canal Zone work and life. It is this "Colón Man image," and the social, cultural, and personal features that give rise to it, that Hodges and the others reveal in the pages of the *LICCW* collection and that richly inform depictions of the figure in creative narratives.

NOTES

1. Harry A. Franck, *Zone Policeman 88: A Close Range Study of the Panama Canal and Its Workers* (New York: Arno Press/The New York Times, 1970).

2. *Letters from Isthmian Canal Construction Workers* (*LICCW*), H. Austin Letter, page 1 of 5. Traditional means of citation have been thwarted by the fact that the collection, obtained from the library of the Afro-Antillean Museum in Panamá City, Panamá, was not paginated. This is most troublesome when I cite from the first seven pages (introduction, list of participants, and glossary). Fortunately, on subsequent pages Ruth Stuhl used headers that include the name of each contestant (in alphabetical order) as well as the number of pages of his/her transcribed submission; all citations refer to this pagination.

3. Contest participant Alfred E. Dottin, writing from Chorrillo, Panamá, said that "when I came here to work I saw tools that I never saw before in my life such as the Jack Hammer, star drills, steel square, etc." (Dottin, page 1 of 2).

4. I have had trouble finding a description of or mission statement for the IHS, but from the two publications I have, it appears to be a social organization started by self-described "Canal Zone brats" to celebrate and record the uniqueness of North American life in the Canal Zone. See www.czbrats.com for more information.

5. Jamaican Daniel Lawson (Lawson, page 1 of 5) and Bajan Jules E. LeCurrieux (LeCurrieux, page 4 of 7) indicated that they documented their experiences while they were in Panamá and employed by the ICC.

6. Austin, Martin, and McDonald seemed to write about what they thought noteworthy; Austin in particular wanted to give credit where it was due, for he used the majority of his submission to rail against practically every injustice he encountered. Participants probably also tried to anticipate what would attract the attention of selection committee members: Antiguan Frederick James peppered his letter with precise descriptions and names of employees, and ended with a recounting of each monetary prize. Still other participants appeared to have had altogether different reasons for documenting certain memories.

7. Precisely because they have passed through previous translations, memories, and time, I have tried to reproduce each entry's word, grammar, punctuation, spelling, and spacing choices as accurately as possible though I exercised editorial discretion only for the sake of clarity or emphasis.

8. One resource, featured in this volume's Conclusion, is Herbert de Lisser's 1915 novel, *Susan Proudleigh*.

9. Despite emphases on the material benefits of Panamá migration, the act also provided migrants with *cultural* capital and stood as an outward sign of their inner ambition, qualities that they could parlay into "commodities": goods, land, status, or even lovers. A cosmopolitan air, an assumed accent, and knowledge about other people and lands also shaped their identities and often translated into community esteem. Cultural capital, as well as individuals' hopes for their migrations, seemed to have been more significant for many Caribbean men and their families than "stories" of death and financial failure on the isthmus. See chapter 1 for a more thorough discussion of "migration images" and other migration traditions in the Anglophone Caribbean.

10. As a messenger, Enrique Plummer too parlayed his access to ICC offices along the canal line into another occupation: unofficial historian of the Caribbean every man. He nuanced this unofficial duty with a complementary investment in community building on the isthmus. Plummer's detailed entry reflects a pride as strong as that of Martineau and Green. Each of these workers-cum-historians also demonstrates the Caribbean workforce's diversity of employment, both official and unofficial.

11. Watkins-Owens claims that, "an unknown but substantial number of Caribbean immigrants came to New York directly from Panama or financed their own or family members' transportation to America with 'Panama money'" (Watkins-Owens 1996: 14).

12. I include Plummer's letter among others written by Caribbean-born respondents because his Spanish/English name identifies him as being an "Afro-Panamanian of Anglophone West Indian descent." Michael Aceto identifies this naming custom among "residents of Bastimentos [an island near the Panamá/Costa Rica border, part of Panamá's Bocas del Toro Province]" who "have resisted pressure to Hispanicize their surnames, which are overwhelmingly Anglophone.... Official Spanish-derived first names are found on all government documents, and they identify individuals as citizens of the Republic of Panama." "Ethnic Personal Names and Multiple Identities in Anglophone Caribbean Speech Communities in Latin America," *Language in Society* 31: 587. Black Panamanians of Caribbean descent often use their "Spanish-derived" first names only in official contexts and on official documents (579); however, like the people of Bastimentos, this ethnic group "conduct[s] their lives in a local English-derived Creole" (578). Aceto recognizes several reasons for this practice, one of which is the desire to "publicly [proclaim] and [emphasize] its Anglophone Creole ethnicity vis-à-vis the dominant Hispanophone national identity in Panama" (585).

13. Caribbean workers were said to have held more than two-thirds of the isthmus's unskilled positions. But, as Michael Conniff documents, they worked at a variety of other positions and at varying rates of pay (Conniff 1985: 31). Of *LICCW* participants, Everton Holder worked as a painter immediately after his 1905 arrival. He was soon promoted to the position of foreman painter and concluded these duties after forty-nine years of service. Interestingly, Holder volunteered as a fireman and served "in the Civilian Defense as Chief Area Warden" during World War II (Holder, page 1 of 3). Among respondents, this kind of volunteerism was rare but not unprecedented. Also rare were workers like Donald Thomas, another participant from Grenada, who worked from 1908 to 1920 as

photographer's assistant (Donald Thomas, page 1 of 1). Simeon T. Wheatley was a teamster who drove a mule wagon; his duties included "deliver coal, kindle, ice and furniture around the Quarters of the White folks Sometimes Commisary Supplies at a section call Empire" (Wheatley, page 1 of 1).

14. Peters, who arrived in Panamá from Nassau, Bahamas on 31 August 1906, stated that "the pay was 2 Balboas a day, those Balboas equal 50¢ U.S. currency" (Albert Peters, page 1 of 4). Arriving three years after Peters, Martin's second-place letter shows some variation in the Commission's wage policy. Martin wrote that he arrived on 2 September 1909 and "we were paid 10c per hour, and work 9 hours a day, giving us the amount of 90 cent daily" (Martin, page 2 of 7). Austin landed at Colón on 9 October 1905 and claimed to have earned $.80 per day, ten cents per hour for an eight-hour day (Austin, page 1 of 5). In their statements of these facts, these men's recollections seem to be of the documentary variety.

15. It is likely that Colón Men took advantage of the de facto legality of what Harry Franck describes as the isthmus's informal economy. He suggests that gratuities greased wheels in the Canal Zone; for example, tipping motivated waiters to provide good service, or any service at all if one was seated too close to closing time (Franck 1970: 211).

16. Contestants described the ways they used to avoid the administration of quinine. Stories about these treatments occupied many who contributed to the collection. Martin described the ICC's quinine policy (all employees were required to take it daily) (Martin, page 3 of 7), but soon the effects of this service became clear. Everyone so treated with the drug suffered some hearing loss. Joseph Gard spent twelve days in the rest house (an intermediary step for those who were not seriously ill or injured) recovering from malaria and "when I came out I was deaf from the Canine" (Gard, page 1 of 2). Austin too recalled quinine-related deafness and deaths that likely resulted when workers could not hear various warnings (Austin, page 2 of 5). If these comments are any indication, the problem was multiplied by the ways Commission officials enforced the ingestion of this preventative. If workers "behave bad" and refused the treatment, Albert Banister claimed, "the man will call the Police you either drink or go through the gate you lost your job you will have to go to a next job where nobody know you and the next [quinine] bottle man don't know you" (Banister, page 1 of 5). And Commission authorities did not stop at firing noncompliant workers; several participants reported that workers were jailed for refusing quinine treatments (Ashby, page 1 of 1; Austin, page 2 of 5). Notwithstanding the drug's benefits and ICC authority in the Canal Zone, Banister's words illustrate that Colón Men found ways to avoid both the medicine and the punishments if they were suspicious of quinine, feared its side effects, or if they objected to the ICC's enforcement policies. Nowhere in the collection is it made clear whether official knew what workers did to avoid ICC rules, an indication that realities existed beyond the purview of the ICC.

17. Constantine Parkinson supports part of Banister's recollection when he stated that Greek and Spanish workers sometimes dug up bodies with money hidden on them (Parkinson, pages 1–2 of 2).

18. Many contestants described these meal coupons they exchanged for food and goods in ICC commissaries (see Peters, page 2 of 4; Martin, pages 1, 2 of 7). Philip McDonald also noted the different increments of coupons in books assigned

to gold and silver employees and the better variety of goods in gold commissaries (McDonald, pages 6, 7 of 9). Parkinson continued in this vein when he stated that Greek and Spanish workers got $40 in meal tickets, which allowed them to purchase wine (Parkinson, page 2 of 2; see also Plummer, page 1 of 5).

19. McCullough discounts Martin's description of food by saying that "most of such declarations date from a later time." He continues: "in fact, the food from the mess kitchens in the labor camps appears to have been quite dreadful to begin with, or at least bad enough that in 1906 some sixteen thousand of the labor force preferred to fend for themselves, cooking their own meals in iron pots" (McCullough 1977: 477). I think it is important to note that McCullough makes these claims after using very few of Martin's words. A larger sampling reveals, as I argue in the text, much about this worker's personality, offering some insight into the jubilant tone of his recollections.

20. George Priestly documents several strikes initiated by Caribbean ICC employees between 1904 and 1914, as well as the labor union participation by Panamanian descendents of Caribbean workers. "Ethnicity, Class and the National Question in Panama," *Emerging Perspectives on the Black Diaspora*, edited by A. W. Bonnett and G. L. Watson (Lanham, MD: University Press of America, 1990): 218–19, 223.

21. Albert Banister remembered things much differently. Speaking for his community of Colón Men, he said "we had plenty to eat good place to sleep good medical attendance you get pay promp rain or shine pay day never putt off there is not a man can say Uncle Sam rub or cheat him on black cent what you aggree to work for that is what Uncle paid you I was admitted at Ancon Hospital about 12 times I had Malaria for five years I got hurt or injur many times God bless the Officials that found out safty commetee" (Banister, page 2 of 5). The founding of the Safety Committee apparently improved the quality of Banister's life because, judging from the way he framed his recollection, it came into being after his twelve hospitalizations. That these men remembered comparable experiences so differently reflects the different realities that inform their memories.

22. Like Enrique Plummer (see note 12 above), Clarke's name suggests that he is an "Afro-Panamanian of Anglophone West Indian descent." Clarke might also be counted among the *LICCW* participants who obtained Panamanian citizenship (Philip McDonald, page 1 of 9; Simeon T. Wheatley, page 1 of 1). It is also possible that Clarke, like other entrants, was a first generation Caribbean-Panamanian. Lessep O. Brown identified himself as being "born in Panama of West Indian parents" (Brown, page 1 of 2); H. B. Clayton "was born October 23, 1892 in the townsite of Gorgona Canal Zone [Plummer's home town] of West Indian parentage" (Clayton, page 1 of 1). As in the case of Plummer and Clayton, place of birth and/or current residence can also identify someone as being of Caribbean descent. Constantine Parkinson, for example, "was born 1894 the 12 of November at a place call Playa de Flor now by the name Fort Sherman this little town was inhabited around french Canal days with mostly Jamaicans and few natives Panamanians" (Parkinson, page 1 of 2). Clarke submitted his letter from Central Avenue in Colón, one of Panamá's few predominantly English-speaking cities, settled by people from the Anglophone Caribbean who arrived on the isthmus during the constructions of the railroad and canal.

23. See Patrice Brown's essay on black workers from the United States, "The Panama Canal: The African American Experience," referenced in the introduction and chapter 1.

24. In Olive Senior's short story "Window," Colón Man Devonshire contends: "the islanders knew that [Negroes from the States] didn't know any better, [behaving in this subservient manner] came as natural to them as eating and sleeping . . . and [islanders] viewed them with scorn" (Senior 1995: 69). Devon thought that because Caribbean workers would return home and in this way escape the ICC's brand of racism, they could perform an inferiority they did not necessarily feel. Upon his return to Jamaica he comes to reevaluate this position. See chapter 4 for a detailed discussion of this story.

25. Martineau appears to have confused historical events here, simultaneously invoking the battle at Majuba Hill (27 February 1881) where South African Boers defeated the English in the first Anglo-Boer War (also known as the Transvaal War or the First War of Independence) and possibly the British (Indian and English) attempt to secure its Mesopotamian oil interests and capture Turkish-controlled Baghdad during World War I (November 1914). Despite the confusion, the Colón Man's interest in these battles is clear. In both instances, successful forces prevailed against extreme geographical, environmental, and human adversities. For useful descriptions of these battles, see www.1914-1918.net/mesopot.htm (Mesopotamia) and www.sahistory.org.za/pages/chronology/thisday/1881-02-27.htm (Majuba Hill).

26. There have been several attempts at acknowledging the contributions of Colón Men and their descendents, the most recent of which was "La Día de la Etnia Negra," first celebrated on 30 May 2001 and founded by Mr. and Mrs. Claral Richards. See http://diadelaetnia.homestead.com/home.html. This form of veneration followed the 15 August 1951 issuance of a stamp commemorating "the part taken by West Indians in the construction of the Panama Canal. The new ten-cent stamp shows a group of laborers at work in Culebra (Gaillard) Cut. It was designed by Mede Bolton, former Panama Canal Architect." www.czbrats.com/Builders/WIStamp.htm. George W. Westerman "conceived the idea that a commemorative stamp would be a fitting memorial to West Indians who worked in building The Panama Canal, and carried his idea to fruition." "West Indian Stamp Appreciation Exercises" program, George W. Westerman Collection, Rare Books and Manuscripts Division, Schomburg Library for Research in Black Culture. The *Jamaica Gleaner* published an article, "Panama Canal workers widows get annuities," to alert eligible women of the new benefit. The annuities resulted from a "new law, passed by the Senate and the House of Representatives and signed by President Nixon" (Friday, 4 September 1970, p. 25, col. 7–8).

3

"Colón Man a Come": Isthmian Migrants in *The Harder They Come* and *In the Castle of My Skin*

I am not a prisoner of history. I should not seek there for the meaning of my destiny.
I should constantly remind myself that the real *leap* consists in introducing invention into existence.

—Frantz Fanon, *Black Skin, White Masks*

the Rastafarian, the calypsonian, the poet, novelist, and dramatist, all entered a new realm of awareness and, as spokespersons of the community, articulated various aspects of the narrative of liberation.

—Patrick Taylor, *Narrative of Liberation*

The greatness of the great batsman is not so much in his own skill as that he sets in motion all the immense possibilities that are contained in the game . . .

—C. L. R. James, *Beyond a Boundary*

I

Fictive Colón Men exist as heroes, historical actors, tools of U.S. and French isthmian authorities, and embodiments of myriad premigration experiences. Interpretive foci, then, cannot rely on the figure as the representative of an ideal postcolonial subject, but instead on its ability to convey a range of lived experiences, those that have been documented as

"Deck scene on the SS Ancon upon its arrival at Cristobal, Panama, from Barbados, West Indies, with 1,500 laborers, September 2, 1909." Photographer unknown. Courtesy of Photographs and Prints Division, Schomburg Center for Research in Black Culture, The New York Public Library, Astor, Lenox, and Tilden Foundations.

well as those that can only be imagined. Thus creative writers draw on mythographic Colón Men to introduce into their texts more than "local color." Writers remember the hopes—realized, unrealized, and unrealistic—that fueled isthmian migration and labor, and through them proffer alternatives to portrayals of the Caribbean subject-as-victim.

George Lamming's creative work equips Caribbean people to reinhabit "the castles of their skins,"[1] a "habitation" undermined by the lack of awareness that he ascribes to the neocolonial moment. Through key figures in his novel *In the Castle of My Skin*, he describes a Barbadian population moving into the postcolonial period but maintaining a colonial mind-set characterized by a pride in its "status" as "Little England" (Lamming 1983: 99) and confidence in an alien authority figure instead of themselves (98). Michael Thelwell, in *The Harder They Come*, imagines a similar population in Jamaica but begins his investigation at the point where its members are primed to confront forces that alienate them from themselves. Lamming and Thelwell are thus engaged in something more than creative expression. They write other realities, but write them *into* prevailing discourses of victimization and dependence. Their articulations of imaginable Bajan and Jamaican subjectivities intend to transform the consciousness of these country's rural and African-descended populations and to complicate predetermined notions about them. They use their Colón Men, and their novel's protagonists, to right/write stories that often only recognize victimization or at best some measure of success in relation to it. Their work declares, as Glissant suitably states, that "our Caribbean reality is an option open to us. It springs from our natural experience, but in our histories has only been [seen as] 'an ability to survive'" (Glissant 1989: 222).

George Lamming has long been concerned with defining "the West Indian writer" and his/her social function.[2] Generally speaking, he maintains that the work of such a writer is to maintain—as its central focus—the Caribbean, its history, and its predicament.[3] This definition refines an earlier view that Lamming asserts in *The Pleasures of Exile* (originally published in 1960). In *Pleasures*, he defines the West Indian writer by his/her relationship to the soil, "for the soil is a large part of what the West Indian novel has brought back to reading; lumps of earth: unrefined, perhaps, but good, warm, fertile earth."[4] The author explains that his earlier definition grew out of a particular historical moment, a time when the land was more significant to the everyday reality of the majority of West Indian people (Dance 1992: 135–36). Both definitions convey Lamming's desire for locally relevant metaphors that communicate the region's concerns. Specifically, the author is concerned with theorizing the Caribbean from the inside out.

Lamming addresses himself to what he perceives as the concerns of the majority of Caribbean people. If the province and responsibility of the writer are the world of the private and hidden self, the world of social relations, and the community to whom the writer is directly responsible,[5] Lamming's writerly self and his community are implicated in (but not wholly constitutive of) each other. The Caribbean writer cannot merely be one who observes and documents his community. In his work, the individual is important as part of a community, but also as a discrete gauge of the effects of slavery/colonialism. His definition of a West Indian writer speaks to the imperative that artistic work be politically and socially relevant. He states that the West Indian writer's imagination is a production of, and in turn produces, society; the writer must, therefore, "be organically related to the political movement of that society in the widest sense."[6]

If Lamming intends "a calculated challenge to the habitual way of seeing that has become a normal part of colonization" (Paquet 1982: 3), such a challenge must disrupt the "truth" of colonial discourse as it functions on multiple levels of a Caribbean reality. Such a writer rejects "escapes to a European autumn pavement, or even to an African homecoming . . . in favour of careful re-examination of the roots of individual and collective personality behind the phenomena of slavery and colonialism in order to confront and interpret the West Indian present."[7] Lamming complicates colonial representations of this reality by enabling those represented to see and use differently myth and emotion that are already viable features of their lives. His new vision contests the primacy of colonial history; his investment in a Caribbean lived reality presupposes the kinds of complication I represent in this and previous chapters.

Lamming's *In the Castle of My Skin* emerges out of an uncommon confluence of historical events.[8] This historical climate elicited from writers of former British Caribbean colonies "a growing awareness of what it meant to be colonized" (Taylor 1989: 183) and a desire to challenge colonialism and its legacy. Although published twenty-six years later, Michael Thelwell's *The Harder They Come* addresses these same concerns. Both writers invoke another historical event, Caribbean migration to Panamá and contribution to the Panamá Canal, to respond to colonialism, importantly offering insight into a process through which liberation from a colonial inheritance can occur. Lamming and Thelwell address the issue of history as it operates in the Caribbean by employing their Colón Men, Pa and Maas' Nattie respectively, as examples of a self that is not fixed by or solely a victim of the legacies of colonialism.

In *The Harder They Come*, Thelwell too seeks a critical model that interprets Caribbeanness from a locally relevant base. His position is effectively stated through the protagonist's grandmother, Miss 'Mando, whose landscape "speaks" volumes:

> between the various homesteads a network of footpaths and trails wound its intricate way, connecting homes and farms into a human community. The

forest, that apparently random jungle, was in reality a testament to human tenacity and labor. . . . [Trees] represented the product of a relationship evolved over many centuries, in a distant, almost forgotten country, between man and the land. The mountain valleys with the strong life-giving sun, heavy rains, and rich deep earth had been there fallow and waiting, it seemed, for them. (Thelwell 1988: 15)

'Mando articulates her land's myriad meanings. What she also reveals is a conception of herself in relation to the land and her community. For the old woman, past and present exist simultaneously, influencing each other symbiotically. Thelwell attempts to reproduce 'Mando's multifaceted experience in Ivan's characterization: he is a product of his personal and social histories. Positing such a vision as feeding the Caribbean artist's muse, Thelwell believes that West Indian writers must reject "fashionable material coming from Europe—existentialism, alienation and all that kind of stuff"—for "works that try to use the experience and culture of the people and try to create the form of literature which is an expression of Caribbean culture and experience" (Dance 1992: 250–51).[9]

These two writers tap into Colón Men's lived and imaginable truths to tell other histories and stories, and to foreground the influential role that such inspiring cultural myths play in Caribbean peoples' responses to oppression. It is important to note, however, that fictional Panamá migrants do not merely celebrate oppositional Caribbean histories and identities, nor do they solely inspire positive action. The literary figures in this chapter are as complicated as the circumstances from which actual migrants evolved.

In this chapter, Lamming and Thelwell use Colón Men's vernacular stories as vehicles through which they demonstrate the innate dignity of Caribbean peoples; these peoples are consequently able to confront the struggles that impact their lives. Through their Colón Men, these writers stress the importance of awareness of self in determining the course of one's life. Significantly, Lamming's Pa channels an alternative and suppressed consciousness to the living. In Maas' Nattie, the Colón Man in Thelwell's novel, the reader encounters a figure who embodies a confidence in the revolutionary potential of culture and community. It is through Nattie's influence that protagonist Ivanhoe Martin performs the author's revolutionary directive. However, it is significant that neither author presents his Colón Man as ideal. In some ways Pa's Panamá experience prevents him from appreciating the similarities between his village's colonial and postcolonial moments. Maas' Nattie's vision is limited in that it is best suited to his past rather than Ivan's present. The Colón Men in these novels do not offer facile solutions, but act as catalysts that move protagonists along unexpected trajectories in their particular contexts.

II

First published in 1953, *In the Castle of My Skin* resonated strongly for those who had never found their Barbadian experience in literature.[10] By making his characters and their community recognizable and more or less conscious of the drama of their lives, Lamming affirms the authority of the formerly denigrated black, peasant, and Bajan perspective, particularly as it equips this population to confront the forces that impact their lives. Pa, who carries the mythographic weight of Colón Men's stories, is the figure in whom many of Lamming's creative and political goals converge.

The novel spans a nine-year period of G.'s childhood, opening on his ninth birthday. It begins with a flood that devastates Creighton's village, a former plantation named for its English slave owner; moreover, the catastrophe physically and symbolically marks the beginning of a more lasting change in the community. The cost of necessary postflood repairs makes landlord Creighton (descendant of "master" Creighton) unwilling to continue his financial obligation to the village; his dwindling interest initiates the village's postcolonial era. Creighton sells out to a consortium headed by Mr. Slime, former schoolteacher and founder of the Penny Bank (a savings and loan) and Friendly Society (a burial society). Villagers can purchase their land at unreasonable rates—that is if their lots have not been claimed by members of Slime's consortium—or move. The final irony is that Slime uses the Bank and Society's resources, existing through the villagers' contributions, to buy Creighton's land. This use of these organizations symbolically demonstrates how villagers contribute to their own disenfranchisement. Pa illustrates both this tragic irony as well as the potential for a transformative politics. Both constitute the legacy the Colón Man passes on to G.

The novel identifies Pa as a Panamá Man as he muses on the dearth of his life's accomplishments. Talking to his partner, Ma, Pa measures himself against the landlord and his estate, both ensconced on a hill high above the village. He says:

> would you say it matter after all, Ma, the strugglin' an' strivin' for this an' the next . . . seems a time come when you want to feel different from what you feel, an' you begin to bother a bit 'bout what others says an' do, an' 'bout what they is. I look up over yonder there at the house on the hill, an' I wonder what it feel like to be big an' great. (Lamming 1983: 85)

Ma reminds him that he was once "big an' great" . . . in Panamá. Pa continues:

> 'tis what I says sometimes to myself. Sitting here or there it come to me how things make a change. Time wus when money flow like the flood through

these here hands, money as we never ever know it before. We use to sing in those times gone by 'twus money on the apple trees in Panama. 'Tis Panama my memory take me back to every now an' again where with these said hands I help to build the canal, the biggest an' best canal in the wide wide world. Me an' my sister dead an' gone, God rest her in her grave, an' as many as me memory can't hold. (ibid)

Expressed as the memories of an "old timer," Pa lists the most commonly known features of canal construction: the amount and significance of Panamá Money and the numerous, unnamed people who died.[11] Pa's recollection dramatizes his pride in his participation in the globally significant project; as he remembers it, the construction's success is closely linked to his own. Lastly, the passage marks the Panamá Man as an historical agent—not as one entirely subjected to history—made so through the work of his own hands.

Panamá affords Pa a sense of self that is shaped through personal achievement ("with these said hands I help to build the canal"), collective work (the "we" to whom he refers in the above passage), and participation in a globally important project ("the biggest an' best canal in the wide wide world"). By emphasizing his hands, Pa identifies the success and achievement of the canal through his body, an eloquent move that links his remembered "self" to the historically/globally meaningful enterprise. Significantly, the language he uses to describe his Panamá experience elevates him, whereas, in the previous passage, he speaks of himself as less than Mr. Creighton. In the end, Pa's conviction about his experience invokes that of *LICCW* contestants; Pa and his "peers" personalize the typical story of Caribbean canal workers. The "memories" of Lamming's Colón Man, and the recollections of *LICCW* participants (see chapter 2), indicate that they took more from canal work than authorities—both in the Canal Zone and, for Pa, in Barbados—could anticipate.

The saga of Panamá Canal migration and labor is also recalled by Lamming's use of the phrase "money was like apples on a tree." This was a familiar refrain in Barbados, said to reflect "the infectious, exciting atmosphere that must have swept the black tenantries" at the time of the construction (Richardson 1985: 116). Pa's character thus embodies the exuberance reflected in this popular phrase. Lamming's use of the saying allows the novel temporal movement (by evoking the historical past and the novel's present) as well as intra- and extratextual movements (by linking Colón Men's literary and historical narratives). By this I mean that as part of a mythography of Panamá migration, Pa recalls the history of the building of the Panamá Canal and the movement between the Central American country and various Caribbean ones, events that occur about fifty years before the novel's 1953 publication. Infused with these mythographies, *Castle's* Colón Man uniquely interprets Creighton village's colonial era and its current movement toward a postcolonial one.

Lamming informs his narrative by bringing together the fictive Panamá Man and mythographies about isthmian migration, on the one hand, and Barbados' peasant and African-descended population on the other. By blending these realities, he taps into and projects the inherent dignity of those relegated to the bottom of Bajan society and then applies the resulting configuration to the novel's coming crisis. This can be seen in the relationship between Pa and Mr. Creighton. Although their social and financial circumstances are vastly different, both are "big an' great." Panamá gives Pa access to the material signs of Greatness—money, coach-and-buggy rides, and "whatever the Great do in the open air" (Lamming 1983: 86). Still, these trappings are not the most significant results of his isthmian migration, particularly since the Colón Man's Panamá Money and the things it buys are gone. He "had been comfortable some years ago, and although much of what he had earned in Panama had been spent in one way or another, he had never been dissolute" (252). However, other signs—his dignity, achievement, and perspective—continue to manifest and determine his contribution to his community. Lamming writes that Pa:

> had always carried himself tidily with the air of a man who reminded others that he knew better times. Everyone remarked his tidiness, and they often said that the old man was great once. He had money and he had also that air of dignity which they associated with the Great. The old man had a mind, and the mind was the man. (ibid)

And if Pa, who is neither rich nor white, is Great, money and white skin–privilege cannot legitimately provide Creighton a position among the Great; the converse is true as well, since poverty and black skin cannot consign Pa to the swineherd. Thus Pa's Greatness disrupts how Greatness and "lowliness" have been defined.

The Colón Man is also unique because he alone is linked to Creighton in this way. Others mimic Creighton-as-master and Creighton-as-colonial authority, but only the Colón Man invokes the landlord's impressiveness. From this position Pa questions "what others say an' do, an' 'bout what they is." Notwithstanding other characters that have mind-set altering experiences, specifically Trumper and the shoemaker, the old man stands out as a character able to exist beyond his current poverty and the limits consigned him by master Creighton's legacies.

Trumper, who travels to the United States on a farm labor program, most closely duplicates Pa's migration experience and its resulting vision. Like the older man, Trumper's knowledge is specifically tied to his experience as a migrant laborer. He says to G., "this world is a world o' camps, an' you got to find out which camp you're in. And above everything else keep that camp clean" (288). As a contracted agricultural worker, Trumper lived in and was identified by his camp. The political implications of his camp metaphor are clear: laborers, primarily African-descended, were in one camp and Euro-American managers were in another. The owners paid the laborers poorly and provided poor working and living conditions thus making it easy to see how economic exploitation and racial oppression are inextricably linked. Trumper identifies with the "Negro" camp because he learns to view his experience as the same as blacks in the United States. Thus he encourages G. to revise the ways the latter defines himself and his People. Trumper parlays this insight into a new vision: he can "know" Slime without personally knowing him.

When G. asks Trumper about the former schoolteacher, who has bought and sold the village by this time, Trumper says he "don't have to think much 'bout [Mr. Slime]. . . . An' I not at all surprised that he do what he do. 'Tis what I learn in the States, an' I know how to handle all the Slimes that come my way" (ibid). This statement, however, reveals that Trumper's knowledge of Slime is incomplete; he makes no mention of the class- and race-based hierarchies that men like Slime accept and duplicate, nor is he immediately concerned by the cooperation between Slime, the consortium, and Mr. Creighton. Consequently, the reader must question whether Trumper can be prepared to handle *them*. G. unwittingly reveals this hole in Trumper's logic when the protagonist states:

> whatever [Trumper] suffered his assurance was astonishing. He had found what he needed and there were no more problems to be worked out. Henceforth his life would be straight, even, uncomplicated. He knew the race and he knew his people and he knew what that knowledge meant. (298)

Trumper is stagnant.[12] He does not consider that his U.S.-forged vision might not be suited to his village's current situation. He collapses the heterogeneous experiences of peoples in the African Diaspora into a reactive, U.S.-defined blackness. As a result, Trumper's migration does not effectively prepare him to face the changing realities of Creighton's village, particularly as they differ from his experiences in the United States. His limited vision also makes apparent the problem of imposing an outside philosophy on his native context.

The shoemaker, like Trumper, has knowledge that gives him unusual insight. Yet again like the young farm worker, the artisan's vision is vague and removed from the village's currently changing situation. The novel demonstrates the difference between the shoemaker's way of seeing and that of the villagers who frequent his shop: Mr. Foster, Bob's father, and the overseer's brother. These men:

> called [Barbados] Little England with the pride of the villager who thought the name carried with it a certain honourable distinction. [The men around the shoemaker's shop] were thinking of what the overseer's brother said.

> The landlord couldn't do without the village any more than they could. The shoemaker thought of that too, but he was suspicious of the attachment. While the others thought of Little England the shoemaker thought there was something suspect in the Englishman's attachment. That is what reading had done for him. (99)

The shoemaker is certain about his suspicions, a certainty fostered by his reading of J. B. Priestly, though "he could never quote this writer's exact words, and he didn't remember the name of the book" (100). Writing about English colonial governors in the colonies and in England, Priestly said that these men "who were not always very educated or even very educable could convince themselves that what was merely a temporary privilege should become a permanent right" (99). The shoemaker cannot articulate his suspicions about expatriots' attachment to "Little England" in terms of Priestly's observation but he knows that the ideas of "J. B. P." are the key to "a big secret" (ibid).

The cobbler's failure to conceptualize and articulate the connection, however, is the least of his problems. Even if he could do both, the other villagers could fully benefit from his observations—they value neither the man nor his insights. When discussing the impending strike[13] with Mr. Foster, the overseer's brother, and Bob's father, the shoemaker sits down at his bench and asks, "Well, what you going to do?"

> There was a trickle of tea along his chin and the cave of a jaw tooth was filled with bread. The men sat quiet and contemplative, feeling for an answer. The shoemaker held the boot on his knees. The thick skin of his brow was heavily creased, and when he chewed the remnants of bread as he spoke, the bones of his face made a ridiculous seesaw movement under the skin. (95)

The narrator does much to make the shoemaker appear ridiculous, and further marks his difference by indicating that he believes that his opinions about the strike, considering that his livelihood would not be immediately affected by it, are purely those of a spectator (96). Lamming portrays the artisan as being in, but not of, the community.

The shoemaker's opinions are as vague as Trumper's. He perceives "something suspect" in the Englishmen's attachment to Barbados and suspects "in a way he couldn't explain" a relationship between Caribbean cricket, his reading of J. B. P., and Barbados and Trinidad's riots. Ultimately his detachment and his inarticulateness prevent him from acquiring or sharing any real insight into Mr. Slime's activities. Through the shoemaker, Lamming offers one of the novel's most meaningful discussions of colonialism and its legacy—that colonial governors often took temporary privileges as rights—but because he appears foolish and is removed, villagers scorn him. Readers, however, may look beyond the author's lampooning of the shoemaker to appreciate his insights. This character's most crucial error is that he does not recognize, until it is too late, that his fate is inextricably tied to that of the village. Rather than relocating when he learns his plot has been sold, the shoemaker tries to remove his shop—the entire structure—from the land and it collapses (299–300). Particularly because he has knowledge that others lack, the cobbler's demise underscores the importance of shared knowledge and community.

It is important to note that Pa, Trumper, and the shoemaker benefit from physical and intellectual movements beyond Barbados.[14] Trumper is an integral part of Creighton's village, but his philosophy is based on a U.S. experience; the shoemaker's selected readings are important, but his alienation prevents him from sharing what he knows with his neighbors. Pa, however, is a unique pedagogic force in the novel. In his Panamá migration, his inherent dignity and communal orientation converge, thus producing an intelligence that survives the denigrating forces acting on the village. Through the Panamá Man readers learn the importance of combining a broader experience of the world with a grounding in one's community, particularly if one is struggling with and toward social change.

Lamming offers an alternative to what he describes as a colonial mindset by representing a view of the village's predicament through Pa's Bajan eyes and ears.[15] Because this character projects his dignity and self-worth through his experiences in Panamá, and because this background continues to influence how he sees and reads his world, he offers a most effective means through which the novel's Barbadian subjectivity is articulated. I resist, however, characterizing Pa's Panamá-influenced perspective simply; even he cannot offer villagers a panacea for their problems. Pa's eyes, though they reflect a shifted perspective, are not immune to deception.

The old man's isthmian experiences dispose him to view the changes Mr. Slime proposes favorably. Slime calls for villagers to be the masters of their fate, owners of their land, and significant wage earners. These ideas resonate for Pa, whose migration afforded him access to the same kind of self-determination. Ma too sees Panamá as the defining moment for Pa and his generation and calls for a "next Panama" for the younger folks; she says "'tis a next Panama we want, Pa, or there goin' to be bad times comin' this way" (86). "A next Panama," for her, will offer the younger generation that which it afforded Pa—the opportunity to reimagine themselves socially and financially. For Pa, Slime appears to inaugurate this next Panamá; however, seeing the former schoolteacher through this imaginable lens disguises how the younger man's vision diverges from that of the Colón Man.

Pa and Ma, the oldest members of Creighton's village, represent the community's opposing perspectives on Slime's proposals (Paquet 1982: 5). Ma represents those who adhere to a religion that, in effect, maintains traditional, hierarchal relationships between former masters and formerly enslaved people. Her faith works against the villagers' interests by fostering a passive belief in God's deliverance "in His own good time" (Lamming 1983: 77). Ma's God encourages her to pray for Mr. Slime, but she cannot support what she sees as his desire for earthly wealth. The old woman prays, "the grace of God go with Mr. Slime in all what he do or don't do, but bank or no bank, the riches o' this life is as naught in the sight of my Savior. 'Cause this world's evil, Pa, 'tis very evil" (ibid). Ma's message is one of deferral, unto God and until a later time, rather than active engagement in that which could yield more immediate benefits. This does not mean, however, that she cannot measure the differences between her own material reality against that of Mr. Creighton. Ma sees that she and Pa could use a new house, but falls back on her faith in God's will rather than work to get one or support someone who proposes how she might get one. She says:

> I don't understan' full well what it mean by politics an' so on, but I know good an' proper what Mr. Slime mean when he say what he say 'bout better house an' so on. . . . What an' what he say 'bout better house is true, but it ain't in my right, Pa, it ain't in my right to put him side by side with Moses, 'cause Moses wus God elect. . . . You got to be careful, Pa, when you quote the holy scriptures, for the Lord Himself says there be some who will get up to prophesy in His name an' the name o' His chosen flock, but beware, beware how they come. The devil got more tricks than what John read 'bout, so you have a care how you call the name o' the Lord's anointed. (78)

Lamming reveals through Ma how religion can hinder colonized and formerly enslaved people, but her Christianity is not uncomplicated. Her belief limits her action, but it also gives her foresight into Slime's future betrayal of the villagers. The ambivalence of Ma's faith suggests that merely rejecting her type of Christianity cannot instigate a lasting change for the old woman or her neighbors. One still has to contend with the effects this kind of faith has on Ma's consciousness. Ma does not interrogate her miseducation, particularly with regard to her own lack of agency and dependence on an absentee "master." Without changing the way Ma's religion shapes how she thinks about herself and about Englishness, eliminating such a faith would be tantamount to replacing Mr. Creighton with Mr. Slime: the face changes, but the system remains the same.

Pa does not share his partner's beliefs, though he is respectful of them. Instead, he values change, particularly if people from the community bring it about. The Colón Man's philosophy is predicated on an active involvement with change where Ma's religion consigns this kind of agency to God. When faith allows Ma some intuition, it prevents her from acting on it. Pa's convictions, on the other hand, require of him a constant and critical engagement with his daily experiences. Consider that this Panamá

Man is excited by, but not completely uncritical of, Slime's proposals. He says "I see sometimes how a thing change, an' when you lest expectin' to besides; you see how that thing change there in front of yuh eyes, an' I wonder to myself if 'tis a change for the better or worse" (Lamming 1983: 76). Unlike Ma, who sifts her opinions and actions through her unwavering trust in God's will, Pa looks at change pragmatically. The old man applies this same critical awareness to what Slime says. The younger man's words are not all that Pa "hears"; the concrete examples of Slime's belonging to and interest in the village weigh into the old man's decision. He says to Ma, "you know as I do how he use to run 'bout here in his shirt tail an' you watch him grow up into a big big school master with everybody having the right respect for him" (78). As a schoolteacher, Slime is the village boy-made-good.[16] He moves on to found the Penny Bank and Friendly Society and gains access to local politics through his involvement with the strike. These accomplishments, for Pa, are what give weight to Slime's words.

Notwithstanding the significance of Mr. Slime's communal activism and ties, in Pa's evaluation the younger man is also important because he has the kind of education the older man respects. The Colón Man says of Slime, "'tis education that's his steering-wheel takin' him here an' there, an' those who ain't got it must show the right an' proper respect for those as has it in plenty, an' Mr. Slime is one o' those" (88). Second, Pa associates Slime with change, tying him to what Ma describes as the evolution from button to zipper: "Yet 'tis change all the same, Ma. I mean the fastener an' zip you talk 'bout. 'Tis change an' in the self-same manner . . . I say 'tis change with Mr. Slime" (83). Finally, Pa reads the former teacher through his Panamá reality, seeing himself and his Panamanian experiences *in* Mr. Slime's activities and choices. This identification ultimately prevents the Colón Man from apprehending Slime's intentions until it is too late. Where Pa has dignity and community at his core, Slime is motivated by his financial ambition and power.

Lamming's novel restores colonized people to the castles of their skin by exploring the ways they react to and participate in history, thus liberating Caribbean subjectivity from its relegated place among the disempowered. But critical engagement—with one's personal, specific, and common realities—is necessary for, as Pa says, "'tis a hell of a thing . . . to have to live with something inside you that you don't know" (90). The novel suggests that such engagement begins with awareness of one's histories, and not merely ones that have been refracted through an English colonial perspective. Again, the novel's Panamá Man is a unique conduit through which such a story emerges. The people of Creighton's village only vaguely recall Barbadian slavery, and know even less about histories that came before—a forgetfulness that is reinforced by an English educational system. Their "father's forebears" speak through Pa (211), informing those who can hear (Ma is the only witness) about a precolonial, preslavery, and spiritually diverse African past in which blacks embraced pantheistic belief-systems as well as ones grounded in the idea that "man was his master and every woman her witness" (210).[17] Tribes that believed in and were in tune with the natural world were also part of these ancient communities. The histories of these peoples were disrupted by the discovery of "silver" that then lead to the Middle Passage and the subsequent erasure of myriad prediscovery realities. As the old man moves closer to consciousness, he ties Barbados' more recent realities to those of his dream-memory. Pa continues:

> the only certainty these islands inherit was that sailor's mistake, and it's gone on and on from father to son 'mongst the rich and the poor: in Slime and Creighton, landlord and politician, those who play at ruling and those at being ruled, and those who are neither one nor the other: the mob that is always good but will never understand the face of the devil nor the equal smile of the deep blue sea. The fate of these islands I do not know, but man must live like a god or a dog, or be a stone that is neither dead nor alive, a pool no wind will ever wrinkle. For there's always two worlds to one man if you're a man, two darknesses to one light, one light, one light . . . (211-12)

While Ma interprets Pa's "one light" through her Christian lens (212), its immediate referent is "one man," one who is aware of the plurality of his worlds in addition to being open to change (unlike the stone or the featureless pool). This man responds to Columbus's mistake and the tradition of artifice (playing at ruling and being ruled) he initiates. Yet the stories Pa channels are not available to the majority and the old man cannot hold all that he conveys at the surface of his consciousness.

Pa suspects more than what the consortium reveals and he fears the truth that his mind can barely grasp. Neither the old laborer nor any other character fully achieves this form of "inside" knowledge. If "unawareness is the basic characteristic of the slave [and] awareness is a minimum condition for attaining freedom" (Lamming 1992: 12), then as a condition of this freedom one must accept its risks (Taylor 1989: 197). Through the Colón Man, Lamming maps a process through which this inside knowledge can be made visible. Pa is not fully aware of Slime's aspirations because he sees the teacher-turned-activist as a younger version of himself; however, the old man's failure to see through Slime becomes part of his awareness and part of the legacy he passes on to G.

The head teacher, who buys Pa's land, meets with the old man to break the news—both of Pa's eviction and his relocation to the Alms House. It is at this meeting that the extent of Pa's critical awareness is revealed. The head teacher:

was one of the villagers who had done well, and although he might have learnt different ways, he knew what affected them most. . . . He understood what the strange men couldn't understand [the villagers' claim on the land] as well as what had seemed meaningless to the shoemaker and Mr. Foster [consortium members' purchase of it]. He had shared both worlds, and in a way it was this double understanding that had urged him to see the old man. (251)

Nonetheless, Head Teacher is not prepared for the direction of Pa's questions. He believes Pa will be concerned about moving to the Alms House; instead, Pa asks "why first of all did Mr. Slime leave the teachin', an' how an' why he come to buy this land since there wus no love an' harmony 'twixt 'imself and Mr. Creighton?" (254). The younger man tells Pa what is generally accepted (Slime's political aspirations), rather than discuss Slime's unseemly affair. But Pa

> didn't worry much about that since he had his own notions about Mr. Slime. "I as much as always says to myself," he said, "that he leave the teachin' in the school 'cause he want to do a teachin' of a bigger kind. My own feelin' wus that the sort of teachin' he wus giving the big people wus sort of bigger than what he give in the school. An' in a sort of way the two don't go together. The education he wus givin' to the children studyin' the books an' so on don't go hand in hand with the education he was givin' the big people from the platform every night. (ibid)

Pa knows more than what the head teacher believes he can know, and this makes the younger man uncomfortable. The old man links Slime with Creighton, but is frightened by the implications of the connection. He "sat shaking a little in the chair. It was unbearable, his failure to understand, his sense of disappointment and his suspicion of the possible disaster that was ahead" (257). In spite of the fear, Pa—and all the villagers—need to know the relationship between the postcolonial and the colonial. While still a schoolteacher, Slime indoctrinates the children into Englishness. As an activist, he replaces it with Afro-Barbadian values, but continues in his lessons of blind reverence and respect for hierarchies established under the former regime. Slime's final substitution places him and those of his class at the top of the hierarchy, thus maintaining villagers' lowly position.

Slime deceives Pa along with the other villagers and, like them, the old man is evicted from his land and home. Yet Pa responds to this betrayal as no other character does. He "hadn't exploded as Mr. Foster and the shoemaker had done, and it didn't seem that his age was totally responsible for his failure to do so. He seemed to feel on another level altogether" (251–52). Pa's experiences allow him to respond differently. When G. asks what the old man thinks of Slime, Pa is simultaneously pragmatic and unsure. He takes into account that the former schoolteacher has changed, and that he may not be the same person he was before the change (Lamming 1983: 303). What the old man's response dramatizes, however, is the ability to survive, as well as to learn from and act on one's knowledge and experience. Slime's betrayal does not defeat Pa. The Colón Man maintains a dignity that predates and survives Slime, one that transcends the implications of the Alms House. This is his legacy. Pa's vision, shaped by who he is, by his role in history, by his experiences in Panamá, is large enough to include Slime's treachery as well as the lessons he enables. Thanks to Pa's isthmian experience, we see that he can entertain contradictory positions. Colonial hierarchies proliferate because of the presumed authority of colonial narratives; therefore, the espousal of perspectives that challenge and complicate this authority offers a most powerful tool in discrediting traditional ways of knowing. This is the kind of education Lamming deems valuable for Caribbean people.

The village's pre-Slime world was one predicated on fixed hierarchies and the harmony achieved through knowledge of one's place in them.[18] This ideology as well as the kind of religious belief Ma represents facilitate Slime's replacement of Mr. Creighton as village master. Considering the outcome of the consortium's purchase of Creighton's village, political naïveté is a luxury Creighton's villagers can little afford.[19] Pa offers a viable option to the familiar states of unawareness and naïveté. The old laborer, like his mythographic counterpart, embodies multiple histories and stories, the result of which is his ability to see his world and himself as more than Slime and Creighton can envision. Pa sees beyond Slime's failure and looks into the unknown. He is afraid, but his response to his fear informs us that one can be defined by how one faces and responds to the unknown rather than by the fear itself.

Although physically removed from the village, Pa continues to exert an influence on the community's consciousness through G., the character most amenable to Pa's legacy (Lamming 1983: 248). The old migrant last appears in the novel with the boy (now eighteen), as the former returns for one last look at his old home. This scene firmly locates Pa in G.'s consciousness as the two play out a symbolic passing of the torch. "[Pa] had rested a hand on [G.'s] shoulder. Then he took it away and as quickly put it back" (302). Pa's touch, at first tentative then sure, binds them. The Colón Man then draws parallels between himself and G. instead of between himself and Slime; this new identification is presented in terms of endings and beginnings: "'We both settin' forth tomorrow,' [Pa] said. 'I to my last restin'-place before the grave, an' you into the wide wide world.'" Referring to the flood as beginning and ending, and linking it to G.'s past as well as his own, Pa recalls:

"'twus a night like this," he said, "nine years ago when those waters roll without end all over this place. 'Twus a flood as I won't want ever to feel for nothin' in the world. . . . "You wus small then," he said, "too small to care much 'bout the calamity that happen. But it wus the beginnin' o' so much in this place. 'Twus strike an' then 'twus riot an' what with one rumour an' a next, now 'tis the land. We see Penny Bank an' Society an' now 'tis the end." (302-3)

Pa communicates G.'s connection to the village (the flood occurs on the boy's birthday and profoundly affects his childish sense of importance), practically expressing it in physical terms. G. and the village define each other, a definition confirmed by the flood and by Pa. Yet where the old man notes endings in the village, we see a beginning for G. After Pa gives the boy a blessing, he takes his leave. It is only at this point in the novel that G. processes the series of events in Creighton's village. This act of evaluation offers an immediate example of the Panamá Man's influence on G. The younger man thinks:

"'Twus a night like this nine years ago when those waters roll." The village/my mother/a boy among the boys/a man who knew his people won't feel alone/to be a different kind of creature. Words and voices falling like a full shower and the old man returning with the pebble under the grape leaf on the sand: You won't see me again, my son. (303)

In G.'s recollection, we find a cacophony of voices: his mother's, Trumper's, and Pa's. It appears, then, that in leaving Creighton's village, the young man will take these people, these stories, with him.

The novel ends and begins with G. and the flood, coming full circle. We hear Trumper in the above passage, but with a new context. G. puts Trumper's vision within a local context, cataloging these experiences so that he may take them with him. Lamming's novels and the situations he fictionalizes are open-ended ("he sees his works as movements in a continuing process");[20] therefore, G. cannot offer a definitive answer to the colonial question in *Castle*. He can only offer his experience into the process. The novel reveals nothing of G.'s future except that which readers can project from his previous behavior. Throughout *In the Castle of My Skin*, but particularly in relation to Trumper, G. is unsure of what he knows and unaware of the import of others' knowledge. His departure is his one decisive act. G., now able to know for himself, carries Pa's legacy; the boy has potential because of his relationship with the old man. As Sandra Paquet argues, "the relationship of G. to his village [is one which] the communal experience is individualized for fictional and political emphasis" (Paquet 1982: 14); thus G.'s potential resonates beyond his individual story to become the potential of his village, of Barbados, and of the Caribbean as a whole.

Both Lamming and Michael Thelwell's novels concern a particularly Caribbean sensibility. They seek a regional critical perspective from which to confront, articulate, and explore a postcolonial Caribbean self. Thelwell describes this perspective as a "peasant world view": the culture and tradition of Jamaica's disenfranchised citizens, specifically their relationship to language, their sense of social relationships, and their religion.[21] Thelwell indicates that he also wants to represent the ways Jamaica's poorer citizens create "a certain organized relationship to the land and to each other and to a sense of tradition. . . . While people may not . . . have a great deal of material comforts, they were certainly self-sufficient" (Dance 1992: 249). For him, strong ties to land and ancestry, as well as a communal interdependence, frame this self-sufficiency. Although these webs of relations mirror those in Lamming's Creighton's villagers, Thelwell's community is firmly located within Jamaica's neocolonial moment; as a result, the Jamaican novel is specifically concerned with identifying and combating the culturally and racially familiar "Mr. Slime," whose danger lies in his masquerade as a wolf in sheep's clothing.

III

Michael Thelwell describes himself as a political activist who writes (252). Accordingly, he intends his novel to support a particular politics in Jamaica. He wrote *The Harder They Come* after being approached by a representative from Grove Press who thought Perry Henzell's film *The Harder They Come* (1973) "had in it the basis for a very good book about Third World experience" (246). Although Thelwell secured a publisher before he wrote a word, which suggests that Grove Press determined the novel's intention, he had prior plans about what he wanted his novel to do. He says that:

> the realities of Jamaican society and culture were being discussed in a much more accurate, a much more meaningful and productive kind of way, and I wanted to make a contribution to that. What I didn't think was that any white publisher in [the United States] would be interested in the kind of book that could do that, so that when Grove Press came up with this idea it struck me that here was precisely the vehicle I was looking for . . . so I thought that since here was a publisher interested in this project it would give me a chance to write a novel about the peasants and the workers in Jamaica, about their culture, about their view of the world. (246–47)

Thus the novel was born.

Thelwell has maintained that the press commissioned a novel that would give a Western audience a detailed view of "the exotic." The film *The Harder They Come* appeared to be an ideal vehicle for this vision because it was set in Jamaica and used Jamaican dialect (English subtitles were added to the film); in addition, because Jamaica was familiar in a tourist context, the film could be accessible from this frame of reference. Thelwell, however, expected that non-Jamaican viewers might not immediately register the film's revolutionary content and thus believed it could offer them a complicated mixture of the familiar and the foreign. Rather than using the film to further a distorted view of Jamaica, Thelwell thought to put the film's ambiguity and revolutionary theme to productive use.

The author expected his novel to disrupt the ways Westerners imagined Jamaica and, at the same time, to propagate the film's revolutionary message to a Jamaican audience. Thelwell invests his novel with the ambivalence and rebellion inherent in the film but grounds both in the family history he creates. An important member of this family is Colón Man Nathaniel Francis, commonly known as Maas' Nattie. Through the influence of this literary Colón Man, Thelwell shapes the novel's Ivanhoe "Rhygin" Martin into a radical Jamaican subject. In so fashioning Maas' Nattie's character, Thelwell echoes the process through which Caribbean isthmian migrants move through mainstream and oppositional canal histories as well as into fictive isthmian narratives. Nattie and his mythographic counterparts reject the narrow confines of traditional historical narratives. Thelwell extends this revisionary process to develop Ivan/Rhygin into a model of a uniquely Afro-Jamaican subject. The novel then projects Rhygin into an urban Jamaican landscape where he makes coherent his generation's nascent struggles against poverty, classism, and U.S. cultural hegemony.

Thelwell borrows from and develops Henzell's multifaceted protagonist to achieve these ends. The film's lead derives from singer Jimmy Cliff's personal history—Cliff left the country to become a singer and was exploited by a record company executive—and that of Ivanhoe "Rhygin" Martin, a 1948 Jamaican outlaw. Thelwell remarks that "[Jamaican] history [is] riddled with, depending on your point of view, either rebel heroes or ungrateful, blood-thirsty savages. A contemporary incarnation of that figure, one Ivanhoe 'Rhygin' Martin, captured Henzell's cinematic imagination" (Thelwell 1991: 140). Thus Henzell's "central figure . . . conflated . . . two ghetto-culture heroes: the outlaw badman and the reggae musician" (141).[22] Incorporating aspects of Jamaica's peasant culture, Thelwell's urban protagonist becomes a more complex figure through which the writer dramatizes Jamaica's changing class politics.

The novel records Ivan's rich culture and the centrality of a history that privileges land, family, community, and a strong sense of self. Maas' Nattie forms a necessary link in this chain and thus exerts a particular influence on the boy. The Colón Man provides Ivan a larger context into which his personal experiences—before and after his move to Kingston—can be placed. The strongly held and practiced folk traditions that Thelwell documents in Ivan's pre-Kingston world explicitly connect to Rhygin's life in the city. Since the film begins with Ivan's arrival in Kingston, the novel's inclusion of Ivan's rural, familial roots signals its importance and therefore marks the continuing influence Nattie has on the boy, even after he leaves his village. Kingston adds to Ivan's experiences by exposing him to a culture largely defined by U.S. films as well as tourist and drug monies. Ivan enters into Kingston's "rude bwai" community, one that patterns itself after North American westerns but also after Jamaican roots music. Through a series of confrontations with "progress," peasant Ivan becomes urban/working-class Rhygin: infamous for killing four police officers and, with the help of Kingston's "suffrahs," existing outside of an oppressive authority longer than anyone believed possible.[23] Although the police eventually kill Rhygin, the identity he espouses and the popular movement he initiates survive him.

Nattie, in and of himself, does not transform the exploitative systems he encounters; he thrives within them, but offers no overt resistance. Yet it is through his influence that the protagonist's revolution becomes possible. The novel foregrounds the significance of a complex and conflicted Jamaican reality and the identity it shapes. The violence and oppression of masters over slaves, and the resulting resistance of African Jamaicans and their claim to the land, form the basis of the novel's contemporary Jamaican reality. Thelwell recuperates these legacies through his analysis of Jamaica's rural peasant and urban working-class populations. He sees in the merging of these two cultures not only the strength to withstand victimization but also the capacity to "re-vision" the urban landscape. By documenting Ivan's life prior to his arrival in Kingston, the author makes clear his interest in the revolutionary possibilities of the culture of Jamaican country people and, specifically, this group's ability to confront an urban culture overly focused on the United States. With this in mind, Rhygin—technically a murderer—is not merely a criminal; his existence outside of the law can be read as a rejection of debilitating Western and upper-class Jamaican influences.[24] Because the author draws a strong correlation between Ivan's upbringing and Rhygin's behavior, one must recognize the former as enabling—or at least supporting—the latter. Therefore, *The Harder They Come* champions the revolutionary features of Jamaican folk and working-class cultures.

The novel's Ivan contains various aspects of the real (combining the personal histories of Jimmy Cliff and Ivanhoe Martin) and the fictional (through his link to Jamaica's Maroons and African and Pan-African warriors). This protagonist, as a part of Kingston's rude bwai community, also represents an urban, roots culture that is influenced by U.S. films, reggae music, and the Rastafarian religion. Thelwell thus weaves historical truths, popular and cultural realities, and political commentary into his fictionalized vision of a Jamaican peasantry-in-transition.

The Panamá Man, like Ivan, exists as a compilation of historical and creative events and personas. Nattie's multifaceted personality and the stories he tells inform Ivan's revolutionary thinking, actions, and cultural identity. Though a simply written character, the Colón Man proves to be a significant part of Ivan/Rhygin's identity.

Ivan identifies Maas' Nattie as a Colón Man, acknowledging the latter's physical superiority, intelligence, and position within their community. Ivan:

> liked Maas' Nattie, who was the richest black man in the district. . . . All the people respeck 'im. He had been to Panama and had made a lot of money digging a canal. Ivan wasn't sure what that was, but all the white men that came to dig it got sick and died, so they had to send for black men. An' Maas' Nattie had gone and had not died. . . . But Maas' Nattie had become a foreman, an' did the job and come back with plenty money which he used to buy up plenty land. (Thelwell 1988: 38)

Mistakenly placed on a list of Panamá's dead, Nattie returns to Jamaica to find his betrothed, Ivan's grandmother Amanda "Miss 'Mando" Martin, married to another man. He invests his Panamá Money in land, continues to migrate, and returns twenty-five years later to end his life where it began. By electing not to represent the most denigrating aspects of isthmian migration and labor, Thelwell casts Nattie as the quintessential Colón Man, a fictional embodiment of *LICCW* respondents' imaginable truths. It is this fictive incarnation that establishes the older man as a strong influence on Ivan.

Thelwell's Panamá Man is deliberately heroic yet, historically speaking, he represents a minority of Caribbean isthmian workers. Because they were not encouraged to improve their skills and because supervisory positions were reserved for North American whites, few of them rose to the level of foreman (Conniff 1985: 31). Still, as Ivan points out admiringly, though "many [others] died . . . he survived and prospered" (Thelwell 1988: 74). Compared to others in the pantheon of literary Colón Men, Nattie is also unusual in that he does not reflect the ambivalences of the migration. It follows, then, that the persona serves a particular narrative function. Thelwell's canal worker needs to thrive unambiguously so that he can properly communicate the recuperative features of Jamaica's peasant culture.

Although Nattie's migration experiences and the money he made could easily have separated him from his community, the opposite occurs. He resumes his place in the village as an elder, advisor, and contributor to its lore. However, the esteem in which the villagers hold him is uncomplicated. The novel reveals this during a communal corn harvest held at Nattie's house:

> Maas' Nattie's mind would wander [after a few drinks] and he would utter phrases in different languages picked up in the travels of his youth. A couple of Spanish sentences might conclude with Marcus Garvey's "Rise up ye

mighty race and accomplish what ye will." Each interjection was met with admiring murmurs since talking in tongues was much respected as a sign of wisdom. (Thelwell 1988: 59)

The content of Nattie's wisdom does not appear to be important to the villagers. They respect that Nattie is wise, but only in so far as his wisdom fits into their already established ways of knowing. They understand and appreciate the phenomena of speaking in tongues, but they do not examine the import and meaning of Nattie's specific knowledge of Marcus Garvey in the context of their present circumstances.

Ivan maintains a different relationship to Nattie and to the import of his stories. Nattie's influence empowers Ivan, encouraging him to know himself as part of a history of revolutionary struggle. Nattie tells Ivan stories

> about Cudjo the maroon warrior and Ma Nannie his sister who was a witch and a warrior too, and about the great Marcus Garvey who was "the black man savior." . . . Maas' Nattie never told Anancy stories or talked about duppi and evil spirits, but spoke of real black men like King Prempeh and King Chaka, and Ras Menelik whose black armies defeated the Italians and took back his country which was in Africa. (38–39)

The Colón Man's stories are about African and Jamaican people in active confrontation with foreign enemies. Nattie's black people are not passive victims of history, nor are they defeated by an inability to act in their own behalf. His stories also reflect a Pan-Africanist consciousness since he positions Nannie and Cudjo within a tradition of black revolutionaries. Historical figures such as Cudjo, Ma Nannie, Garvey, Prempeh, Chaka, and Menelik were individuals who fought for their communities. Perceived of as wise because of his travels, Nattie's voice carries authority as he teaches Ivan to appreciate individuals-in-communities as agents in historical struggles against foreign domination.

Although Ivan says that Nattie tells tales about "real men" rather than about ghosts and evil spirits, suggesting that he finds duppi stories unbelievable, he accepts Ma Nannie's witchcraft without comment. Ivan's exposure to the spiritual traditions of Jamaican people generally, and specifically those of his village, coexist with his historical education; this interrelationship allows the boy to value both forms of knowledge. Thus Nattie's stories offer the protagonist a template for an activist Jamaican identity.

The first quarter of the novel introduces Ivan's country beginnings, particularly the influence of his grandmother and Maas' Nattie. The old man is particularly relevant because of the cultural and historical traditions associated with him. Nattie's migrations allow him to place his Jamaican reality (exemplified by his stories about Nannie and Cudjo) within the context of the African Diaspora. Along with Miss 'Mando's influence, Nattie synthesizes his Pan-Africanist and revolutionary visions with notions of roots, family, and land. Ivan receives these insights but, importantly, interprets them through his own worldview, one that distinguishes him from his neighbors. Many join Nattie in remarking on Ivan's specialness, saying "there was something about Ivan that fit the name Rhygin. He was so full of life and energy, so full of questions. There was nothing that didn't interest him, and nothing that he didn't think he could master" (17). Ivan blends this confident and inquiring spirit, and the soon-to-be gained knowledge of Kingston, with inheritances from his grandmother and the Colón Man. Rhygin is, then, a vessel for the revolutionary features of local and Diasporic black communities; as such, he alone is equipped to shift the vision of Kingston's poor community away from the United States and toward a Jamaican lived reality.

Because Ivan translates the Colón Man's lessons through an urban vision, the boy is much more than a cipher. Nattie espouses his own activist politics, but his ways are his, specific to his reality. Ivan, who encounters different enemies, can recognize them because of Maas' Nattie's influence, but bests them because he becomes Rhygin. The protagonist creolizes Nattie's lessons by accommodating them to an urban reality. Merging his inheritances from his grandparents, Nattie, peasant traditions, and his life in Kingston, Rhygin's "self" is cosmopolitan and embraces Pan-Africanism and Jamaica's cultural influences.

Ivan's blended vision does not prevent him from holding Nattie in high regard. The boy develops a taste for Kingston after hearing some "town" music at a local café; he is then determined to go there and become a singer. On the eve of his journey, Nattie reinforces Ivan's relationships to family and land, moving through Ivan's homestead, pointing out the gravesites of the boy's grandparents and uncles. The migrant tells Ivan, "you come from somewhe', from decent people dem, people whe' nevah ha' no heap a money—but dem nevah poor neider. And you raise up decent, to know what right an' to have manners. Bwai, don't grow 'way from you raisin', eh?" (110). The old man seeks to ground Ivan in the moral values of his traditional culture, ones that will help him navigate his present and future. Although Nattie never "physically" appears in the novel again, his influence continues to be apparent.

Thelwell threads references to Nattie throughout the remainder of the novel. For example, Ivan reads his first experience outside of the village through one of Nattie's stories. While on the Kingston-bound bus, Ivan passes a cane field in flames. The only context he has for interpreting this scene is "Maas' Nattie's stories of slaves in revolt burning down the plantations" (112). Ivan knows there are "no more slaves" and continues to wonder about the fire until another passenger enlightens him:

"Is just burn dem a burn off de leaf dem. Mek it easier fe cut de cane."
"Den, it no burn up de cane too?"

"Dem say it no harm it. But sometime when de workers dem strike, or if dem have some dispute dem will burn up de cane still." (113)

Ivan thinks Nattie will be pleased to know that, in response to "some dispute," the "black man was still a burn down the canefields" (ibid). These passages demonstrate that the boy does not leave his country-based knowledge behind; his history lives with him and shapes the ways he sees the present. The newness of his experiences excites him, but does not replace or topple the coherence of his rural life. Ivan retains Nattie's association with an activist tradition, one in which black people—enslaved and free—aggressively respond to oppression and exploitation. Ivan demonstrates that he has learned the Colón Man's lessons about the strength of community and personal activism.

Excitement continues to color Ivan's trip to Kingston, but upon his arrival he is quickly confronted with the dangers Nattie warned him against. Ivan falls victim to the city: he is robbed, jobless, and homeless for his first few months in Kingston.[25] At his lowest point, Ivan knows himself solely in terms of his current poverty and the ways he figures in the purview of Kingston's middle- and upper-class blacks. This is a point where Nattie's stories fail Ivan: in the old man's tales, blacks confront foreign, easily identifiable enemies. It seems that Ivan cannot imagine middle-class blacks as enemies and thus does not defend against their perceptions of him. Instead, he "could feel a shrinking, a constriction, a closing up and sealing off of something that had always been part of him" (170).

Ultimately, a familiar "something" rescues Ivan from his alienation and poverty. Hungry, he tries to steal a sweetsop from a market woman. She catches him but sees in him something more than "thief." Even in his degraded state, the woman recognizes him as a kindred spirit, one born of a familiar relationship to "country." She says she can see that "is not here [Ivan] belong" (176). The woman gives him the fruit and tells him that "because a man sleep in a fowl-nest, it doan mean say fowl-nest is 'im bed" (ibid). Significantly, it is now that he can recall his old self, but his experience of Kingston necessarily informs this self, infusing it with and extending it beyond Nattie's migrations and tales. Immediately after this interaction Ivan remembers a job opportunity. Revived by his encounter with the market woman, and soon to be employed, Ivan moves closer to Rhygin. Working as a handyman for Preacher, Ivan earns money, falls in love with Elsa (Preacher's "ward"), and records his song "The Harder They Come."

One of the benefits of working for Preacher is that it allows Ivan to frequent the cinema. At his first show, he finds "young, black, poor, 'suffrahs' and the children of 'suffrahs,' they constituted an audience so rapt and attentive, so impressionable and apparently uncritical that their identification [with film characters] was almost total" (147). From a slightly different position, Ivan appreciates the stark morality depicted in these films:

the world of the movie was harsh and brutal, yes. But it was also one where justice, once aroused, was more elemental and deadly than all the hordes of evil. He thought Maas' Nattie would approve of such a world. (149)

Considering Ivan's severe sense of justice, his attraction to films (particularly Westerns) is not surprising. As a regular at the movies, he becomes known as Rhygin among the rude bwais, many of whom take the names of their favorite film characters: Bogart, George Raft, Hitler (195). Ivan's nickname, however, is uniquely Jamaican while his peers take the names of U.S. actors. Although Ivan is as drawn to these North American films, as are the other suffrahs, Thelwell makes it clear that Ivan is attracted to the righteousness rather than the glamour represented by U.S. culture.

After Ivan enters into Kingston's rude bwai community, he invokes Nattie twice more. In both cases, the comparison of urban revolutionaries to the Colón Man leaves him dissatisfied. He first recalls Nattie when a group of Rastafarians attempts to "take" Kingston and purge it of its spirit of colonialism; city police quickly disperse their demonstration (209). Ivan also sees something of Nattie in the spiritual convictions of a Rastafarian called Peter/Pedro. Each reference suggests a similarity to aspects of Nattie's stories or personality, but what Ivan finds lacking is the Panamá Man's revolutionary directive, the component of his tales and his personal migrations that encourages people to act in their own best interests. Ivan—shaped by Nattie, the maroon spirit of his grandfather, and his stay in Kingston—wants more than the symbolism the Rastas offer and more than Ras Peter's passive spirituality. The current climate in Kingston demands more.

When Ivan and a friend discuss that climate, they conclude that the people are more bitter than ever. They attribute this demoralization to the negative effects of tourism, an abusive police force, and crippling poverty. Rastafarianism and reggae/roots music relieve some of these stressors, but Ivan's background enables him to imagine something more than the temporary alleviation of suffering. His violent and justified response to an attempted assassination by police epitomizes the revolutionary spirit he has inherited.

Ivan is marked for death because he refuses to pay Jose, a police informant who controls Kingston's ganja traders, for "protection." In retaliation, Jose enlists the police to make an example of Ivan. When he escapes, killing several policemen in the process, "Ivan" no longer exists—he is now Rhygin:

> the feeling of power and invincibility flooded him again. "Star-bwai can' dead! Star-bwai can' dead! Pedro, Maas' Nattie unu no see! Ras Suffrah look! Babylon get a blow!" (349)

"Star-bwai" is a term that alludes to Rhygin's identification with the male leads in U.S. films. At his first town movie, he learns that the lead cannot die until the last reel. But where these imported films feature white men from the United States, Rhygin's drama features a Jamaican. He transforms the films that have influenced him by inserting himself in the role of lead. As the police attempt to coerce the marijuana traders into betraying Rhygin, we see that this "outlaw" vindicates this community, one oppressed by poverty and lack of opportunity, and manipulated for the benefit of the upper classes. Members of the urban working class, consequently, protect Rhygin, for he strikes a blow for them all. Where the rude bwais used to mimic heroes from U.S. westerns and gangster movies, they now have Rhygin. These young Jamaicans find in Rhygin the same kind of inspiration Ivan draws from the heroes in Nattie's stories. Rhygin struggles against, and bests, Babylon. Rhygin's place in Kingston's urban community marks the evolution of Nattie's influence; rather than struggling against individual agents of systems of power, Rhygin addresses the larger system itself. Through actions enabled by his activist/outlaw identity, he reaches for the justice he has long been seeking.

"The Harder They Come," the song Ivan records for the corrupt record producer, Mr. Hilton, represents Ivan's creolized persona:

> The . . . song had an assertive and rebellious spirit heightened by the up-beat semireggae rhythm Hilton put around it. The words were only one element—the voice was good, rich toned and flexible, easy with the music—but the total effect was a combination, a fusion of words, melody, and rhythm into a passionate affirmation of a vision as hard, resistant, stubbornly desperate and macho as shantytown itself.
> Ah say
> De harder dey come
> Is de harder dey fall
> One and aall
> But I'd raddah be a free man in mah grave
> Dan living as a puppet or a slave
> So, as sure as the sun will shine
> I'm gonna get mine (281)

In becoming Rhygin, Ivan dramatizes the identity that his nickname suggests. Nattie's teachings and Ivan's maroon spirit, combined with the communities of which he becomes a part in Kingston, authorize Rhygin's rebellion. Kingston's urban dwellers claim Rhygin and celebrate his exploits. Sightings of him and tales about his feats proliferate and are documented by graffiti that appears all over the city: "*Rhygin was here/But 'im jus' disappear!*" (356). He has become a local figure who challenged the roles prescribed for poor and working-class Jamaicans. Rhygin asserts his selfhood and dignity and, simultaneously, undermines the authority of those in power. Once inconsequential in the purview of the powerful,

Ivan makes himself consequential and then removes himself from their habitual way of seeing and legislating him.[26]

Elsa, Ivan's lover, eventually turns Rhygin in (so that the ganja traders can resume trading), and the police kill him as he attempts to board a ship to Cuba (390). Although physically absent from the remainder of the novel, Rhygin has become an integral part of the consciousness of the people of Kingston. Hearing the end of Rhygin's song on the radio, a boy muses:

> "Wait," the boy said. "Ah t'ink dem ban dah song de?" But he had little time to wonder. He had to deal with more urgent matters, the approach of the posse.
> "Bram, Bram, Bram!" He leapt from cover, guns blazing.
> The posse returned fire. "You dead!" the sheriff shouted. "Cho man, you dead!"
> "Me Ah Rhygin!" the boy shouted back. "Me can' dead!" (391–92)

The Harder They Come ends with these boys "playing Rhygin." Where the rude bwais previously reenacted U.S. cowboy and gangster movies, these young boys now perform Rhygin's life. U.S. culture shapes the experiences of the former group; the latter, however, celebrate a Jamaican hero. Ivan/Rhygin is an outlaw-hero-revolutionary who replaces the heroes of U.S. films, reorienting the identity of Kingston's suffrahs toward home.

Maas' Nattie, emblem of Colón Men's mythographies, reflects Thelwell's political and social goals for his novel. Thus the author, identifying as a "West Indian writer," fulfills what he sees as such a writer's role in revisioning Caribbean identities and histories. Highlighting the importance of Nattie's influence illustrates Thelwell's vision for a renewed Jamaican subjectivity.

IV

Thelwell and Lamming employ male protagonists and principally male environments in their fictional studies of colonialism's social and psychic legacies. Prominent female characters appear in both novels, Miss 'Mando in *The Harder They Come* and Ma in *Castle*, acting as transmitters of peasant and spiritual cultures. Yet in this guise, 'Mando and Ma are startlingly familiar representations of the Caribbean female subject, particularly when read against the innovative characterizations of their respective protagonists. Thelwell's novel, however, is more determinedly grounded in a masculinist social and political ideology, an interpretation that permits a critique of the role gender plays in the author's examination of Jamaica's changing landscapes. Within the volatile environment that Thelwell's novel navigates, gender identities—whether rural or urban—remain strangely static.

Whether hemmed in by the features of the Rhone/Henzell film, or informed by the cultures that structure the novel (rude bwai and Rastafarian traditions in particular), Thelwell's depiction of Rhygin's revolutionary persona is contingent upon, perhaps even enabled by, an aggressively masculine identity. Hunted by the police, Rhygin meets Delores at a bar and they proceed to a hotel. Thinking himself the seducer, Rhygin soon learns that Delores, conspiring with Jose, plans to use her sexual prowess to "incapacitate" him for the police. Rhygin escapes this trap, and Thelwell's language conflates his sexual and masculine identities with his legendary status:

> Naked and gleaming like a newborn baby, his turgid penis standing out woman-slick and reeking of carnality, a pistol in either hand, Rhygin stepped out the door and truly into legend. (Thelwell 1980: 348)

This character's experiences coalesce in this moment, but the sexually potent and dangerously violent masculinity evident in this passage is visible while Ivan still lives up-country.

'Mando tries to teach the young Ivan a lesson in community; the boy takes away from the demonstration a wholly different meaning. While navigating the bush to tend to the family farming plot, 'Mando hears a hawk "sending his shrill hunting call keening into the valley" (40). Ivan believes the noise will *prevent* the hawk from catching its prey, but his grandmother teaches him otherwise. The hawk's call is designed to disengage potential prey from the protection of the bush—but more importantly, from the protection of community. Finally, apparently too afraid of the hawk's menace, one parakeet "broke cover and started across the valley with frantic, desperate wing strokes" (41). The hawk catches this lone bird, but 'Mando intones, "'*fraid kill* 'im. If 'im did stay ina the guava trees wid the rest of 'im generation dem, the hawk never coulda catch 'im. But is 'fraid 'im 'fraid cause 'im to fly out. You see?" (42). What Ivan's "sees" is:

> it must have been terrible to sit there watching the shadow of death circling over, hearing that grating scream until you couldn't stand it anymore, couldn't force yourself to sit still any longer, until nerve and control went and panic took over. Yes, 'fraid can kill you. (ibid)

Ivan's interpretation of this scene reveals an aspect of his personality that distinguishes him from Miss 'Mando. He feels sorry for the doomed bird while demonstrating no feeling for the "wisdom" of the birds whose collective inaction spared their lives. Interpreting his final statement ("yes, 'fraid can kill you") from the perspective of the novel's end, this scene marks Ivan's determination *not* to be afraid. The fearlessness and individualism that this scene illustrates become concrete when Ivan most demonstrably rejects the values of his community.

During a shelling match (a communal harvesting tradition), Joe Beck tells the story of a king who promises his capricious daughter to any man who can catch a wild bull single-handedly (the man who successfully completes the task can also successfully "tame" the princess). Two brothers take up the challenge. After some weeks, the younger one returns beaten and bloody and without the bull. He nonetheless claims the princess because, "is over a hundred mile I run [the bull]. . . . But Ah couldn' ketch him. The las' Ah see the bull, 'im an' me breddah drop down over a cliff. Both a dem *mus'* dead. So since me don't love dead, me turn back" (50). The king agrees to let him marry his daughter, an arrangement that seems to please her. However, the older brother, wearing the bull's head and hide, turns up at the wedding feast. Joe Beck asks those at the shelling match how they would resolve the situation; after some debate, he tells them the rest of the story. The king rejects the older brother's claim because he was too single-minded in his pursuit of the bull and, "there was no living with a man whose will knew neither fear nor limits" (53). Where the older people at the match agreed, saying that "age had taught them that a spirit of compromise, to bite one's tongue, to 'take low,' to be flexible, was the most important quality that life taught if one was to live in human society" (ibid), Ivan was outraged.

He "was on his feet, inarticulate and stuttering from his sense of outraged justice." He would not be pacified by Joe Beck's comment that "justice is not a straight t'ing you know, is a crooked and curvy t'ing" (ibid). One might merely attribute this difference of opinion to age, but the following comment puts a gendered spin on the community's differing opinions. Ivan is convinced that the older brother was cheated, but cannot find support among the crowd. He ultimately gives up, saying, "he didn't really like shelling matches: too much woman and pickney and petty talk. Bet you if it was a digging match nobody would agree with such a decision [as the king's]" (54). For Ivan, men and men's work (at a digging match) support his sense of justice. This is an interesting position to take since men actively participate in both the shelling match and Joe Beck's story. Therefore, the *attitudes* expressed by those at the shelling match are what the boy defines as "woman and pickney and petty." The boy considers lessons of community (taught by Miss 'Mando), patience, and compromise (embraced by Ivan's community) the province of women and children. The converse, that is lessons of individualism, fearlessness, and stark and swift justice, are taught and held by men, but men of the "tallowah" sort.[27]

Those who cleared Miss 'Mando's land at a previous digging match suit Ivan's definition of "man." They were "hard-handed black men, proud of their strength and their ability to do muscle-tearing, heart-stopping work under the merciless sun, and to sing defiantly as though challenging the work as they did it" (54). Physical labor and a defiant relationship to it, as well as a black-and-white sense of justice, shape Ivan's ideas about manhood. Though appearing to be partially unhinged from biology (men *and* women at the so-called woman shelling match) and partially determined by the situation (the shelling versus the digging match), Ivan's definition of "man" is physical and demonstrative—rather than contemplative and cerebral—attributes often linked to masculinity. Adding Rhygin's overtly sexual behavior nuances the physicality central to the young boy's definition. Thelwell intimately ties Ivan's definition of masculinity to his achievement as rhygin/Rhygin: the results of his exploits reorient Kingston suffrahs toward their urban and working-class reality and away from the corrupting influence of upper-class Jamaicans and U.S. culture. The exploits themselves are as frightening (as are those of the older brother in Beck's story) as they are awe-inspiring. Rhygin's death at the end of *The Harder They Come*, and Thelwell's depiction of women as left behind (Mirriam, Ivan's country girlfriend), sexually available (Delores), or treacherous (Delores and Elsa) stand as signs of the limits of this masculine characterization.

The features that "make" Ivan/Rhygin a legendary man similarly make the mythographic canal worker, but with a different outcome because the figured is paired with (rather than supported by) female protagonists. Chapter 4 introduces a critique of masculinity through the bejeweled and free-spending Tack Tally (Claude McKay's *Banana Bottom*), Devonshire (Olive Senior's "Window"), and Poyah (Eric Walrond's "Panama Gold"). Despite being irreverently remembered in song and oral histories, this figure allows for a gender critique that is relevant to the study of culture and migration in the Caribbean region. Tack, Devonshire, and Poyah, in their relations with their female protagonists, critique the kind of masculinity Thelwell depicts. These three characters also enable a critique of industrialization and traditional social relations in the Canal Zone as well as back home.

NOTES

A portion of this chapter was first published as "Colón Man Version: Oppositional Narratives and Jamaican Identity in Michael Thelwell's *The Harder They Come*," *Identity: An International Journal of Theory and Research* 2.2 (2002): 157–76. Reprinted with permission.

1. Patrick Taylor traces Lamming's title to a poem by Derek Walcott "in which the poet states in rage: 'You in the castle of your skin, I among the swineherd.'" *The Narrative of Liberation: Perspectives of Afro-Caribbean Literature* (Ithaca, NY: Cornell University Press, 1989): 194. Taylor then remarks that Lamming, through his novel, seeks "to restore the castle to its rightful place. This does not mean moving from the village to the castle, as it does for the dependent bourgeoisie. It means recognition by the villager of his heritage and dignity" (ibid).
2. Sandra Pouchet Paquet, *The Novels of George Lamming* (London: Heinemann, 1982): 119.
3. Daryl Cumber Dance, "George Lamming," *New World Adams: Conversations with Contemporary West Indian Writers* (1984. Leeds, UK: Peepal Tree Books, 1992): 135. Craig Tapping interprets this theoretical/cultural imperative in *In the Castle of My Skin*:

> about halfway through [the] novel . . . a group of villagers has gathered to discuss Empire, Marcus Garvey, and the disjunctions between the history they've lived and the history they've been taught. This community wants another version of the past, which would offer them another, more empowering explanation for the present and another, more inspiring agenda for the future. [Through this scene,] Lamming articulates what contemporary theorists might call the epistemological dilemma of post-colonial fiction.

"Children and History in the Caribbean Novel: George Lamming's *In the Castle of My Skin* and Jamaica Kincaid's *Annie John*," *Kunapipi* 11.2 (1989): 53.
4. George Lamming, *The Pleasures of Exile*, foreword by Sandra Pouchet Paquet (Ann Arbor: University of Michigan Press, 1992): 46.
5. George Lamming, "The Negro Writer and His World," *Presence Africains* 8–10 (1956): 325.
6. "George Lamming," *Kas-Kas: Interviews with Three Caribbean Writers in Texas: George Lamming, C. L. R. James, Wilson Harris*, edited by Ian Munroe and Reinhard Sander (Austin: African and Afro-American Research Institute/University of Texas at Austin, 1972): 12.
7. Helen Tiffin, "The Tyranny of History: George Lamming's *Natives of My Person* and *Water with Berries*," *Ariel* 10.4 (1979): 37.
8. Patrick Taylor states:

> this indigenous literature in the British Caribbean was a response to a number of international developments: the social transformation brought about by the Russian and, later, Cuban revolutions; economic depression and social unrest, particularly in the period between the European wars; and the growing quest for self-determination, beginning in places such as Ireland, India, and Egypt in the immediate postwar period and spreading throughout the colonial world. In the Caribbean, nationalist-oriented labor movements arose in the 1930s and initiated a momentum that would eventually lead to independence in many West Indian colonies. This nationalist movement was accompanied by a cultural reawakening among the intellectuals and a renewed respect among the popular classes for things African or "Ethiopian." European intellectual trends were also influential: socialist realism and Marxism, the concern for the "unconscious," the "primitive," and the non-European. So, too, were black movements such as the Harlem Renaissance and Negritude. (Taylor 1989: 187–88)

9. This statement suggests that Thelwell is against any theory/interpretive model that does not originate in the Caribbean. I would argue, rather, that what he reacts to is the impulse to privilege critical tools standardized outside of the region—nuanced with non-Caribbean historical, cultural, and social mores—over those of the Caribbean. I also interpret his statement as a warning against the uncritical use of such models.

10. Brathwaite describes his experience reading Lamming's first novel poetically: "breathing to me from every pore of line and page was the Barbados I had lived. The words, the rhythms, the cadences, the scenes, the people, their predicament. They all came back. They all were possible." "Timehri," *Is Massa Day Dead? Black Moods in the Caribbean*, edited by Orde Coombs (Garden City, NY: Anchor Press/Doubleday, 1974): 32. Michael Thelwell laments a similarly absent Jamaican reality. "*The Harder They Come*: From Film to Novel," *Grand Street* 10.1 (1991): 135–65.

11. Counted among the dead, Pa's sister is also one of the few Caribbean women who appear in narratives that discuss migrants to Panamá. Scanty and vague references appear in each of the works that I use in this study. The protagonist in Herbert de Lisser's *Susan Proudleigh* becomes a Panamá Woman through her determination to change the life she lives in Jamaica. (A discussion of this character and her migration narrative appears in the conclusion.)

12. Edward Baugh finds "something glib and possibly naive about the new Trumper, which highlights by contrast the greater complexity of G.'s personal quest and anguish." "Cuckoo and Culture: *In the Castle of My Skin*," *Ariel* 8.3 (1977): 24; see also Taylor 1989: 222.

13. Lamming includes reference to Trinidad's oil field labor riots (1937) as a context for the strikes that affect workers in Creighton's village (100). Dockworkers want to strike for better "conditions" but aside from wages they are unclear about what "better" conditions would be (95). The call for the strike began at the grassroots level but educated/middle-class people intervene (96); Slime positions himself as spokesman and negotiates with Creighton on their behalf (107).

14. Sandra Pouchet Paquet writes that "it is significant that all important steps in education come to the village from outside the school system," citing the shoemaker's chance reading of J. B. Priestly and Trumper's U.S.-influenced black consciousness. *The Novels of George Lamming* (London: Heinemann, 1982): 20.

15. Derek Walcott states that "[his] generation had looked at life with black skins and blue eyes, but only [by their] own painful, strenuous looking, the learning of looking, could [they] find meaning in the life around [them], only [by their] own strenuous hearing, could [they] make sense of the sounds [they] made." "What the Twilight Says: An Overture," *Dream on Monkey Mountain and Other Plays* (New York: Farrar, Straus, Giroux, 1970): 9. Here Walcott stresses the need not only to be aware of an assumed vision, but also to be attentive to the process through which one learns to look through different eyes.

16. Few in Creighton's village are aware that head teacher forces Slime to resign because of the latter's involvement in a scandalous affair with the principal's wife. Later, after the village is sold and claimed by the consortium, Pa is the only one who suspects that there is more behind the teacher's career change than Slime's interest in politics.

17. Lamming uses the word "dream" to describe the story Pa narrates, but the writer makes it clear that this word cannot accurately describe the old man's vision. Pa says "from part of you that's neither flesh nor bone in a sleep before your last and longest, I come to say what I say. . . . Tomorrow you won't remember the visit made by your father's forebears, for what you call a dream the morning after has quite a different meaning from what your silence made safe the night before" (211). Since the Colón Man locates the narrative within each individual, in the "part that neither flesh nor bone," the perhaps "memory" might best describe it. These memories live in—but are not necessarily accessible to—everyone in Creighton's village.

18. Carolyn T. Brown, "The Myth of the Fall and the Dawning of Consciousness in George Lamming's *In the Castle of My Skin*," *World Literature Today* 57.1 (Winter 1983): 40.

19. Gordon Rohlehr, "Possession as Metaphor: Lamming's *Season of Adventure*," *Journal of West Indian Literature* 5.1–2 (August 1992): 12. Rohlehr continues by saying that "there can be no compromise with this deadness [an outsider's version of history], and no easy reconciliation of ancestors until the inner truth of historical encounter is revealed, and there is open acknowledgement of guilt, and reparation" (ibid).

20. Rudolf Bader, "George Lamming," *International Literature in English: Essays on the Major Writers*, edited by Robert L. Ross (New York: Garland Publishing, Inc., 1991): 147.

21. Daryl Cumber Dance, "Michael Thelwell," *New World Adams: Conversations with Contemporary West Indian Writers* (1984. Leeds, UK: Peepal Tree Books, 1992): 245.

22. Thelwell defines "rhygin" as an adjective meaning "spirited, vigorous, lively, passionate with great vitality and force; aggressive. Probably a form of [the] English *raging*" (398).

23. Significant to the novel, but outside the scope of this book, is Thelwell's critique of progress in Jamaica. Ivan, some years after he leaves the country, returns to find everything changed. His ancestral home has returned to bush, taking his family's burial ground with it. Maas' Nattie's farm has been claimed by white American "Ras Tafarian warriors." Village land is being mined for bauxite and the mining process covers the once-lush landscape with rust-colored slime. The people of his youth have moved on, died, or joined the tourist industry that caters to North Americans. Thus unmoored, Ivan is free to become Rhygin: he returns to Kingston and buys the guns that catapult him into legend.

24. Thelwell notes that

> not only was [the film *The Harder They Come*] Jamaican in story, theme, social issues, and music . . . it was *working-class* Jamaican in language and point of view—so much so, in fact, that it is deeply resented to this day by the more backward and shallow elements of the middle classes there, in whose view it projects the wrong image of the country. (Thelwell 1991: 136)

25. In many ways, Thelwell uses Kingston as a symbol of the debilitating features of colonialism, neocolonialism, and classism. The author, although conscious of the economic motivations for rural-to-urban migration (as can be seen

in Nattie's migrations), downplays Ivan's migration in favor of Jamaica's rural communities. Thelwell celebrates rural cultures that foster a self-reliance and reliance on community through his depiction of Ivan when he is faced with the debilitating effects of urban life.

26. It is important to reiterate that Ivan/Rhygin is a lawbreaker. He sells ganja and murders/assaults several policemen. In addition, Rhygin's murders and run from the law can be seen as profoundly selfish; all the other ganja traders are negatively impacted by his actions—the police prohibit them from trading (their only source of income) until they divulge Rhygin's whereabouts. I do not point these out to judge the protagonist, but rather to highlight the range exhibited in his characterization. Ivan's rebellion is a predictable consequence of the position that lack of opportunity and exploitation relegate him. Ivan/Rhygin is a product of intricate realities that necessarily influence his response to what he perceives as threats. Nevertheless the protagonist's identity and behavior, in their complexities, challenge the simplistic definitions that circumscribe his urban experience.

27. In a footnote, Thelwell defines "tallowah" as "sturdy, muscular" and uses it to describe the victorious older brother in Joe Beck's story (Thelwell 1980: 51).

4

"With him watch chain/a knock him belly": Migration, Masculinity, and the Colón Man in *Banana Bottom*, "Window," and *Tropic Death*

"It's the Panama Canal," said Priscilla. "Our Negroes are not the same after contact with the Americans. They come back ruder."

Bita replied, "But they make more money there, though. [At] least two dollars a day, they say. And here they get only a shilling. Eight times more gain over there."

"And a loss of eight times eighty in native worth. They come back hard-drinking and strutting with bad manners, loud clothes and louder jewelry."

—Claude McKay, *Banana Bottom*

[Poyah] faced Ella, piling up the goods on the counter. "I's a man, man," he said, meeting Ella's frosting eyes. "I wuz a brakesman in Palama, don't fomembah dat. I wuz de bes' train hooper on de Isthmus!"

—Eric Walrond, "Panama Gold"[1]

At the personal level, the high incidence of sickness, industrial accidents and death on the canal and railroad projects ruined the hopes of many an emigrant. However, thousands found the venture profitable economically, and educationally in terms of the exposure to people of different languages and customs. Consequently, by the time the post-1904 wave of emigration to Panama was in progress, "foreign travel was accompanied by such an aura of accomplishment, that it came to be regarded as a necessity in order to 'become a man', to know the world,

"West Indian laborers lined up at pay car, Culebra, Panama, January 12, 1908." Photographer unknown. Courtesy of Photographs and Prints Division, Schomburg Center for Research in Black Culture, The New York Public Library, Astor, Lenox, and Tilden Foundations.

and to understand life. Thus . . . emigration became highly desirable
and sought after, even for its own sake . . ."

—Velma Newton, *The Silver Men: West Indian
Labour Migration to Panama, 1850–1914*

I

The ubiquity of the Colón Man trope suggests that it embraces, even embodies, a communal image of isthmian migration. Interpretations of the figure's varied appearance in several genres, therefore, point to previously inaccessible elements of this particular migration. This chapter is particularly concerned with the migrant-as-dandy, known for his jewelry, assumed accent, cosmopolitan air, and North American–styled clothes. Frequently appearing in Jamaica, men fitting this description embodied the economic success and cultural capital available through isthmian labor and incited others to migrate to Panamá (Senior 1978: 64). This Panamá Man was also familiar in Barbados where "the swaggering show-off was the most colorful stereotype recalled of Panama returnees by old Barbadians. . . . The strutting self-importance, distinctive dress, and jingling pockets of Panama veterans often set them apart from everyone else" (Richardson 1985: 149). So familiar was this representation that he came to characterize *the* Panamá returnee. A close study of literature, songs, and poetry that features the Colón Man-as-dandy, factoring in meanings contained in these specific genres, uncovers migrant and community expectations for migrations, generally, but specific demands for isthmian migration because its size, financial, and personal benefits. The range of communal responses to returned Panamá migrants, and these men's impact on their home communities, measure the Panamá Man's adherence to and/or deviation from the migration image. Finally, these responses to migrant's "embodiment" (i.e., performance) of his migration reveal local expectations for his identity as a man as well as his potential mate's identity as a woman.

Relatively few migrants returned home if they could not show off their finery, so the fancy Colón Man evolved into a myth so powerful that it withstood "rumors" of hardship, disease, and death in Panamá. For their part, those who did not migrate only seemed interested in stories that affirmed their positive images of isthmian migration.[2] This might explain why so few examples of the unsuccessful Panamá migrant exist. The following incidental song characterizes the Panamá Man who is down on his luck. Mr. Charles Barton of La Boca, Panamá (a city populated by Jamaican migrants and their families), recalls this song, entitled "Come from Colon":

> Come from Colon wid him big empty trunk,
> Not a boot to him foot, not a ting to him front,
> Rub him dung, in him Santampee
> Give him a rum, can't even buy cawfee,
> Rub him dung. (Cramer 1946: 257)

As an incidental song, "Come From Colon" documents the experience of at least one such returnee, but more importantly the communally accepted definition of and response to him. Despite the fact that this repatriated worker stands in contradistinction to his flashy brother, his community embraces him, perhaps acknowledging the courage it took for him to leave and return to his home island. The following lines, however, attest to how anomalous the image of the pitiable Colón Man was. Collected in Barbados and also fitting the definition of a social/incidental song, "Panama Man" portrays another man who returns from the isthmus without any money:

> 1. Oh de Panama man 'ent got no money,/Still de Panama man want love,/Wen de Panama man come back from sea/An' de Panama canal.
> CHORUS
> But 'e cahn get me/Widout de money/To buy me a taffeta dress!
> If de Panama man gwine court wid me,/He gwine treat me like a queen.
> If de Panama man gwine court wid me,/He gwine treat me like a queen.
> 2. Look de Panama man come home from sea/As skinny as a Church rat,/An' all he had in he grip fo' me/Was a wide-brim Panama hat
> 3. When de Curaçao man come back to Bim/He bring me a calico dress,/ When de Panama man come back to Bim/All he bring is de Spanish caress. (*Folk Songs of Barbados:* 66–67)

The humor evident in both songs reflects the social context in which they are sung and performed; in "Panama Man," however, the humor implies a critique of the poor canal worker who nonetheless wants some reward for his migration (he has no money but nonetheless wants "love"). Even when the Colón Man-as-dandy is lampooned in song, yet envy and/or jealousy, and a grudging respect, motivate this ribbing.[3] Whether informed by derision or jealousy, humor nonetheless serves to individuate the migrant's need or cockiness, making failure a problem of the individual and allowing the home community to maintain their migration image.[4] Making fun of Panamá returnees might also reflect humorists' desire to avoid critical engagement with the social, economic, and political hierarchies that militate against migrants' success.

One can understand the durability of the successful Panamá Man myth since migration images, once established, are generally difficult to displace. These images are subject to changes in an individual's value systems or significant changes in his/her factual environment (Thomas-Hope 1992: 31), but the success of altering messages is largely determined by the strength of the image prescribed by family and neighbors, "authorities" who hold views similar to that of the prospective traveler (32). "Noh Lickle Twang!," a poem by Jamaica's Louise Bennett, exemplifies this point.[5] In the poem, the protagonist berates her son who goes to the United States "An come back not a piece betta/Dan how [he] did goh wey" (Bennett 1966: 209). The fact of the boy's migration was supposed to be confirmed by commodities ("gole teet or/A gole chain" [210]) or some other demonstrative capital (a "lickle language" [209]). As his emigration was supposed to stand as a sign of his and his family's ambition, the absence of identifiable markers of his success overseas plays as public humiliation when he returns home. This explains his mother's disappointment at his empty hands. The popularity of this poem, and the fact that it received wide circulation through Bennett's performance of it, indicates that the general expectations for any migratory act were commonly known and held. The commonness of this belief, then, explains why returned isthmian workers needed to demonstrate—in the forms of clothes, jewelry, and affections—how successful they were in Panamá. The migrant who fails to demonstrate his or her migration in this way could suffer consequences: "The expectations of relatives, especially those in the extended family, could [put] a strain on family relations" (Watkins-Owens 1996: 19).

"Come from Colon" and "Panama Man" reflect another communal response to returned Panamá migrants who do not fulfill the image for this movement. These songs importantly reflect the relationship between a man's reputation and his faithfulness to the Colón Man image. Colón Men's oppositional histories and memoirs reveal men who, demoralized by their inability to make money, refused to return home; others projected other types "capital" (assumed accents, and perhaps a change of clothes) in an attempt to approximate the image of the successful isthmian migrant. As the image and reality of Panamá migration collided in the Canal Zone, Colón Men eased the contradiction by employing legal, illegal, and other means to amass money—or they chose not to return to the Caribbean. The failure to return with Panamá Money to purchase material goods, land, and/or to court a woman would put a migrant's identity as "man" in question. The myth and reality of the successful migrant, then, merged to create a world that Colón Men literally *had* to inhabit.[6] This was the case for Bajan "Moneytree" Alleyne who so wanted to live up to the myth that he spent *all* of his Panamá Money on sweets for the children and loans to adults in his St. Philip parish community (Richardson 1985: 149).

The persona of the Panamá Man gains authority from the migration images of many in the Caribbean, yet its strength may also derive from the ways it mirrors other socially relevant definitions of masculinity. This can be seen in the song "Panama Man," one of few that positions the emigrant in relation to one who has not migrated, significantly a woman. The song, therefore, permits a reading of the migration in terms of a masculinity informed by the imaginable possibilities of canal work. "Noh Lickle Twang!" demonstrates that the desire to and the act of migration signaled a man's (and thus his family's) assertiveness and ambition. In as much as the accumulation of experiences, gained through emigration, work, and contact with new people and things were thought to be necessities for one to "become a man" (Newton 1984: 170), then the Colón Man's identity as "man" was at stake. Moving into the unknown world, surviving the isthmus' myriad dangers—of the work-, nature-, and human-related varieties—and returning proved migrants' mettle. Lastly, surviving long enough to return home was significant, but returning with money (or other kinds of capital) marked returnees as especially manly.[7]

Though the absence of women in the Canal Zone forced Colón Men to cope, particularly with regard to cooking and other domestic chores, their coping strategies reinforced rather than toppled traditional gender identities. Men who opted to cook and wash for themselves became proficient with activities that *LICCW* participants described as women's work, and they were able to eat better and save money (see chapter 2). Yet when women were available for these tasks, Martinican women engaged by the ICC or partners personally secured, Colón Men hired them. This absence of women to carry out domestic work opened up a niche for women who wanted to pursue their entrepreneurial ambitions in the Canal Zone,[8] but when Colón Men returned home successfully, their cultural and financial "capitals" gave them access to some features of hegemonic masculinity (patriarchal head of household "bought" by economic dominance), ones that they invariably parlayed into traditional relationships with women (see Beckles 1998: 93; Downes 2003: 312, 319–20).

Through analyses of fictive narratives, one can explore how the gender profile of migrants and the women they court promotes the idea of relationships based on exchange, particularly with regard to the more mythologized, financially successful Colón Man. But if mythographic canal laborers draw from the complexities of various isthmian narratives, the female characters with whom they are linked are strangely static. Caribbean migration to the Canal Zone was predominantly male, as are mythographies that evolve out of this environment, images of the migration, as well as its myths. However if fictive and some historical narratives are rendered through imaginable truths, dandified Colón Men expose the figures' masculinist imaginings.[9] In narratives that feature the Colón Man-as-dandy, women function as the fulcrum around which the mythologized isthmian migrant pivots.

In *Banana Bottom*, "Window," and "Panama Gold" (exemplary among Eric Walrond's isthmian narratives), money and masculinity take on local tones, the first two concerned with Jamaica's social structure and the last with modernity in a Barbadian context. Unlike Colón Men in chapter 3, Tack Tally (*Banana Bottom*), Devonshire ("Window"), and Poyah ("Panama Gold") are distinguished by their Panamá Money and its benefits, their irreverent, cocky attitudes, and by their attempts at seducing their female protagonists. Tack's community marks him as an upstart because of his inappropriate advances toward protagonist Tabitha Plant, his social better. Olive Senior's Panamá Man elaborates upon class and racial relationships that are more crudely drawn in McKay's novel; Devonshire's Panamá-derived money and confidence subtly exposes the complexity of long established racial and gender norms that define characters' relationships to each other. Poyah's upward mobility is more explicitly tied to his sense of himself as a man, but he expects his money to render the meanings of his dark skin insignificant and allow him to claim light-skinned Ella as a potential mate. These writers use the Colón Man-as-dandy to ground their considerations of diasporic African identities, color and class hierarchies, and modernity in Caribbean contexts. The complexity that this incarnation of the Panamá Man introduces into each of these texts helps to unveil each author's narrative goals. The introduction of the insistently male and inherently complex Colón Man thus upsets existing analyses of—and introduces unexpected interpretations of—each writer's work.

II

Many have studied Claude McKay and his oeuvre from the perspectives of biography and literary criticism.[10] None, however, have examined his use of the Panamá Man or Panamá in *Banana Bottom*. This focus not only expands on critiques of Bita Plant's persona in some critical treatments, but it also allows for an examination of Jamaica's intraracial class structure. Although I do not pretend that Colón Man Tack, in and of himself, is integral to understanding the novel, his position within isthmian mythographies marks him as a discomfiting figure and as such he threatens the simple characterizations that structure McKay's novel.

Critics are divided on whether *Banana Bottom* and its protagonist are successfully constructed,[11] a fact that I attribute to the author's treatment of Jamaica's difficult class/status and gender issues. McKay presents Bita Plant as a character whose English education does not irreparably separate her from the traditions and people of her childhood. In fact, the former enables her full appreciation of the latter. Thus McKay presents her as a successful blend of the best of English and Afro-Jamaican customs. Yet there are moments when inconsistencies erupt through the façade of Bita's New World black identity, most often evident when she confronts the former Panamá Man, Tack Tally. McKay introduces a previously unseen version of the Colón Man as well as unique insights into the Panamá experience. He represents the migrant and migration in relatively complicated ways and, as such, they disrupt the protagonist's more simplistic characterization.

Banana Bottom, a novel taking its name from a fictitious Jamaican village, begins with Tabitha Plant's return from England, where she has had "seven years of polite upbringing" (McKay 1961: 1). Bita is afforded this rare opportunity because, after being assaulted at twelve years of age, she is adopted by the Reverend Malcolm Craig and his wife Priscilla, white missionaries in the nonsectarian, nondenominational Jubilee Free Church. Throughout the novel, the narrator declares that "the [assault] gave [Mrs. Craig] the idea of taking Bita to train as an exhibit" (17), a plan that is not lost on Bita (109). The protagonist returns to the town of Jubilee (*not* Banana Bottom, the place of her birth) to fulfill the Craigs' intentions for her: that she marry Herald Newton Day, the seminary student intended to replace Rev. Craig (109), and, through said union, become the first "cultured native couple to [succeed to] one of the finest missions in the colony" (36). At first acquiescing because of her perceived debt to the Craigs, Bita ultimately rejects their plans in favor of the people and traditions of her youth. Through comparisons between Bita (the champion of selected English and Jamaican intellectual/cultural traditions), Mrs. Craig (representative of Western civilization and religion), and Colón Man Tack Tally (symbol of U.S. materialism and Afro-Jamaican "superstition"), among other characters, McKay argues that an effective New World black subjectivity is best forged through a blend of selected English intellectual and Jamaican cultural traditions.

This chapter's opening epigraph is the novel's first reference to Panamá Man Tack Tally. Creatively illustrated in it are issues that often appear in stories about Caribbean isthmian workers. Bita expresses the commonly held belief of its economic benefit; Mrs. Craig, on the other hand, is concerned that returned Colón Men, who have profited from their contact with the English, deevolve through contact with Euro-Americans. The missionary remembers that:

> there was quite a stir about a blade from Banana Bottom called Tacky or some such name. He got in wrong with the police here drinking mad. They say he respects nothing and nobody. He talks Yankee, the nasal accent with the Negro dialect. And they say it's as funny as it's awful. He has been to Panama three times, and each time comes back with more money. Don't know how he does it, for he doesn't seem to stay long enough to work for it. (35)

Priscilla suggests that Tack is not only negatively influenced by his contact with North Americans (signified by his lack of respect), but that he accrues his wealth through criminal means. A drinker in Jamaica, migration to Panamá seems to have facilitated this Colón Man's moral decline. However, it is also possible that Mrs. Craig responds negatively to Tack's Panamá-derived self-assurance, the ramifications of which she finds intolerable. Tack's Panamá Money facilitates his movement out of traditional economic and social relationships with Jamaica's white, affluent, and respectable citizens.[12] Despite the waves caused by his movement up Banana Bottom's social ladder, the Panamá Man represents a larger threat to the structures themselves. Images of successful Colón Men, coincidentally made real by returning migrants, encouraged those who witnessed the transubstantiation (from myth to reality) to duplicate it. Yet for Mrs. Craig, Tack represents a threat to the world (and people) she knows. This chapter's epigraph indicates that she is not used to the breed of black man that the returned Canal Zone worker represents. Priscilla relies upon a different (deferential) kind of person thus, for her, Tack is decidedly out of place. She says, "times may be hard here and our black folk terribly poor. But I like them better so than when they come back peacocks from Panama" (35).

Bita's benefactor has reason to fear the Colón Man's influence because Tack has an entourage. Decked out in his Panamá gold and American-style clothes, "wherever he went he was accompanied by an admiring gang. For that gang, everything that Tack said and did was charged with importance. For he had not only gone to Panama like many, but he had come back with the gold" (66). Changed economic relations were not the only kind enabled by migration to and money made in Panamá. What Mrs. Craig describes as Tack's lack of respect might be his attempt to act upon his newly acquired knowledge of his own agency. Tack "personifies" the potential for social and economic transformations because he is different from his Banana Bottom peers, a change evident in his Panamá Money and purchases, but also in his attitude. He no longer adheres to rules that prescribe the behavior of those in his premigration social class.

Priscilla's fear of a potential social revolution inflects her perception of Tack, but she is not alone in this fear. Even some members of the Colón Man's community find cause to look askance at him, and for reasons similar to Mrs. Craig's. These characters subscribe to conventional hierarchies and resent disruptions to them. Unlike the uniformly high regard in which George Lamming's Pa and Michael Thelwell's Nattie are held by their communities (chapter 3), Tack's peers ambivalently—and simultaneously—hold him in high *and* low esteem. His gang generally admires his clothes and money, but find his manners wanting. When the Panamá Man makes a lewd remark about Bita, one of Banana Bottom's own who "made it" (McKay 1961: 51), readers learn that "although Tack's gang admired his success and delighted in the drinks he provided, they were envious of him and secretly resented his Panama ways which were equivalent to bad manners—his bold and forward talk about the finest type of village folk as if everybody could be cooked together in the same Panama pot" (67). They do not appreciate the "social leveling" that Tack's crudeness implies, and further believe that:

> with all his Panama success, Tack was in peasant parlance, a hurry-come-up. That was the native word for *nouveau riche*, only more inclusive, as it meant not merely a have-nothing who had risen to be a have-something, but also one of bad reputation. (68)

Although villagers critique the Panamá Man's behavior, their resistance to cooking everybody "together in the same Panama pot" suggests not only that distinct social groups exist, but also that they are sacrosanct. Tack Tally wears his Panamá experiences as ostentatiously as he wears his gold, and he flaunts his disregard for accepted rules of behavior. He does not adhere to the opinion, offered by a black shopkeeper, that demands "the lower . . . look up to the higher an' de higher to the highest" (108), for he approaches Bita as he would approach women of lower social standing. (Significantly, Tack's community does not demand respectful behavior for women, but for members of the upper classes.) The Colón Man and Bita both come from the same town, but the Plant's are landed and Bita receives an English education. Money alone does not give Tack purchase on Bita's station, particularly since he lacks the necessary education and manners to furnish him complete access to the higher social registers.[13]

Still, it is significant that Tack maintains his membership in Banana Bottom's community despite his challenge to its mores. By labeling him a "hurry-come-up," the community defines him in their terms and, therefore, understands him as one of their own. Villagers are savvy enough to embrace and critique a character like Tack Tally. Banana Bottom's relationship to Bita, however, is not as nuanced. Her family's property and associations, in addition to her education, unambiguously position her as a "better." This characterization is so unyielding that the people of Banana Bottom consider Bita's rejection of the Craigs' world a downward movement, mainly because the missionaries disinherit her but also because she returns to the town of her birth.

Within this novel, a book intended to advance an ideal Westernized black subjectivity, a more revolutionary truth develops: the Colón Man brings his unruly, aberrant self to *Banana Bottom*, posing a threat to the roles whites prescribe for blacks as well as those that the upper classes prescribe for the lower ones. Thus Tack proffers the most efficient challenge to Bita's persona, highlighting the fact that—in its seamlessness—her cultural negotiation runs contrary to the reality of the novel's more common folk. McKay tries to write the differences and contradictions that are part of Banana Bottom's reality out of his protagonist. In this regard, he imposes his narrowly defined identity on the community's broader experience, thus making Tack Tally's interpretative value all the more important. The mythographic Colón Man works against McKay's narrative impulse toward coherence. This is perhaps why the figure is unceremoniously dispatched from the novel.

While Tack is undoubtedly one of Banana Bottom's own, he is not protected from the harsh views of his neighbors. Pap Legge, the father of his current girlfriend, Yoni, finds him an unsuitable mate and publicly expresses his feelings. As a hurry-come-up and possibly a criminal, Tack is not "good enough" for Yoni. Hearing that his daughter was seen with the Colón Man, Legge confronts the younger man in a fit of rage. Pap's verbal and physical assaults end when the old man collapses, dead, at Tack's feet (147). Tack believes he has murdered Legge though the old man dies of a heart attack. It is noteworthy that this confrontation permits the narrator to recollect another Panamá Man.

Readers learn that "it was nine years since there had been anything like . . . it. That time when a poor fellow returned from Colon a little off his head, and one day murdered an old cripple in his cabin" (148). If *Banana Bottom*'s depictions of the mentally unstable Colón Man and Tack Tally are the only measure, one would have to affirm Priscilla Craig's vision of Panamá. However, McKay returns to the economic benefits of migration. The narrator indicates that a hurricane, with its necessary clean up, temporarily alleviates a job shortage on the island; nevertheless, the windfall is short-lived:

> and when there was nothing left to do [formerly employed blacks] used their savings to take ship to Panama. The Panama Canal was the big hope of the poor disinherited peasant youth of Jamaica and all those islands of the Caribbean Belt . . . all those who did not like to sport the uniform of the army and police force. (293)

Isthmian migration is an economically enabling force and—at the same time—a psychologically damaging one. One might interpret these differing representations as inconsistencies in the novel; however, if framed as mythographies of Panamá Canal migration, they imaginatively construe the ambivalences evident in the migration as well as Colón Men's impact in the region. As such, the novel's depiction of isthmian workers duplicates villagers' ranged of responses to Tack Tally.

McKay seems to back off from the complexity of this position since he has Tack inexplicably take his own life and disappear from the remainder of the novel.[14] When he does reappear, a preacher uses him to warn his congregation against adherence to "primitive" religions (153). Still, Tack—as a Colón Man and as part of Banana Bottom—works against the limits McKay imposes on the character and provides a productive challenge to the notion of Jamaicanness Bita represents. This idea is best supported by a close look at a scene that features both the Panamá Man and *Banana Bottom*'s protagonist.

During a visit to Banana Bottom, Bita visits her childhood haunts. As she moves through the woods on her way to "Martha's Basin, where the girls used to bathe" (116), she encounters five naked boys who are examining themselves for signs of manhood; they dash into the water when they register her presence. When Bita reaches Martha's Basin:

> she slipped off her slight clothes and plunged into the water and swam round and round the hole. Then she turned on her back to enjoy the water cooling on her breasts. Now she could bear the sun above burning down. How delicious was the feeling of floating! To feel that one can suspend oneself upon a yawning depth and drift, drifting in perfect confidence without the slightest intruding thought of danger. (117)

The language that McKay uses in this passage alludes to the unproblematic way he envisions Bita's cultural negotiation. Despite the current conflict between Bita and Mrs. Craig, the scene indicates that her English-educated self can be sustained by a reemersion in her childhood culture.[15] This symbolic baptism revives Bita so much that she painlessly recalls her schoolgirl days, particularly an unrequited crush on a white boy and a memory of an eatery in Munich where "it seemed that all the guests were observing her and commenting, but not offensively" (ibid). Buoyed by her childhood reality, she can think about her connection to the English world "without the slightest intruding thought of danger." But reading *against* McKay's intention for this scene demonstrates that Bita's rebaptism in the culture of her childhood is not sufficiently recuperative.[16] As the protagonist continues to enjoy this placid setting, someone forces her out of her reverie and out of her idealized persona.

Coming out of her dream and out of the water, Bita discovers that her clothes are missing. At first she thinks that the boys she saw previously are playing a trick on her and is not angry (118). She looks for her clothes behind a mangrove tree and:

> suddenly she heard a slight sound like the shearing of a limb and from the smaller end of the mangrove trunk she saw the face of Tack Tally grinning at her through a rose-apple branch.
> "You ugly monkey!" Bita cried. "I'll have you arrested, I will." And she started towards him. (ibid)

Despite the sustenance of Jamaican culture, represented by the protagonist's immersion in the pool, an intruding "thought" of danger *does* trespass on her protected space. Another character might have disrupted the protagonist's reverie and possibly produced a different effect, evinced by Bita's first thought that the schoolboys hid her clothes. However, since the novel has already marked Tack as a disconcerting figure, it is significant that *he* threatens the simple transcendence the swimming hole scene represents. It is also important that from this ideal space Bita responds to Tack's intrusion by drawing on a common black stereotype as well as a predictable class privilege. Strangely, the protagonist does not threaten Tack in Jamaican English. As a hurry-come-up, Tack is linguistically and culturally known in a Jamaican context, so Bita's expletive choice is all the more curious—particularly since this scene is the first in which she fully occupies a rural Jamaican space. Finally, the "Westernness" of the protagonist's curse is accentuated by her invocation of the police, an authority charged with protecting the property and respectability of the upper classes.

When Bita observes the boys at their swimming hole, McKay does not indicate that her voyeurism is abnormal; in fact, he renders it innocuous by treating it casually: rather than acknowledging as inappropriate the way she participates in the boys' genital examinations, Bita says that, because of the heat, she understands their truancy (116). Neither is she angry when she believes that these boys hide her clothes. Tack's age and the sexual tension invoked by his presence notwithstanding, the latter scene has an ominous quality the former lacks. The sustenance and protection present in Bita's folk-cultural rebaptism is quickly shattered by Tack's introduction into the scene—that is, by the disruption he embodies. In the final analysis, Bita's stereotypically charged response to Tack's intrusion reveals an aspect of her English training that the author refuses to address. The protagonist's two worlds, therefore, are not as easily merged as McKay would have readers believe.

The novel reveals another disturbance not far from the surface of Bita's persona. The girl is rudely reminded of her blackness, and the notion of inferiority that has been attached to it, by a white landowner's assertion that she is "only a nigger gal" and, therefore, not entitled to respectful treatment. The man offers this comment after Bita rejects his sexual advances; he feels she should be honored to receive them from a man of his color and class and tries to force himself on her. Jubban, her future husband and drayman to her father (Jordan Plant), is conveniently on hand to prevent the rape. Later, when the protagonist ponders what it means to be "only a nigger gal," she laughs at the absurdity of the insult, likening it to a little poisonous insect:

> the constant image of the [insult] so insignificant and yet so insistent brought sharply home to Bita the sense and humour of the ridiculous in all things and

she exploded with laughter, loud, lilting, riotous shaking, rustic black laughter until the [insult] was frightened, fits of laughter, gales and torrents and storms of laughter, until it was scared and vanished to hell away. (269)

McKay's word choices and metaphor diminish both the impact and import of the landowner's comment and, more importantly, his *behavior*. The author also fails to locate the epithet and the landowner's attitude in their historical contexts of slavery, colonialism, colorism/racism, and patriarchal power, realities not easily diminished or dismissed. McKay's trivialization of the attempted rape scene, as well as his remedy for it, suggest that such prejudices can be vanquished by the very persona it creates: Bita's "rustic black laughter," apparently a sign of her "original" black self, makes the insult "[vanish] to hell away." The protagonist's response to Tack's intrusion and her response to the white landowner indicate that she is not sufficiently critical of the racial prejudices that inhere in an English tradition. In short, the protagonist's claim on Englishness is selective; she benefits from its intellectual and cultural traditions but attempts to leave its other features behind. Bita simplifies her folk experience for she lacks the complexity of the community who admires and envies Tack, resents his deviance from its norms, and includes him as one of its own. She too rejects what the author characterizes as "primitive superstition," African-derived belief systems to which many in Banana Bottom subscribe.

Although Miss Plant reclaims Banana Bottom and its villagers after she returns from England, she is not—nor has she ever been—the *same* as them. Her father, Jordan, was a "better" peasant (he had plenty of good land but no formal education) and was a friend of an influential white man (Malcolm Craig's father). When Bita returns to the village after breaking with the Craigs, villagers consider her a failure rather than a prodigal daughter. McKay describes her as a representative of "the folk," but she is clearly different from the landless, uneducated, and obeah practicing majority of Banana Bottom. It appears, then, that the protagonist's relationship to the folk is limited to her appreciation of music and selected religious observations, and she can only embrace these because she has been away.

Rather than separating her from Banana Bottom's community, Bita's education enables her appreciation of its traditions. Accompanying the Craig's housekeeper to the local market for provisions:

Bita mingled in the crowd, responsive to the feeling, the colour, the smell, the swell and press of it. It gave her the sensation of a reservoir of familiar kindred humanity into which she had descended for baptism. *She had never had that big moving feeling as a girl when she visited the native market. And she thought that if she had never gone abroad for a period so long, from which she had become ac-*

customed to viewing her native life in perspective, she might never have had that experience. (40, emphasis added)

Although both Tack and Bita have migrated from and returned to Banana Bottom, only Bita's brand of education enables her to view the village through an anthropologist's lens. Rather than becoming critically aware of how blackness operates in an English context, or understanding Afro-Jamaican traditions in their own syncretic milieus, Bita merely learns to celebrate the "feeling, the colour, the smell, the swell and press" of them. The protagonist's Englishness supports her immersion in these *expressions* of culture, but it does not afford her insight into the community's people, worldview, or moral reality.

Returning to the confrontation scene between Bita and Tack, one must evaluate McKay's characterization of the girl in light of the limits of her folk persona and the epithet she uses to rebuff the isthmian returnee. McKay fails to consider that, in attaining an English education, the protagonist is simultaneously exposed to its disabling perspective on black inferiority; he does not explore how the psychic experiences of slavery, colonialism, and racism might affect Bita's hybridized persona. Instead, the author suspends critical engagement with the unsuitable parts of English culture and draws on simplified images of Jamaican folk culture. The Colón Man's intrusion into Bita's folk-based, yet educationally nuanced, safe space challenges the notion that a Western education can be purely benevolent and the implication that Jamaican culture can be purely emotive.

The kind of cultural mixture that McKay espouses cannot accommodate the range of meanings that Tack introduces into the novel. Furthermore, the Colón Man's position within his community moves along a continuum and, as such, he makes a mockery of the simplified ways Jamaicanness and Englishness exist in the novel. Even the people of Banana Bottom demonstrate a level of complexity that resists the author's narrative construction. The Colón Man's intricate characterization, and the complexity revealed by McKay's description of Jamaican migration to Panamá, makes visible the inadequacy of the kind of cultural negotiation that he advocates through Bita Plant.

I do not want to belabor my point, particularly since critiques of *Banana Bottom* have already found that McKay unsuccessfully portrays an ideal identity for blacks in the New World. (It goes without saying that other critics find *Banana Bottom* successful in other ways.) Scholars often remark on the author's structural and thematic laziness, the novel's uneven quality, improbable characters and situations, missed opportunities for complication, and easy resolutions. Reading *Banana Bottom* through its references to Tack Tally and isthmian labor affirms these insights into the novel's shortcomings; yet this frame extends the conversation by bringing the Colón Man's mythographies to bear on McKay's vision of the New World black subject. The tension that Tack introduces into *Banana Bottom* takes the novel along other critical paths.

The emigrant allows examinations of Jamaican social and class structures. Tack Tally also draws attention to the role that gender plays in the novel. Tack's maleness is an important part of his disruptive persona, manifested when he invades Bita's swimming hole but also when he lustily describes her. Importantly, an extension of this critique shows that the protagonist is not as "new" a representation of the New World subject as she is purported to be.

Tack's masculinity as well as his social standing are informed by his migration and contribute to his challenge to Bita's characterization. As a result of both, his advances toward the protagonist put her femaleness at issue, particularly as it defines her as an appropriate mate. From the Panamá Man's perspective, his travels and Panamá Money make him Bita's peer and her femaleness makes her available. This is the point at which the Panamá Man comes up against his community's mores. This position is evident in a letter Tack sends after he intrudes on the protagonist at Martha's Basin. Tack writes:

> I beg to apolojoys for trying to mek a little plesantry wid you as a genelman and you not a lady as big to apreachiate it. I not jest a fool country naygur not know nothing, but I is a pusson travelled far abroad jest lak yousef and I is acquented wid all the etykwets. Thas why I wait until you was all alone by yousef to get a good introduction to you. I is sorry you did tek it in sech a bad way and insult me lak a dawg but I is willing to forgive you and even be a frien to you ef you will tek that back. And ef you apreachiate freinship between female and male I doan want to praise mesef too much but I doan tink you can fine a finer pusson than me in Banana Bottom. (131)

Thus the Colón Man establishes himself as an able suitor. In his mind, his migration has flattened the status and economic hierarchies that separated him from the protagonist.

Citing Bita's adoption and educational opportunity, scholars have argued that she is unique among Caribbean literature's typically dependent female characters, but that at the time of the novel's publication, such a figure could only exist in fiction.[17] Notwithstanding the impractical choice of a dark-skinned female protagonist, within her literary context, Bita's revolutionary aspect is largely cultural. With regard to women's gender identities, she embodies the most traditional female behaviors. Interestingly, her educational opportunities are curtailed by her choice of the roles of wife and mother. Thus the only way readers can determine Miss Plant's cultural negotiation to be successful is through her marital choice of the dark-skinned and earthy Jubban over the more status/class and color appropriate, the light-skinned and educated Herald Day.[18] Bita continues triumphantly by giving birth to her son, Jordan, thereby transmitting her influence to her progeny.

Both Tack and Jubban are Banana Bottom's native sons. They also lack formal education but are nevertheless successful in their chosen endeavors. Yet while Tack Tally is radical enough to pry Bita out of the Craigs' world and project her back into Banana Bottom, he is too radical (in his challenge to established class norms) to merge comfortably with Bita. Jubban, on the other hand, is grounded—both literally (Jubban is a farmer) and figuratively (in his rural Jamaican identity). He is linked to the protagonist through her father (Jubban works for Jordan Plant and takes over the farm upon Plant's death) and he conveniently appears in the novel to protect Bita from total immersion in the basest aspect of rural Jamaican culture, when she becomes entranced by the drums played at a religious performance (250, 252), and from the grossest form of Anglo-Jamaican authority when the landowner tries to rape her (263). Through their union, Jubban supports Bita's renewed claim on the suitable features of her Afro-Jamaican past and his Jamaicanness complements her English orientation. Their union is not only contingent upon the protagonist's biological femaleness, but also on her adherence to the traditionally female role of cultural transmitter. This "common" portrayal is all the more surprising in light of the unusual context in which McKay places her.

A traditional and stable female subject, importantly one who produces a male heir, anchors the cultural revolution that McKay envisions for blacks in the Diaspora. Despite her appreciation of the best that Englishness and Jamaicanness have to offer, Bita can only *give birth* to the New World black. The revolutionary identity that McKay puts forth, therefore, requires Bita to be heterosexual and fertile. It also seems to demand a particular class position since Bita's status is not reduced by the loss of the Craigs' patronage; she descends from "better" peasants and is the sole heir to English ex-patriot Squire Gensir's estate. Though McKay writes the dark-skinned and female Bita as his ideal, the character affirms traditional gender and class roles. Rather than enabling a significant revolution, Bita's education and inheritances bind her to domestic duties of wife and mother. Her son will therefore accrue the benefits of her experiences. In addition to his father's quiet strength and aptitude with things related to the land, Jordan begins his life with all the qualities McKay deems necessary for blacks in the Diaspora.

From this perspective, baby Jordan stands in stark contrast to Tack Tally. Each of these males shares inheritances (money and peasant roots), but in Tack these features take on a superficiality that does not seem to threaten Jordan. The inference, then, is that Panamá Money (and the things it buys) only appear to make him a "better" peasant for Tack Tally still cannot access the ranks of his betters. The Colón Man believes himself to be Bita's peer (131), but he lacks the "etykwets" that would endorse his imagined status, etiquettes that Jordan has as his birthright.

As *Banana Bottom*'s antagonist, Tack Tally initiates critiques of gender and identity that offer new insight into this Harlem Renaissance novel. The Panamá Man makes use of his Panamá-derived status to approach Bita, behavior that subsequently undermines the protagonist's blended identity at the same time that it upholds her traditional gender and class ones. Similarly set in a Jamaican village, Olive Senior's "Window" positions these identities as central to the story. Devonshire is typical of the strutting, self-confident, and financially successful Colón Man, however his premigration status and Panamá-defined manliness (characterized by his physical, material, and moral selves) make what McKay represents as fixed class hierarchies more complicated. Moreover, Senior depicts racial and gender identities as integral to class as it is represented in the story, making any resolution of the tensions between the main characters all the more elusive.

III

"Window" documents the relationship between Carmen Jasper, her youngest daughter, Bridget, and Ma Lou, who has lived with and worked for the Jaspers all her life. Despite the racial difference (Ma Lou is black), these women form a family, a bond affirmed by the filial bond between Bridget and Devonshire, Ma Lou's grandson. Since Mr. Jasper abandoned his family, poverty also seems to unite these characters, or so Devon believes (70). Through her skill at managing the household, Ma Lou is the Jaspers sole financial support. In fact, because Carmen refuses to leave her bed after her husband's departure, Ma Lou acts as Brid's mother. Returning to his family after five years in Panamá, Devon uses his newly acquired carpentry skills to make the Jasper home habitable. Ma Lou is well pleased with this, but in response to Devon's other proposal—that he marry Brid, use his Panamá Money to buy their property, and thereby rescue everyone from the squalor in which they lived—she "refused to listen to him anymore, threw her apron over her head and cried the living eyewater for his boldness" (Senior 1995: 68). The class issues triggered by Tack Tally's return to Banana Bottom resurface in "Window." Yet Senior's attention to the connection between race, class, and gender in the Jamaican context, as well as her use of the short story form, mirror her subtle treatment of Dev's migration and return.

At first, Devon embraces the Panamá Man myth. He "arrived in fullblown Colón style—a brown draped suit, complete with watch chain with dangling charms and a fat gold watch inside his fob pocket, matching brown derby, yellow boots, and a walking-stick with the head of a wolf carved in ivory on the handle" (57). He also makes sure he is seen in his finery because he walks "up and down the whole district to show off his clothes, his Panama strut, his American accent, and his Panama gold rings—like all the other young men who came back from foreign" (59). Yet other behaviors mark Devon as different from most Panamá returnees: after a few weeks, he tires of the performance (64) and begins to think seriously about the fit between his new, postmigration self and his old rural Jamaica. He is now a master carpenter and "he could make it, he felt sure, for he had been taught by the Americans and nobody could beat them when it came to modern, efficient ways. The country was ripe for people like him, he knew" (65). This progression from superficial performance to a critical entrepreneurial perspective, both resulting from experiences gained through his migration, marks Devon's difference from his fictive peers and best represents the complexity of the issues engaged by him.

Devon, as isthmian returnee, turns his critical gaze to truths that informed and reshaped his views on social realities in the Zone and his Jamaican village. After his grandmother's dramatic response to his proposed marriage, he thinks, "while he had gone away and been changed so much, nothing here had changed" (68). His sacrifice in living "with Jim Crow" seemed for nothing; Devon and his Caribbean peers learned "the habit of averting your eyes when the white American women walked by and smiling when they addressed you as 'Boy,' got used to saying, 'yassuh,' 'nosuh,' to everything their white husbands said" believing them to be temporary inconveniences, survivable because Caribbean men had a home to which to return and because they were British subjects, "equal to any man before the law. British law" (69). With Ma Lou's pained response still ringing in his ears, Devon begins to think that his Jamaica is more like the Canal Zone than he first believed. "Here [in Jamaica] they were simply expected to recognize the invisible signs, to be born knowing their place" where in Panamá "silver" and "gold" signage clearly marked one's place (ibid).

The racial and class norms that Ma Lou takes as a matter of course, and that Devonshire believes have paced his personal change, encourage Carmen to instruct Brid that "Black people were born to be poor . . . nobody expects any better from them" (61). Brid later asks her elder sister, Jesse, why they (the Jaspers) are poor. Jesse says, "we weren't born poor . . . we're only poor because Papa ran away and left us and there was nobody to look after the place. Mama got sick and everything" (ibid). This is a familiar refrain, but Brid still needs convincing. Jesse obliges:

> "Bridget, you'll understand when you're older," Jesse said. "God gave you beautiful skin and long lovely hair and you should thank him for it and take

care of it. Some day a man will come along who will appreciate those things and you'll be glad then that you don't have ol'nayga skin and picky-picky hair." (ibid)

Both Carmen and Jesse's words and behaviors demonstrate how much race and class combine to form their perception of themselves. The degree to which the elder Jaspers' self-perception hinges upon gender norms is also significant here. Carmen succumbs to some mysterious illness when her husband leaves (63) and Jesse "lived for . . . a man to come along," so much so that she too abandons her mother and sister to improve her prospects in Kingston (61). Mr. Jasper's abandonment locks Carmen into the domestic space, and propels Jesse into a different though equally domestic one. Neither of these women seem to let this departure and the concomitant decline in their fortune unseat their assessment of their white, nonpoor, and female selves. Brid, however, is not as certain about what her white skin and "tall" hair mean. In his own way, Devon is similarly confused.

When Dev shares with Ma Lou his plan for acquiring the Jasper home and land, and marrying Bridget, she says, "You go away is true and do well for yourself. . . . But that still don't give you no right to think you can marry white people daughter. Don't even bother to think of it. You want to kill off Miss Carmen?" (67). Ma Lou associates this boldness to the attitudes her grandson learns in Colón:

> "You see that now. You come in just like all them Colón man there. And I did think you have a little more sense in yu head. Go to Colón and make a little money and you all come back same way—*thinking you just as good as everybody else. Wanting to change the whole world overnight*. Out to create nothing but bad blood and confusion." (68, emphasis added)

Devon responds: "Gran, what confusion you see me creating? . . . You behaving as if is something criminal I proposing" (ibid). He is genuinely confused by Ma Lou's reaction because he believes that he has the answer to his—and his family's—prayers. In short, despite the racial difference, he views Carmen, Brid, Ma Lou, and himself as "family," a feeling Brid shares.

The youngest Jasper sees a symbiotic relationship between the Scotchman fig and the silk-cotton tree in the yard as a metaphor for the relationship between the Jaspers and Ma Lou:

> Brid used to think that their lives and Ma Lou's were intertwined like the Scotchman fig which grew on to the big silk-cotton tree, twisting and embedding itself into the trunk of the other to such an extent that it was hard to figure out which was the silk-cotton and which the fig. (63)

However, what Brid describes as a mutually beneficial relationship, Ma Lou and Carmen—because both believe that whiteness equaled high and separate status, even if blacks and whites shared the same life—imply is a more parasitic one. The Jaspers survive because "it was Ma Lou who made all the decisions now . . . she who planted the crops and sold what needed to be sold to earn them a little cash, she who went to market to buy; it was she who fed them and looked after them, for Mama was now helpless as a child" (ibid). What was once an occupation has now become who Ma Lou is. Brid's metaphor thus marks the tension between the truth of the family's shared, daily reality and the "truth" of Ma Lou/Carmen's vision of it.

Colón Man Devon is similarly caught between the real and the imagined, as his surprise at Ma Lou's reaction suggests. He is concerned that his more-than-imaginable, postmigration self might no longer fit in Jamaica's rural society. On the one hand, his isthmian-acquired skills make him the "right man" for Jamaica (65); on the other, these same skills and the critical perspective informed by his migration make him the wrong man since he is no longer comfortable with a country where "people like him were expected to remain [whites'] semi-slaves and servants" (69).

Throughout the story, both Devon and Brid recall the closeness they shared before he left for Panamá. It takes some time before the Panamá Man grasps that he cannot return to this idyllic space, a realization that Bridget comes to almost immediately. She hides from him for weeks until he comes upon her by chance. Remembering the Devon of her youth, she is confused by the man he has become: "he had grown almost a foot taller in the five years he was gone, and had filled out. Looked like a real grown-up man. . . . But she wouldn't come out and talk to him because she was dismayed to see the old Dev vanished and this impressive, self-assured stranger in his place" (58). Brid believes that the new Devon outclasses her, making her ashamed of her poverty and her sister and mother's false pride. Carmen and Ma Lou find Dev's changes almost meaningless; although his migration changes his status by improving his finances and skills, his race remains the same. The same is true for the Jaspers in that their white skin confirms their higher class even though their financial status has changed. Only Bridget's interpretation of and behavior toward Devon reverses this traditional maxim.

The only time that Brid can imagine herself in the Colón Man's presence, and that he can imagine fulfilling his isthmian dreams with her, is at night while he stands outside the house. He restlessly wanders about, but invariably ends up standing beneath Brid's window. Because she is equally restless, she witnesses Dev's first nocturnal visit and then, over the course of the story, comes to anticipate and then live for them. The story ends, on the night before Devon is to leave the village (he is undone by the implications of Ma Lou's disapproval), with Bridget,

> instead of staring at her window and condemning herself for her cowardice, she forced herself to imagine the very actions she was so afraid to carry through. To her surprise, she found that she could actually envision herself getting off the bed, walking to the window and, with a sense of wonder at her boldness, throwing open the shutters. (74)

Brid only *pictures* herself opening the window, leaving readers to wonder whether or not she can act on her imaginings. Neither can it be known whether Devonshire confronts her as he promises himself he will (71). This uncertain ending is characteristic of Senior's creative oeuvre, a technique that further complicates situations that her stories portray complexly. With regard to the themes in "Window," the ambiguous ending compounds complications not only in Devon's experiences in the Canal Zone and Jamaica, but also those that result from clashes between his imaginable and lived realities in both places. The vividness of Brid's imagined behavior leaves readers with hope, and yet the power of Ma Lou's words and beliefs echo beyond the story's conclusion: what is the likelihood that Devon can "change the whole world overnight," even if the change would only require a fuller embrace of his family's daily reality?

Its ambiguous ending pushes readers experience of "Window" far beyond its eighteen pages, if only for the time it takes to speculate about the possibilities of Bridget's "real" versus her imagined behavior. The length of this creative piece also has an effect on how Senior fashions her characters. She does not have much space to make them resonate for readers, so their features must be conveyed quickly and richly. This writing method might explain Devonshire's deeply nuanced portrayal: he is an artisan, a dandy, financially successful, and cosmopolitan in his thinking and insights. The combination of these descriptors translates into the Colón Man's naïveté as well as his wisdom. Most subtle, however, is Devon's applied knowledge for he does not simply impose his Canal Zone-inspired racial critique upon his Jamaican experience as Trumper imposes his U.S. experience upon his Barbadian reality (see chapter 3); Devon recognizes the similarities *and* differences between his two societies. Brid's characterization benefits from Dev's complexity because the two are so closely linked. Both consider themselves "family" and appear to be equally attracted to each other. Most significantly, perhaps, is that Brid and Devon exist in and try to negotiate a world that is more complex than that occupied by the other characters.

Olive Senior's characterization of the Colón Man in "Window," perhaps because of the demands of the genre, both takes up and extends issues raised in McKay's novel. Both Dev and Tack challenge prescribed racial and status norms; Ma Lou and Carmen Jasper's opinions reflect those of the Banana Bottom community. Yet where McKay's novel has a decidedly unambiguous ending (neatly tying up the author's goals for the protagonist), Senior puts her complicated representation of the Panamá Man in service of similarly complex local concerns. Eric Walrond's short stories anticipate Senior's emphases. Walrond employs these strategies of characterization similar to Senior's, and invokes Panamá Canal mythographies, to describe the relationship between Colón Man Poyah and Ella, the female protagonist in "Panama Gold." In some ways, Walrond's thematic situations prefigure that between Senior's Devonshire and Bridget. Walrond poses his critique of gender identities and traditional and modern lifestyles through a failed relationship between a repatriated Colón Man and a local woman. This story also instigates a critique of the benefits of isthmian migration and it takes up the themes of color and class introduced by Olive Senior in "Window." These and similar themes are taken up and complicated in additional stories in *Tropic Death*.

IV

Eric Walrond's collection contains ten stories, seven of which are set in Barbados or Panamá. Of the remaining three, one is set in Demerara, another on a ship en route to Honduras from Jamaica, and the title story is set in Barbados, aboard a ship, and in Panamá. I am most interested in the stories set in Panamá or that feature isthmian migrants and migration in their plots. These tales reveal Walrond's intricate, rich, and oppressive view of the Caribbean and his ambivalent view of the benefits of isthmian migration.

Unlike Michael Thelwell and Claude McKay, both of whom celebrate the Jamaican landscape and the people most closely identified with it, Walrond's evaluation of Bajan and Panamanian geographies is more pessimistic. He resists the impulse to mythologize either the land or "the folk," opting instead for a critical and creative vision that approximates the unpredictable relationships between people, land, and industrialization/modernization. Walrond's environments are malevolent, but he nonetheless respects them and those who make their living in them.[19]

Critical reviews of *Tropic Death* reference the writer's "impressionistic style" and his "eye for exotic detail."[20] These stylistic observations neglect the collection's equally important narrative issues, such as the author's disabling natural milieus (a vision rarely used by Caribbean writers). Eric Walrond perceived his extraliterary world as unstable and, meaningfully, creatively represented this instability in his short stories. The author was born in British Guiana (now Guyana) and lived in Barbados, Panamá, the

United States, and England. His experiences of these places, as well as the effect of being so frequently uprooted, are evident in *Tropic Death* (Bogle 1986: 474).[21] The author's connection to the isthmus during the construction of the U.S. canal explains his familiarity with Panamá as a subject, but his vision of the Caribbean and his personal relationship to it echo the uncertainties inherent in isthmian migration and labor. One can also draw a causal relationship between Walrond's personal life and his creative interest in Caribbean isthmian migration. He won a Guggenheim fellowship and intended to use it to support research for "a series of novels and short stories on native life in the West Indies" (Ramchand 1970A: 74). Although he made the trip in 1928–1929 he never produced the work, "but in 1940, from a Wiltshire [England] address, [Walrond] wrote to Mr. Henry Allen Moe, Secretary General of the Guggenheim Foundation explaining his lack of productivity." In this and subsequent letters, he writes that "as a depression casualty I have had my ups and downs; my quest for security in a world in which nothing is stable led me astray" (ibid). It is through this equivocal personal perspective that Walrond critiques isthmian migration and the treatment of Caribbean workers. He imbues his Colón Men and descriptions of isthmian migration with this kind of equivocation and then uses this perspective to examine the impact of modern/industrial culture on the premodern Caribbean.

"The Wharf Rats," Walrond's most famous story, epitomizes the distinct culture of Caribbean people in the Canal Zone. In highlighting the ethnic diversity of this population, the author directly engages narratives that characterize people from this region as an amorphous army of "blacks" or "West Indians." "Panama Gold" also takes issue with indistinct depictions of the Panamá Man and his migration experience. This story features Poyah, a returned Colón Man who parlays his Panamá Money into a dry goods shop; he personifies the successful migration image, but he also manifests the unprecedented and modern aspects of canal construction. These features, in addition to the type of masculinity he projects into his romantic interest in Ella Heath, enable multipronged analyses of Bajan agricultural and social traditions particularly as they stand up against an encroaching modern culture. Walrond turns a cynical eye toward the type and effect of industrialization offered by canal work in "Subjection." Apparently a story about Colón Men's victimization at the hands of North American canal authorities, the story elaborates on what "victim" means for Caribbean men in the context of the Zone. Skillfully depicting a range of laborers' responses to a marine's brutality, the author again enters into a dialogue with historical narratives that homogenize the experiences of Caribbean isthmian workers. Lastly, "Subjection" includes an oppositional version of the "official" story of the protagonist's murder, and as such dramatizes the work of Colón Men's fictive tales.

The stories in *Tropic Death* comprise decisive parts of Panamá Canal mythographies. Each contributes to discourses about Colón Men and the canal enterprise, but the collection reveals much more about specific and underrepresented effects of this migration for the Caribbean generally and Barbados in particular. Walrond begins to document the pan-Caribbean community in "Wharf Rats," on the surface a story about obeah and unrequited love. It features Philip, the oldest son of Jean Baptiste, a native of St. Lucia (Walrond 1954: 68). The boy is a "good-looking, black fellow" (69) who "loved to see others happy" (71). Maffi is the Trinidadian helper in the Baptiste household and a practitioner of obeah; her inexplicable jealousy of Philip and Maura, the Panamá-born daughter of Tortola mulattoes (70), also distinguishes her. Unbeknownst to Maffi, Maura is in love with San Tie, Philip's Chinese- and African-descended Jamaican friend, and she uses the Baptiste boy to pass messages to him. Misinterpreting the young peoples' frequent meetings, Maffi avenges herself on Philip: while diving for coins tossed overboard by European tourists, a shark devours Philip and his younger brother, Ernest. "The Wharf Rats" ends with Maffi humming "an *obeah* melody" (84).[22] This short story embraces a racially/ethnically and nationally diverse Canal Zone that moves beyond the U.S. emphasis reflected in other narratives. It also manifests the degree to which this Central American space is rich with Caribbean cultural practices.

Walrond quickly makes it clear that his Panamá is multinational, multiethnic, and multiracial. The story begins with the assertion that "among the motley crew recruited to dig the Panama Canal were artisans from the four ends of the earth." Specifically:

> down in the Cut drifted hordes of Italians, Greeks, Chinese, Negroes—a hardy, sun-defying set of white, black and yellow men. But the bulk of the actual brawn for the work was supplied by the dusky peons of those coral isles in the Caribbean ruled by Britain, France and Holland. (67)

The author provides readers with a fictional example of the oft-overlooked fact that canal construction drew laborers from all over the world, but specifically from the circum-Caribbean region. This Pan-Caribbean perspective becomes more character-identified as "Wharf Rats" progresses. Consider that Jean Baptiste, Philip's father:

> like a host of the native St. Lucian emigrants, forgot where the French in him ended and the English began. His speech was the petulant *patois* of the unlettered French black. Still, whenever he lapsed into his Majesty's English, it was with a thick Barbadian bias. (68)

Walrond's depiction of the different nationalities on the isthmus moves in concentric circles toward a single character: the narrator describes the

Canal Zone's diversity, continues by referencing the variety within its Caribbean segment, and finally represents this multiplicity in one Jean Baptiste. In this character, Panamá, St. Lucia, and Barbados (perhaps Baptiste absorbs the influences from the large numbers of workers from this country) merge. Baptiste can also claim stronger affiliation with the Francophone Caribbean because Celestin, "his second wife, [was] a becomingly stout brown beauty from Martinique" (69).

As a Canal Zone resident, Baptiste not only adds to the country's diversity but also takes from it, evinced by his after-work ritual. Upon returning home, "[Jean] would discard his crusted overalls, get in starched *crocus bag*, aping the Yankee foreman on the other side of the track . . . and loll on his coffee-vined porch" (ibid). Homogeneity is neither a feature of the isthmian labor force nor an aspect of the culture brought or encountered by emigrants. The ethnic and cultural variations evident in Jean Baptiste and members of his household also extend to Europeans on the isthmus. With the addition of a "red-bearded Scot" (73) and the German tourists who toss coins to Philip and Ernest (81), Walrond affirms the image of the Central American country as an international crossroads.

Yet within this "melting pot," Walrond differentiates his Caribbean community by emphasizing its spiritual and cultural practices. Setting the stage for obeah's role in this story, he emphasizes the degree to which Caribbean people in Panamá believe in it. The narrator says:

> one refuted [stories about obeah] at the price of one's breath. And to question the verity of the *obeah*, to dismiss or reject it as the ungodly rite of some lurid, crack-brained Islander was to be an accursed pale-face, dog of a white. And the *obeah* man, in a fury of rage, would throw a machete at the heretic's head or—worse—burn on his doorstep at night a pyre of Maubé bark or green Ganja weed. (68)

While attempting to signify the strength of this belief-system within the Caribbean-Panamanian community, the quotation also raises the specter of white/black, U.S./Caribbean tensions on the isthmus. Walrond characterizes obeah as something to which *all* Caribbean-descended people subscribe, upon fear of being a "dog of a white." One might interpret the obvious hyperbole as an indication of the extent to which such a relationship to whites was undesirable.[23] Significantly, this quotation exposes workers' attitude toward North American whites but also their disdain for black Caribbeans who kowtow to them. By setting up obeah's role in this story, Walrond represents the Zone as a tumultuous international, interracial contact zone. The author's word choices also speak volumes about the U.S. presence in and cultural contribution to it. Jean Baptiste *apes* his Yankee bosses, indicating the man's senseless mimicry and possibly the bankruptcy of the behaviors he copies. Read in conjunction with the curse of being a "pale-face, dog of a white" the author negatively critiques the U.S. presence on the isthmus.

"The Wharf Rats" is a character sketch or, more precisely, a sketch of the Caribbean portion of the isthmian population. It paints Panamá's Colón People as pan-Caribbean, where more traditional isthmian narratives describe these people in racial and/or regional terms as "blacks" (McCullough 1977: 170), "black men from the West Indies" (473), or "English-speaking blacks from the West Indies—from Jamaica mostly" (147). It is hard to tell whether these workers were homogenized for the sake of expedience or due to a lack of interest, but this story opposes such reductions. By documenting the Canal Zone's diversity, "The Wharf Rats" complicates how the canal project is remembered historically.

If this story builds upon common representations of the largest segment of the ICC's workforce, "Panama Gold" extends this process by turning its attention toward the Caribbean and the experience of the repatriated Panamá Man. Set in Barbados, "Panama Gold" describes protagonist Ella as a lonely old maid with an intense respect for the land, that which it nurtures, and Bajan folktales and foodways. Readers learn that "all of nature gave flavor to Ella, [and] wrought a magic color in Ella's life" (Walrond 1954: 38). With his Panamá-derived masculinity and money, Colón Man Poyah fancies himself a suitable beau; the protagonist, however, prefers her own way of life and rejects him because of his "possessions," namely his materiality, dark skin, and handicap. The story ends by suggesting that Ella reconsiders this decision, but only upon Poyah's death (he dies in a fire that engulfs his shop). Seemingly a tale about a missed romantic opportunity, "Panama Gold" explores—through contrasting male/female, industrial/agricultural, and Barbadian/U.S. associations—the growing conflict between industrial/modern and agricultural economies in Barbados, the benefits—but more significantly—the costs of Panamá Money, and features of the Bajan personality.

"Panama Gold" lends itself to the view that an ideal Caribbean subjectivity can result from the union of Bajan, peasant Ella and Colón Man Poyah; such an identity would reflect the best of both worlds.[24] However this interpretation can only be sustained if one overlooks details that communicate Walrond's ambivalence about such a union. A critical attempt to marry these characters in fact demonstrates the impossibility of such an outcome, particularly since U.S. industrial and Bajan agricultural traditions make up its constitutive parts. Given Walrond's allusions to Ella's aggressive independence and Poyah's materialistic masculinity, a "relationship" between the protagonist and the Colón Man appears, if not impossible, at least fraught with complication. Ella's characterization further alludes to the author's equivocal vision of the folk. While Walrond endows her with a love of the land and local folklore, he complicates her representative "folkness" by expressing spiteful color prejudices through her. Poyah's certainty of the attraction of his manhood (stemming from his Panamá-derived possessions and his damaged body) also undermines his representation. Any critical claim that a resolution is achieved through the two main characters' union masks the story's more pressing concerns, namely Walrond's ambivalence about the value of isthmian migration and its attendant effect on agriculturally oriented Barbados.

Poyah and Ella become acquainted through Lizzie (Ella's neighbor) who directs the protagonist to his shop to buy salt. We are thus introduced to the Panamá Man in the familiar incarnation as a financial success and local entrepreneur (Richardson 1985: 153). Walrond records the conversation between the two women as follows:

> [Lizzie] "Why yo' don't go up de road an' get a bag o' salt?"
> [Ella] "Up whey?"
> [Lizzie] "Up at Missa Poyah's shop."
> [Ella] "Who 'im are—whey he come from?"
> [Lizzie] "Palama, soul . . . Yes, chile, he are a Palama man." (Walrond 1954: 36–37)

Poyah returns to Barbados with enough money to open a shop although it was exceedingly difficult for Caribbean workers legally to earn large amounts of cash. The story does state, however, that some part of Poyah's Panamá Money is compensation for a work-related accident. Where his successful economic situation marks this Panamá Man as common among his fictive counterparts, Poyah is unique among historical, lyrical, literary, and epistolary figures in that he is physically marked by his work on the isthmus: he lost a leg in a work-related accident. This distinguishing feature makes Poyah's Panamá Money personally significant: it becomes a part of him as much as the cork that replaces his leg.

In an exchange with Pettit Bruin, "the village idiot," the Colón Man makes known the connection between his damaged body, Panamá Money, and the canal enterprise. Pontificating, he says:

> "Pay me? Man, yo' should o' see how fas' dey pay me! Pay me fas' enough, indeed! Five hundred pounds! Ev'y blind cent! Man, I wuz ready to sick Nelson heself 'pon dem. At a moment's notice, me an' de council wuz gettin' ready fo' ramsack de Isthmus and shoot up de whole blasted locks! Hell wit' de Canal! We wuz gwine blow up de dam, cut down de wireless station an' break up de gubment house! If dey didn't pay me fo' my foot!" (42)

George Lamming's Colón Man expresses a bodily connection to the successfully completed waterway in his reference to his hands and the structure they helped produce (see chapter 3). Poyah's claim, however, is rendered in financial terms and linked to his physical loss. And, much like

Senior's Devon, Poyah establishes his right to the canal through his status as a British subject. Where Pa defines his own greatness in terms of the canal's, and Lamming uses Pa's migration to reflect his innate dignity, Poyah asserts his Britishness—he let canal authorities "understand quick enough dat [he] wuz a Englishman and not a bleddy American nigger" (42).[25] Through an aggressive pride in his British identity (different from Bita Plant's largely cultural Englishness) and the money earned in Panamá, Walrond's Colón Man is wholly defined through his relationships with Western powers. Although this story, like "Wharf Rats," intimates some intra-/inter-nation tension (between blacks in Barbados and those in the United States, and between blacks and whites), Poyah nonetheless presents himself in terms of British and ICC authorities.

As a Panamá Man, Poyah is an activist, British, rich, proud, and ethnocentric. He also asserts a masculinity distinguished by his work in the Canal Zone. "'I's a man, man' [Poyah] said . . . 'I wuz a brakesman in Palama, don't fomembah dat. I wuz de bes' train hooper on de Isthmus!'" (44). Announced as Ella enters his shop, Poyah intends this comment to be impressive. For her he catalogues his attributes, his shop and his manhood, both drawn from his migration. The Colón Man also has an image of isthmian migration to speak for him because it announces his desire for self-improvement. Panamá affords Poyah a means through which he articulates a masculinity characterized by the knowledge and experience necessitated by canal work. The danger involved in migration to the Panamanian isthmus, the potential for unparalleled earnings, the cosmopolitan environment surrounding construction all combined to distinguish Poyah as a "man." And if migration can inform one's sense of himself as a man, the unprecedented nature of isthmian migration extends to Poyah the status of alpha male.

Walrond goes to great lengths to describe Ella as single and conscious of this state, despite the fact that the story opens with her apparent ease with her independence, crops, and animals. Members of her village of Low'rd (Lower Side), however, are preoccupied by the absence of a man in her life. In fact, Lizzie's daughter, Capadosia, harshly criticizes Ella because of it, and loudly enough for Ella to hear: "Capadosia, [cuts] her eyes at [Ella] and [murmurs], 'come complainin' 'pon me—de old hag—why she don't go 'n get sheself a man?'" (35). Poyah's hypermasculinity, if paired with Ella, might make her more acceptable to their community, if Capadosia's comment is an accurate representation of their views. Yet despite the girl's invective, the protagonist does not seem to want a man. She has, after all, her land and livestock.

The author describes Ella as godlike in her ability to create. She splices dissimilar trees and plants, and crossbreeds pigeons and ground doves, in order to breed new life. In doing these things, Ella conveys an aggressive fertility. In fact, though she is single, her desire to create seems quite urgent: "sometimes, unmoved by their genetic dissimilarity, Ella'd use drastic, aggressive methods . . ." to produce her offspring (40). It is important to note that her fertility is self-contained as she can create new life without a man. If she is melancholy about being alone, and concerned by Capadosia's words, there is nothing to indicate that these feelings result from a desire to reproduce. In other words, if Ella wants a man, she does so for reasons other than procreation.[26] She is certain of her ability to breed life on her own, confirmed by the zeal with which she approaches it.

Walrond gives some insight into Ella's view on female/male relationships, though only in relation to plants and animals. In his descriptions of the protagonist's behavior, he suggests that she is aware of how nature participates in unusual pairings; to be precise, the protagonist knows how *she* can initiate such pairings. With regard to her own "pairing," Ella must necessarily lean toward the unusual.

We learn that the protagonist's success with birds and plants extends to animals. The narrator indicates that:

> sows fared prodigiously at the hands of Ella. She filled huge, fat-stinking troughs of slime for them. Ella's boars grew tusks of flint-like ivory. Vicious, stiff-haired boars who ate up the sow's young, frothed at the mouth at [her dog] Jit's approach, tried to stick their snouts between Ella's legs whenever she ventured in the pen. (40)

The language in this passage suggests that Ella's male animals are particularly deadly—and virile. This, interpreted in relation to her certainty about her procreative skills, insinuates a vexed relationship to physically aggressive types of masculinity. Continuing, the narrator says:

> under Ella's tutelage the one cow she owned streamed milk. From fat luscious udders filled skillet after skillet. . . .
> Gay, lonely girl, her bare arms yellow in the blazing February sun, the words of a West Indian madrigal issued from her lips:
> Do Mistah Bee don't chase me 'way
> Fo' de gals nex' do' will laugh at me
> Break me han' but let me stan'
> Break me han' but let me stan' . . . (ibid)

The writer tellingly uses more evocative, less violent language to describe Ella and her female animal. This song, finally, tells of a man (Mr. Bee) who must not reject a woman too harshly so as to protect her from outsiders' judgments. Ella overhears how Capadosia describes her, so she has some insight into her standing among her neighbors. In light of her ability to reproduce and her relationship to her animals, the song Ella sings speaks more of her relationship to her community than to a mate. The madrigal, in relation to the previous quotations, exposes the tension between the protagonist and her neighbors. Ella is both in line and, to some extent, at odds with the mores of her community: she is tied to and successful on the land, and respects local foodways and folklore, but disregards their prescribed definitions of womanhood (Capadosia's comment suggests that it is unusual for a woman like Ella to be single). As "Panama Gold" unfolds, it continues to define Ella along these lines and, as a result, makes a relationship between her and Poyah less and less likely. When the protagonist finally comes face to face with him, it is abundantly clear that such a union will never happen. Walrond centers his characterization of Ella around a femaleness defined by independence and connection to nature, a direct challenge to Poyah's kind of masculinity, one contingent upon material goods and an aggressive demeanor.

Ella is content with her lifestyle, but if her relationship to her plants and animals is not sufficiently suggestive, Heath could not be any more explicit in her denunciation of the Colón Man's handicap, his color, worldliness, and material possessions. A "natural" and "fertile" relationship between the two, therefore, is far from being either. Ella rejects Poyah because she finds his skin too dark, but she expresses her prejudice as a condemnation of the Panamá Man's money and possessions. As a result, what might simply be interpreted as an example of intraracial and/or social class prejudices in Barbados is also a critique of the materiality of and modernization afforded by labor on the Panamá Canal.

Upon first seeing Poyah at his shop, Ella says to herself "Gahd, he are black in troot" and, "with a stab to the breast, she [notes] the protrudent tip of the cork leg" (Walrond 1954: 43). Poyah thus makes a doubly negative impression on her. This does not, however, prevent him from calling on Ella at her home. When the Colón Man comes courting, Ella's disapproval of him is biting and very specific in its conflation of the isthmian worker's handicap, color, and materiality. Heath rants:

"All dem bag o' flour yo' 'a' got, an' dem silk shut, an' dem gold teets, an' dem Palama hats yo' a spote round heh wid—dem don't frighten me. I is a woman what is usta t'ings. I got me hogs an' me fowls an' me potatoes. *No wooden foot neygah man can frighten me wit' he clothes or he barrels o' cologne. . . .*"
Yellow kerchief mopping his brow, he walked off . . . peg step, peg step . . . leaving Ella by the well, gazing with defiance in her being . . . (45–46, emphasis added)

Ella obviously takes exception to everything that defines Poyah in this story. Indeed, each of his "faults" can be seen as building on the others, forming a structure that Ella invokes to unman him. Because she is a woman who is used to things, none of the Colón Man's qualifications impress her. And since the things with which Heath is accustomed are agricultural, the comparison to Poyah's "things" leaves his wanting. Confronted with Ella's cultural superiority, the Colón Man and his Panamá Money are superfluous.

Soon after Ella shames Poyah into retreat, his shop catches fire and she tries to contribute her bucket of water to relief efforts. At the scene, she frantically searches for the Panamá Man, but all she finds are traces of him: "A straw valise, label spattered—decker's luggage—an old shirt—one or two stray sacks of split peas—the money canister" (49). These signs of his migration underscore the Colón Man's signification of modernity and materiality: the fire reduces him to the sum of his defining Panamá parts. "Ella realized how for nothing was her bucket of water" only after she learns that Poyah has died in the fire (ibid). This ambiguous ending leaves more questions than answers: Is Ella unable to bring Poyah anything? If she can bring him something, would it be useless and/or no longer necessary? Does she try to bring him her folk self and does it come too late for him? Is Poyah, as a symbol of a particular kind of progress, not viable in a Bajan context? Is Ella, as a perversely fertile and happily single woman, a transgressive Caribbean female? Is Poyah, wounded but still "masculine" because of his migration, out of place in Barbados?

These questions leave readers with a suspicion that, with the Panamá Man denigrated and dispatched, Ella nostalgically stands for a past where Bajans were tied more closely to the land. Still one cannot ignore the prejudices that allow readers to pity the rejected Poyah. The strangeness that characterizes Ella and Poyah's relationship suggests that a union between modern and traditional cultures might be inevitable but fraught with problems, and that gender relations in Barbados were similarly vexed. The ambiguity that surrounds his death, particularly Ella's part in the rescue effort, prevents our interpretation of it as necessary or wholly desirable. Walrond's ambivalent ending promises neither the maintenance of an idealized Barbadian reality—Ella's aggressive fecundity and prejudices indicate that her worldview is problematic—nor the pure valuelessness of modern progress signified by Poyah's money.

What both of these positions do reveal is how intrinsically interconnected Poyah and Ella are. They define each other despite the fact that they repel each other. "Panama Gold" casts Poyah, that is his maleness, as bringing this definition/repulsion paradigm about; it is the absence—and potential "presence"—of a man in Ella's life that marks her as unusual and defines the tension in the story. Walrond deliberately identifies Poyah as male through his work and injury in the Canal Zone, thus setting up a sequence that begins with Caribbean migration to the Panamanian isthmus. In other words, the author links Barbados' (and the Caribbean's) fraught movement into modernity to conflicted gender identities that are constituted by troubling features of isthmian migration.

"Subjection" is as an allegory of the Caribbean worker in the Canal Zone. In this, the story anticipates the conflict in "Panamá Gold" as the former story powerfully enumerates the problems faced by the canal's Caribbean workforce. Ballet, a young Panamá Man who supports his aging mother, intervenes in an altercation between Mouth and a nameless white marine. Ballet receives no support from his fellow laborers (they distance themselves from the affair), but he still confronts the marine. The soldier shifts his attention to Ballet and threatens to kill him as a lesson to others who might intercede in the execution of canal authority, in its myriad forms. The marine stalks and ultimately murders the protagonist, thereby making an example of him, but only to those who had knowledge of the initial altercation. Rather than the brutal murder of a Good Samaritan, the Quarter Marshall officially records the Colón Man's death as the only casualty of a "native labor uprising" (Walrond 1954: 112).

"Subjection" questions the "beneficial" aspects of isthmian migration by conflating Mouth's beating with the kind of work Colón Men perform. The technique allows readers to link Ballet's objection to the marine's abuse of Mouth to the kind, in fact, the *value* of the work canal laborers perform. In the process, the story skillfully documents a range of laborers' responses to the U.S. marine's brutality, elaborating on what "victim" and "victimization" mean in the context of canal construction. Ballet and his peers behave as cowards, but framed within Walrond's cost/benefit analysis of Panamá migration, their behavior can be seen as a consequence of canal work.

Lastly, this story's ending confirms its status as an oppositional narrative of the days of canal construction. As such, it complicates the official version of the story recounted in the *Canal Record* (the ICC's official publication) where what begins as a marine's lesson in authority ends as an effectively controlled "native uprising."[27] A consideration of *both* official (recognized, historical) and oppositional (fictive, imaginable) accounts of Ballet's murder provides access to an effaced isthmian experience and, perhaps most significantly, the meaning contained in it.

In this tale, Colón Men are little more than living machines. Walrond creatively depicts this by imagining workers as moving parts of a pulverizing machine:

> Toro Point resounded to the noisy rhythm of picks swung by gnarled black hands. Sunbaked rock stones flew to dust, to powder. In flashing unison rippling muscle glittered to the task of planing a mound of rocky earth dredged up on the barren seashore. (99–100)

Black canal workers are presented as objects through the attention drawn to pieces of them—their gnarled hands and rippling muscles. Notably, their parts do not cohere into whole men who can determine how their work is performed; such parts, therefore, can be easily acted upon. When viewed merely as pieces of a pulverizing machine, it cannot be surprising that, in some ways, Colón Men perceive of themselves in the same way.

Walrond spends a lot of time describing Ballet and his peers' responses to the marine's assault on Mouth. This omnipotent (because he is unnamed) white man bludgeons Mouth, partially severing the boy's ear, while vowing:

> "I'll show you goddamn niggers how to talk back to a white man—"
> About twelve, thirteen, fourteen men, but only the wind rustled. A hastening breath of wind, struck dead on the way by the grueling presence of the sun. (100)

The sun, in its ferocity and unquestioned authority, is the marine incarnate; Mouth specifically, and all who witness the beating, are "struck dead" like the wind. Every Colón Man who observes the boy's beating cowers under this demonstration of ICC supremacy. Walrond frames the assault as a display designed to "unman" workers. Rather than actors and agents, "Subjection's" Colón Men accept not only the marine's authority, but also the emasculated roles to which it consigns them.

Ballet chastises his coworkers and initiates a conversation that defines their lack of motivation. It is important to note that even in his willingness to speak on Mouth's behalf, Ballet's words are equally directed at himself. It appears, then, that the bravery associated with the migration image can be affected by certain realities on the isthmus. Addressing his coworkers, Ballet says:

> "Unna is a pack o' men, ni'," cried Ballet, outraged, "unna see de po' boy get knock' down an' not a blind one o' wunna would a len' he a han'. Unna is de mos'—"
> But one man, a Bajan creole, did whip up the courage of voice. "Good God, giv' he a chance, ni'. Don' kick he in de head now he is 'pon de groun'—" and he quickly, at a nudge and a hushed, "Hey, wha' do you? Why yo' don't tek yo' hand out o' yo' matey' saucepan?" from the only other creole, lapsed into *ruthless impassivity*. (100–101, emphasis added)

Several of the men refuse to get involved "in de backra dem business" and blame Mouth for initiating the assault, asserting that "de boy ain't got no business talkin' back to de marinah man—" (101). At last, they encourage Ballet to mind his own business. By describing these Panamá Men's inaction as "ruthless impassivity," Walrond suggests an *active* passivity. Ballet's fellow workers *choose* to be silent as a familiar survival strategy, a choice that can be misread as paralyzing fear (Devonshire's peers make a similar choice). In any case, they exhibit a degree of choice that calls into question their status as mere victims. Therefore Ballet's choice is linked to that of his peers as one of many possibilities open to these Colón Men, possibilities that are likely to be destructive but ones that could not be available if they were completely divested of the ability to choose—a characteristic often applied to Caribbean workers in more traditional canal narratives.

Walrond makes it clear that Mouth's beating is more than a conflict between two individuals. Neither is it an individual act of prejudice or assertion of power. It might have begun as either of these, but in front of an audience it becomes a message to any laborer who believes in his "rights" as an ICC employee—and as a human being. The marine distinguishes between "correcting" a single, cheeky boy like Mouth and forestalling the self-assertion that Ballet represents:

> Mouth, the boy at issue, one of those docile, half-white San Andres coons, was a facile affair. Singly, red-bloodedly one handled it. But here, with this ugly, thick-lipped, board-chested upstart, there was need for handling of an errorless sort.
> "I'll git you yet," the marine said, gazing at Ballet quietly, "I'll fill you full of lead yet, you black bastard!" (101)

The marine's ominous thoughts and behavior are unmasked, exposing an environment that begs the question: how can Colón Men work and thrive under this imaginatively remembered system? The marine's tactics demonstrate that canal authorities were prepared to handle Colón Men who asserted their rights. Ballet's mother describes working for North American whites as "[getting] under the heel o' de backra" (104). Ballet asserts himself and stands up for Mouth, but faced with Mouth's severed ear, he must recognize the danger of the situation. Through this story, Walrond poses an important question: why work under such conditions, and to acquire money and goods, at the cost of one's dignity and self-respect, even one's life? He seems to sympathize with these Colón Men; however, he is ambivalent about the value of the progress that canal work represents even if solely viewed in terms of its economic benefit.

Ballet mirrors this ambivalence because, contemplating the marine's threat, he is not sure that he wants to go to work. But

> a stab of pain corrugated Ballet's smooth black brow. His mother's constant dwelling on the dearth of the family fortunes produced in him a sundry set of emotions—escape in rebellion and refusal to do as against a frenzied impulse to die retrieving things.
> The impulse to do conquered, and Ballet rose . . . (104)

This passage clearly weighs the problem of working for things against the loss of aspects of one's humanity. Walrond complicates this conflict by showing how violence toward and objectification of Caribbean canal workers impacts their sense of themselves, not only as laborers, but also as people. In this way he acknowledges how the protagonist and his peers participate in their own objectification.[28] His emphasis on the high cost associated with earning Panamá Money suggests that nonmonetary motivations played significantly in prospective Colón Men's reasons for migration; money alone cannot sufficiently explain why Caribbean men continued to put up with abuse like the kind meted out by the unnamed marine.

Walrond delays the story's denouement by describing Blanche and Ballet's sexual encounter on his way to work, demonstrating that the harsh reality awaiting his worker-self does not subsume his other selves, notably his sexual/masculine self (106–7). The dalliance affirms the survival of this aspect of Ballet's manhood, the one place in the story where his authority is unwaveringly expressed and felt ("unquestioningly the force of such a wiry, gluey, gummy impact as [Blanche and Ballet's coupling] left her heels a little broader" [107]). Therefore the marine, as representative of the isthmian authority, cannot wholly subsume Ballet's reality. Nonetheless, the marine ultimately catches up with the Panamá Man. Ballet, heeding neither his own nor Mouth's fears about returning to work, comes face-to-face with the white man's murderous eyes. He flees from them, finding refuge in a storage shed. Tracking Ballet there, the marine hollers:

> "Where the hell are yer, yer lousy bastard—yer—come sticking in yer mouth where yer hadn't any goddamn business? Minding somebody else's business. I'll teach you niggers down here how to talk back to a white man. Come out o' there, you black bastard."
> Behind the wheel, bars dividing the two, Ballet saw the dread khaki—the dirt-caked leggings.
> His vision abruptly darkened.
> Vap, vap, vap—
> Three sure, dead shots. (112)

The marine murders Ballet, not for anything that he says or does, but for what his actions imply: his refusal of the role consigned him by North American whites and by canal authorities, as well as his belief in his own transgressive—because it countermands that prescribed by others—humanity.

Whereas this Colón Man's behavior might positively influence those who witnessed it (those, that is, who can overcome their terror of the marine's violence), no one removed from the spectacle can benefit from the events leading up to Ballet's murder. His story is never officially recorded. "Subjection's" last lines inform readers that "in the Canal Record, the Q. M. at Toro Point took occasion to extol the virtues of the Department which kept the number of casualties in the recent native labor uprising down to one" (ibid). This erasure enacts additional violence by striking Ballet's story from the official record and thereby enabling the fiction of U.S. benevolence in the Canal Zone to continue. In light of this erasure, "Subjection," as one fictive narrative among isthmian mythographies, has a broad reach. It manifests the importance of telling isthmian stories through multiple genres; not only can this add narratives that would otherwise remain unseen, but genres contribute their rules, structures, and ideologies to the meanings of isthmian migration and labor.

The Colón Men in "Subjection" stand along side more celebratory figures, adding to rather than contradicting previous characterizations. Walrond's telling of this aspect of the isthmian experience, complementing mythographies of Colón Men and Caribbean isthmian migration, contributes to the ritual of telling and retelling of workers' stories, approaching the complexity of the migration itself. Rather than seek a representative Panamá Man, making meaning from the varied tellings signifies the process through which alternative visions of Panamá migration, labor, and workers—oppositional views of the Caribbean's Panamanian realities—can revise the representations in mainstream historical narratives. By identifying and layering diverse stories of Colón Men and the isthmus, I am not concerned with finding "answers"; instead this project, and this process, is instructive because it foregrounds a viable method of addressing (countermanding?) the authority of one type of isthmian narrative.

Walrond raises all of these issues in the above stories. "Subjection" communicates the writer's uncertainty about Caribbean labor on, hence migration to, Panamá. The author suggests that the costs may be too high; yet he does not counter the vain and possibly inescapable quest for material possessions with another option.

What is truly tragic is that official accounts do not acknowledge the complication that fictive narratives like "Panama Gold," "The Wharf Rats," and "Subjection" embrace. While not offering any conclusion, these stories are valuable because of the unofficial isthmian experiences they describe. Exemplary Colón Man (Pa or Nattie) and their dandified counterparts (Tack or Poyah) must be placed along side Ballet and his coworkers. Collectively reading these recurring isthmian references underscores the importance of alternative realities in investigations of Caribbeanness.

V

The Colón Man can be seen as a trope because of its frequent and varied appearances in Caribbean literary, cultural, and nonfictional forms. Various writers use the figure to present Panamá as part of the region's historical, economic, and social realities, and to make deductions about Caribbean subjectivities. Memories, histories, and stories about this migrant intertwine to create a mythography that complicates ideas about Caribbean victimage, confirms the interpretive value of oppositional histories and stories in speaking the region's realities, and positions imaginable truths at the center of examinations of Caribbeanness. In a phrase, the trope of the Colón Man embodies the "creative friction" that characterizes the confrontation between Caribbean workers, their migration and work, on one hand, and Panamá, Panamanians, and North Americans on the other.

While the mythographic Colón Man is a valuable tool in the exploration of literary Caribbeanness, the subjectivity it identifies is a masculine one. This becomes most evident here because Tack Tally, Poyah, and Devon relate to female protagonists, *Banana Bottom*'s Tabitha "Bita" Plant, "Panama Gold's" Ella Heath, and Bridget Jasper in "Window." As a consequence, these Colón Men permit not only a critique of masculinity, but also a critique of the trope itself, that is, its theoretical currency. This kind of critique can be seen in this chapter as interpretations offered through the Colón Men begin a dialogue about gender identities despite the absence of women among isthmian mythographies. This gender analysis adds another facet to the Caribbean's Panamanian experience, invoking the inaccessibility of women's narratives while, at the same time, affording insight into the possible "look" of their lived realities through the lens provided by Colón Men's mythographies. These workers imaginable truths also inform readers how masculinity, in relation to isthmian migration, has been defined. Colón Men's imaginings about themselves as men, and creative writers' use of these imaginings, supplement official stories and contribute previously submerged ones about workers' lives in the Canal Zone and back home. However, when the official story is thin, as is the case with Panamá Women, emphasis on—and the value of—fictive contributions are particularly relevant.

The next chapter, featuring the canal worker in Maryse Condé's *Tree of Life: A Novel of the Caribbean*, gets at some of the problems of gender identities, historical and imaginable truths, and Caribbean isthmian migration by taking "disorder" and "chaos" as concepts central to investigations of Caribbeanness. Condé-the-critic values disorder and complication, and thus uses them as ideologies to advocate oppositional Caribbean realities. Chapter 5 begins by tracing Condé's attempt to perform this theory of disorder in her fiction. The trope of the Colón Man, already a complex device, profitably gauges the author's success at enacting her version of disorder in *Tree of Life*. But where previous chapters foreground fictive stories (while historical ones always operate in the background), to reconstruct the life and legacy of Condé's Panamá Man, Albert Louis, the narrator relies on a process that simultaneously brings his history, histories, and stories to light.

NOTES

A portion of this chapter first appeared as "Mythographies of Panamá Canal Migrations: Eric Walrond's 'Panama Gold,'" in *Marginal Migrations: The Circulation of Cultures within the Caribbean*, edited by Shalini Puri, 43–76. Oxford: Macmillan Press/Warwick University Caribbean Studies, 2003. Reproduced from *Marginal Migrations*, Warwick University Caribbean Studies Series, by kind permission of Macmillan Caribbean, a division of Macmillan Publishers, Ltd.

1. Claude McKay, *Banana Bottom* (1933. San Diego: Harvest Books/Harcourt, Brace, and Company, 1961); Eric Walrond, "Panama Gold," *Tropic Death* (New York: Collier Books, 1954).

2. Thomas-Hope states, "persons abroad prefer to transmit information which demonstrates that their migration has been successful and those in the Caribbean who have not yet migrated are seeking positive information about migration as well. The image of migration itself becomes the key factor in determining the ways in which the experiences abroad are interpreted both by migrant and potential migrant from their two perspectives within the same value judgement framework" (Thomas-Hope 1992: 32).

3. The song, appearing as an epigraph in the Introduction, is a prime example. Olive Senior (1978) uses it to represent the attitude of those removed from the attractions of isthmian migration with regard to Colón Men (and, soon, other returned migrants) who strutted around with the migration-bought finery.

4. Austin Clarke, introduction, *Nine Men Who Laughed* (Toronto: Penguin Books, 1986). Thanks to Kali Gross (Assistant Professor of History and Politics, Drexel University) for bringing this book—and Clarke's ideas on the uses of laughter—to my attention.

5. Louise Bennett, "No Lickle Twang!," *Jamaica Labrish* (Great Britain: Collins Clear-Type Press, 1966: 209–11). Velma Pollard has describes this perspective with regard to Jamaican peasant and urban working classes ("Imagination and Reality"). Thomas-Hope also attributes this particular take on migrants and migrations to the lower classes: "migration and its related attributes [higher wages, goods, new "walks" and "talks"] had not only made its social and economic impact felt in the islands, but it had become incorporated into the entire fabric of lower class values" (Thomas-Hope 1978: 76).

6. Michelle Rowley, Assistant Professor of Women's Studies at the University of Cincinnati, helped me process my readings on Caribbean masculinities and

articulate the dynamic between realities and mythologies of Colón Men's migration-forged masculinity.

7. Bonham Richardson affirms this point: "it is therefore entirely reasonable to suggest that migrants who returned were held in greater esteem than those who had remained. Those who had gone away and successfully returned with gifts for loved ones and tales of perils overcome had beaten the system, while those who had stayed behind had not" (Richardson 1983: 19). The returned migrant, because he had traveled to *and* returned from foreign with signs of his migration, earned (at least) *twice* the cultural capital of migrants who remained away.

8. Remarking on the lack of restaurants during the early phases of construction, IHS contest participant Amos E. Clarke claimed to have bought food from "two colored women [who] carried trays on their heads with hot coffee, bread and butter, to the work-place in the morning time, price 10¢ U.S. currency. The name of these two Jamaican women, one Marian Cunningson and one Caroline Lowe" (*LICCW*, A. E. Clarke, page 1 of 3). Clarke links these two women with food, placing them within a familiar domestic context, but it is important to note that Cunningson and Lowe were courageous migrants and independent entrepreneurs.

9. Discussing "Le Torrent," a play about the Haitian Revolution, Joan Dayan remarks:

> what is most striking about the celebratory reversals of the play—Dessalines's defection from the French, the mulatto sons joining with the African-born Ti-Noël, and the recognition of "the African soul" and "the regeneration of the race" by none other than the [white] planter Delcourt, as he praises his 'black madonna'—is that Sister Rose remains constant. In her varying guises, she abides all the changes. Whether called "slave," "mother," "kindness," "luck" or "lady of sorrows," she is the passive recipient of history. (Dayan 1995: 50)

In imagining the Haitian nation, "Le Torrent" addresses the country's most pressing issues: establishing itself as an independent, black republic (Dessalines's defection from the French); healing the rift between its black and mulatto populations, as well as other legacies of Haiti's colonial occupation (the union between Ti-Noël and his mixed-race sons); and using the white planter to celebrate Sister Rose's representation of "the African Soul" and racial regeneration. Dayan points out that the Haitian nation evolves out of Rose's regulated persona; she enables, not a revolution in the systems and institutions that made Haiti, but allows black men to replace white men at the reigns of power.

10. Three significant texts are Tyrone Tillery's *Claude McKay: A Black Poet's Struggle for Identity* (Amherst: University of Massachusetts Press, 1992), Wayne F. Cooper's *Claude McKay, Rebel Sojourner in the Harlem Renaissance: A Biography* (Baton Rouge: Louisiana State University Press, 1987), and A. L. McLeod's *Claude McKay: Centennial Studies* (New Delhi: Sterling Publishers Private, 1992). The following critical treatments of McKay and his work are significant here: Leota S. Lawrence, "Three West Indian Heroines: An Analysis," *CLA Journal* 21.2 (December 1977): 238–50; Helen Pyne-Timothy, "Perceptions of the Black Woman in the Work of Claude McKay," *CLA Journal* 19.2 (December 1975): 152–64; George E. Kent, "Claude McKay's *Banana Bottom* Reappraised," *CLA Journal* 18.2 (December 1974): 222–34; Kenneth Ramchand, "Claude McKay and *Banana Bottom*," *Southern Review* 4.1 (1970): 53–66.

11. Kenneth Ramchand finds in the text an inspired examination of Afro-Caribbean identity, while George Kent posits that McKay fails to take his ideas about identity to their logical conclusions. Helen Pyne-Timothy argues that Bita is an example of McKay's "ideal black woman" and approves of his representation of her and other female characters in the author's oeuvre. On the other hand, Leota S. Lawrence considers the protagonist implausible because she embodies a "romanticized version of West Indian womanhood" (Lawrence 1977: 242).

12. Richardson speaks on this point with regard to Barbadian Colón Men. Local planters were, at first, supportive of Panamá migration by black plantation workers; these white men saw workers' desire to migrate as a sign of the their industry. But this attitude failed to acknowledge that these migrants might no longer continue to accept traditional racial relationships. In fact, "the money sent and brought home from Panama . . . would help to bring about socioeconomic changes, including the ability of black Barbadians eventually to seek new and more equitable adjustments to old problems" (Richardson 1992: 142). Returned Barbadian Colón Men *recognized* that they could positively influence their social circumstances by migrating, and thereby inaugurate new and more equitable social relations. Conditions unique to Jamaica necessarily influenced the extent to which returned Colón Men could change local conditions, but *Banana Bottom's* fictional intervention in this regard, not to mention the precedent set by Bajan returnees, suggests that Jamaican returnees could have similar impact in their country.

13. Pollard discusses how tensions around "class passing" informed Jamaicans' responses to repatriated Panamá migrants ("Imagination and Reality"). She argues that the currency that the migration bought the migrant and his family sometimes allowed them to move up Jamaica's social and economic ladders but in the absence of additional class markers (education, upper-class mores and manners, light skin, etc.), this movement was fraught with bumps and detours.

14. Believing that he murdered Pap Legge, Tack plans to challenge obeahman Wumba for failing to protect the Colón Man from evil. Apparently intended as some kind of revenge, Tack hangs himself at the home of the absent obeahman (151).

15. By this point in the novel, the protagonist has begun to feel uncomfortable with the role consigned her by her adoption and education. She recognizes herself as the Craigs' "experiment" and, although she has accepted Herald Newton Day's marriage proposal, she "was occupied all the time now devising means to be as little as possible alone in the company of her intended" (109). The final break between Bita and the Craigs comes when she engages in an inappropriate flirtation with Hopping Dick, who was "a dandy all right, but not a little ratty sort like Tally" (167). Immersed in the reality of her childhood, the protagonist can effortlessly draw on the security of that experience, standing as it does in stark contrast to her discomfort in the world of Jubliee.

16. Ramchand finds Bita's "escape from the world of the Craigs into the world of Banana Bottom . . . a plausibly organized dramatic process"; further, he considers her movement from Jubilee to Banana Bottom predictable because "the heroine has always belonged to [the village]: [Bita says that] 'whatever I was trained like or to be, I know one thing. And that is that I am myself'" (Ramchand 1970: 65). Ramchand judges the reassertion of Bita's childhood identity best expressed in the swimming scene (ibid). Finally, he emphasizes the protection that

Jamaican culture affords *Banana Bottom*'s protagonist and elaborates on this idea through his interpretation of Bita's marriage to Jubban, a dark-skinned farmer whom she chooses instead of the more "suitable," light-skinned, middle-class Herald Newton Day.

17. Tyrone Tillery argues that McKay's use of a dark-skinned and female protagonist is incredible: "McKay's choice of Bita as his protagonist to lead a cultural rebellion is implausible. Given the male-dominated character of Jamaican society at the time, it is unlikely a woman, especially a dark-skinned one, would have had the freedom and independence of a Bita" (Tillery 1992: 207n15). Despite this implausibility, the biographer acknowledges that McKay's choice might signify his attempt at authorial distance more than his desire to create a realistic situation (131, 132). See also Richard Prieb, "The Search for Community in the Novels of Claude McKay," *Studies in Black Literature* 3.2 (Summer 1972): 27.

18. Day, incidentally, escapes to Panamá after being caught in a compromising position with a goat (McKay 175-76). Watkins-Owens mentions Paule Marshall's aunt who was "banished" to the isthmus for having a child out of wedlock (Watkins-Owens 25) and Glenville Lovell's 1995 novel includes a character whose broken heart drives him to the isthmus. *Fire in the Canes* (New York: Soho Press, 1995).

19. Enid Bogle, "Eric Walrond (1898–1966)," *50 Caribbean Writers: A Bio-bibliographical Critical Sourcebook*, edited by Daryl Cumber Dance (New York: Greenwood Press, 1986): 478. Kenneth Ramchand, "The Writer Who Ran Away: Eric Walrond and *Tropic Death*," *Savacou: A Journal of the Caribbean Artists Movement* 2 (1970): 70 (hereafter cited in the text as Ramchand 1970A). Ramchand comments on Walrond use of harsh landscapes and puts him in the context of literature of the Harlem Renaissance, finding that "Walrond is both moving his material away from conventional social realism and protest against the social order, and seeking to balance or complicate the tone of the narrative by adding elements that lie outwith the sphere of satire, protest or indignation" (69–70).

20. *The Norton Anthology of African American Literature*, edited by Henry Louis Gates Jr. and Nellie Y. McKay (New York: W. W. Norton, 1997): 1195. Sterling Brown, in an excerpt from comments published in *The Massachusetts Review* (reproduced on the collection's cover), describes the collection as "a brilliantly impressionistic series of portraits of the author's native West Indies."

21. This collection, therefore, seems to prefigure the critical movement toward disorder and complication in Caribbean Studies, evinced by Maryse Condé's "Order, Disorder, Freedom, and the West Indian Writer" and Joan Dayan's *Haiti, History, and the Gods*.

22. Though she downplays the extent to which West Indians in Panamá believe in obeah, Louise Cramer collects a song that mentions it, tracing the song's origins to Trinidad. Maffi hums "Trinidad is a *damn* fine place/But *obeah* down dey" (Walrond 1954: 84, emphasis added). This reference appears to be a more risqué version of the song "Trinidad Is a *Very* Fine Place" that begins:

> Trinidad is a very fine place,
> But de Obeah doung deh!
> Trinidad is a very fine place,
> But de Obeah doung deh!

> Why, why, why, why, why de Obeah doung deh,
> Why, why, why, why, why de Obeah doung deh.
> Blanchie gal a why ya doin' doung here?
> Why de train bring me doung.
> Blanchie gal a why ya doin' doung here?
> Why de train bring me doung.
> Why, why, why, why, why de train bring me doung.
> Why, why, why, why, why de train bring me doung.
> Beg de doctor for a pique dress
> But he gi me muslin.
> Why, why, why, why, why he gi me muslin.
> Why, why, why, why, why he gi me muslin.
> Trinidad is a very fine place,
> But de Obeah doung deh!
> Trinidad is a very fine place,
> But de Obeah doung deh! (Cramer 1946: 263)

23. Michael Dash asserts that Walrond falls into the often ubiquitous representations of Caribbean savagery (typified by the Haitian revolution and vodun) circulating during the Harlem Renaissance (Dash 1988: 56–57). Perhaps, but the detail Walrond offers (obeah man, Maubé bark, ganja weed) distinguishes his rendition, tweaking the often generic characterizations. It is also significant that no whites appear in the story, an omission that affords the story an insider's revelatory tone instead of an outsider's/anthropologist's perspective.

24. In his exegesis of "Panama Gold," Kenneth Ramchand finds a romantic relationship between Ella and Poyah most significant. He says that "the association of Ella with fertility rituals is obviously a celebration of her connections with the earth, but it also looks forward symbolically to the opportunity coming into her life with Mr. Poyah" (Ramchand 1970A: 72). From this perspective, then, the protagonist's relationship with the Colón Man, or another man, is preordained. If reading this story as a literary enactment of Caribbean identity, the Westernized Colón Man married to Ella's Bajan self advances a New World black subjectivity similar to that which McKay espouses through Tabitha Plant. Ramchand continues by remarking on Ella's likely survival when her union with Poyah does not materialize. The critic interprets the protagonist's use of a tale to stave off her fear (she recalls a "Portuguese legend" of a black man whose punishment for an attempted theft is having his eyes gouged out by crows; Ella chants "Sh, carrion crow, me no dead yet" to protect herself from a similar fate) this way:

> in her continuing loneliness, Ella is dying slowly, and though the story-line is still to be unfolded we are allowed to anticipate through the [carrion crow] legend both that Ella will lose her opportunity with Mr. Poyah, and that for all that, [her] will to survive shall not be defeated ("Sh, carrion crow, me no dead yet"). (73)

The lesson of this legend, as the critic interprets it, is that without Poyah, Ella's survival is somehow uncertain.

25. One must read Poyah's boastful comments in relation to the almost total control wielded by the ICC in the Canal Zone. French and English authorities were deployed in Panamá to attend to the welfare of its subjects, but their authority was

mitigated by the fact of Colón Men's voluntary migration and contingent on the Commission's interest in workers' complaints. The authority of English colonial officials was also diminished by the prickly relationship between the United States and England over the building of a trans-isthmian canal (see chapter 1). One must also consider the different representations of isthmian labor offered by repatriated Colón Men and those who remained in the Canal Zone. Because Poyah survives the isthmus and returns home, he has earned his "bragging rights" (Richardson 1992: 152; see also Richardson 1893: 19). His Panamá, therefore, has been interpreted through his successful travel to *and* return from the isthmus. It is also likely that in response to the unfamiliar North American racism, Poyah (a representative English colonial subject) relies on his foreign status; again the success of this strategy would have been contingent upon U.S. authorities' recognition of this position.

26. Readers' only insight into Ella's view on children comes through her strained relationship with Capadosia: Lizzie beats the girl for being rude, an action supported by Ella as she remarks on the unruliness of girl-children (35).

27. I have not come across an historical version of "Subjection," however McCullough describes the systematic exclusion of black workers' experiences from official canal records, namely "the Canal Record—a reliable, admirable publication in most other respects" (McCullough 1977: 575).

28. In *The Harder They Come*, Michael Thelwell makes a similar claim with regard to the progress, in the form of the tourist industry, that encroaches on Jamaica's rural population. However through Rhygin, as through Walrond's Ballet, both writers demonstrate that progress does not inevitably and irreparably reduce Caribbean people to passive victims. Rhygin translates his diverse, creolized experiences into revolutionary action; Ballet challenges white authority without any kind of support. Yet one cannot overlook the fact that each protagonists dies at the hands of the authorities they resist, leaving open the likelihood that these characters are not as important as the possibilities they can set in motion. Fictively speaking, such a position holds, but in the context of the meanings of Panamá migration and canal construction for Caribbean people, a larger sociological study must be engaged.

5

Out of One, Many People: Disorderly Narrations and the Colón Man in Maryse Condé's *Tree of Life: A Novel of the Caribbean*

> It was not for nothing that Théodora had bled herself dry to send [Albert] to the school in town! He signed proudly with a beautiful paraph, and this is the first document I have of his: his name at the bottom of a two-year contract to dig the Panama Canal. The year was 1904; the month, March; the day, Tuesday. Tuesday, March 14, 1904.
>
> —Maryse Condé, *Tree of Life*

> [Condé] has replaced the ideological weight of *discours* with a maximum of *récits* or tellings and retellings that urge the reader to attend, not to the Truth, but to the process by which a community comes to understand itself.
>
> —A. James Arnold, "The Novelist as Critic"

> Disorder meant the power to create new objects and to modify the existing ones. In a word, disorder meant creativity.
>
> —Condé, "Order, Disorder, Freedom, and the West Indian Writer"[1]

I

In several interviews about *Tree of Life*, Maryse Condé (née Boucolon) acknowledges the autobiographical aspects of the novel; yet, from interview to interview, her representations of what these aspects are vary. For example, in a review appearing in *Essence*, Condé claims that, through a

"Acting Panamanian Governor Hugh M. Arnold congratulating Wilfred 'Big Man' James of Jamaica, West Indies, on the eve of his departure after forty-one years of service with the Maintenance Division, n.d." Photographer unknown. Courtesy of Photographs and Prints Division, Schomburg Center for Research in Black Culture, The New York Public Library, Astor, Lenox, and Tilden Foundations.

"niece," she became aware of her "uncle Albert";[2] in an interview with VéVé Clark, the writer identifies Albert as her half-brother—the son of her father's first wife—and as Bébert in the novel.[3] These two stories more or less correspond (though they slightly confuse the *novel's* genealogy), but both contradict claims the author makes in "The Role of the Writer." In this essay, Albert (called Bert) is her *grandfather's* son by a first wife and, therefore, Condé's half-uncle (the author, however, describes him as her "great uncle").[4] Bébert is Bert's son by a woman named Marie; Bébert's child is Condé's second cousin, Nadia, and the author's link to this branch of the family (Condé 1993A: 697–98). Condé is similarly unclear about an autobiographical point relevant to other novels, namely where her mother was born: in Marie-Galante, a small island off the coast of Guadeloupe (Clark 1988: 89),[5] or in Guadeloupe (Condé 1993A: 699).

Condé's disinclination to expose her family history might appear to be a minor point, but it is within this context that I position her use of Colón Man Albert Louis. The variety of Condé's familial narratives can be interpreted in myriad ways. The inconsistencies revealed above might be the result of a fitful muse (memory) summoned through a less-than-perfect medium (Condé's ability to remember).[6] It is also possible that Condé received these stories in the manner in which she then passed them on, as mythographies that become more or less complex as they travel from family member to family member (and from memory to memory). The most simple explanation is that the author unintentionally made some mistakes. Yet if one reads Condé's rendering of her autobiographical "pieces" through her views on memory, not to mention her investment in "disorder,"[7] her familial tellings and retellings suggest a disinclination to fix meaning as well as a disbelief that "identity" can be known definitively. Lastly, with regard to this book's investment in imaginable truths and the variety of Colón Men's mythographies, one can interpret the different accounts of Condé's family's history as a subversion of the idea that any one version or voice can relate *the* truth of the novel's origins. Its truth lies, therefore, somewhere among these narratives' similarities and contradictions. The confusion visible in Condé's renditions of her personal ancestries, therefore, can been seen as a performance of her writerly ambition.

Claude Elaïse Louis, also known as Coco, narrates *Tree of Life*, a story of the Louis family. Through a few written documents, numerous family photos, personal interviews, historical facts, vague stories, and her own memories (some "real," others imaginatively reconstructed), Coco assembles a genealogy that begins with her great-grandfather, Albert Louis. Her forebear, vowing not to die a misused—though happy—plantation worker like his father, Mano (Condé 1992: 6), abandons Guadeloupe's cane fields to pursue racial justice and financial success in Panamá. This search begins on the isthmus where Albert works on an explosives team and where he meets his first wife,

Liza. After Liza dies in childbirth, Albert briefly returns to Guadeloupe; he reappears with enough money to liberate his mother, Théodora, from the Boyer-de-l'Etang plantation and set her up in a house in La Pointe. It is there that Théodora raises Albert's son, Albert (called Bert). The Colón Man returns to Panamá, where he works with multinational partners in a mortuary business. He continues to migrate, in search of gold, and ends up in San Francisco; once there, he lives and works in Chinatown. The racially motivated murder of his best friend, Jacob, sends Albert fleeing through Panamá and back home to Guadeloupe. He remarries and fathers the line that eventually produces Coco.[8] Albert's travels and business ventures make him rich and foster in him a Pan-Africanist consciousness; ultimately these, plus humiliations, broken dreams, and a strange mixture of greed and color- and class-based chauvinisms, are what he passes on to his descendants. Coco, as one of the "illegitimate" Louises, is motivated to trace and retrace Albert's legacy as a means of finding her place because "it is the branches and above all the roots that do the healing" (38).

In *Tree of Life*, Condé addresses Coco's feelings of being out of place through the narrator's mediation of her family's history, histories, and stories. In addition, this individual's—and individual—*histoire*, dramatized in "A Novel of the Caribbean," conveys the author's desire to explore, fictionally, a Caribbeanness that is not hemmed in by what she describes as "stereotypes" that characterize Caribbean literature. Further, Coco's process of genealogical exploration is self-reflexive in that it draws attention to itself rather than its conclusion (a reconstituted Louis clan). Condé, therefore, seeks neither to use Coco to codify a Guadeloupean subjectivity, nor embody a representative Caribbeanness. The writer intends to foreground not only Coco's reconstructive process, but also the "disorderly" scraps that contribute to it. It is significant, therefore, that Albert Louis is a Panamá Man and that Panamá is so prominently featured in this novel. For the Caribbean region as well as for potential laborers, isthmian migration was distinguished by its ambivalences and its imaginable (real though unrealized, possible but unprecedented) truths. Borrowing and modifying a phrase from Condé, the "creative disorder" (or imaginable truths) of Panamá Canal mythographies and the author's narrative goals come together in Coco's attempt at reconstructing the Colón Man's complicated legacy.

The Panamanian leg of Albert's migration trajectory begins with his dissatisfaction with the money he receives for work on the Boyer-de-l'Etang plantation. This is a position shared by other isthmian workers, if the following work song, "Come Out A Merican Cut," is any indication:

> Before me work fe bit a day
> Before me work fe bit a day

> Before me work fe bit a day
> Me wid come out a Merican Cut,
> Dem a bawl, oh, come out a Merican Cut,
> Dem a bawl, oh, come out a Merican Cut.
> Come out a Merican Cut,
> Come out a Merican Cut. (Cramer 1946: 253)

This work song was sung to encourage workers to act in concert while performing repetitive tasks (like laying railroad ties or crushing stone) and to make their work proceed evenly and steadily (248). It was also sung as call-and-response, with a gang's leader calling out a line to which members of the gang responded. Thus the song sets up a suggestive environment where timing, type of labor, and, arguably, the feeling (if not subject) of the song were shared by laborers.[9] The lyrics of "Come Out a Merican Cut" support the contention that high wages pulled Caribbean workers to the Canal Zone, but they also communicate workers' sense of the value of their labor. They knew that "a bit," or 4.5 pence (253), was a poor measure of their labor and that their work would be better appreciated on the "Merican" project. Literary Colón Man Albert Louis and his lyrical counterparts use their ability to migrate to resist the devaluation of their labor.

But canal authorities, while expressing their appreciation for Albert's work in financial terms, offered only a minor respite from the type of oppressions he faced in Guadeloupe. Once on the isthmus, he quickly realizes that rather than changing his situation, he merely changed location. Coco tells us:

> it did not take Albert long to realize that he had changed nothing but the color of his rags.
> The Canal Company cared only about its American employees. For them, it was bringing in fortunes from Wall Street. For them, it was draining the coastal area and constructing pleasant bungalows complete with running water. For them, it was planting signs in the ground: RESERVED FOR WHITES, WHITES ONLY.
> Like the rest of his countrymen who were putting up mud and straw lean-tos around Gatun, Bohio, Baja [sic] Obispo, and Culebra, Albert settled in close by the stagnant waters of the Chagres. (Condé 1992: 12)

The racism Albert observes, in addition to the death of his first wife, irreparably damage him. However he learns more than sorrow from these events. He develops a disdain for blacks, whites, and mulattoes that confounds most analyses. Albert Louis also cultivates an overwhelming greed, the beginning of which he attributes to North Americans in the Canal Zone. It is difficult, therefore, to know where to place this isthmian worker among the pantheon of fictive Colón Men.[10] But perhaps this is Condé's objective. By writing Albert as a "mis-fit," the author does not intend him to be known completely or absolutely. The Caribbeanness she espouses through him is equally complex.

Tree of Life's Panamá Man is as equivocal as he is because of Condé's concern with multiplicity, "incoherent" identities, disorder, and memory. In response to the omnipresent image of the "messianic" Caribbean male returning from abroad to revolutionize his country, she promotes a flawed and contradictory Albert.[11] And, though her novel is putatively about the Louis family and is framed by the life and experiences of its isthmian migrant ancestor, the *process* through which Coco renders her story dramatizes a general as well as a specific history.[12]

The conflicting information gleaned from interviews and in her characterization of the Colón Man illustrates Condé's belief in the unpredictability of memory and, to a different extent, history. In explaining her exploration of these terms in her later works, she makes the following claim:

> it seems to me that I now depart from the stage of writing history and reach the stage of writing memory. You know the difference that Pierre Nora made between history and memory. He says that in history, you have a rational organization of facts. You select facts. You organize them and you try to see their meaning. On the contrary, memory is something totally disorganized; there's no rule, there's no order. It comes from all corners, and builds up, and *you have to find meaning in the complexity of things*. Also memory is not made only of the things which are supposed to be important. Memory is made of a lot of trivialities, a lot of unnecessary things. (emphasis added)[13]

Contemporary historiography has certainly progressed well beyond the simple organization of selected facts that Condé dismisses here. However, the author's complex notion of memory as a source of creative inspiration converges with current theoretical preoccupations. In an interview she says:

> history is something official. Memory is in the mind of the people. It is something which may be very minute, very unimportant, but it can change a whole life. Memory may be something very trivial, very banal. But not to the person who lives that life. (Condé 1995A: 548–49)

Condé declares her investment in writing complex memories that are significant to the lives she portrays. Her writing style and characterizations, then, reflect her desire to find meaning in the complexity of things and to understand the sometimes disparate elements at play when people and cultures come in contact.[14] Through the disorder that often frames her narratives, Condé subjects the status quo to disrupting rearrangement and challenges.

Maryse Condé challenges the conventions of Francophone Caribbean literature by foregrounding memory, disorder, gender, and geographic diversity as significant aspects of her exploration of Caribbeanness. As an example of her critical praxis, *Tree of Life* recovers cultural memories that do not mar official versions of Caribbean realities, but instead draw attention to the "untidiness" of history by placing written and oral histories and stories along side it. Women's contributions, often not included in official records, are prominently featured in *Tree of Life*. The author's project is driven by the narrator's voice and Coco's process of un-covering, discovering, and re-covering her forebear. Although Condé is offhand when she talks about why she made Albert a canal worker (below), her Panamá Man nonetheless responds to many of her writerly concerns.

II

From the first page of *Tree of Life*, the reader is forced to contend with Albert's paradoxical attributes. In the absence of a written birth certificate, the not-yet-born narrator[15] determines the Colón Man's age through "natural" means:

> the people of the plantation simply remembered his being born in the year of the terrible hurricane that downed trees and cabins from one end to the other of both Basse- and Grande-Terre and swelled to overflowing the tranquil Sanguine, which usually provided the islanders with just enough water to fill their water jars and wash their clothes nicely white. (Condé 1992: 3)

Coco defines Albert's birth in terms of a natural disaster, something uncontrollable and destructive. It is most interesting, however, that she tells us that the villagers *choose* to link his birth to the hurricane, rather than rely on a written record of it: "As everyone knows, they paid scant attention to birth certificates in those times" (ibid). The ambiguous "they" can refer to Guadeloupean whites who did not think it necessary, during the postemancipation period, to record the births of formerly enslaved people. However, the pronoun might also refer to "the people of the plantation" (the next available referent), particularly their ability to signify their own reality/realities. The latter perspective foregrounds the recording method that villages find most meaningful, one that resonates in their world.[16] The people of the plantation, therefore, accept the hurricane as a sign of Albert's birth. They also choose to "know" the event in relation to their daily lives—that is, in terms of their laundry and thirsts. The Colón

Man's birth, therefore, does not merely read as a lamentation on the hurricane's destruction; it is an arcane and mundane phenomenon of communal and individual importance.

In contrast to the destructive effects associated with the time of his birth, the next important event in Albert's life, his migration to Panamá, is recognized in opposing terms that also resonate with his neighbors. A character called Eudora traditionally celebrates Palm Sunday by reenacting Jesus' death and resurrection; Albert's migration occurs during this time and "thus the departure of [Coco's] forebear remained linked with the idea that suffering precedes a very great happiness" (4). Coco again conceives of her forebear in relation to incongruities: the death of Jesus Christ, Eudora's simulated death, and their rebirths, "after which the entire village would gather in [Eudora's] hut to celebrate" (ibid). Finally, Coco's description of Albert and his migration concludes with her relation of a fact of his birth: Albert was born with a caul (5). A familiar phenomenon in various folkloric traditions, children born with cauls are said to have the gift of "second sight"; considering these in relation to Albert and his equivocal persona, one can imagine the Panamá Man as embodying a vision of/for his family.

While the Colón Man is a recurrent figure in Caribbean literature, he is often not central to texts in which he appears. Nevertheless, *Tree of Life's* Colón Man serves a vital narrative role. He imbues the text with isthmian mythographies, inserting a productive tension within a novel that pivots around creative disorder. Coco's reconstruction of her forebear's legacy duplicates the productive cacophony initiated by him. The narrator's recollections of the Colón Man are shaped by both imagination and memory; both forms allow her to bring together significant pieces of his story.

I see some of Coco's contributions as memory because they can be traced to a source, such as interviews with prostitutes who knew her great-uncle Bert (78). She also makes use of written documents, such as letters, receipts, and contracts (Albert's ICC contract, for example [9]) to reclaim her ancestor. Such tangible pieces are often made known through an "omniscient" narrative voice, one less personal than Coco's other voice (for example, the former does not use "my" to refer to Albert as forebear). The presence of traceable pieces of the forebear's history, read in conjunction with Coco's imaginable truths about him, not only weaves together the real and the imaginable but also affirms the interpretive authority of the latter. Imaginable possibilities come into play when traceable pieces are not present, such as when the narrator recounts conversations between Albert and other characters, all of which occur before she is born. Although readers can assume that Coco has done her homework, the novel does not substantiate this assumption; accordingly, Coco's memories and imaginings are all self-validating. They are true because they are possible.

Through Coco's omniscient voice, readers are made aware of a conversation between young Albert and a returned Panamá migrant named Samuel that catapults the forebear off the Boyer-de-l'Etang plantation. Samuel says:

> the Americans were afraid of nothing. Now they were tampering with the very structure of the world and cutting continents in two. In Panama they were digging a canal that would allow their ships to sail more quickly from New York to San Francisco on the Pacific coast and were sending out a call to workers from around the world. To this superhuman end they had set up a hiring hall in the very center of La Savane in Fort-de-France. Two thousand seven hundred and eighty men had already left. (Condé 1992: 7)

Samuel's comments insert into the fictional world of the novel certain verifiable historical truths.[17] Yet the conversation is one to which the narrator could not have had access (Albert is still single, therefore has not yet sired the line that will produce Coco). This mix of history and fiction shapes the way readers "know" Colón Man Albert Louis, not in a mere linear fashion but as one reconstructed through various forms of official and unofficial histories, as well as through "personal," "remembered," and invented stories.

Albert's characterization thus far speaks volumes: he embodies the unpredictability of nature and the banality of people's everyday lives. Through Condé's representation of Coco's re-creative process, the reader witnesses the convergence of imaginable truths, unofficial and official narratives of Guadeloupe's contribution to canal construction, as well as the author's writerly interventions. Albert is not intended to be "an exemplary hero devised to teach lessons" (Pfaff 1996: 70) or an idealized Guadeloupean subject; instead, the mixture of features that distinguish him encourages readers to appreciate who he is, flaws and all, and acknowledge his complicated influence on his progeny.

Albert's work in the Canal Zone appears to cultivate his most vicissitudinous features, for they become most evident while he works there. His spirit is irreparably damaged by the racism he experiences in Panamá and later in San Francisco. This spiritual/psychic damage manifests itself mentally, but Albert's wounds are further inscribed on his body, a body that simultaneously signifies his status as a Panamá Man. Since working in Panamá, Albert always wears a black serge suit, black patent-leather boots, and a Panamá hat (Condé 1992: 23). But unlike the myth of the dandified Colón Man, Albert's tailor-made wardrobe projects a more dignified carriage and signals his wealth.

Beneath his this dignified façade, however, the Colón Man's body, specifically his damaged leg, denotes a more troubled isthmian reality. Motivated by a nascent Pan-Africanist consciousness, Albert avenges blacks' suffering upon the body of a white prostitute (one for whom he is a regular customer); he beats her while shouting "Devil! You belong to the race of devils! But we'll be rid of you someday!" (37). And because

> neither the American nor the Panamanian administration appeared to react quickly enough [in carrying out a just punishment,] one night some men attacked Albert, leaving him unable to move on the dirty bed of empty bottles that clogged the mud streets of Colón. Somehow Albert managed to avoid being taken to the hospital. . . . *Throughout his life Albert would suffer pain from the aftereffects of his wounds and fractures.* (37, 38, emphasis added)

The beating does not help Albert recognize the flaws in the way he acts on his black consciousness; instead, the attack leaves scars that constantly remind him—not of his behavior—but of the humiliations he has suffered because of his race and color. Yet his humiliations and their physical reminders do not lessen his contempt for black people or his thirst for money. Albert wears his canal experiences on his body as a display of his personal contradictions; his work in the Canal Zone, it seems, is a fitting vehicle through which the Panamá Man's contradictions are manifested since his migration is cast as salvation and hell.[18]

Early on, the Colón Man demonstrates a contradiction in the way he perceives and responds to the traditions of peoples of color. After his beating, he relies on and commits himself to herbal cures:

> since he seemed to be on the verge of death, Centinela [one of his mortuary business partners] went to the San Blas Indians at Limon Bay and brought back armloads of leaves, roots, and dried plants from which she concocted potions, unguents, and poultices. . . . As the decoctions of passionflower root had done him the greatest good, flushing the bad humor from his blood, he was careful to plant some wherever he lived. The passionflower displays a mauve and lightly perfumed bloom that has little medicinal value. It is the branches and above all the roots that do the healing. (38)

Previously, however, he is adamant in refusing Mama Beah's offer of similar treatments for his first wife. When Liza falls sick:

> Mama Beah, who had seen such things before, offered to treat her with herbs, but Albert lost his temper. . . .
> "You niggers, still sticking to your leaves and roots! Your plasters and poultices! That's why the white man walks all over you. Haven't you seen the Americans' doctors?" (19)

Coco never makes an issue of Albert's shifting attitudes, though her previous descriptions of the forebear prime readers to expect such inconsistencies. In fact, rather than a discussion that would reconcile Albert's contrary response to herbal treatments, Coco offers us additional complications.

Albert's rejection of Mama Beah's remedies stems from his belief in the superiority of whiteness. The quasi-omniscient narrator simultaneously reveals that although Beah and members of her community value their traditions, they so strongly believe in the differences between whiteness and blackness that they reject useful advancements initiated by officials of the Isthmian Canal Commission. Thus readers cannot judge Albert without also questioning his community's different, but equally disturbing, position. After Liza falls ill and Albert rejects Mama Beah's help, the Colón Man's Panamá community asks:

> what did [Albert] think his wife was going to bring into the world? A white baby, perhaps? It's not good to forget what color you are. It was like that cradle he bought from a Chinaman in Colón and covered with a square of netting, as the Americans recommended be done. Foolishness! Foolishness and pretension, all of it! (15)

The use of mosquito netting to arrest the spread of malaria and yellow fever was well known among sanitation officials on the isthmus, putting Albert at the forefront of modern medical science.[19] However, his disdain for his peers as well as for their traditions makes his behavior appear pretentious rather than enlightened. The Colón Man's poor relationship to other Caribbean people in Panamá coincides with a community whose awareness of sanitary advancements is sorely lacking. What begins as a difference of opinion gets tied up with issues of inculcated racism/inferiority and ends as a personality trait later in Albert's life.

The Colón Man's "contempt" for black people might better be described as his inability to separate the people from their circumstances. In his desire to escape poverty, racism, and oppression, conditions he understands as the lot of black people because of slavery and colonialism, Albert conflates the people with their oppressive circumstances. He says as much to his mother after Liza dies:

> I wanted to take [Liza] far from Gatun. Gatun is mud, mud and affliction, mud and sickness. I heard it said the American white men were digging the Canal—a thing the French white men couldn't do—to show that they're the greatest of all the whites. But let me tell you, it's our hands, our gorilla paws they call them, that're doing the work. Doing the digging. Doing the cutting. Doing the hauling. Putting it together piece by piece. Mama, I met Negroes there who talk English, who talk Portuguese, Spanish, who talk Dutch! But the common language, Mama, is poverty! So, I wanted to take her far from Gatun, here maybe, and give her own house on the hill. (Condé 1992: 25–26)

In Albert, then, is an inseparable mix of an autodidact's Pan-Africanism and Marxism as well as an insightful race consciousness, all learned from his personal experiences on the isthmus.

His personal insights find a powerful incarnation in the figure of Marcus Garvey, whom Albert first hears speak at a rally on the isthmus. The activist's speech exposes Albert to philosophies that profoundly influence his life. After this event, he no longer drowns his sorrow over Liza's death in rum and prostitutes, but instead loses himself in the study of math and the natural sciences. He incorporates Garvey's teachings into his personal philosophy, committing his favorite phrase to memory: "I shall teach the Black Man to see beauty in himself" (34).[20] But like his self-imposed abstinence, Albert's solidarity with "the Black Man" cannot withstand his body's other needs. The Panamá Man resumes his visits to his favorite prostitute then (as previously mentioned) assaults her in a fit of Pan-Africanist fury. Albert's racial consciousness and self-schooling also give way to his desire for wealth, however he can accumulate it.

Louis's tenure in Panamá teaches him to be a great businessman, that is if "great" is defined in terms of the ability to make money. He not only recognizes the ways the Americans capitalize on black labor; he emulates them. As a mortician, Albert profits from "work accidents, epidemics, and delirium tremens" on the isthmus (31); this venture ends abruptly after a period of anti–West Indian violence (41) that drives Albert to San Francisco, where he enters into the laundry business:

> Albert entered into partnership with Chi Lu Lee, the proprietor of a laundry on Washington Street. The entire trade of washing and ironing laundry was run by the Chinese, who trotted from house to house, their baskets on their backs. But Albert had ideas. It was not for nothing that he had gotten the hang of such things in Panama! He pushed Chi Lu Lee into buying a horse, all skin and bones, and a cart for delivering the laundry; now they were always ahead of their competitors. . . . Chi Lu Lee employed three "brothers," paying each one no more than a bowl of rice and five bowls of tea. Albert took on three more, and eliminated the rice. (44–45)

Louis subsequently parlays his Panamanian and San Franciscan successes into flourishing import/export and real estate businesses in Guadeloupe. He builds a tenement yard to house country folk seeking work in the city. The altruism implied by this real estate venture is immediately negated by Albert's failure to maintain his property and his lack of sympathy for his impoverished tenants. Although the project gives him the reputation of a slumlord and exploiter of "the people," he is also celebrated for being the dark-skinned, uneducated man who broke into a business world that was once restricted to Guadeloupe's light-skinned, educated elite. Ironically, his color and lack of education make him a pariah among the class to which his money and businesses give him access. Condé's representation of Albert's diverse traits prevents readers from consolidating his character, therefore his persona, evolving out of his personal affronts and financial motivations, extends into his family tree.

For most of Albert's descendants, particularly his son Jacob and granddaughter Thécla, the Colón Man's reality and motivations remain mysteries. Jacob, Thécla's father, builds upon Albert's financial success and assumes his father's Pan-Africanism; the son's birthright also includes the Colón Man's physical and mental agonies. Thécla, however, fails to apprehend her grandfather's legacy and translates this incomprehension into a confused relationship to her family and its middle-class way of life. But because healing can come from a knowledge of (the passionflower's) branches and roots (38), we anticipate different trajectories for Albert's son and granddaughter. But their shared disaffection from Albert leads to tumultuous lives that postpone the satisfaction of this healing.

The uniqueness of Coco's mediation of her forebear's legacy is best revealed in contrast to its impact on two of Albert's other descendants. Jacob, Albert's first son with his second wife Elaïse, and Thécla, Jacob and Ultima's (called "Tima") only child, know the forebear more intimately than Coco; their knowledge, however, does not offer either of them the insight the narrator achieves. Jacob succeeds Albert in the family business and is a direct heir to the latter's black consciousness and failed dreams. The son, however, improves upon his father's financial success and is a committed, though overbearing, family man where Albert's self-involvement prevents him from being a father to his children. Thécla is spoiled by her father and socially isolated by her mother's chauvinisms. Through both parents, Thécla learns to be arrogant toward and intolerant of almost everyone. She gains a desire to work for "the people" from her uncle Jean, but rather than becoming liberated by it, she is thrown into a confusion that ends with her desertion of Guadeloupe and marriage to the white "enemy." Condé dramatizes Thécla's confusion through the character's sexual relationships and grandiose but inchoate literary projects. Jacob and Thécla assume Albert's dreams, disappointments, and complications, and nuance them in their own peculiar ways. They do not, however, benefit from the forebear's complexities as Coco does.

Jacob becomes most important to Coco's retelling of the Louis's history when he replaces a clerk in his father's store. Hating his unapproachable father, Jacob believes he will equally despise Albert's business. This turns out to be a monumentally false assumption; Jacob surpasses Albert in his business acumen as well as in the abuse of his economic power. The younger Louis "did not know that [Albert's "hot odorous lair"] was as well the temple of a god to whom, like Albert, even more than Albert, he also would become a devotee: money!" (Condé 1992: 97). At eighteen, Jacob "improved" the tenement yard by partitioning rooms in two, thereby doubling the number of tenants as well as his rental income. He sinks this profit into farmland where he grows staple crops for his family and sells the excess.

Guadeloupe's governor recognizes Jacob's financial achievements and invites him on an economic mission to New York (121). When the young Louis tells his father about the trip, Albert is most interested in the opportunity to correspond with Marcus Garvey. The contents of this letter, in addition to the results of its delivery, confirm that Jacob is truly his father's son; he reenacts Albert's obsession with Garveyism. Jacob delivers the letter to UNIA headquarters in Harlem on the day of Garvey's death and learns, via Brother Ben, about "torture, lynchings, and segregation . . . ," an education that takes this Louis along the "long march of his newfound brothers from the plantation to the ghetto" (129).

Jacob takes Albert's consciousness one step further and forms the "Negroes Arise Party" upon his return to Guadeloupe. "The party's program was rather vague. It could be summed up in Marcus Garvey's splendid phrase: 'I shall teach the Black Man to see beauty in himself'" (132). Again like Albert, Jacob's dreams and aspiration for "the Black Man" are literally beaten out of him. When news of the "Negroes Arise Party" spreads, Jacob and the Louis family are universally and publicly castigated. His business practices are scrutinized, his family's (that is, Albert's) exploits are rehashed, and, at a sparsely attended party rally, Jacob is stoned (134). Jacob

> learned his lesson. He set aside his fine ideas and let Tima lecture him:
> "Go on, if you're dying to die! If you want to leave me with a fatherless child!" . . .
> He cared about nothing now but making money, even more money, and spoiling his Thécla. . . .
> He never complained. He confided in no one. Nevertheless all those who gazed into his eyes knew that in those waters a great dream had drowned! (134)

In his renewed dedication to family rather than politics (though his financial ambitions are a constant), Jacob strengthens his relationship with his younger brother Jean, and together they try to work through the mystery surrounding the suicide of Bert (their half brother) and his erasure from the family record.[21] Yet his financial ambitions and greed predictably undermine this commitment. Jacob's trip to France, his attempt to gather news about Bert and Bert's son, ends abruptly when

> a registered letter brought him news that a fire had broken out in the tenement yard! In those days fires were a common occurrence in La Pointe. Not a Lent went by without fire breaking out in the working-class districts! So Ja-

cob could have slept easily if that fire had not caused the death of an entire family. . . .
   Once more, the left- and right-wing newspapers joined in an attack on those black Shylocks who were drinking the blood of their brothers and had had the nerve, sometime earlier, to try to pass themselves off as defenders of the race. Jacob's assistant, insulted, threatened, and for days on end forced to keep the dockside store's steel curtain lowered, begged him to come home. (171–72)

Once recalled to Guadeloupe, Jacob never again tries to find his half brother and nephew. Undoubtedly the unresolved relationship between Jacob's economic goals and his dedication to "family" (his Guadeloupean and diasporic African ones) prevent him from facing his personal responsibility to the exiled Bert and Bébert.

Thécla is like her father in that she is unsuccessful in profiting from her own and her family's intricate histories and stories; her journey, however, is geographically and physically wide-ranging. Thécla attempts to resolve her contradictions geographically (she travels to and studies in France, England, the United States, Jamaica, Haiti, and Guadeloupe), intellectually (she begins, but never completes, several dissertations on black peoples: "The Influence of the Harlem Renaissance on the Intellectuals of Haiti" among others), and sexually (through her men: Gesner Ambroise, Denis Latran [a middle-class mulatto and Coco's father], Manuel Pastor [whose father's life was similar to Albert's (192)], Earl Pastor [Manuel's brother], Terrence Cliff-Brownson, and ultimately her white French husband Pierre Lavasseur). Thécla's search ends with the white man because, through this union, she relinquishes all responsibility to "the people": "all [she] wants is to live [her] own life! Not all among us are a royal ceiba tree meant only to provide shade for others!" (226).

The tone that Coco uses to retell her mother's story is various: it reflects the yearning as well as the hatred felt by an abandoned and unloved child, and it traces the emergence of learned insight that finally allows her some compassion. The narrator says:

> my mother possessed neither my forebear's helpless desire to serve, nor my grandfather's muddled sensitivity and humility; even less the generous and naïve idealism of my great-uncle Jean. She was arrogant because [of] self-doubting. Pretending to disdain the esteem of the bourgeoisie since she knew she could never earn it. An outsider due to an excess of ambitions impossible to satisfy! For me, my mother was a sham! (174)

Coco traces Thécla's conflicted self to the childhood where it takes shape. Jacob and Tima's pampering of their only child makes her unfit for society; both her schoolmates and teachers find her unbearable. In turn, Thécla holds others—her fellow Guadeloupeans—in contempt because, in effect, she is taught to do so. "At enormous expense," readers learn, "[Jacob] would buy [Thécla] French apples or Muscat grapes, so that the little girl remained unaware of the bananas and mangoes that grew on trees to feed the hunger of underprivileged children her own age" (142). Thécla's loathing of Guadeloupe also stems from the rigid order imposed on her young life by her protective parents. Their desire to shield her from the world leaves her little to do but fear, and as a response to this fear, develop contempt for everything outside of her limited experience. From this closed world, Thécla wages her attack against her parents and family who she holds responsible for her dark skin; she is consumed by contempt for Guadeloupeans, and her own unattainable social aspirations. This same family perversely fosters in Thécla a commitment to "the people." After proclaiming herself the (metaphorical) murderer of her parents, Thécla says:

> They made me ashamed. I blamed them for being too black. Being uneducated. My mother didn't know anything about anything. She could only talk about her recipes and her dreams. "To make *dombwé* and peas, you take . . ." And at the same time she thought of herself as sprung from the thigh of Jupiter. Because of her money she had contempt for everyone. As for him, as for him . . ." (205)

Escape from this world is foremost in Thécla's mind; her desire to flee indicates that she cannot appreciate, hence wants to erase, the vagaries of the Louises' lived realities.

Thécla identifies and soundly rejects her family's faults, yet she is unable to recognize their strengths. By her own estimation, Thécla's mother, as black as her daughter and additionally "handicapped" by her lack of education, can think of herself as "sprung from the thigh of Jupiter." Still readers cannot uncritically celebrate Tima's sense of self, for she is contemptuous of those less successful than herself. Nor can we simply castigate Thécla, because we see her behavior in a broader context. The path to her ultimate humiliation—her failed affair with upper-class and light-skinned Denis Latran (he refuses to marry her) and the child conceived from it—begins with her flight from her own family. Thécla's unresolved familial conflict ends with a patriarchal, patronizing white man. Perhaps because of her status as "illegitimate" and her place in the Louis family tree, Coco is the repository of the clan's most contradictory features; yet these features allow her to make sense of her birthright where Jacob, Thécla, and even Albert cannot.

Coco introduces herself rather straightforwardly: "I, Claude Elaïse Louis, was born in secret at a small private hospital in the fifteenth arrondissement of Paris, on the night of April 23, 1960" (Condé 1992: 185). The factors that contribute to her conception, however, are not so simple.

She is the result of Thécla's desperation to enter into Guadeloupe's bourgeois society, denied her because of her color and peasant ancestry. Coco, therefore, symbolizes her mother's failure and embodies her mother's social ambition and her hatred for/envy of Denis Latran and his kind. In order to "find" her self (Coco is "lost" because she is exists outside of the Louises' world), Coco has to collect and recompose the life experiences of family members. It is telling, then, that *Coco* is the Louis who brings Bert and Bébert back to Guadeloupe; as outsiders, they each suffer most from the Louis's idiosyncrasies. Through Coco, the two branches of the Louis clan are finally combined. They are not "blended" or otherwise brought together in a way that would erase the particulars of their stories; rather Coco brings Bert and Bébert home, exposing the Louises' role in their "murder" and adding them to the ancestral record. Coco's process begins with Thécla, whose internal conflict Coco blames on her great-uncle Jean: "great-uncle Jean [is] responsible for the confusion that reigns in [Thécla's] head, for those contradictions she was never able to resolve between her disdain for the people, her fierce desire for social advancement, and her dreams of Negro liberation" (174).

III

Three generations of Louises (Bert, Jacob and Bébert, Thécla) receive Albert's legacy and duplicate it in their unique, though equally troubled ways. Claude Elaïse Louis, on the other hand, recounts a different, less troubled story and she wants to tell it differently. What she uncovers about Albert assists her process. Where Coco begins by *discovering* and *retelling* the Louises' histories and stories, she (and the novel) ends when she *claims* them. She ingeniously tells the tale of her people by using visual, oral, and written records, versions of official and unofficial histories, memory, and imaginable truths. Because she avails herself of such a polyphony of narratives, the reader is not inclined to interpret any one of them as *the* best feature through which the Louises can be revealed. And even though the story begins with Albert, Coco does not recount a patriarch's legacy. The narrator's inheritance is best revealed, then, through Coco's recuperative process. Her strategy encourages the consideration of all details, whether large, small, or inconsequential, for they all nourish her family's tree.[22] Condé reveals her commitment to alternative histories and memory through Coco's genealogical method.

The narrator's project is imbricated in a postcolonial literary tradition of protagonists on identity quests, both personal and national. But unlike most protagonists in this tradition, Coco does not compose a "whole truth" from the various fragments that make up the lives of her people.[23]

She cannot resolve anyone's conflict, neither can she form a coherent identity for herself. Such a whole is denied by the varied aspects of her story, and by the methods she uses to tell it. What the narrator can do is establish her place among the Louises, a family she understands because she accepts and reflects their complexities.

Condé's manipulation of narrative voice in *Tree of Life* demands that readers struggle with the multivoiced way in which Coco tells the Louises' contradictory tales. The author's interest in memory as oppositional history allows her to move beyond official versions of the truth that ignore or devalue what may be the most meaningful parts of an individual's life. Memory and alternative truths are therefore Coco's primary means of recovery and the novel's complex structure exemplifies how Coco tells her story "differently."

The novel appears to proceed in a linear fashion, beginning with Albert and moving through to Coco. But the Panamá Man's story is refracted through Coco, an indication that the narrative unfolds from the "end" to the "beginning." This trajectory is further complicated because Coco is not "born" until 185 pages into the novel. Thus readers cannot consider the Louises' experiences as cause-and-effect. Condé, therefore, upsets a "patriarchal" history of the family that only recognizes as worthwhile events that relate to the forebear's reality. Nor can we say that Coco is who she is because Albert was who he was. She uniquely locates herself among the Louises and, by the end of the novel, the narrator is more than the sum of her forebears' experiences.

Coco's perspicacity stems not only from the self-reliance developed in response to her abandonment by her mother. She has also developed special insight from her childhood experience; Coco does not learn to read or write until she is about fourteen years old. This lack puts established ways of knowing and doing beyond her. She says:

> having passed my twelfth birthday, I barely knew how to read and write. I was equally murdering three languages. . . . Therefore I was handed over to Madame Lafleur, a retired teacher of exceptional quality who had worked wonders with retarded children. (Condé 1992: 296)

The strength of Lafleur's teaching skills notwithstanding, Coco remains so stubbornly illiterate that her inability to read is classified as a disability. However, Coco's achievements in the novel recast her peculiar literacy as a successful strategy. Her ways of knowing are informal and disorderly, but creatively so. Teacher Lafleur, or Friend Antonine as Coco calls her, attempts to teach the girl to add in the following manner: "1 sunflower + 2 geraniums/3 thistles + 4 daises/5 cornflowers + 6 jonquils . . ." Coco quickly gives up on this type of aptitude:

Alas, to such a point would I lose my way in this bed of flowers never seen and never smelled that Friend Antonine gathered up her courage in both hands, and . . . wrote to my grandfather Jacob that I needed the attentions of a specially trained instructor. In France, perhaps? While waiting for my . . . grandfather to . . . have a serious talk with [Thécla], I was free to devote time to my passion: the search for Bébert. (296–97)

Coco rejects Lafleur's education because it is delivered through an irrelevant, foreign cultural context. Freed from such lessons, the narrator can trace her "illegitimate"/illegitmate's history.

Coco finally learns her lessons, but under the instruction of Aurélia Louis, who, we soon learn, is Coco's relative. Aurélia is also a special education teacher. Aurélia's lessons, like Coco's informal ones, are "special" because Coco finds them both personal and relevant. Aurélia helps Coco learn her lessons, and in a "special" and more palatable manner than Madame Lafleur could offer. Coco validates this form of education, saying:

it is my unforeseen—yet no doubt foretold somewhere—meeting in a dreary dungeon of a special school with Aurélia Louis that healed me, that unstopped my stopped-up ears, that unsealed my sealed lips and set free, high and clear, the song of my muffled voice. For it took us quite a lot of nerve, and the voicing of it, to merge our knowledge and set it in order, to compare it, to fill in the holes, to deduce, to infer, to understand why two dead men were absent from the roll call of our name. Two dead men. Two suicides. (323–24)

Bert and Bébert's inclusion in Coco's story transforms her recounting of Albert's legacy.

The narrator returns to Guadeloupe at the request of her grandfather; he is recovering from an illness and wants to ensure that he see her at least one more time. In a conversation between the two, Coco responds to Jacob in a way that suggests a break from her family's conflicted relationships with "the people" and their people. Lamenting his political failure, Jacob tells his granddaughter:

"In this country they don't want the Negroes to succeed! Up until this very day it's in the cane they want to see them, the straw *bakoua* hat on their heads!"

[Coco] dared to suggest:

"Maybe they can't accept Negroes doing what the others do, walking all over their fellow man to succeed?"

At which his mouth fell open, and then he groaned:

"Where did you get that nonsense? Coco, you've really changed! Have you, too, started in to reading that Marx?" (344–45)

Neither Albert nor Jacob can reconcile their desire for wealth with the vicissitudes of their black consciousness. Thécla's reconciliation of her ambitions is indefinitely deferred by her marriage to a doting and rich white man. Coco's daring response to her grandfather, while not offering a definitive answer (she does, after all, pose it as a question), is the first sign of a revision of Albert's legacy; it intimates another possible way of living it. Jacob's failure to understand his granddaughter confirms the distinction between Coco and previous Louises; it does not occur to him that there are innumerable ways to succeed and definitions of success, different from his chosen path and his kind of success. The narrator's perspective, that is her experience with oppositional rules and ways of knowing, enables a vision that permits the above rejoinder. Finally, she can claim and validate her own reality.

Coco's handling of Albert's inheritance, declared obliquely in her conversation with her grandfather, is more forcefully related below. She recounts her histories, in an almost uninterrupted stream of words, to a woman who asks who she is. She declares:

> "I am the illegitimate daughter of Thécla, herself the legitimate and much-desired daughter of Tima and Jacob, Jacob himself the favorite son on the one side, unloved on the other, of Bonnemama Elaïse, known as God's Own Child, and of Albert, called the *Soubarou*, who went off to sweat away his sweat and toil his toil in Panama in order to earn some gold and learn that when it comes right down to it, it buys nothing!"
>
> And I left her lost in speculation. I, I was no longer ashamed. I had planted my flag on the island. (Condé 1992: 351)

Significantly, this is not a literal recounting of the Louis's lineage. It diverges with Coco's claim that "when it comes right down to it, [gold] buys nothing." As in her conversation with Jacob, Coco offers a previously unheard of finale. Her revision of her forebear's story, the primacy of gold to his vision, demonstrates that his experience, more than Thécla and Jacob's and even more than her recovery of Bert and Bébert, seems to enable her acceptance of the family's histories.

At its conclusion, *Tree of Life* reveals a subjectivity in Coco that resembles, yet is distinct from that of other members of the Louis clan. Abruptly, Gesner (Thécla's first lover) entreats Coco to do her part with regard to blacks' liberation. He asks her to contribute her talents, as other Louises have tried to do. His speech encourages Coco to do what the novel has already achieved. Gesner says to her:

> And you, too, you can, you must do something. You don't know it yet, and I can't show you the way, I who haven't gone to all those schools. . . . I'd say it's hardly begun. The entire field remains to be deciphered, with its weeds,

its Guinea grass and its touch-me-nots clawing at the ankles. We, we're weary. The villainess has beat us. But you, you are the child of our tomorrows. Think about it! (367)

Coco acknowledges Gesner's charge by tracking through her perplexing heritage:

> I found nothing to say, inwardly rebellious and fearful at the promise he was attempting to wrest from me. The role he meant to burden me with. The task he meant to assign me. Sensing nevertheless in the secret of my heart that my soon-to-be adult age, once the tribute to my dead was paid, would be unable to escape it.
> And anyway, how could I deny the blood of my entire ancestry—and this is the other aspect of this story, my story—beginning with my forebear Albert with his fine teeth made for devouring the world, he who left to sweat out his sweat in Panama and raise gold only to realize when all is said and done that gold buys nothing. From Albert up to my mother, yes, even she, especially she, who bled from all her failures and was consumed by all her disillusions before taking refuge on the far side of the world. And not forgetting my poor grandfather Jacob, bound to the floor of his shop. And my great-uncle, my great-uncle Jean patriot hero martyr, who bounteous blood had permeated out land . . . ? (367–68)

Tree of Life ends with this ellipse. Although my chapter cannot simulate this ending, it is an aptly inconclusive conclusion to the preceding discussion. Condé intends to write a Guadeloupean story that is concerned with its process and memories rather than its end. Invested in this manner of discovery, the author draws on countless narratives because this kind of process best articulates a Caribbean lived reality in its documentable as well as its imaginable and transformative effects.

IV

Comparing the title of the French edition of Condé's novel, *La vie scélérate* (1987), to its English translation helps to introduce the competing and coexistent complexities central to her use of the figure of the Colón Man. *La vie scélérate* translates as the wicked or wretched life, a meaning/attitude not immediately invoked by the phrase "tree of life." Condé asserts that *Tree of Life* was packaged to sell in a U.S. market. One can appreciate the marketing benefits of such a strategy; however, the author objected to the way the "exotic" color and art on the book's cover,[24] along with its English title—insofar as *Tree of Life* is "A Novel of the Caribbean"—relegate the novel and its author to a "part of the world where life is supposed to be more colorful than in the USA" (Condé 1993A: 697). The world to which the novel's North American packaging consigns it is, presumably, less complicated than the United States. This renaming of the novel represents the imposition of a single, foreign reality upon the complicated lived reality of the region. The French title, however, more closely captures Condé's goals for the novel.

In response to a question derived from a literal translation of the French ("Why is life wicked?"), Condé says:

> you never get from life what you expect. When you do make some gains, you realize how much more is missing that you will never acquire. These are the vicious circles that make life so wicked, *secerat* [Creole spelling], as my mother used to say. (Clark 1988: 133)

The word *secerat* and the author's elaboration on the French title illustrate her attempt to fictionalize the complexity of (the Louises') lives and highlight her investment in lives that are particularly meaningful in a Caribbean context. Condé's invocation of her mother and her use of "a common proverb in Guadeloupean creole" (Pfaff 1996: 69) suggest that these lives are undoubtedly, and culturally, Guadeloupean. As such, the author opposes the notion of a merely paradisiacal Caribbean and, by extension, of equally simplistic subjectivities.

The lives revealed by Coco Louis's reproduction are both wicked and benevolent; furthermore, the narrator's process underscores the plurality of the lives treated in the novel. *Tree of Life* contains multiple lives—at least those of Coco's great-grandfather Albert, her grandfather Jacob, her mother Thécla, as well as her own. The plurality even extends further, into a broader Caribbean context, because *Tree of Life* is, after all, *A Novel of the Caribbean*. Coco's telling and retelling of the Louis genealogy, a reflection of Condé's investment in memory and disorder (not to mention the writer's determination to counter simplistic images of the Caribbean), nicely complements Albert Louis's role in the novel. The process through which Coco reconstitutes her lineage mirrors the piecing together of Caribbean laborers' isthmian mythographies. Albert similarly reflects these complex processes; his character reflects many of the features of historical as well as fictive Panamá narratives. The factually irreconcilable—but imaginarily real—features of Albert's self and life, not to mention those of his descendants, direct one's attention to the process through which Coco reveals her forebear's realities. Though the protagonist traces her lineage back to its putative origin, her forebear remains an obscure focal point. Thus Coco comes to know and claim her self and her family, not through her identification of Albert Louis, but through her discovery of him, in all his impenetrabilities.[25] Coco's achievement, as a consequence, is in her examination of rather than conclusions about Albert's legacy.

NOTES

1. Maryse Condé, *Tree of Life: A Novel of the Caribbean*, translated by Victoria Reiter (New York: Ballantine Books, 1992); Condé, "Order, Disorder, Freedom, and the West Indian Writer," *Yale French Studies* 83.2 (1993): 121–35; A. James Arnold, "The Novelist as Critic," *World Literature Today* 67.4 (Autumn 1993): 711–16.
2. "Maryse Condé: Unraveling the Unexplored," *Essence Magazine* 23.10 (February 1993): 52.
3. Maryse Condé, "'I Have Made Peace with My Island': An Interview with Maryse Condé," interviewed by VéVé Clark, *Callaloo* 12.1 (1988): 91. Françoise Pfaff, *Conversations with Maryse Condé* (Lincoln: University of Nebraska Press, 1996).
4. Maryse Condé, "The Role of the Writer," *World Literature Today* 67.4 (Autumn 1993): 697–98, cited in the text as (Condé 1993A).
5. Maryse Condé, "No Silence: An Interview with Maryse Condé," interviewed by Barbara Lewis, *Callaloo* 18.3 (1995): 545, cited in the text as (Condé 1995A).
6. One can also read Condé's lack of specificity as examples of her deliberate unreliability. She is similarly hard to pin down on her views on a Caribbean audience (whether or not she has an audience in mind while she is writing) and her belief in solidarity among peoples in the African diaspora (Condé says this is impossible, yet she advocates a Pan-West Indian identity [Condé 1993A: 698n17]). I have found other inconsistencies, but the above are most significant to this study.
7. Condé says "in a Bambara myth of origin, after the creation of the earth, and the organization of everything on its surface, disorder was introduced by a woman. Disorder meant the power to create new objects and to modify the existing ones. In a word, disorder meant creativity" (Condé 1993: 130). I discuss more thoroughly how the author manages disorder and defines memory in the text.
8. Albert Louis is the youngest son of Mano and Théodora. He meets Liza in Panamá and they have one son, Bert. With his second wife, Elaïse Sophocle, forebear Albert fathers Jacob, Serge, René, and Jean. Jacob marries Ultima Lemercier; their daughter is Thécla Elaïse Jeanne Louis. Thécla has a child with Denis Latran, and this child is Claude Elaïse "Coco" Louis. Turning to another branch of the Louis family, Bert has a child (who he also names Albert [called Bébert]) with a white Frenchwoman named Marie. Bébert and Lucette Legendre have one daughter, Aurélia Louis, who meets Coco in France and acquaints her with this previously unknown branch of the Louis family.
9. Eileen Southern's *The Music of Black Americans: A History, 3rd Edition* (New York: W. W. Norton, 1997). Although Southern documents African American musical traditions from 1619 to 1996, her descriptions of songs of narration/social comment and work songs are applicable here. Through songs of narration, enslaved people could "comment on their problems . . . they could voice their despair and hopes" (156); these types of songs could also sum up the things enslaved people most hated such as minor irritations, dread at not meeting deadlines, tortures, or the auction block (160). She posits that work songs were primarily intended to persuade workers to work quickly (making the rhythm of the songs more important than the lyrics), but they also alleviated the monotony of their tasks. These songs were particularly useful with gang labor, when the required

work needed workers to act in unison and when workers, ending their workdays, gathered on their ways home. Thus work songs and songs of narration/social comment can be said to embrace a collective experience. I want to thank folklorist Nomalanga Dalili, Ph.D., for directing me to Southern's book.

10. Condé's isthmian migrant shares, to some degree, features of canal workers who appear in previous chapters. Like George Lamming's Pa (*In the Castle of My Skin*) and Michael Thelwell's Nattie (*The Harder They Come*), Louis has a sense of his worth human worth. He shares with Claude McKay's Tack Tally (*Banana Bottom*), Olive Senior's Devonshire ("Window"), and Eric Walrond's Poyah ("Panama Gold") financial success and clothes, and their transgressive attitudes as well. Condé's Colón Man projects the dignified carriage that characterizes Pa and Nattie, and he is successful in business like Nattie and Poyah. In the denigrating features of his experience on the isthmus Albert mirrors the portrayal of Walrond's Ballet in "Subjection." Finally, Albert subscribes to the teachings of Marcus Garvey, as does Maas' Nattie, and he is as politically astute as Pa.

11. If "it is an accepted fact that French Caribbean literature was born with *Négritude* during the 1930s," this philosophy marks the moment when Francophone Caribbean literature's interpretive community took shape. "Language and Power: Words as Miraculous Weapons," *CLA Journal* 39.1 (September 1995): 19. In an earlier essay, Condé lists the de facto rules for West Indian literature that evolved out of this movement, as well as Marxist/social realist philosophies, as follows:

1. Individualism was chastised. Only the collectivity had the right to express itself.
2. The masses were the sole producers of Beauty, and the poet had to take inspiration from them.
3. The main, if not the sole, purpose of writing was to denounce one's political and social conditions, and in so doing, to bring about one's liberation.
4. Poetic and political ambition were one and the same. (Condé 1993: 123)

These guidelines were revised, to reflect a specifically Caribbean focus, after the success of Jacques Roumain's *Masters of the Dew* (1941. New York: Collier Books, 1971). This novel, Condé claims, "established a model which is still largely undisputed to this day." A minor revision of these rules occurred, dictating that West Indian literature should be set only on one Caribbean island, depict a male protagonist who seeks to redeem his society and who is assisted by a fertile, but desexualized female (126). Edouard Glissant contributes his notion of *antillanté*, and Jean Bernabé et al. adds *créolité* to the above criteria; both additions speak to characterization and language in West Indian literature.

Condé finds such dictates restrictive at best. At worst, they enable the suppression and misunderstanding of Caribbean women's writing (Condé 1995: 20; Condé 1993: 131) and proffer an idyllic and unrealistic image of an African motherland and a geographically and racially limited Caribbean (Condé 1995: 24–25). Finally, conventions that so define West Indian literature eschew a social reality of the region, specifically the existence of what the author describes as less-than-heroic Caribbean men (Condé 1993: 133). She finds it illogical, therefore, that rules for literature demand a strong, male protagonist with a supportive and auxiliary female. Condé responds to these rules with her notion of disorder. See Wangari

Wa'Nyatetu-Waigwa's "From Liminality to a Home of Her Own? The Quest Motif in Maryse Condé's Fiction," *Callaloo* 18.3 (1995): 554 for further analysis of Condé's critique of *Négritude*.

12. *Tree of Life*'s Caribbean subjectivity is Guadeloupean in that it is defined by color and class issues peculiar to this island; it is also Caribbean in that the Colón Man and other characters in the novel migrate to the isthmus, the United States, Europe, and other Caribbean countries. Condé asserts the former in response to the erasure of blacks' ethnic differences that she perceives in *Négritude*. Yet she also espouses a "West Indian identity, regardless of colonial language and political status," and defines it in terms of this region's tradition of migration (Condé 1993A: 698). Rather than limit her fictional explorations to one island (she says that "even the most superficial study of literature from the West Indies demonstrates that every writer keeps to his or her island" [ibid]), the author's rendition of Caribbean identity is not limited by geographical boundaries.

13. Mohamed B. Taleb-Khyar, "An Interview with Maryse Condé and Rita Dove," *Callaloo* 14.2 (1991): 357. Condé cites Nora's introduction to a series of essays entitled *Lieux de la mémoire*, edited by Pierre Nora (Paris: Gallimard, 1984).

14. Leah D. Hewitt concurs when she acknowledges that "Condé's novels move back and forth between contemporary culture and myth, between fiction and history, eventually harmonizing them so that the reader often wonders where historical facts leave off and story-making takes over." "Condé's Critical Seesaw," *Callaloo* 18.3 (1995): 641. Although I disagree with Hewitt's contention that Condé "harmonizes" these varied aspects (I believe she leaves them as disharmonious as she finds them), what the critic describes as the author's "seesaw" movement between ideologies can also be read through Condé's investment in disorder or creativity.

15. Because *Tree of Life* has only one narrator—Coco—she speaks throughout Part One of the novel even though the events occur before her birth. However, there are times—in this section and throughout the book—when it is difficult to identify the narrative voice. Thomas Spear sees this as Condé's trademark "omniscient characterization in which the narrative point of view floats from one character to another. [It has been shown] how this aids in the reader's sense of distance from Condé's texts and from her narrators." Thomas C. Spear, "Individual Quests and Collective History," *World Literature Today* 67.4 (Autumn 1993): 726. Anthea Morrison finds that "Condé stretches the first person narrative to the limit, allowing [Coco] a quasi-omniscience as she meticulously relates the adventures of her forebears . . ." "Emancipating the Voice: Maryse Condé's *La vie scélérate*," *Callaloo* 18.3 (1995): 617. This creative strategy also discourages reader identification with a fixed narrator and thus shifts this focus onto Coco's process. I distinguish between an "omniscient" narrator and Coco, memory and imagination, for clarity's sake, to identify different layers of the narrative process; the novel does not necessarily present these features as distinct categories. I will continue to discuss this narrative technique in the text.

16. Condé has commented on the significance of culturally meaningful events that function as historical markers. She claims that "if you write a history of Guadeloupe, you are going to talk about the war, the First World War and the Second World War. You are going to explain the problems of immigration, how many

people went to live in France, and so on. If you ask people what is important, they may never mention these things. They are going to mention the hurricane of 1928 or 1989" (Condé 1995A: 549).

17. Oppositional histories of the U.S. canal venture support Samuel's statements. For example, Michael Conniff mentions the labor recruiting station in Fort-de-France (Conniff 1985: 27; see Cramer 1946: 246) and Lancelot Lewis discusses how the news about work on the isthmus was spread through word-of-mouth (Lewis 1980: 33). Condé herself points to an official/unofficial version of Panamá history to explain her characterization of Albert. She says "in the States in 1985–86, I met with Leonardo Sidney, a researcher who had uncovered the story of his Guadeloupean grandfather's work in helping build the Panama Canal. His research got mixed into my thinking and *La vie scélérate* resulted. . . . The history of my family alone might have been interesting, but could not sustain interest in a novel. West Indians working in Panama was true; however, I had to add imagination to those facts" (Clark 1988: 131, 133). In another interview, Condé says that Sidney "showed [her] some documents, and [she] interviewed him about his grandfather and included that information in the novel" (Pfaff 1996: 67).

18. While Samuel's tales about the Panamanian El Dorado give shape to Albert's desire to migrate, his behavior on what will be his last payday for plantation work reads as a performance of his dissatisfaction with his life.

19. Dr. William C. Gorgas, colonel in the U.S. Army and widely held to be an authority on tropical diseases, proved the effectiveness of this mosquito-netting "treatment" in curbing the spread of malaria and yellow fever in the Canal Zone (McCullough 1977: 407).

20. Garvey's rhetoric begins to assuage some of Albert's pain, but any lasting effect of such a remedy is denied the forebear, a denial metaphorized by Garvey's rejection of Albert. Spotting the Colón Man in a crowd (Albert is tall and striking in his Panamá gear), Garvey asks about him; when an aide reports that Albert profits from death and American exploitation of black labor (the Colón Man is working as a mortician at this time), Garvey wants nothing to do with him (Condé 1992: 33–34). This thwarted relationship between the Colón Man and Marcus Garvey is also an example of Condé's less-than-strict adherence to historical truth: Garvey was in Panamá during the 1920s (Conniff 1985: 10), nine years after Albert's fictional departure for San Francisco, California.

21. As previously mentioned, Bert is Albert's son by first wife, Liza. The Colón Man unceremoniously ships the boy to France to learn a trade. Despondent over this separation from family and friends, and ostracized by the Louises because of his marriage to and child by a white French woman, Bert kills himself. Bert's son Bébert, also rejected by the Guadeloupean Louises, meets the same fate.

22. The silences that dot Coco's narration are intentionally absent from this list of "details," most notably the one that surrounds the ten years she was raised by a foster mother. See Anthea Morrison, "Emancipating the Voice: Maryse Condé's *La vie scélérate*," *Callaloo* 18.3 (1995): 616–25 for a thoughtful analysis of this and other textual silences.

23. Caribbean literature includes many examples of creative examinations of this personal, national, postcolonial identity quest. Michelle Cliff's *Abeng* (Trumansburg, NY: Crossing Press, 1984) and *No Telephone to Heaven* (New York: Vin-

tage International/Vintage Books, 1989), as well as George Lamming's *In the Castle of My Skin*, represent compelling examples of this.

24. *Tree of Life*'s cover is a bright orange. In the foreground, within a snake-filled frame, is a large brown-skinned woman in a flowered dress who seems to contort herself to fit within the frame. Two small men, one in a suit and hat and the other more casually dressed, occupy the upper right corner of the picture and look at the woman, over her left shoulder. The English title and cover art also carry biblical associations: the "tree of life" and snakes invoke images of a paradisiacal Eden and of a paradise lost, no doubt resonant images of the Caribbean for U.S. readers. Interestingly, recent scholarship on the Caribbean and tourism note the ambivalences created by conflicting meanings of "paradise" for colonizers and pleasure-seekers versus that for indigenous, formerly enslaved/indentured peoples, and tourist industry employees. Ian Strachan's "Paradise and Plantation: The Economy of Caribbean Discourse" (Ph.D. diss., University of Pennsylvania, 1995), published as *Paradise and Plantation: Tourism and Culture in the Anglophone Caribbean* (Charlottesville: University of Virginia Press, 2002).

25. Spear recognizes this feature in Condé's work. He says that "for [her] characters preoccupied with self-discovery, the 'search' itself is more important than any point of arrival where one's supposed 'authenticity' would be found—that is, where one's past, or individual identity, would become clearly defined" (Spear 1993: 724). He continues by pointing out that such quests may never end in conclusions: "a major force propelling forward both [Condé's] characters and her narratives is that which aims to discover links to a past and an identity (perhaps forever beyond grasp)" (725).

Conclusion: Panamá Woman a Come

Immigrant women performed a variety of essential tasks for the canal work force. They cooked for men in camps established along the construction line. They also washed and mended clothes, nursed the sick, and maintained boarding houses. Only a small proportion of the women engaged in these chores were on the canal payroll; most were self-employed or worked for others. As a result, very little information about women is available in canal records, making it difficult to trace their experience in Panama. Two things are certain, though. Canal construction would have taken longer and been more unbearable without women, and women worked as hard as men yet earned less and had less job stability.

—Michael Conniff, *Black Labor on a White Canal*

In the next apartment a girl was singing—[Susan] knew the words, she had heard them in Jamaica:
"Ef I did hear what me mammee did say
I wouldn't be in dis wort'less Colon."
But no one had warned her against Colon; she had wished to come to this place, she was here, she must make the best of it. She listened to the singing. It seemed to her that, despite the words, the singer's voice was cheerful.

—Herbert G. de Lisser, *Susan Proudleigh*[1]

I

Histories offer unique accounts of Panamá Canal workers from the Caribbean. Creative narratives bring to light different truths about Colón Men, their migration, and their labor. Mythographies of Panamá Canal migration evoke the meanings of historical and imaginative canal narratives, valuing and revaluing each narration to communicate workers' imaginable truths. A mythographic approach to the study of Caribbean isthmian workers, therefore, offers insight into experiences that are not available in any one narrative form. Such an approach is particularly important for stories—and characters—that are not adequately represented in *any* isthmian narrative. In the above epigraph, for example, Conniff notes that female migrants from the Caribbean often did not appear in canal authorities' records. Anecdotal and creative narratives, however, not only confirm these women's presence but they also recast migration behaviors that have solely attributed to men.[2]

Some of the letters that constitute the *LICCW* collection included references to specific and/or atypical women (see chapter 2). These infrequent representations of women on the isthmus—in addition to those that appear in literary and lyrical narratives—allows one to speculate about women who were part of the Caribbean segment of the Canal Zone population. The assortment of women who appear in Colón Men's memoirs, black and white, from the Caribbean and the United States, suggest that female migrants did not adhere to any particular "type." Their literary and lyrical counterparts similarly defy simplistic categorization.

In trying to create a stable workforce, canal authorities did not limit their attention to Caribbean workers' living and eating conditions. Officials came to believe that a married man would be a more dependable worker and encouraged white North Americans to bring their spouses to the Canal Zone. For Colón Men, the ICC contracted women from Martinique to achieve this end. Some argue that the workers themselves initiated this change by refusing to work without women (www.czbrats.com). According to *LICCW* participant Harrigan Austin, "the government brought many French women from Marknique and those who wanted went to those in authority and took themselves wives and became responsible for them" (Austin, page 2 of 5). Austin and Alfred Dottin judged this to be beneficial since before these women came, workers had to do their own cooking and washing as well as perform the duties for which they were contracted (Austin, page 2 of 5, Dottin, page 1 of 2). However, this domestic benefit was not always beneficial since it could give canal authorities an inordinate amount of control over laborers' lives.

Albert Banister remembered that it was ICC policy to deny housing and other services to those who were not legally married. Seeming to refer to unions between Colón Men and Martinican women, he claimed "many people get married for six months but it did not last for their was no love they just went for a short time but bad luck catch them so marriage did not last but it was the law of the Canal Zone don't stand for bad life" (Banister, page 3 of 5). Barbadian John Prescod's entry was not explicit, but it suggested that men were fined if officials discovered their nonsanctioned unions. Opening with a story about a man who was almost certainly his roommate, Prescod stated:

> One of men leave the camp go the bush in Mandinga to sleep   12 o'clock midnight ploice knock at the roon door   open the door   go in   you married   no   come one put yer shose un to to jail   in the morning court house at Empire judge say you married   no sir . . . $10 and the woman $10.00 (Prescod, page 2 of 2)

Considering that most Colón Men earned about $1.00 per day, the amount of these fines was exorbitant.

G. Mitchell Berisford was married and determined to better manage his money. Yet his methods did not involve housing authorities. "One day," he began:

> I gotted my Commisary book, 10.00   and my wife came for it to spend, she went to the Commisary and baught cake and ice cream and went home gotted her friends and had a spree over me, when I went home the evening I saw the ice cream dishes what they use and the crumbs of cake all over the table, not a crumb leave for me, pots cold, stove cold, and no dinner, and she was away,   hungry killing me and nothing to eat, great expearance, I had to make a devorce on her. (Berisford, pages 2–3 of 3)

In these recollections, women provided domestic services for the good of Colón Men, and thus the construction enterprise itself. Even Berisford's wife, although she shirked her wifely duties by not having her man's food ready when he finished his day's work, affirms that women were intended to provide domestic support for men. Mrs. Berisford and her friends, enjoying the benefits of Berisford's Commissary privileges, obviously had other "duties" in mind, ones that had little to do with her husband or the ICC. In her "unsanctioned" behavior, Mrs. Berisford was not alone.

Lancelot Kavanagh tells an amazing story of one such female. "It was at this station," he averred, "that an Engineer slipped at a switch broke his leg and when taken to the Hospital found she was a woman working among the men all the time" (Kavanagh, page 2 of 3). Kavanagh does not describe this cross-dressing woman—and I have found no other reference to this story—but because she worked as an engineer she was probably white and North American.

The *LICCW* collection contains details about Caribbean and other female isthmian migrants who only briefly appear in most construction histories. Histories published at the beginning of the twentieth century as well as in Bonham Richardson and Olive Senior's nonfictional studies of isthmian migrants from Barbados and Jamaica, respectively, reference such women (chapter 1). Creative writer George Lamming mentions two Panamá Women, Pa's sister and G.'s grandmother, in his novel *In the Castle of My Skin* (chapter 3). In chapter 4, Claude McKay's Tack Tally (*Banana Bottom*) and Eric Walrond's Poyah ("Panama Gold") hope to build upon their Panamá-derived status by including their female protagonists among their possessions. In song, Anglophone Caribbean women are similarly described as status symbols, "things" Colón Men can or cannot "buy" with their Panamá Money. Finally, Colón Man Albert Louis, forebear in Maryse Condé's *Tree of Life*, meets and marries his first wife while employed by the ICC (chapter 5). These brief references, fleshed out by the broader depictions that appear in Colón Men's memoirs, make parts of Caribbean, U.S., and Panamanian social, economic, and cultural realities known. If, as demonstrated by "Panama Gold's" Ella Heath and "Window's" Brid (chapter 4), not to mention the errant Mrs. Berisford, Caribbean women challenged behavioral norms established for women, then migration to Panamá might have likewise offered women a similar option.

Herbert de Lisser's *Susan Proudleigh*, alleged to be "the first West Indian novel of emigration," is located within a complex that includes Colón Men's mythographies but that also represents the status- and color-informed migration image of a Jamaican woman.[3] Thus de Lisser's novel stands in contrast to the women depicted in men's mythographies (such as the Barbadian song "Panama Man" and, to a lesser extent Walrond's "Panama Gold") who function as ciphers through which masculinist migration narratives find voice.

In *Susan Proudleigh*, dark-brown-skinned Susan is the eldest daughter of Mr. and Mrs. Proudleigh. Supported by regular portions of Tom Wooley's weekly paycheck, Susan and her family live in well-positioned and -appointed rooms in a Kingston yard. The status Tom's support affords proves tenuous when Susan learns of his flirtation with black but beautiful Maria Bellicant, a woman Susan considers her social inferior. Subsequently, the protagonist comes to believe that her aspirations, thwarted in Jamaica, can be realized by moving to the Panamanian isthmus, a move enabled by another man, Mr. Samuel Josiah Jones. When Jones fails to live up to the protagonist's expectations, she leaves him for Mr. Mackenzie, an older and stable Colón Man.

While Susan initially defines her social advancement in terms of her associations with a series of men, during the course of the novel the limits that this kind of mobility places on her becomes clear to readers though

Susan elects to capitulate to them as she returns to Jamaica and plans to marry Jones. De Lisser draws on descriptions of the people and culture of Jamaica, and Jamaicans' labor migration to the Panamanian isthmus, to explore and critique the urban poor's concerns with status.[4] Significantly, canal mythographies assist in these literary goals in that their ambivalence mirror de Lisser's characterization of the ambitious, status-conscious, independent, dependent, radical, and conservative Susan. In *Susan Proudleigh*, isthmian migration, labor, and social realities create an apt setting for thematic veins that run through de Lisser's novels: the contours and impact of poor black and brown women's independence, these women's class/status[5] concerns; and Jamaican social life and customs. De Lisser avails himself of the myriad incentives for Jamaican labor migration to Panamá (adventure, hope for possible economic security, fear of illness or death, historical and imaginable truths) to represent Jamaican social customs, particularly as they constitute the most available options for ambitious working class and peasant women.

II

Herbert de Lisser's oeuvre lends itself to a mythographic reading because it examines Jamaica and Jamaicans from the perspectives of journalism, history/sociology, and literature. His body of work also depicts Jamaicans as they migrate to and live in other countries. Focusing on his representations of black and brown, rural peasant and urban working-class women—Jamaicans who occupy much of his fictional and nonfictional attention—one finds information that is duplicated, elaborated on, and challenged in each of the disciplines de Lisser employs.

De Lisser traveled to Panamá several times before the canal's 1914 completion (Roberts 110, 111);[6] in 1913 he published *Twentieth Century Jamaica*, a study that includes chapters on Jamaican people and customs. *Susan Proudleigh* was published in 1915. Reading across the novel and the two travelogues/histories/sociocultural studies, one finds, in the author's description of migrants and their motivations, versions and re-visions of the story of black Jamaicans' social and status aspirations.

The tenth chapter of *In Jamaica and Cuba*, entitled "A Visit to Panama," begins with an important and nuanced description of Panamá-bound passengers:

> The deckers who have come over on this ship . . . are all Jamaicans. There is something pathetic about them, though perhaps they themselves do not perceive it. For weeks and months before they left their homes they had been thinking of this voyage and preparing for it. They had saved a little money,

but most likely had found it was not enough; so the household gods[7] were sacrificed? [sic] the chairs and tables, perhaps even the bed, had to be sold before the necessary sum could be made up to pay for the passage and to lodge in the Treasury the 25s. demanded by the government for repatriation purposes.

Now the emigrant may not find life easier in Panama, he may find it harder; but at the very least he will find it different, and that is what he craves. He will return home some day, but never will he forget his experience 'over sea'; and in after years the memory of life in a labour camp where the rain fell in torrents daily, or in fetid, unbeautiful Colon, where all night long the shrill shrieks of railway engines broke in upon the silence, and where the squalor of tenements reared upon piles planted in sodden earth was equaled only by the squalor of the streets—this memory will come back to him, and even the hardships of that time will seem to him an experience worth having. (*In Jamaica and Cuba* 154–55)

De Lisser describes these migrants as "pathetic," but the subsequent lines suggests that "determined" or "strongly motivated" might be more appropriate modifiers. Emigrants' willingness to replace the property that gave them status among their peers (*Twentieth Century Jamaica* 50) with another currency—the act of migration itself and isthmian migration in particular—can represent the level of their dissatisfaction with things in Jamaica. Yet de Lisser's second paragraph reveals a more complex picture of migrants' desire for change (craving for something different), for tools to live an acceptable life at home (repatriation), and their heroic behavior in overcoming adversity and simultaneously gaining experiences (memory of Panamanian hardship admirably recalled). One must note, too, that de Lisser does not list money as the primary motivation for this movement; it is certainly a tool that helps them live better at home, but it is one of many tools that contribute to the desire to migrate.

Acting in his journalist's guise (and likely as a "brown" Jamaican[8]), de Lisser disdainfully depicts lower class migrants, yet this does not mask the insights that come through his writings. Where in *In Jamaica and Cuba* de Lisser frames his description of migrants with the word "pathetic," in the novel he adds to this disparaging remark by documenting their imaginable social realities, hopes, fears, and expectations as they prepare to leave Jamaica. Susan "too wanted to go away," the omniscient narrator writes, but at the same time she recalls tales told by returning workers:

> True, returning emigrants told of fearful fevers, and unsympathetic policemen, and months of continuous rain, and the dark impenetrable jungle; but the bright fantastic picture painted by imagination cast no shadow in spite of all these dreadful tales. The emigrants who returned to Jamaica almost invariable went back. (de Lisser 1915: 82)

The desire to return to a place where illness and death, the abusive power of U.S. and Panamanian authorities, and the vagaries of nature work against migrants' aspirations seems incomprehensible. But truths about disease and hardship must certainly be understood in relation to Colón Men and Women's migration images and imaginable truths. Earlier in the novel, Susan proclaims, "after all, whatever y'u meet in this world it is you' luck. If you to dead in Colon, you will dead there. If you to come back to Jamaica, y'u will come back" (62).[9] Belief in her "luck" allows Susan to imagine an outcome for herself belied by other migrants' negative experiences, Panamá's geography and climate, Panamanian and U.S. authorities' oppressive behaviors, or (as I will discuss below) the whims of Tom and Sam, and the staid personality of Mackenzie. Yet despite this belief, and what the narrator describes as the West Indian's ability to "face with a calmness which springs from his deep-rooted fatalism" (126), Susan, Jones, and their companions summon their faith to help them manage the unknowable features of their impending migration and to interpret the portentous comet that marks their voyage to Panamá. *Susan Proudleigh* exhibits a mixture of knowledges, facts, and fictions (word of mouth about life on the isthmus, personal imaginable truths, faith, and fear), in its depiction of the lead character's emigration.

The novel corroborates the oft-cited economic motivations for Caribbean isthmian migration, but Susan's story looks beyond them. At their first social event in Colón, a "subscription party" held at "Mrs. Driscole's establishment" (172–73), Jones joins a group of men discussing the Jamaican and U.S. governments' failure to care for Jamaican citizens working on the isthmus. Considering himself among like-minded individuals, Jones confidently states: "a man can't get a good job in his own country, an' when he come to a God-forsaken foreign land he has no protection at all. In Jamaica you have to die of starvation, an' here you lucky if you don't die of neglect" (180). Jones states that one's failure to thrive financially in Jamaica makes isthmian migration desirable; however, this movement does not guarantee improvement as workers encounter problems of a different sort. Economic analyses suggest that a salary that bests that which could be earned in the Caribbean is "good," but improved finances do not dispose of one's troubles. Later, Samuel Jones further qualifies this perspective on isthmian labor. Offering a veiled critique of Mr. Mackenzie, the man for whom Susan leaves him, Jones sings his own praises. He says:

> I am thinkin' of returning to me native land. The temperature of Panama is deleterious to my constitution, an' they have no decent administration in the country. Some people, of course, are contented with it. If you kick some people it will please them. But Samuel Josiah Jones is of a different

characteristic; besides, I am one of those men who can make a living in me own country, an' I didn't come here to pass all me life digging dirt for American people. (230)

Susan's decision to marry Mac hurts Sam and he responds with bravado. His claim that he can make a living in his own country suits this context, but it must also be interpreted with his earlier statement that "in Jamaica you have to die of starvation." Because the financial benefits of isthmian migration and labor necessarily coexist with their less attractive features, one must maintain the possibility that money may and may not have encouraged this Jamaican Colón Man. Perhaps, then, the lesson isthmian mythographies teach us is that attention might better be paid to the negotiations migrants make in order to move to, and work and thrive in Panamá, rather than on that which pushes—or pulls—them to the isthmus. Jones speaks to such a negotiation above when he links making money on the isthmus to the ability to return to Jamaica and to work for himself, sentiments expressed in historical and creative narratives alike.[10] Home, therefore, still figures prominently for Colón Men, as well as for Panamá Women who share their "desire to go somewhere" (122). Caribbean workers' economic motivations for Panamá emigration are almost always attended by other meanings, such as the desire for adventure, self improvement, coping strategies with regard to natural and economic problems at home, and a strong sense of personal worth, the latter being a truth that is most contrary to histories' descriptions of life and labor in Panamá.

Jones frames his decision to migrate as a response to an invitation extended by "Mr. Hewet, an American man that was down here three months ago hiring labourers"; Hewet "sends for" Jones, and Jones heeds the call (de Lisser 1915: 81). Samuel's skills (he is a trained railroad mechanic) make him valuable to the recruiter, but his bravery in facing "the perils of the deep" on the Panamá-bound ship (121) as well as the cultural capital of the migration itself give him status among the people he leaves behind. Jones's interactions with his peers and his invitation to work on the canal assure him of the likely success to be had in the Canal Zone. But while Panamá mythographies enable this interpretation of men's motives and achievements, women's migration remains largely unexplored. The latter group did not have skills that U.S. canal authorities deemed fundamental (literally speaking) to the building of the canal therefore their services were not contracted to the degree that men's services were. If one relies on official and/or historical truths for answers, the reasons for and meanings of women's migration are harder to deduce. Creative fiction then becomes a crucial source of information.

The factors that make Susan's emigration possible are slowly revealed over the course of the novel. Serendipitous personal, social, and historical events make her isthmian adventure possible, some of which correspond to Jones and other males' reasons and others that uniquely characterize her own experience. Occurring on the first page of the novel, Susan Proudleigh's concern with her standing among her neighbors forms the most significant piece of this picture. Chapter I, entitled "Susan's Dilemma," begins with the protagonist's complaint, "I know I am hated in this low neighbourhood. But I don't see what them should hate me for, for I never interfere wid any of them." Her sister, Catherine, responds, "them hate y'u because you are better than them, and because y'u don't mix with them" (1). Susan's dark brown (rather than black) complexion, her "thin and pouting" lips, "her hair, curly but fairly long," and "her eyes, large, black, and vivacious" are what make her "better" (6); readers soon learn that the location of her house, her household goods, and her haughty attitude also factor into her status. Susan and Catherine's conversation reflects what de Lisser argues in *Twentieth Century Jamaica*: "between all the several sections of the Jamaica [sic] people there is a certain amount of jealousy, and this jealousy is often expressed in terms of colour. There is also, as is inevitable in every country, a good many individual dislikes and perhaps hatreds, and often these are also expressed in terms of colour" (*Twentieth Century Jamaica* 52; de Lisser 1915: 70). While the author downplays the import of racial/color prejudices in his vision of twentieth-century Jamaica, the focus on black and brown people in *Susan Proudleigh*, particularly the extent to which "dark brown" Susan "classes off" from particular (i.e., black) members of her "low neighbourhood," signals a pervasive social issue. Dark brown and poor since her father cannot to work, Susan—with her family in tow—goes to great lengths to construct and maintain distance between the Proudleighs and black Maria Bellicant, her mother (Mother Smith), as well as lower status "others" in the yard.

De Lisser notes that "property, personal worth, education" can signify higher status in members of the same class, items that can be as meaningful as—and sometimes more meaningful than—color (*Twentieth Century Jamaica* 50; Watkins-Owens 1996: 13). Susan's features and color, but significantly Tom's gifts and money, "purchase" her and her family's standing. The Proudleighs live in "a little house . . . which opened on the lane" as opposed to others that face inward, toward the central yard (de Lisser 1915: 2); they count "two American rocking chairs [and] . . . an iron bed with a straw mattress" among their "household gods"; "only married people of her class usually had as much" (38–39). These "gods," as well as Susan's haughty attitude, solidify the family's status—in their own eyes, but significantly in the behavior of other yard inhabitants:

> [Susan] carried herself with an air of social superiority which was gall and wormwood to the envious; and often on walking through the land she had

noticed the contemptuous looks of those whom, with greater contempt, she called the common folks and treated with but half-concealed disdain. On the whole, she had rather enjoyed the hostility of these people, for it was in its way a tribute to her own importance. (2)

Within the novel's black, majority community is waged a pitched battle for social position, a fight over "leftovers" because the "meal" is perceived of as being out of reach. En route to a church-sponsored picnic, Susan and her friends:

> passed handsome villas; those were the houses, they thought, where the rich people lived, people so much above their own station in life that they never dreamt of envying them. The white and the higher classes of fair coloured people belonged to one world. They belonged to another. But envy and hatred did not embitter the relations of one class with another, though their interests in life were superficially as different as was the yard-room or little front house from the spacious-looking residence with its garden of tropical shrubs and flowers blooming in front of it. (70)

What the narrator describes as a lack of interclass animosity manifests as an overabundance of intraclass hatred and envy. Apparently small stakes—orientation of one's home, the number of goods, degree of color, ability to migrate to Panamá—become profoundly meaningful to Susan and the people in her yard. Status is the fulcrum on which these intraclass relationships pivot; therefore, the protagonist deems her ability to achieve, maintain, and improve upon her social position as vitally important.

De Lisser characterizes Susan's desire and ability to migrate as part of her strategy of acquiring cultural capital, but also as one of few status-accruing opportunities available to her and her "kind." Like the layered narratives that result in Colón Men's mythographies, Susan Proudleigh's migration narrative is an intricate one. The men with whom she can associate (e.g., manipulate) largely define her chances for "upward mobility" within her social class, in Jamaica but also en route to and in Panamá. Even when independent opportunities for improved social standing are available (running a small shop, performing domestic work), Susan does not find them nearly as attractive. Though the novel illustrates some of the limits of status earned through men and includes examples of women who make it on their own, both options of which Susan is aware, she nonetheless holds fast to her men.

The novel establishes Susan's fight against being, or rather, against being perceived of as, "common" as a motivating factor in her decision to travel to the isthmus of Panamá. Her fight proves to be a personal struggle, as well as one contingent on forces outside of herself (keeping a man), as Susan must be vigilant in maintaining behavior that indisputably locate her within the "conventions of recognized propriety" (100). When Maria challenges Susan's supremacy over Tom, they engage in a "tracing match" on a crowded lane that ends in a tussle (18). The shame over her behavior stems from her horror of street scenes for "people of her class did not participate in them" (ibid). The fight, as well as being "handled" by a policeman, results in Susan being classed with the "common folkses." "You common folks," says the policeman, "are ignorant to the extreme. You ever see white ladies fight in the street?" He continues, "white people don't fight in de street, because them is ladies and gentleman" (19). Here, color and social position combine. Being of a high class, or an aspirant to social heights, can be seen as an approximation of upper-class behaviors and color. Without the color, money, or education of the upper classes, Susan must work hard to overcome these "failings" in order to achieve her ambition.

In an attempt to regain her standing in the yard, Susan brings Maria up on assault charges, a move that causes her social demise. Rather than adjudicate Susan's case and Maria's countersuit, the judge brokers a compromise that enrages Susan, leaves Maria feeling victorious, and leads to Tom's dismissal from his job (49). The speed that the Proudleighs fall illustrates the tenuousness of their advanced social position, contingent as it is on Tom's financial contributions. Without them, "the front house would have to be given up, and perhaps some of her furniture sold." Susan muses that "she would miss all that she had become accustomed to. She might have to face actual want—she who had for one full year enjoyed what she considered luxury . . ." (51).

Tom, fearing that his dismissal will prevent him from finding comparable employment in Kingston, decides to try his hand in Panamá (50). Susan's options, however, are not as immediately clear. She does not have the "influence to secure a position as a barmaid," nor the color since "small shops . . . usually employed young women fairer than she was" (41). The kind of job open to her, "as nurse in one of the wealthier families of Kingston," is not attractive because to "domestic work she had a strong aversion" (42).[11] For the post-Tom Susan Proudleigh, her financial and social advancement are contingent on her "luck," in earning money through acceptable employment . . . or in finding another generous lover. Falling back on her resourcefulness, Susan rents a shop and "stocked it with the things she knew would sell," "bread and 'grater cake' . . . cocoa-nut oil, sugar-cane, mangoes, bananas, and flour-cakes . . . Rosebud cigarettes . . . firewood" etc. (57, 58). With the help of her sister (who helps at the counter) and mother (who prepares the cakes), she makes good money.[12] This job and the money it brings in protect Susan from "interference" of the kind Maria produces (60), yet she is not satisfied. After tallying her profits for the week, the protagonist tells Catherine:

> "Yes, I am independent now," returned Susan, with a touch of pride in her voice; "but I sick of this life. Every day it's de same thing. I 'ave to work too hard, an' sometimes I don't make as much in a day as I use to spend on car ride when Tom was here. I feel so tired. . . . I going to save up money meself an' go to Colon, even if Tom don't send for me." (53–54)

Although she is able to earn her own money, Susan prefers taking an allowance from a lover. In this she appears manipulative and lazy, but considering her concern with how she is seen, her comments,[13] can also be interpreted as an evaluation of the cultural capital produced by shop keeping versus keeping company with Tom.

Susan's wish to move to Panamá can be interpreted similarly. There she can easily make money (her father has heard that "you can earn money there like water" [54]), but importantly, this emigration buys the same kind of capital that Tom's company buys. When Maria learns that Susan "got another intended with plenty of money, and was going to Colon," her response is practically the same as her response to Susan's airs, house, and property: "'dis world don't level,' was Maria's bitter comment on Susan's undeserved good fortune" (85). That Susan ultimately enjoys a community of similarly positioned women—her social equals—on the isthmus attests to the migration's value among Kingston's "upwardly mobile" (166).

As soon as she arrives in Colón, the protagonist's intention to climb the social ladder cannot be clearer. Tom's money helps her move up some rungs, as does her relocation to the isthmus; additionally, the novel illustrates that a relationship with a man—the more formal (that is, legal) the better—can secure even the most ambitious woman's social goals. A young woman's "engagement" to a young man of means, better yet her marriage to said type of man, is her best opportunity to demonstrate that she is worthy of respect; the wedding ring is a material sign of this worthiness. When Jones reneges on his promise to marry her,[13] begins spending too many nights out in Colón with his friends, and too much money on strong drink, she considers Mackenzie's marriage proposal. She thinks:

> Mackenzie was a steady man. If she married him, she could become a member of a church. That would mean a definite rise in the social scale; her respectability would then be beyond challenge, beyond question. The ring on her finger would be the outward and visible sign of her right to respectful treatment on earth below, and also the promise of an uninterrupted passage to heaven in the unfortunate event of death. (192)

The novel is littered with so many variations on this theme that its import is impossible to overlook. The strength of this conviction, despite her resentment at being wholly dependent on Jones while in Colón (152) and her success at making her own way, confirms this idea as a particularly powerful cultural marker. *Susan Proudleigh* suggests that women such as Susan (dark brown or black and poor) need a man in order to accrue the status they crave. The power of this belief can even be seen when Susan's husband dies in a landslide at Culebra; she recognizes that she continues to be extended the highest level of respect (296). The protagonist claims to be indifferent to marriage (108) but is nonetheless giddy at the possibility of achieving it (128). Even when demonstrably irresponsible Jones lustily seeks her hand in marriage, approaching her only nine days after Mackenzie's death, Susan seems to acquiescence. Through Susan's inheritances from Mac (insurance money and land in Jamaica), she achieves as a dark brown woman can: by skillfully managing money, men, and migration.

Yet de Lisser's heroine is far from definitive on any of these points. As mentioned above, she can earn her own money but instead prefers to take what her man offers. She marries Mackenzie because of the standing she can accrue through him, but complains that he is not exciting and questions whether the benefit is worth the boredom. Marriage provides her an escape from dependence on negligent Sam (190, 235), but soon after moving in with Mac at Culebra, she says "'Marriage is dull . . . you are not you' own mistress. It is true you 'ave a honourable position, but what is the good of that if it don't make you happier?'" (221; see also 236, 255). Susan is so disillusioned that she considers eschewing respectability by running away with Samuel rather than stay married to Mac (270). She is so dissatisfied that she even questions the "honor" that marriage affords: it does not demonstrably change her material condition—or her standing among her isthmian community (246); as she describes it, her marriage flings her out of one life and into an unfamiliar and less pleasurable one (201). Susan states that she will never marry again (307), that she "is all right now, an' [she] can live comfortable without anybody" because of Mackenzie's life insurance and property in Jamaica (308).

Finally, although she (faintly) suspects that Sam will "go on the same way in Jamaica as [he] went on [in Colón]," she agrees to marry him "in Parish Church," but on the sly since she is so newly widowed (309). *Susan Proudleigh* ends on this note as Susan, Jones, and Mr. Proudleigh see "the grey-green mountains of Jamaica rising into view as the ship drew nearer the shore" (ibid). The ambivalence that characterizes Susan's views on her social standing, independence, and marriage might be read as a critique of the protagonist herself, or of her preoccupations. Susan says that her ability to live in the manner to which she is accustomed, without a man, is easier said than done. She seems to resent this but is not willing to do the kind of work that will allow her to be truly independent (152–53);[14] she will and does, however, secret away part of the money Sam gives her to achieve this end (154).

Susan chooses to secure an "intended" or a husband rather than availing herself of options prescribed for women of her color and class. This decision suggests that women like Susan has few options for social advancement; another possible interpretation is that a shrewd woman like Susan can make many things happen. Through his representation of characters and events in the novel, Herbert de Lisser enables the critique of status, color, and gender concerns as they manifest among people in a Kingston yard. *Susan Proudleigh* charts the negotiations in which the main character engages in response to the social realities that impact her life. In this, the novel demonstrates what can result when one considers Panamanian labor migration from myriad perspectives. Meanings that, in one genre, appear fully represented, comprise only one part of a bigger picture when read through other genre perspectives.

Within the pantheon of Panamá Canal mythographies, de Lisser's 1915 novel adds a woman's concern with status to the migration narratives that appear in this book. The ambivalence of Susan's characterization lends itself nicely to the contexts of Jamaican and Caribbean labor migrations; her shifting position on marriage and social standing mirrors the beneficial as well as the detrimental consequences of isthmian migration. Imaginable truths, as well as the documentable aspects of isthmian migration and work, like Susan's savvy, allowed migrants the tools through which they could change their realities—even when it appeared they had little impact on the enterprise. If, as Rhonda Cobham argues, "the problem of placing de Lisser, politically, ideologically and as a creative writer, can only be resolved if we consider the contradictions within his personality . . . as a reflection of the contradictions within Jamaican society" (9), then the study of Panamá Canal workers from the Caribbean must similarly embrace similar contradictions. Such an examination must not only attend to the inherent contradictions of canal construction project itself, but also those of Colón Men and Women's many-faceted migration narratives.

NOTES

1. This, de Lisser's second novel, was so popular that it was adapted for the stage and performed by a Jamaican theater group. See Rhonda Cobham's "The Literary Side of H. G. de Lisser (1878–1944)," *Jamaica Journal* 17.4 (November 1984–January 1985): 4.

2. Generally referring to Caribbean migration, Thomas-Hope is informative on this point: "from the point of reliance on wage labour, the lower-class woman, just as much as males of the same social status, has a high migration potential because of her equally high level of motivation for securing employment and ultimately some measure of upward mobility" (Thomas-Hope 1992: 4). Recent works elucidate the experiences of Panamá Women. Eyra M. R. Rivas's *El trabajo de las mujeres en la historia de la construccíon del Canal de Panamá, 1881–1914* (2000) and Agatha Williams's "La mujer antillana en la construccíon del Canal," *La Prensa*, Viernes, 8 March 1991, 19B. Williams documents that Panamá Women lived alongside male workers in Colón and in shanties constructed along the canal line. Such women were also subject to the same illnesses as the men. Whereas women from Martinique, contracted as *"calidad telegrafios"* and washerwomen by the ICC, were the most-documented female Caribbean migrants, Williams's article identifies migrants from Jamaica, Barbados, Trinidad, St. Lucia, and Guadeloupe. When not contracted by the U.S. canal commission, these women often worked for themselves, selling goods along the canal line or taking in laundry (19B).

3. Kenneth Ramchand, introduction, *Jane's Career: A Story of Jamaica* by Herbert George de Lisser (New York: Africana Publishing Corporation, 1971): ix.

4. In a typewritten note included in de Lisser's *Twentieth Century Jamaica* (Kingston, Jamaica: The Jamaica Times Limited, 1913), the Archbishop of the West Indies (Enos Nuttall) describes the author as "a coloured gentleman, a native of Jamaica, highly intelligent, cultured, and a very able writer of the journalistic type." De Lisser was counted among Jamaica's colored class through his "very old Jamaican ancestry, Portuguese-Jewish on the paternal side with a modicum of African blood. There was also a Hebrew strain on the other side, [de Lisser's] mother having been a Miss Isaacs of Kingston." W. Adolphe Roberts's *Six Great Jamaicans: Biographical Sketches* (Kingston, Jamaica: The Pioneer Press, 1951): 105. De Lisser worked as a library assistant at the Institute of Jamaica, but began his journalism career as a proofreader at the *Daily Gleaner*, advanced to reporter at the *Jamaica Times* and the *Daily Telegraph*, and was promoted to editor at the *Gleaner* at 26 (Ramchand 1971: vi; Roberts 106, 109). He brought his researcher and journalist's eyes to creative writing, particularly (for my purposes) the works that took peasant and working class black and brown women as his subjects. De Lisser eschews a crass kind of journalistic "objectivity" for detail and research (Roberts 104) that gives his fiction "life and character," and provides a "picture of the Jamaican native which impresses one very strongly as true" (W. Somerset Maugham letter to de Lisser, quoted in Roberts 119–20). Though his literature was not overtly political (Cobham 9), it can be interpreted as such particularly in de Lisser's attention to the problems of black domestic workers (*Jane's Career*). I argue in the body of this chapter that the subtly depicted social realities in *Susan Proudleigh*, informed as they are by the author's research and interest in Jamaican people, also carry meanings beyond those exemplified by the story's twists and turns.

5. Here and throughout this chapter, I do not intend to use "class" and "status" interchangeably. I define "class" as the larger social grouping into which "status" constitutes a smaller part. The *Oxford Desk Dictionary and Thesaurus* (American Edition) defines "class" as "any set of persons or things grouped together, or graded or differentiated from others" and "status" as "rank; social position; rela-

tive importance" or "prestige" (see also OED Online, http://80-dictionary. oed.com.metalib.bc.edu/entrance.dtl). In a twentieth-century Jamaican context, membership in the upper class was typically defined by white skin and money; as one moves down the hierarchy, members' skin color darkens and the amount of money decreases. While Susan's possessions and money can furnish her status among people in her class, they cannot give her access to the upper classes where, in addition to color, lineage, education, and behavior also play significant parts.

6. Herbert de Lisser, *In Jamaica and Cuba* (Kingston, Jamaica: The Gleaner Company, 1910): 155.

7. OED Online defines "household gods" as "the *Lares* and *Penates*, divinities supposed to preside over the household, whose images were kept in the *atrium* or central room of the house; *fig.* the essentials of home life" (http://80-dictionary.oed.com.metalib.bc.edu/entrance.dtl). I find its usage in this context meaningful as the phrase infuses household goods with religious importance, evincing the significance that their sale imparts to migrants and their migration. This interpretation of the phrase carries over to the author's usage in *Susan Proudleigh* where he lists the items that distinguish Susan and her family from others in the yard (de Lisser 1915: 39). I discuss the role these "gods" play in Susan's depiction in the text.

8. Aleric Josephs, and others, use "mixed race," "colored," "brown," and sometimes even "creole" to describe Jamaicans of mixed racial ancestry. "Mary Seacole: Jamaican Nurse and 'Doctress', 1805/10–1881," *Jamaican Historical Review* 17 (1991): 49. For a discussion of the problems of terminology used to describe nineteenth-century Jamaicans, see Gad J. Heuman's *Between Black and White: Race, Politics, and the Free Coloreds in Jamaica, 1792–1865* (Westport, CT: Greenwood Press, 1981), xix–xx; Hilary Beckles's "On the Backs of Blacks: The Barbados Free-Coloreds' Pursuit of Civil Rights and the 1816 Slave Rebellion," *Immigrants and Minorities* 3.2 (1984): 185n1; Sandra Gunning's "Traveling with Her Mother's Tastes: The Negotiation of Gender, Race, and Location in Wonderful Adventures of Mrs. Seacole in Many Lands," *Signs: Journal of Women in Culture and Society* 26.4 (2001): 949n1.

Color conflicts between black and brown Jamaicans might also inform de Lisser's characterization, as can be seen in the following examples. Susan's contempt for Maria is couched in terms of color prejudice: "because Maria, though black, was comely, Susan had made a point of ignoring Maria's existence; she had never thought of Maria as a possible rival, however, so confident was she of her ascendancy over her lover, and so certain was she that Maria could never be awarded the prize for style and beauty if Susan Proudleigh happened to be near" (de Lisser 1915: 5; see also *Twentieth Century Jamaica* 50).

9. In *The Silver Men*, Velma Newton similarly finds that "luck," more than the realities of death, disease, and racist bosses, informed migrants' views on their success—or failure—on the isthmus: their "bad luck" in having a low-paying job in the Caribbean could be changed, bringing "good luck," by migrating to Panamá (Newton 1984: 172).

10. Circular migration, or the practice of frequently moving between Panamá and a given Caribbean country, is a feature of isthmian migration that has been in-

frequently addressed in historical and literary isthmian narratives. This kind of movement thwarted attempts to document the number of workers from the circum-Caribbean region since some circular migrants were probably counted several times (see *LICCW* entries by Joseph Gard, page 2 of 2, Albert Peters, page 3 of 4, Rufus Lucas, page 2 of 3, Harrigan Austin, page 4 of 5). Richardson describes "oscillating" migration as a, "strategy more often . . . adopted by the black lower classes" of St. Kitts/Nevis. Members of the upper classes from this country tend to make their migrations permanent (Richardson 1983: 173).

11. Among rural Jamaican women, a similar stigma attaches to the most available type of work. De Lisser finds that "in some parts of the island field-work is almost the only form of employment open to women. But most of the girls dislike it, and public sentiment revolts at the idea of girls of tender age working along with boys and men under circumstances conducive to the most thorough demoralization. The aim and ambition of every decent countrywoman, therefore, is to secure for her girls good places as domestic servants" (*Twentieth Century Jamaica* 98). Whether in urban or rural contexts, workingwomen value their ability to support themselves, a position that also supports the strength of Susan's desire to maintain her social position. De Lisser notes, "no grown woman likes to return home, except on a short visit, and as a person of independent means. Very rarely will the girl who has 'taken the world upon her shoulders' consent to let her people know that she is in desperate straits. She loves her independence, she takes a certain pride in being able to manage her own affairs and direct the course of her own life" (103).

12. Rhonda Cobham comments on what can only be described as the author's bias against black Jamaican men. According to de Lisser, these men are "good humoured and impulsive, an admirable imitator when well taught but with no inventive faculty whatever. . . . He is sometimes brave to recklessness and sometimes a deplorable coward" (3; quoted from de Lisser's "Marriage," *Jamaica Times* 25 August 1900, p. 8). This might explain his characterization of Mr. Proudleigh, a man trained as a carpenter but whose arthritis (conveniently) prevents him from plying his trade; he takes as his due money "loaned" him by Susan's lovers, and from his daughter's, or his wife's occupations. Cobham describes de Lisser's representations of black men when she writes, "in both *Jane's Career* and *Susan Proudleigh* de Lisser is often satirical at the expense of his black male characters, using the pragmatism and resourcefulness of his attractive heroines to highlight what he sees as the laziness and misplaced aggression of black Jamaican men" (4).

13. Susan and Jones's passage to Colón is overshadowed by a comet, seen by the migrants as "a flaming portent . . . emerging suddenly out of the mysterious depths of space" (125). Most interpreted this as a sign that the world would soon end. So that he and Susan can "die right," Jones proposes that they get married as soon as they land in Colón (126, 127). Samuel changes his mind when it is clear that the world will not end (151–52).

14. When Susan decides to return to Jamaica, she leaves her sister and Aunt Deborah in Colón because "of course [they] can do better here" (298). Deborah and Catherine work as private laundresses, a profession in which they make "four

or five times as much at this work as they would have done in Jamaica" although the work is not as "genteel" as dressmaking (the occupation the older Proudleigh preferred). The earning potential in washing clothes allows her to maintain some of her status because, "she had hired a girl to help her; particularly, to go for and to take home the clothes, for that neither she nor Catherine would consent to do" (225). Other Caribbean women followed this route, whether they were formally engaged by the ICC or self-employed (Conniff 1989: 67, Haskin 1913: 161).

Bibliography

Abbot, Henry L. *Problems of the Panama Canal*. New York: MacMillan, 1907.
Abbot, Willis J. *Panama and the Canal in Picture and Prose*. London: Syndicate Publishing Company, 1913.
Abrahams, Roger D. *The Man-of-Words in the West Indies: Performance and the Emergence of Creole Culture*. Baltimore: Johns Hopkins University Press, 1983.
Aceto, Michael. "Ethnic Personal Names and Multiple Identities in Anglophone Caribbean Speech Communities in Latin America." *Language in Society* 31: 577–608.
Anderson, Benedict. *Imagined Communities: Reflections on the Origin and Spread of Nationalism*. London: Verso, 1983.
Arnold, A. James. "The Novelist as Critic." *World Literature Today* 67.4 (Autumn 1993): 711–16.
Ashcroft, Bill, Gareth Griffiths, and Helen Tiffin. *The Empire Writes Back: Theory and Practice in Post-Colonial Literatures*. London: Routledge, 1989.
Bader, Rudolf. "Characterization and the Colonial Myth," in *International Literature in English: Essays on the Major Writers*, edited by Robert L. Ross, 143–52. New York: Garland Publishing, 1991.
Barriteau, Eudine, ed. *Confronting Power, Theorizing Gender: Interdisciplinary Perspectives in the Caribbean*. Kingston, Jamaica: University of the West Indies Press, 2003.
Barrow, Christine. "Introduction and Overview: Caribbean Gender Ideologies," in *Caribbean Portraits: Essays on Gender Ideologies and Identities*, edited by Christine Barrow, xi–xxxviii. Kingston, Jamaica: Ian Randle Publishers/Centre for Gender and Development Studies, University of the West Indies, 1998.
Barry, Tom, Beth Wood, and Deb Preusch. *The Other Side of Paradise: Foreign Control in the Caribbean*. New York: Grove Press, 1984.
Baugh, Edward. "Cuckoo and Culture: *In the Castle of My Skin*." *Ariel* 8.3 (1977): 23–33.

Beckles, Hilary McD. "On the Backs of Blacks: The Barbados Free-Coloreds' Pursuit of Civil Rights and the 1816 Slave Rebellion." *Immigrants and Minorities* 3.2 (1984): 185n1.

———. "Sex and Gender in the Historiography of Caribbean Slavery," in *Engendering History: Caribbean Women in Historical Perspective*, edited by Verene Shepherd, Bridget Brereton, and Barbara Bailey, 125–40. Kingston, Jamaica: Ian Randle Publishers, 1995.

———. "Centreing Woman: The Political Economy of Gender in West African and Caribbean Slavery," in *Caribbean Portraits: Essays on Gender Ideologies and Identities*, edited by Christine Barrow, 93–114. Kingston, Jamaica: Ian Randle Publishers/Centre for Gender and Development Studies, University of the West Indies, 1998.

Benítez-Rojo, Antonio. *The Repeating Island: The Caribbean and the Postmodern Perspective*, translated by James Maraniss. Durham, NC: Duke University Press, 1992.

Benn, Denis. *Ideology and Political Development: The Growth and Development of Political Ideas in the Caribbean, 1774–1983*. Mona, Jamaica: Institute of Social and Economic Research/University of the West Indies, 1987.

Bennett, Louise. "No Lickle Twang!" *Jamaica Labrish*. Great Britain: Collins Clear-Type Press, 1966: 209–10.

Bernabé, Jean, Patrick Chamoiseau, and Raphäel Confiant. "In Praise of Creoleness." *Callaloo* 13.4 (1990): 886–909.

Besson, Jean. "Changing Perceptions of Gender in the Caribbean Region: The Case of the Jamaican Peasantry." *Caribbean Portraits: Essays on Gender Ideologies and Identities*, edited by Christine Barrow, 133–55. Kingston, Jamaica: Ian Randle Publishers/Centre for Gender and Development Studies, University of the West Indies, 1998.

Bhabha, Homi, ed. *Nation and Narration*. London: Routledge, 1990.

Biesanz, John, and Mavis Biesanz. *The People of Panama*. New York: Columbia University Press, 1955.

Birney, Earle. "Meeting George Lamming in Jamaica." *Canadian Literature* 95 (Winter 1982): 16–28.

Bishop, Joseph Buchlin. *The Panama Gateway*. New York: Charles Scribner's Sons, 1913.

Bogle, Enid E. "Eric Walrond (1898–1966)." *50 Caribbean Writers: A Bio-bibliographical Critical Sourcebook*, edited by Daryl Cumber Dance, 474–82. New York: Greenwood Press, 1986.

Bolt, Jonathan. *To Culebra: A Play in Two Acts*. Salt Lake City: Gibbs Smith Publisher/Peregrine Smith Books, 1989.

Boyce-Davies, Carol, ed. *Moving Beyond Boundaries, Volume 2: Black Women's Diasporas*. New York: New York University Press, 1995.

Boyce-Davies, Carol, and 'Molara Ogundipe-Leslie, eds. *Moving Beyond Boundaries, Volume 1: Dimensions of Black Women's Writing*. New York: New York University Press, 1995.

Brathwaite, Edward Kamau. "Caribbean Man in Space and Time." *Savacou* 11/12 (September 1975): 1–11, 106–8.

———. "Timehri." *Is Massa Day Dead? Black Moods in the Caribbean*, edited by Orde Coombs, 29–45. Garden City, NY: Anchor Books/Doubleday, 1974.

———. *Contradictory Omens: Cultural Diversity and Integration in the Caribbean*. Mona, Jamaica: Savacou Publications, 1974.

———. *The Development of Creole Society in Jamaica, 1770–1820*. Oxford: Clarendon Press, 1971.

Brown, Carolyn T. "The Myth of the Fall and the Dawning of Consciousness in George Lamming's *In the Castle of My Skin*." *World Literature Today* 57.1 (Winter 1983): 38–43.

Brown, Patrice C. "The Panama Canal: The African American Experience." *Prologue: Quarterly of the National Archives and Records Administration* 29.2 (Summer 1997): 122–26.

Bryce-Laporte, Roy S. "Crisis, Contraculture, and Religion Among West Indians in the Panama Canal Zone," in *Blackness in Latin America and the Caribbean: Social Dynamics and Cultural Transformations. Volume I: Central America and Northern and Western South America*, compiled, edited, and with a general introduction by Norman E. Whitten Jr. and Arlene Torres, 100–18. Bloomington: Indiana University Press, 1998.

———. "Voluntary Immigration and the Continuing Encounters between Blacks: The Post Quincentenary Challenge." *The Annals of the American Academy of Political and Social Science* 530 (November 1993): 28–41.

———. "Black Immigrants: The Experience of Invisibility and Inequality." *Journal of Black Studies* 3 (1972): 29–56.

Bryce-Laporte, Roy S., and Delores M. Mortimer, eds. *Caribbean Immigration to the United States*. Washington, DC: Smithsonian Institution, 1976.

Bryce-Laporte, Roy S., Delores M. Mortimer, and Stephen R. Couch, eds. *Sourcebook on the New Immigration: Implications for the United States and the International Community*. New Brunswick, NJ: Transaction Books, 1980.

Bush, Barbara. *Slave Women in Caribbean Society, 1650–1832*. Bloomington: Indiana University Press, 1990.

Canby, Vincent. "Films that Refuse to Fade Away." *New York Times* 14 July 1974, Section 2: 1+.

Cartey, Wilfred. *Whispers from the Caribbean: I Going Away, I Going Home*. Los Angeles: Center for Afro-American Studies/University of California, 1991.

Cassidy, F. G., and R. B. LePage. *Dictionary of Jamaican English*. New York: Cambridge University Press, 1967.

Césaire, Aimé. *Lyric and Dramatic Poetry 1946–1982*, translated by Clayton Eshleman and Annette Smith. Charlottesville: University of Virginia Press, 1990.

———. "Notebook of a Return to the Native Land," in *Aime Cesaire: The Collected Poetry*, translated by Clayton Eshleman and Annette Smith, 32–85. Berkeley: University of California Press, 1983.

Chakrabarty, Dipesh. "Postcoloniality and the Artifice of History," in *The Postcolonial Studies Reader*, edited by Bill Ashcroft, Gareth Griffiths, and Helen Tiffin, 383–88. London: Routledge, 1995.

Chamberlain, Mary, ed. *Caribbean Migration: Globalised Identities*. New York: Routledge, 1998.

———. *Narratives of Exile and Return*. London: MacMillan Press/Warwick University Caribbean Studies, 1997.

Chambers, Iain. *Migrancy, Culture, Identity*. London: Routledge, 1994.

Chidsey, Donald Barr. *The Panama Canal: An Informal History.* New York: Crown Publishers, 1970.

"The Chinese in the English-Speaking Caribbean." *Encyclopedia of World Cultures, Volume 3,* edited by James W. Dow. Boston: G. K. Hall & Co., 1995.

Christian, Barbara. "The Race for Theory." *Culture Critique* 6 (Spring 1987): 51–63.

Clark, VéVé. "'I Have Made Peace with My Island': An Interview with Maryse Condé." *Callaloo* 12.1 (1988): 86–133.

Clarke, Austin. "Introduction." *Nine Men Who Laughed.* Toronto: Penguin Books 1986.

Cliff, Michelle. *No Telephone to Heaven.* New York: Vintage International/Random House, 1989.

———. *Abeng: A Novel.* Trumansburg, NY: Crossing Press, 1984.

Cobham, Rhonda. "The Literary Side of H. G. de Lisser (1878–1944)." *Jamaica Journal* 17.4 (November 1984–January 1985): 2–9.

Cocks, Jay. Review of "The Harder They Come." *Time Magazine* 19 February 1973: 64.

Collier, Eugenia. "Claude McKay." *50 Caribbean Writers: A Bio-bibliographical Critical Sourcebook,* edited by Daryl Cumber Dance, 284–93. New York: Greenwood Press, 1986.

Collin, Richard H. *Theodore Roosevelt's Caribbean: The Panama Canal, the Monroe Doctrine, and the Latin American Context.* Baton Rouge: Louisiana State University Press, 1990.

Condé, Maryse. *Crossing the Mangrove,* translated by Richard Philcox. New York: Anchor Books/Doubleday, 1995.

———. "Language and Power: Words as Miraculous Weapons." *CLA Journal* 39.1 (September 1995): 18–25.

———. "Order, Disorder, Freedom, and the West Indian Writer." *Yale French Studies* 83.2 (1993): 121–35.

———. "The Role of the Writer." *World Literature Today* 67.4 (Autumn 1993): 697–99.

———. *Tree of Life: A Novel of the Caribbean,* translated by Victoria Reiter. New York: Ballantine Books, 1992.

———. *I, Tituba, Black Witch of Salem,* translated by Richard Philcox. Charlottesville: University of Virginia Press, 1992.

Connell, R. W. *Masculinities.* Berkeley: University of California Press, 1995.

Conniff, Michael L. *Black Labor on a White Canal: Panama, 1904–1981.* Pittsburgh: University of Pittsburgh Press, 1985.

Coombs, Orde, ed. *Is Massa Day Dead? Black Moods in the Caribbean.* Garden City, NY: Anchor Books, 1974.

Cooper, Carolyn. *Noises in the Blood: Orality, Gender, and the "Vulgar" Body of Jamaican Popular Culture.* Durham, NC: Duke University Press, 1995.

———. "'Only a Nigger Gal!': Race, Gender, and the Politics of Education in Claude McKay's *Banana Bottom.*" *Caribbean Quarterly* 38 (1992): 40–54.

Cooper, Wayne F. *Claude McKay, Rebel Sojourner in the Harlem Renaissance: A Biography.* Baton Rouge: Louisiana State University Press, 1987.

Cornish, Vaughn. *The Panama Canal and Its Makers.* London: T. Fisher Unwin, 1909.

Coser, Stelamaris. *Bridging the Americas: The Literature of Toni Morrison, Paule Marshall, and Gayle Jones.* Philadelphia: Temple University Press, 1994.

Coulthard, G. R. *Race and Culture in Caribbean Literature*. New York: Oxford University Press, 1962.
Cramer, Louise. "Songs of West Indian Negroes in the Canal Zone." *California Folklore Quarterly* 5 (1946): 243–72.
Craton, Michael. *Testing the Chains: Resistance to Slavery in the British West Indies*. Ithaca, NY: Cornell University Press, 1982.
Cromartie, John, and Carol B. Stack. "Reinterpretation of Black Return and Nonreturn Migration to the South 1975–1980." *Geographical Review* 79.3 (1989): 297–370.
Cross, Malcolm, and Gad Heuman, eds. *Labour in the Caribbean: From Emancipation to Independence*. London: MacMillan Press/Warwick University Caribbean Studies, 1988.
Cubena (Carlos Guillermo Wilson). *Chombo (novela)*. Miami: Ediciones Universal, 1981.
Cudjoe, Selwyn. *Caribbean Women Writers: Essays from the First International Conference*. Wellesley, MA: Calaloux Publications; Amherst: University of Massachusetts Press, 1990.
———. *Resistance and Caribbean Literature*. Athens: Ohio University Press, 1980.
———. *The Role of Resistance in the Caribbean Novel*. Ithaca, NY: Cornell University Press, 1975.
Dance, Daryl Cumber. *New World Adams: Conversations with Contemporary West Indian Writers*. 1984. Leeds, UK: Peepal Tree Books, 1992.
———, ed. *50 Caribbean Writers: A Bio-bibliographical Critical Sourcebook*. New York: Greenwood Press, 1986.
Danticat, Edwidge. *Breath, Eyes, Memory*. New York: Soho Press, 1994.
Dash, J. Michael. *Haiti and the United States: National Stereotypes and the Literary Imagination*. New York: St. Martin's Press, 1988.
———. *Literature and Ideology in Haiti, 1915–1961*. Totowa, NJ: Barnes and Noble Books, 1981.
———. "Haitian Literature—A Search for Identity." *Savacou* 5 (June 1971): 81–94.
Davidson, Adenike Marie. "Spirituality and Black Manhood in Earl Lovelace's *The Wine of Astonishment* and Michael Thelwell's *The Harder They Come*." *In Process: A Graduate Student Journal of African-American and African Diasporan Literature and Culture* 1 (Fall 1996): 74–90.
Davies, Carol Boyce, and Elaine Savory Fido, eds. *Out of the Kumbla: Caribbean Women and Literature*. Trenton, NJ: Africa World Press, 1990.
Davis, Raymond A. "West Indian Workers on the Panama Canal: A Split Labor Market Interpretation." Ph.D. diss., Stanford University, 1981.
Dayan, Joan. *Haiti, History, and the Gods*. Berkeley: University of California Press, 1995.
De Lisser, Herbert George. *Jane's Career: A Story of Jamaica*. 1914. Introduction by Kenneth Ramchand. New York: Africana Publishing Corporation, 1971.
———. *Susan Proudleigh*. London: Metheun & Co. Ltd., 1915.
———. *Twentieth Century Jamaica*. Kingston, Jamaica: The Jamaica Times Limited, 1913.
———. *In Jamaica and Cuba*. Kingston, Jamaica: The Gleaner Company, 1910.
———. "Myrtle and Money." *Planters' Punch* (1941–42): 3–6, 15–17, 19–22, 24–25, 27–33, 35–38, 42–43, 46–50, 52–65, 68–70, 72–74, 76–78, 80–86, 88.

De Moya, E. Antonio. "Power Games and Totalitarian Masculinity in the Dominican Republic," in *Caribbean Masculinities: Working Papers*, edited by Rafael L. Ramírez, Víctor I. García-Toro, and Ineke Cunningham, 105–45. San Juan, Puerto Rico: HIV/AIDS Research and Education Center—University of Puerto Rico, 2002.
Diawara, Manthia. "Englishness and Blackness: Cricket as Discourse on Colonialism." *Callaloo* 13 (1990): 830–44.
Downes, Aviston D. "Boys of the Empire: Elite Education and the Socio-Cultural Construction of Hegemonic Masculinity in Barbados, 1875–1920." Unpublished paper shared through e-mail.
———. "Gender and the Elementary Teaching Service in Barbados, 1880–1960: A Re-examination of the Feminization and the Marginalization of the Black Male Theses," in *Confronting Power, Theorizing Gender: Interdisciplinary Perspectives in the Caribbean*, edited by Eudine Barriteau, 303–23. Mona, Jamaica: University of the West Indies Press, 2003.
———. "From Boys to Men: Colonial Education, Cricket and Masculinity in the Caribbean, 1870–c. 1920." Unpublished paper shared through e-mail.
Eagleton, Terry. *Literary Theory: An Introduction*. Minneapolis: University of Minnesota Press, 1983.
Edwards, Bryan. *The History, Civil and Commercial, of the British Colonies in the West Indies*. 1793. London: John Stockdale, 1819.
———. *A New Atlas of the British West Indies*. Philadelphia: James Humphreys, 1806.
Elder, J. D. *Folk Songs from Tobago*. London: Kamak House, 1994.
English, Peter. *Panama and the Canal Zone: In Pictures*. New York: Sterling Publishing/Oak Tree Press, 1973.
Erisman, H. Michael. *Pursuing Postdependency Politics: South-South Relations in the Caribbean*. Boulder: Lynne Rienner Publishers, 1992.
Essence Magazine, review of *Tree of Life* by Maryse Condé. February 1993: 52.
Fanon, Frantz. *The Wretched of the Earth: The Handbook for the Black Revolution that is Changing the Shape of the World*, translated by Constance Farrington. New York: Presence Africaine, 1963.
———. *Black Skin, White Masks*, translated by Charles Lam Markmann. New York: Grove Weidenfeld, 1967.
Farmer, Paul. *The Uses of Haiti*. Monroe, ME: Common Courage Press, 1994.
Ferguson, Moira. *Colonialism and Gender from Mary Wollstonecraft to Jamaica Kincaid: East Caribbean Connections*. New York: Columbia University Press, 1993.
Ferguson, Russell, Martha Gever, Trinh T. Minh-ha, and Cornel West, eds. *Out There: Marginalization and Contemporary Cultures*. Cambridge, MA: The MIT Press, 1990.
Ferreira Habersham, Rhonda. "Education of the Colonial Woman through the Eyes of the Novelist," in *Caribbean Portraits: Essays on Gender Ideologies and Identities*, edited by Christine Barrow, 225–33. Kingston, Jamaica: Ian Randle Publishers/Centre for Gender and Development Studies, University of the West Indies, 1998.
Folk Songs of Barbados, compiled by Trevor Marshall, Peggy McGeary, and Grace Thompson. Bridgetown, Barbados: McMarson Associates, 1981.
Franck, Harry A. *Zone Policeman 88: A Close Range Study of the Panama Canal and Its Workers*. New York: Arno Press/The New York Times, 1970.

Froude, James Anthony. *The English in the West Indies*. London: Scribner, 1888.
Garvey, Marcus. *African Fundamentalism: A Literary and Cultural Anthology of Garvey's Harlem Renaissance*, edited by Tony Martin. Dover, MA: Majority Press, 1991.
———. *Message to the People: The Course of African Philosophy*, edited by Tony Martin. Dover, MA: Majority Press, 1986.
———. *Philosophy and Opinions or, Africa for the Africans, Volumes I and II*, edited by Amy Jaques-Garvey. Dover, MA: Majority Press, 1986.
———. *The Marcus Garvey and Universal Negro Improvement Association Papers*, edited by Robert A. Hill. Berkeley: University of California Press, 1983.
———. *The Poetical Works of Marcus Garvey*, edited by Tony Martin. Dover, MA: Majority Press, 1983.
———. *More Philosophy and Opinions of Marcus Garvey, Vol. 3*, edited by Amy Jaques Garvey and E. U. Essien-Udom. Totowa, NJ: Frank Cass & Co., 1977.
Gates, Henry Louis Jr., and Nellie Y. McKay, eds. *The Norton Anthology of African American Literature*. New York: W. W. Norton, 1997.
Gilroy, Paul. *The Black Atlantic: Modernity and Double Consciousness*. Cambridge, MA: Harvard University Press, 1993.
———. *Small Acts: Thoughts on the Politics of Black Cultures*. New York: Serpent's Tail, 1993.
———. *"There Ain't No Black in the Union Jack": The Cultural Politics of Race and Nation*. London: Hutchinson, 1987.
Glissant, Edouard. *Caribbean Discourse: Selected Essays*, translated by J. Michael Dash. Charlottesville: University of Virginia Press, 1989.
Gmelch, George. *Double Passage: The Lives of Caribbean Migrants Abroad and Back Home*. Ann Arbor: University of Michigan Press, 1992.
Goveia, Elsa. *A Study on the Historiography of the British West Indies to the end of the 19th Century*. Washington, DC: Howard University Press, 1980.
———. *Slave Society in the British Leeward Islands at the End of the 18th Century*. New Haven, CT: Yale University Press, 1965.
Griffin, Farah Jasmine. *"Who Set You Flowin'": The African American Migration Narrative*. New York: Oxford University Press, 1995.
Gunning, Sandra. "Traveling with Her Mother's Tastes: The Negotiation of Gender, Race, and Location in *Wonderful Adventures of Mrs. Seacole in Many Lands*." *Signs: Journal of Women in Culture and Society* 26.4 (2001): 949n1.
Hall, Stuart. "Cultural Identity and Diaspora." *Colonial Discourse and Post-Colonial Theory: A Reader*, edited by Patrick Williams and Laura Chrisman, 392–403. New York: Columbia University Press, 1994.
Harlow, Barbara. *Resistance Literature*. New York: Methuen, 1987.
Harris, Wilson. *The Palace of the Peacock*. London: Faber and Faber, 1988.
———. *Tradition, the Writer and Society: Critical Essays*. 1967. London: New Beacon Press, 1973.
———. *History, Fable, and Myth in the Caribbean and the Guianas*, introduction by Selwyn Cudjoe. 1970. Wellesley, MA: Calaloux Publications, 1995.
Haskin, Frederic J. *The Panama Canal*. Garden City, NY: Doubleday, Page & Company, 1913.
Hatch, Robert. Review of "The Harder They Come." *The Nation* 3 May 1973: 316.
Henri, Florette. *Black Migration: Movement North 1900–1920: The Road from Myth to Man*. New York: Anchor Press, 1976.

Henry, Paget. *Caliban's Reason: Introducing Afro-Caribbean Philosophy.* New York: Routledge, 2000.

Henry, Paget, and Paul Buhle, eds. *C. L. R. James's Caribbean.* Durham, NC: Duke University Press, 1992.

Heuman, Gad J. *Between Black and White: Race, Politics, and the Free Coloreds in Jamaica, 1792–1865.* Westport, CT: Greenwood Press, 1981.

Hewitt, Leah D. "Condé's Critical Seesaw." *Callaloo* 18.3 (1995): 641–51.

Hill, Howard C. *Roosevelt and the Caribbean.* Chicago: University of Chicago Press, 1927.

Hobsbawm, Eric, and Terence Ranger, eds. *The Invention of Tradition.* Cambridge: Cambridge University Press, 1983.

Hodge, Merle. *Crick Crack Monkey.* London: Heinemann, 1970.

Hulme, Peter. *Colonial Encounters: Europe and the Native Caribbean, 1492–1797.* London: Routledge, 1986.

Hulme, Peter, Francis Barker, and Margaret Iversen, eds. *Colonial Discourse/Post Colonial Theory.* Manchester, NY: Manchester University Press, 1994.

Hurston, Zora Neale. *Their Eyes Were Watching God.* Urbana: University of Illinois Press, 1991.

Isthmian Historical Society. *Letters from Isthmian Canal Construction Workers*, edited and introduced by Ruth C. Stuhl. Balboa Heights, C. Z., 1963.

James, Cyril Lionel Robert. *The Black Jacobins: Toussaint L'Ouverture and the San Domingo Revolution.* New York: Vintage Books/Random House, 1989.

———. *Beyond a Boundary.* Durham, NC: Duke University Press, 1993.

JanMohamed, Abdul R. "The Economy of Manichean Allegory: The Function of Racial Difference in Colonial Literature." *"Race," Writing and Difference*, edited by Henry Louis Gates, Jr., 78–106. Chicago: University of Chicago Press, 1985.

Johnson, Willis Fletcher. *Four Centuries of the Panama Canal.* London: Cassell and Company, 1907.

Josephs, Aleric. "Mary Seacole: Jamaican Nurse and 'Doctress,' 1805/10–1881." *Jamaican Historical Review* 17 (1991): 49.

Kael, Pauline. Review of "The Harder They Come." *Reeling.* Boston: Little, Brown & Company, 1976.

Kent, George E. "Claude McKay's *Banana Bottom* Reappraised." *CLA Journal* 18.2 (December 1974): 222–34.

———. "A Conversation with George Lamming." *Black World* 22.5 (March 1973): 4–14, 88–96.

Kincaid, Jamaica. *Lucy.* New York: Farrar, Straus, Giroux, 1990.

———. *A Small Place.* New York: Farrar, Straus, Giroux, 1988.

———. *Annie John.* New York: Farrar, Straus, Giroux, 1985.

King, Nicole. "C. L. R. James and Formulations of Caribbean Cultural Identity." Ph.D. diss., University of Pennsylvania, 1994.

LaFeber, Walter. *The Panama Canal: The Crisis in Historical Perspective.* New York: Oxford University Press, 1989.

Lamming, George. Personal interviews. July 1996, July 1994.

———. *The Pleasures of Exile.* Foreword by Sandra Pouchet Paquet. Ann Arbor: University of Michigan Press, 1992.

———. *In the Castle of My Skin.* Foreword by Sandra Pouchet Paquet. Ann Arbor: University of Michigan Press, 1991.

———. *In the Castle of My Skin*. 1953. New York: Schocken Books, 1983.
———. *The Emigrants*. London: Allison and Busby, 1980.
———. "The Negro Writer and His World." *Presence Africaine* 8–10 (1956): 318–25.
Las Casas, Bartolome de. *History of the Indies*, translated and edited by Andree Collard. New York: Harper and Row, 1971.
Lawrence, Leota S. "Three West Indian Heroines: An Analysis." *CLA Journal* 21.2 (December 1977): 238–50.
Lemann, Nicholas. *The Promised Land: The Great Black Migration and How it Changed America*. New York: Knopf, 1991.
Lewis, Barbara. "No Silence: An Interview with Maryse Condé." *Callaloo* 18.3 (1995): 543–50.
Lewis, Gordon K. *Main Currents in Caribbean Thought: The Historical Evolution of Caribbean Society in Its Ideological Aspects, 1492–1900*. Baltimore: Johns Hopkins University Press, 1983.
———. *Notes on the Puerto Rican Revolution: An Essay on American Dominance and Caribbean Resistance*. New York: Monthly Review Press, 1974.
———. *The Growth of the Modern West Indies*. New York: Monthly Review Press, 1968.
Lewis, Lancelot. *The West Indian in Panama: Black Labor in Panama, 1850–1914*. Washington, DC: University Press of America, 1980.
Lorde, Audre. *Zami: A New Spelling of My Name: A Biomythography*. Freedom, CA: The Crossing Press, 1982.
———. *Sister Outsider: Essays and Speeches by Audre Lorde*. Freedom, CA: The Crossing Press, 1984.
Lovell, Glenville. *Fire in the Canes*. New York: Soho Press, 1995.
McCain, William. *The United States and the Republic of Panama*. New York: Russell and Russell, 1965.
McCullough, David. *The Path Between the Seas: The Creation of the Panama Canal, 1870–1914*. New York: Simon and Schuster, 1977.
McKay, Claude. *Gingertown*. 1932. Freeport, NY: Books for Libraries Press, 1972.
———. *Banjo: A Story Without a Plot*. 1957. New York: Harcourt, Brace, Jovanovich, 1970.
———. *A Long Way from Home*. 1937. New York: Arno Press, 1969.
———. *Banana Bottom*. 1933. San Diego: Harvest Books/Harcourt, Brace, and Company, 1961.
McLeod, A. L. *Claude McKay: Centennial Studies*. New Delhi: Sterling Publishers Private, 1992.
Major, John. *Prize Possession: The United States and the Panama Canal, 1903–1979*. New York: Cambridge University Press, 1993.
Maloney, Gerardo. *El Canal de Panama y Los Trabajadores Antillanos: Panama 1920: Cronologia de una Lucha*. El Dorado: Ediciones Formato 16/Universidad de Panama, 1989.
Manley, Michael. *The Politics of Change: A Jamaican Testament*. London: Deutsch, 1974.
Marshall, Paule. *Soul Clap Hands and Sing*. Washington, DC: Howard University Press, 1988.
———. *Praisesong for the Widow*. New York: Dutton, 1984.
———. *Reena and Other Stories*. New York: Feminist Press/CUNY, 1983.
———. *Brown Girl, Brownstones*. 1959. Old Westbury, NY: Feminist Press, 1981.

Martin, Tony. *The Pan-African Connection: From Slavery to Garvey and Beyond*. Dover, MA: Majority Press, 1984.

———. *Marcus Garvey, Hero: A First Biography*. Dover, MA: Majority Press, 1983.

Mellander, G. A. *The United States in Panamanian Politics*. Danville, IL: Interstate Printers & Publishers, 1971.

"Middle America and the Caribbean." *Encyclopedia of World Cultures, Volume 3*, edited by James W. Dow, 55–59. Boston: G. K. Hall & Co., 1995.

Miller, J. Hillis. "Narrative." *Critical Terms for Literary Study*, edited by Frank Lentricchia and Thomas McLaughlin, 66–79. Chicago: University of Chicago Press, 1990.

Miller, Hugh Gordon. *The Isthmian Highway: A Review of the Problems of the Caribbean*. New York: Macmillan, 1929.

Millett, Richard, and W. Marvin Will, eds. *The Restless Caribbean: Changing Patterns of International Relations*. New York: Praeger, 1979.

Mintz, Sidney W. *Caribbean Transformations*. Baltimore: Johns Hopkins University Press, 1984.

Mintz, Sidney W., and Sally Price, eds. *Caribbean Contours*. Baltimore: Johns Hopkins University Press, 1985.

Mohammed, Patricia. "Refining Gender Methodology: Studying Masculinity Through Popular Song Lyrics." *Caribbean Masculinities: Working Papers*, edited by Rafael L. Ramírez, Víctor I. García-Toro, and Ineke Cunningham, 33–56. San Juan, Puerto Rico: HIV/AIDS Research and Education Center/University of Puerto Rico, 2002.

Morrison, Anthea. "Emancipating the Voice: Maryse Condé's *La vie scélérate*." *Callaloo* 18.3 (1995): 616–25.

Munro, Ian H. "George Lamming." *50 Caribbean Writers: A Bio-bibliographical Critical Sourcebook*, edited by Daryl Cumber Dance, 264–75. New York: Greenwood Press, 1986.

Munro, Ian, and Reinhard Sander. *Kas-Kas: Interviews with Three Caribbean Writers in Texas: George Lamming, C. L. R. James, Wilson Harris*. Austin: African and Afro-American Research Institute/University of Texas at Austin, 1972.

Naipaul, V. S. *A Turn in the South*. New York: Knopf, 1989.

———. *The Enigma of Arrival: A Novel*. New York: Knopf, 1987.

———. *Finding the Centre: Two Narratives*. London: A. Deutsch, 1984.

———. *The Return to Eva Peron with the Killings in Trinidad*. New York: Knopf, 1980.

———. *Guerrillas*. New York: Knopf, 1975.

———. *The Loss of El Dorado, a History*. New York: Knopf, 1970.

———. *The Mimic Men*. London: A. Deutsch, 1967.

———. *Middle Passage: Impressions of Five Societies: British, French and Dutch in the West Indies and South America*. London: A. Deutsch, 1962.

Neptune, Harvey. "Manly Rivalries and Mopsies: Gender, Nationality, and Sexuality in United States-Occupied Trinidad." *Radical History Review* 87 (Fall 2003): 78–95.

Nettleford, Rex. *Mirror, Mirror: Identity, Race, and Protest in Jamaica*. 1970. New York: Morrow, 1972.

Newton, Velma. *The Silver Men: West Indian Labour Migration to Panama, 1850–1914*. Mona, Jamaica: Institute of Social and Economic Research of the University of the West Indies, 1984.

Nora, Pierre, ed. *Lieux de la memoire*. Paris: Gallimard, 1984.
Ober, Frederick A. *A Guide to the West Indies, Bermuda and Panama*. New York: Dodd, Mead & Company, 1913.
Oviedo, Gonzalo Fernandez. *Natural History of the West Indies*, translated and edited by Sterling A. Stoudemire. Chapel Hill: University of North Carolina Press, 1959.
Palmer, Colin A. "Identity, Race, and Black Power in Independent Jamaica." *The Modern Caribbean*, edited by Franklin W. Knight and Colin A. Palmer, 111–28. Chapel Hill: University of North Carolina Press, 1989.
Panama Canal. Written and produced Andy Thomas. A&E Home Video, 1993.
The Panama Canal 50th Anniversary: The Story of a Great Conquest. Washington, DC: United States Government, 1964.
Paquet, Sandra Pouchet. *The Novels of George Lamming*. London: Heinemann, 1982.
Parker, Richard. "Culture, Political Economy, and Sex/Gender Systems: Masculinity in Latin America and the Caribbean." *Caribbean Masculinities: Working Papers*, edited by Rafael L. Ramírez, Víctor I. García-Toro, and Ineke Cunningham, 1–32. San Juan, Puerto Rico: HIV/AIDS Research and Education Center/ University of Puerto Rico, 2002.
Pepperman, W. Leon. *Who Built the Panama Canal?* London: J. M. Dent and Sons, 1915.
Petras, Elizabeth McLean. *Jamaican Labor Migration: White Capital and Black Labor, 1850–1930*. Boulder: Westview Press, 1988.
Pfaff, Françoise. *Conversations with Maryse Condé*. Lincoln: University of Nebraska Press, 1996.
Pollard, Velma. "Imagination and Reality: The Profile of the Colon-man in Jamaican lore and literature." Paper presented at the 26th Annual Caribbean Studies Association Conference, St. Maarten, 27 May–2 June 2001.
Price, David. W. *History Made, History Imagined: Contemporary Literature, Poiesis, and the Past*. Urbana: University of Illinois Press, 1999.
Prieb, Richard. "The Search for Community in the Novels of Claude McKay." *Studies in Black Literature* 3.2 (Summer 1972): 22–30.
Priestly, George. "Ethnicity, Class and the National Question in Panama: The Emerging Literature." *Emerging Perspectives on the Black Diaspora*, edited by Aubrey W. Bonnett and G. Llewellyn Watson, 215–37. Lanham, MD: University Press of America, 1990.
Pyne-Timothy, Helen. "Perceptions of the Black Woman in the Work of Claude McKay." *CLA Journal* 19.2 (December 1975): 152–64.
Ramchand, Kenneth. Introduction. *Jane's Career: A Story of Jamaica*, by Herbert George de Lisser. New York: Africana Publishing Corporation, 1971.
———. "Claude McKay and *Banana Bottom*." *Southern Review* 4.1 (1970): 53–66.
———. "The Writer Who Ran Away: Eric Walrond and *Tropic Death*." *Savacou: A Journal of the Caribbean Artists Movement* 2 (1970): 67–75.
Ramcharitar, Raymond. "The Detours of Caribbean Literary Theory: Has Caribbean Scholarship Been Undermined by Intellectual Insecurity?" Paper presented at the "Caribbean Literary Studies" Conference, University of Miami, Coral Gables, FL, 28 September–1 October 2000.
Ramírez, Rafael L. et al. "Introduction." *Caribbean Masculinities: Working Papers*, edited by Rafael L. Ramírez, Víctor I. García-Toro, and Ineke Cunningham, vii–xi. San Juan, Puerto Rico: HIV/AIDS Research and Education Center/ University of Puerto Rico, 2002.

Reddock, Rhoda. "'Man Gone, Man Stay!': Masculinity, Ethnicity and Identity in the Contemporary Sociopolitical Context of Trinidad and Tobago." *Caribbean Masculinities: Working Papers*, edited by Rafael L. Ramírez, Víctor I. García-Toro, and Ineke Cunningham, 147–72. San Juan, Puerto Rico: HIV/AIDS Research and Education Center/University of Puerto Rico, 2002.

"'Rhyging' Killed by Police." *The Daily Gleaner* 9 October 1948, Special Edition.

Richardson, Bonham C. *The Caribbean in the Wider World, 1492–1992: A Regional Geography*. Cambridge: Cambridge University Press, 1992.

———. *Panama Money in Barbados, 1900–1920*. Knoxville: University of Tennessee Press, 1985.

———. *Caribbean Migrants: Environment and Human Survival on St. Kitts and Nevis*. Knoxville: University of Tennessee Press, 1983.

Richter, David H., ed. *The Critical Tradition: Classic Texts and Contemporary Trends*. New York: Bedford Books/St. Martin's Press, 1989.

Rivas, Eyra Marcela Reyes. *El trabajo de las mujeres en la historia de la construccíon del Canal de Panamá, 1881–1914*. Instituto de la Mujer de la Universidad de Panamá, 2000.

Roberts, W. Adolphe. *Six Great Jamaicans: Biographical Sketches*. Kingston, Jamaica: The Pioneer Press, 1951.

Rohlehr, Gordon. "Man's Spiritual Search in the Caribbean Through Literature." *Troubling of the Waters*, edited by Idris Hamid. San Fernando, Trinidad: Rahaman Printery, 1973.

———. "Possession as Metaphor: Lamming's *Season of Adventure*." *Journal of West Indian Literature* 5.1–2 (1992): 1–29.

Roumain, Jacques. *Masters of the Dew*, translated by Langston Hughes and Mercer Cook. 1941. New York: Collier Books, 1971.

Rubenstein, Hymie. "Return Migration to the English-Speaking Caribbean: Review and Commentary." *Return Migration and Remittances: Developing a Caribbean Perspective*, edited by William F. Stinner, Klaus de Albuquerque, and Roy S. Bryce-Laporte, 3–34. Washington, DC: Research Institute on Immigration and Ethnic Studies/Smithsonian Institution, 1982.

Russell, Carlos E. *An Old Woman Remembers . . . : The Recollected History of West Indians in Panama, 1855–1955, A Prose-Poetry Monologue*. New York: Caribbean Diaspora Press, 1995.

Said, Edward. *Culture and Imperialism*. New York: Knopf, 1993.

———. "Reflections on Exile." *Out There: Marginalization and Contemporary Cultures*, edited by Russell Ferguson, Martha Gever, Trinh T. Minh-ha, and Cornel West, 357–66. Cambridge, MA: MIT Press, 1990.

Samuels, Wilfred D. *Five Afro-Caribbean Voices in American Culture, 1917–1929*. Boulder, CO: Belmont Books, 1977.

Scott, James C. *Domination and the Arts of Resistance: Hidden Transcripts*. New Haven, CT: Yale University Press, 1990.

Seacole, Mary. *Wonderful Adventures of Mrs. Mary Seacole in Many Lands*. 1857. New York: Oxford University Press, 1988.

Segal, Lynne. *Slow Motion: Changing Masculinities, Changing Men*. New Brunswick, NJ: Rutgers University Press, 1990.

Senior, Olive. "Window." *Discerner of Hearts and Other Stories*. Toronto: McClelland & Stewart, 1995. 57–74.

———. *Working Miracles: Women's Live in the English-speaking Caribbean*. Bloomington: Indiana University Press, 1991.
———. *Summer Lightening and Other Stories*. Essex: Longman Caribbean Writers, 1986.
———. "The Panama Railway." *Jamaica Journal* 14 (1980): 66–77.
———. "The Chinese Who Came from Panama." *Jamaica Journal* 14 (1980): 78–79.
———. "The Colon People." *Jamaica Journal* 11.3/12.4 (1978): 62–71, 87–103.
Smith, Faith. *Creole Recitations: John Jacob Thomas and Colonial Formations in the Late 19th Century Caribbean*. Charlottesville: University of Virginia Press, 2002.
Smith, Michael Garfield. *The Plural Society in the British West Indies*. Berkeley: University of California Press, 1965.
Southern, Eileen. *The Music of Black Americans: A History, 3rd Edition*. New York: W. W. Norton, 1997.
Spear, Thomas C. "Individual Quests and Collective History." *World Literature Today* 67.4 (Autumn 1993): 723–30.
Spivak, Gayatri Chakravorty. *Death of a Discipline*. New York: Columbia University Press, 2003.
Stinner, William F., Klaus de Albuquerque, and Roy S. Bryce-Laporte, eds. *Return Migration and Remittances: Developing a Caribbean Perspective*. Washington, DC: Research Institute on Immigration and Ethnic Studies/Smithsonian Institution, 1982.
Strachan, Ian G. "Paradise and Plantation: The Economy of Caribbean Discourse." Ph.D. diss., University of Pennsylvania, 1995.
———. *Paradise and Plantation: Tourism and Culture in the Anglophone Caribbean*. Charlottesville: University of Virginia Press, 2002.
Taleb-Khyar, Mohamed B. "An Interview with Maryse Condé and Rita Dove." *Callaloo* 14.2 (1991): 357.
Tapping, Craig. "Children and History in the Caribbean Novel: George Lamming's *In the Castle of My Skin* and Jamaica Kincaid's *Annie John*." *Kunapipi* 11.2 (1989): 51–59.
Taylor, Patrick. *The Narrative of Liberation: Perspectives of Afro-Caribbean Literature, Popular Culture, and Politics*. Ithaca, NY: Cornell University Press, 1989.
Thelwell, Michael. *The Harder They Come*. 1980. New York: Grove Press, 1988.
———. "*The Harder They Come*: From Film to Novel." *Grand Street* 10.1 (1991): 135–65.
Thomas, John Jacob. *FROUDACITY: West Indian Fables by James Anthony Froude*. London: New Beacon Books, 1969.
Thomas-Hope, Elizabeth. *Explanation in Caribbean Migration: Perception and the Image: Jamaica, Barbados, St. Vincent*. London: MacMillan Press/Warwick University Caribbean Studies, 1992.
———. "The Establishment of a Migration Tradition: British West Indian Movements to the Hispanic Caribbean in the Century after Emancipation." *Caribbean Social Relations*, edited by Colin G. Clarke, 66–81. London: University of Liverpool/Centre for Latin American Studies, 1978.
Tiffin, Helen. "Post-coloniality, Post-Modernity and the Rehabilitation of Post-colonial History." *Journal of Commonwealth Literature* 23.1 (1988): 169–81.
———. "The Tyranny of History: George Lamming's *Natives of My Person* and *Water with Berries*." *Ariel* 10.4 (1979): 37–52.
Tillery, Tyrone. *Claude McKay: A Black Poet's Struggle for Identity*. Amherst: University of Massachusetts Press, 1992.

Urgo, Joseph R. *Novel Frames: Literature as Guide to Race, Sex, and History in American Culture.* Jackson: University Press of Mississippi, 1991.
Van Mol, Kay R. "Primitivism and Intellect in Toomer's *Cane* and McKay's *Banana Bottom*: The Need for an Integrated Black Consciousness." *Negro American Literature_Forum* 10.1 (Spring 1976): 48–52.
Wa'Nyatetu-Waigwa, Wangari. "From Liminality to a Home of Her Own? The Quest Motif in Maryse Condé's Fiction." *Callaloo* 18.3 (1995): 551–64.
Wa'Thiongo, Ngugi. *Decolonising the Mind: The Politics of Language in African Literature.* London: Heinemann, 1986.
———. *Homecoming: Essays on African and Caribbean Literature, Culture and Politics.* 1972. New York: L. Hill, 1973.
Walcott, Derek. "The Muse of History." *Carifesta Forum: An Anthology of 20 Caribbean Voices,* edited by John Hearne, 111–28. Kingston: Institute of Jamaica/ Jamaica Journal, 1976.
———. "The Caribbean: Culture or Mimicry?" *Journal of Interamerican Studies* 16.1 (1974): 3–13.
———. "What the Twilight Says: An Overture." *Dream on Monkey Mountain and Other Plays.* New York: Farrar, Straus, Giroux, 1970. 1–40.
Walmsley, Anne. *The Caribbean Artists Movement, 1966–1972: A Literary & Cultural History.* Port of Spain, Trinidad: New Beacon Books, 1992.
Walrond, Eric. *Tropic Death.* 1926. New York: Collier Books, 1954.
———. "The Voodoo's Revenge." *Opportunity: A Journal of Negro Life* 3.31 (July 1925): 209–13.
Waters, Mary C. *Black Identities: West Indian Immigrant Dreams and American Realities.* New York: Russell Sage Foundation/Harvard University Press, 1999.
Watkins-Owens, Irma. *Blood Relations: Caribbean Immigrants and the Harlem Community, 1900–1930.* Bloomington: Indiana University Press, 1996.
Watson, James. *Between Two Cultures: Migrants and Minorities in Britain.* Oxford: Blackwell, 1977.
George W. Westerman Collection, Photographs and Prints Division, Schomburg Center for Research in Black Culture, New York Public Library.
George W. Westerman Collection, Rare Books and Manuscripts Division, Schomburg Center for Research in Black Culture, New York Public Library.
Westerman, George. *The West Indian Worker on the Canal Zone.* Liga Civica Nacional, 1951.
———. *A Minority Group in Panama.* Liga Civica Nacional, 1950.
———. *Toward a Better Understanding.* Liga Civica Nacional, 1946.
Williams, Agatha. "La mujer antillana en la construccíon del Canal." *La Prensa,* Viernes (8 March 1991): 19B.
Williams, Eric. *From Columbus to Castro: The History of the Caribbean 1492–1969.* New York: Vintage Books, 1984.
———. *Eric Williams Speaks: Essays on Colonialism and Independence,* edited by Selwyn Cudjoe. Wellesley, MA: Calaloux Publications; Amherst: University of Massachusetts Press, 1993.
———. *The Negro in the Caribbean.* 1942. New York: Negro University Press, 1969.
———. *Capitalism and Slavery.* New York: Capricorn Books, 1966.
———. *Documents of West Indian History.* Port-of-Spain, Trinidad: PNM, 1963.

Index

Note: Page references in *italics* indicate a photograph.

Abbot, Henry, 34
Abbot, Willis J., 26, 61
Adamic aesthetic, xiv
Africa: pantheistic belief systems of, 104, 123n17; peoples and language groups of, xviii
African-Caribbean cultural traditions, 6, 63, 104
African Diaspora, 112–13
ague, 39
Allick, Helon, 16n11, 70, 71
Ancon, Panamá, 26
Anglophone Caribbean, 3, 7, 42, 43, 200
Antigua, canal workers from, 64, 65
Area Studies, xviii
Arnold, Hugh M., *170*
Austin, Harrigan, 70, 76, 78, 83, 85n6, 198

Bahamas, canal workers from, 65
Banana Bottom (McKay), 5, 12, 120, 131–42, 162, 200
Banister, Albert, 70, 71, 72, 78, 79, 87n16, 88n21, 198–99
Barbados: anti-emigration laws of, 44; canal workers from, xi, 12, 27, 29, 64, 65, 69, 78, 79, 80; impact of Panamá Money on, 44–45; skills acquired by returnees, 45–46; songs about Panamá Man, 15n6
Barton, Charles, 127
Bas-Obispo Canal Zone, 66
Beckles, Wesley, 70
Belgrave, Allan C., 74–75
Bennett, Louise, xi, 129, 163n5
Berisford, G. Mitchell, 70, 199
Bidlack Treaty, 22, 24
Black Labor on a White Canal: Panama, 1904–1981 (Conniff), 14n4
Blaine, James, 23
Boer War, 23
border crossings, xiii
bottom-up history, 3, 14n4, 34
Braithwaire, Donald, 2
Brathwaite, Edward Kamau, xiii, xvii, 122n10
Brewster, John, 2
Brewster, Joseph, 66, 80
Britain: colonies in the Caribbean, xi, xiv, 8, 44, 93, 94, 101, 102, 103, 106, 108; control of Panamá territory, 21–23, 24

229

British Guiana, 147
British Honduras, 64
Brown, Joseph, 72
Brown, Lessep O., 72, 88n22
Brown, Patrice, 89n23
Bryce-Laporte, Roy, 14n4
Bunau-Varilla, Phillipe, 23, 24, 48n7
Butcher, John, 30, 69, 80

Caliban's Reason (Henry), xii, xix
California, 22, 26–27
call-and-response song, 173
Camp Bierd, 30
Camp Coiner, 30
Canal history, xiv, 1–10, 19, *20*, 21–47
Canal Record, 63, 157
Canal Zone: creation and control of, 23–24; disease and illness in, 15n9, 66, 79. *See also* Isthmian Canal Commission (ICC); labor; women
Caribbean histories, xi–xvi, xxiin11, 1–13, 14n4–5
Caribbean League, 44
"Caribbean Man in Space and Time" (Brathwaite), xvii
Caribbean philosophy, xii–xiii, xvi, xxin5
Caribbean Studies, xvii, 11
Central America, trans-isthmian canal activities in, 19, 22
Cesaire, Aime, xiii
Chamberlain, Mary, 53n26
Charles V, 21
Chase, Leonard A., 73
Chinese workers, 13n3, 28
Christian, Barbara, xvi
Clark, Vévé, 171
Clarke, Aaron, 83
Clarke, Amos E., 77, 164n8
Clarke, Wesley D., 72, 81, 88n22
class, Panamá Money and interclass movement, 12, 41, 45, 165n13, 206–8, 211–12n5
Clayton, H. B., 88n22
Clayton-Bulwer Treaty, 22, 23
Cliff, Jimmy, 110
Cobham, Rhonda, 210, 213n12

Colombia: canal workers from, 28, 65; negotiations with the U.S., 23–24
Colón, Panamá, 27, 30
colonialism, xi, 8, 44, 93, 94, 101, 102, 103, 106, 108
Colón Man: anecdotal descriptions of, 62–63; avoiding ICC housing and food policies, 30, 34; experiences of, 6–7, 10, 64–85; fancy characteristics of returnees, 11, 41, 125–63, 165n12, 167–68n25; features and characteristics of, 3, 5, 9; illness and death rates of canal workers, 28, 31–32; literary figures of, 91–124; moneysaving methods of, 71–73, 86–87n13; motivations for isthmian migration by, 7–8, 12, 13n3, 32, 36, 37–41, 46, 52n24, 67, 84–85, 166n18, 203–5, 212n9; myth and reality of a successful migrant, 127–31, 164n7; mythographies of, xi, xx, 10, 38, 93, 117–20, 131–62, 175–90, 198, 200–210; populations in Panamá of, 35–36, 57n43; postconstruction lives of, 83–84; racial stereotypes of, 3, 10, 25, 34, 39; recognition of accomplishments of, 25–26, 28, 31, 34–37, 46, 47, 63–64, 69, 79–81, 89n26, 97–98, 152–53, 157–61, 170, 202–3; relationships with white bosses, 71–72, 76, 77–79; as superior workers, 77–85; vernacular stories of, 91–124
"Colón Man a Come," 3–4
"The Colon People" (Senior), 14n4
colorism/racism, 8, 32, 51n18, 51n20
"Come from Colon," 128, 129
"Come Out A Merican Cut," 172–73
Compagnie Nouvelle du Canal de Panama, 16n15, 23, 24, 27, 28, 31
Compagnie Universelle du Canal Interoceanique, 16n15, 27, 28, 31
Comparative Literature, xvii–xviii
Condé, Maryse, xi, xviii–xix, 1, 3, 5, 12–13, 162–63, 169–90, 191–95
Conniff, Michael, 14n4, 36, 86–87n13, 197, 198

Corbin, Ethelbert A., 2
Cramer, Louise, 5, 47, 166–67n22
creolization, xiii
Cristobal, Panamá, 28, 92
Culebra, Panamá, 126
Culebra Cut, 34, 36, 89n26
cultural capital, 41, 52n24, 86n9, 130
Cunningson, Marian, 164n8

The Daily Gleaner, 60
Darling, Charles, 24
Dayan, Joan, 9, 164n9
death rates: associated with canal construction, 4, 7, 15n9, 27; documented and undocumented worker deaths, 31; in railroad workers, 15n9, 27
de Lesseps, Ferdinand, 27
de Lisser, Herbert, 5, 13, 200–210, 211n4
Dessalines, Jean-Jacques, 1, 9–10
Disability Relief, 64
disease: ague in workers, 39; in the Canal Zone, 4, 7, 15n9, 25, 27, 31, 66, 79; ICC resources for sanitation and health, 50–51n17, 68–69, 87n16, 179, 194n19; malaria, 15n9, 39, 68, 79, 88n21, 179, 194n19; yellow fever, 15n9, 68, 79, 179, 194n19
Dominica, canal workers from, 65
Dottin, Alfred, 69, 70, 85n3, 198
Dottin, Austin, 198
Douglas, Nehemiah E., 70
Drake, Francis, 21
Dunbar, John, 2

education, 42
Emancipation, 7, 8, 43
Emmanuel, Victor, 2
Emperador, 28
The English in the West Indies (Froude), xiv, xv
epistolary narratives of workers, 65–85
Essence, 169
ethnic and cultural studies, xvii–xviii

Fanon, Frantz, xiii, xxin5
fictive narratives, 7, 16n11

Fields, J. B., 69
Fields, J. S., 69
folk culture, songs in, 5, 6, 12, 15n6, 47n1, 128, 129, 130, 173, 191–92n9, 200
Folk Songs of Barbados (Marshall), 5
Forde, Rufus, 80
France, construction of a canal across Panamá by, 22–23, 27
Franck, Harry, 63–64, 87n15
Francophone Caribbean writers, xix
Frederick, James, 72
French Guiana, 75
Froudacity (Thomas), xv
Froude, James Anthony, xiv–xv, xvi
Fulani language group, xviii
Fulbe peoples, xviii
Fumigating Gang, 68

Gallagher, Ed, 69
Gamboa, Panamá, 81
ganja trade, 115, 117
Gard, Joseph, 87n16
Garner, John, 69, 80
Garvey, Marcus, 112, 180, 182, 194n20
Gatun, Panamá, 82
Gay, Douglas, 43
gender, 54–55n32–37, 117–18, 130. See also masculinity; women
genre, 3, 6–8, 10–11, 64–65
Germany, 23
Gittens, Thomas, 77
Glissant, Edouard, xvi, 93
globalization, xviii
Goethels, George, 81
gold: discovery in California, 26–27; employee classification of, 32–33, 51n19–20
Gorgas, William C., 31, 194n19
Graham, Joseph, 72
Green, Prince George, 66–67, 81–82, 86n9
Grenada, canal workers from, 64, 65
Guadeloupe, canal workers from, 169–90, 193n12
Guyana, 147
The Guyana Quarterly, xiii

Haiti: liberation from France, 9; postrevolutionary image of, 17n20; practice of *vodou* in, xxiin11, 9, 17n20, 167n23; violent slave revolt in, xiv
Haiti, History, and the Gods (Dayan), 9
The Harder They Come (1973), 108–9
The Harder They Come (Thelwell), 5, 12, 93–95, 108–17
Harris, Wilson, xi–xv, xvii, xxi–xxiin7–8, 8–9
Harrod, Ernest, 69
Haskin, Frederic, 26, 35
Hausa, xviii
Hawaiian Islands, 22
Hay, John, 23
Hay/Bunau-Varilla Treaty, 24
Hay-Herrán Convention, 23
Haynes, Johnny, 69
Hay-Pauncefote Treaty, 23
hegemonic masculinity, 42, 55n34, 55n37
Henry, Paget, xii–xiii, xvii, xix, xxin5
Henzell, Perry, 108, 109
Heremakhonon (Condé), xviii–xix
Hermon, Peter, 84
history: bottom-up, 3, 14n4, 34; creative appropriation of, xiv; disorder and untidyness of, 169–90; top-down, 4, 14n4, 34, 35
History, Fable, and Myth in the Caribbean and the Guianas (Harris), xiv
Hodges, George, 80–81, 84–85
Holder, Everton, 86–87n13
Honduras, canal workers from, 65
Hunt, Clifford, 84

I, Tituba, Black Witch of Salem (Condé), 3
imaginable possibilities, 7–8, 10, 38, 176
imaginable truths, xi, xvi, 6, 7–8, 13, 37, 65, 73, 172
imagination, role of, xix, xxin4
imaginative arts, xiii
imperialism/colonialism, xi, 8, 44, 93, 94, 101, 102, 103, 106, 108
indenture, xi, xiii

India, canal workers from, 28
In Jamaica and Cuba (de Lisser), 202
In the Castle of My Skin (Lamming), 5, 12, 93–95, 96–108, 117, 200
Ireland, canal workers from, 28
Isthmian Canal Commission (ICC): documented and undocumented workers of, 26, 36; gold/silver classifications of workers by, 32–33, 51n19–20; minimizing work-related complaints by, 30; race/color in policies of, 32–33, 61–64, 76–77; recruitment of workers by, 11, 25, 26, 29, 50n15, 54n30, 130, 198; repatriation of workers by, 46; room and board provided by, 29–30, 33–34, 49–50n13, 73–74, 87–88n18–19. *See also* Colón Man; labor
Isthmian Historical Society (IHS), 5, 64, 68, 69, 85n4
isthmian migration: circular migration in, 36, 212–13n10; as cultural capital, 41, 52n24, 86n9, 130; as defining masculinity and Caribbeanness, 130–31, 161, 162, 163–64n6–7; imagined possibilities of, 7–8; motivations for, xii, xx, 3, 4, 12, 37–41, 46, 52n24, 66, 67, 84–85, 166n18, 203–5, 212n9; perceived and actual reality of, 38–47, 52n24, 53n27, 72; by women, 130–31, 169–210, 211n2

Jamaica: British colony of, xiv; canal workers from, xi, 28, 64, 65, 76, 78, 81, 108–17, 123–24n23–24, 200–210, 212n8; government restriction on emigration, 28–29; history of slavery in, xx–xxin2; labor unions in, 44, 56n40; railroad labor recruits from, 27
Jamaica Gleaner, 89n26
James, C. L. R., xiii, xv
James, Frederick, 72, 85n6
James, Wilfred, *170*
Jim Crow, 143

Kavanagh, Lancelot, 76, 199
Kirby, Jerry, 69

La Boca, Panamá, 30, 127
labor: African-descended Caribbean workers in, xi, xx, 6, 63, 104; anecdotal descriptions of, 25–27, 39–40, 59, 61–65; Chinese workers in, 13n3, 25; exploitation and opportunistic use of black workers, 5, 12, 49n10; as *extranjeros*, 15n8; gold and silver classification of workers in, 32–33, 51n19–20; illness and death rates of, 7, 15n9, 27–28, 31–32; name-changing practices of, 16n11, 71, 86n12; narratives of personal experiences of, 64–85; North American workers in, 25, 26, 27; for the Panamá Railroad, 3, 4, 15n9, 16n15, 22, 23, 25, 27, 32–33, 39–40; pay rates of, 29, 32–33, 51n19, 70–71; recruitment of, 11, 54n30, 92; room and board for canal workers, 29–30, 33–34, 49–50n13, 72–74, 87–88n18; single and married workers, 30, 198–99; skills acquired by, 45–46; stereotypes about workers, 3, 10, 25, 34, 39; West Indian workers, 2, 4, *126, 170*; working and living conditions of, 11–12, 15n8, *20*, 88n20. *See also* Colón Man; isthmian migration; women
LaFeber, Walter, 26
Lamming, George, xi, xiii, 5, 6–7, 12, 93–95, 96–108, 117, 121n3, 133, 152, 200
language: influence of translator's choice, xviii; language groups in Africa, xviii
Latin America, 19
La vie scélérate (Condé), 189–90
Lawson, Daniel, 81, 85n5
LeCurrieux, Jules, 75, 85n5
Lesseps, Ferdinand de, 4
"Le Torrent," 164n9
Letters From Isthmian Canal Construction Workers (Isthmian Historical Society), 5, 64, 66, 68, 70, 71, 73, 75, 76, 82, 85, 85n2, 97, 111, 130, 198, 200
Lewis, Lancelot, 14n4, 40, 47n1
LICCW. See Letters From Isthmian Canal Construction Workers (Isthmian Historical Society)
limbo, xxii
lock-type canals, 27, 49
Loomis, Francis, 24
Lorde, Audre, 8
Loulan, J. A., 26
Lowe, Caroline, 164n8
Lucas, Rufus, 75
lwa, 9

Macarie, Henry, 71
Major, John, 26
malaria, 15n9, 39, 68, 79, 88n21, 179, 194n19
Manifest Destiny, 22
Mark, John Thomas, 79
Marshall, Trevor, 5, 15n6
Martin, George H., 64, 67–68, 69, 70, 73–74, 82, 83, 84, 85n6, 87n14, 88n19
Martineau, E. W., 67–68, 78–79, 82, 86n9, 89n25
Martinique, recruitment of women from, 50n15, 130, 198
masculinity, 5, 41–42, 54–55n32–37, 120, 125–68
Maynard, Manassah, 72
McCullough, David, 15n9–10, 26, 32, 35, 61, 77, 88n19
McDonald, Philip, 76, 85n6, 87–88n18–19
McEnnis, Luther, 68
McKay, Claude, xi, 5, 12, 120, 131–42, 200
McKenzie, Z. H., 83
migration: as act of resistance, 13; circular migration pattern of, 36, 212–13n10; as form of masculine indoctrination, 42; global migrations, xvii; intellectual migration, xvii; internal migrations, xvi, xvii; songs of, 6; voluntary and

involuntary, xiii. *See also* isthmian migration
Mitchell, Alfred, 66
Moe, Henry Allen, 148
Mohammed, Patricia, 6
Monroe Doctrine, 22, 52n22
Moses, Charles, 69
mosquitoes, 68
Murtaugh, William, 69
Muslim populations in Africa, xviii
mythographies, xi, xx, 38, 93, 117–20, 131–62, 175–90, 200–210

Naipaul, V. S., xiii
Nettleford, Rex, xiii
Nevis, canal workers from, xxin4
New Granada, 22, 23, 47–48n2
New Mexico, 22
Newton, Velma, 14n4, 16n11, 52n25
New World writers, xiv
Nicaragua, British settlements in, 22
Nigeria, xviii
"Noh Lickle Twang!" (Bennett), 129, 130, 163n5

Old World writers, xiv
oral history, 5
Outlook, 61

Paily, Henry, 71
Palace of the Peacock (Harris), xiii, xv–xvi
Pan-Africanism, 112–13
Panamá: Canal Zone in, xvi, 15n9, 23–24, 66, 79; citizenship of Afro-Caribbean workers, 15n8; climate of, 31, 49n9; historic international interests in, 21–24; independence of, 24, 47–48n2, 48n5; multinational control of, 21–22; railroad construction in, 3, 4, 16n15, 22, 23, 25, 27, 32–33, 39–40; segregation and racial prejudices in, 21, 32, 51n18; trade crossroads of, 19. *See also* Colón Man; isthmian migration; labor
Panama and the Canal in Picture and Prose (Abbot), 26

Panamá Canal: construction of, *20*, 26–47; end of construction of, 81–84; illness and death associated with, 4, 7, 27, 28, 31–32; investors in, 22–24, 48n4; work-related accidents during building of, 152, 177–78. *See also* Colón Man; isthmian migration; labor; Panamá Money
The Panama Canal (Haskin), 26, 35
Panamá City, 27, 30
"Panama Gold" (Walrond), 120, 131, 147, 148, 151–56, 157, 162, 200
Panamá Man, 13n3, 73, 79
"Panama Man" (song), 15n6, 128, 129, 130
Panamá Money: class mobility with, 41, 45, 165n45, 205–8, 211–12n5; financial possibilities of, 4, 7, 11, 29, 40, 66, 73; risk and sacrifice associated with, 157–62, 168n28; sent to home and family by workers, 45, 52n25, 56–57n42; social impact of, 12; songs about, 15n6. *See also* Colón Man; isthmian migration; labor
Panama Money in Barbados (Richardson), 14n4
Panamá Railroad: construction and completion of, 4, 23; French backing of, 16n15; illness and death during construction of, 15n9, 39–40; recruiting labor force for, 25, 27; segregated payment systems of, 32–33, 51n19; U.S. use of, 22; women workers on, 66
"The Panama Railway" (Senior), 14n4
Panamá Woman, 122n11, 197–214
Paquet, Sandra, 107, 122n14
Paraiso, Panamá, 30
Parkinson, Constantine, 88n22
Parks, Amos, 79
Patterson, Orlando, xiii
Pauncefote, Julian, 23
Pedro Miguel, Panamá, 30
penny dreadfuls, 42
Penters, Albert, 70

Pepperman, W. Leon, 26
Peters, Albert, 64, 66, 87n14
peuls, xviii
The Pleasures of Exile (Lamming), 93
Plummer, Enrique, 68, 71, 78, 86, 88n22
poeisis, xvii
poeticist school of Caribbean history, xii, xiii
Prescod, John, 83, 199
Priestly, J. B., 100

Quimby, B. C., 69
quinine, 87n16

race/color, defining categories of workers by, 8, 12, 76–77
Ramchand, Kenneth, 165n11, 165n16, 166n19, 167n24
Rastafarian religion, 110, 115
Red Tank, Panamá, 30
reggae music, 110, 115
rhygin, 115–18, 120, 123n22
Richards, John Altyman, 66
Richardson, Bonham, 14n4, 15n7–8, 40, 44, 51n24, 52n25, 63, 164n7, 200
"The Role of the Writer" (Condé), 171
Roosevelt, Theodore, 23, 48n5
rude bwai, 110, 115, 118

Salem Witch Trials, 3
Santa Cruz, Panamá, 30
sea-level canal, 49n11
Senior, Olive, xi, 5, 12, 14n4, 15n7, 52n24, 89n24, 120, 131, 142–47, 163n3, 200
shelling match, 119–20
silver, employee classification of, 32–33, 51n19–20
Silver City, Panamá, 30
Silver Man, 13n3
The Silver Men: West Indian Labour Migration to Panama (Newton), 14n4
slavery, xi, xiii, xxn2, 3, 8, 43, 56n40, 113
Smith, Walter D., 80
Sokoto Palisades, xviii
songs, 6, 12, 191–92n9, 200

"Songs of West Indian Negroes in the Canal Zone" (Cramer), 5, 47n1
South Africa, 23
Spain: canal workers from, 78; control of Panamá, 21, 22, 24
Spear, Thomas C., 193n15, 195n25
Spivak, Gayatri Chakravorty, xi, xvii–xviii
sports, hegemonic masculine norm of, 42
SS *Ancon*, 92
St. Kitts, canal workers from, xxin4
St. Lucia, canal workers from, 27, 64, 65, 70
St. Vincent, canal workers from, 64, 65
starvation, 72
Stevens, John, 15n9, 25, 61–62, 74
Stuhl, Ruth, 64
Suazo, Alfonso, 64
"Subjection" (Walrond), 148, 157
Suez Canal, 27
Susan Proudleigh (de Lisser), 5, 13, 200–210, 213n11
Swettenham, Alexander, 29

Taft, William, 29, 34, 62
Taylor, Patrick, 121n1, 121n8
teleopoesis, xvii
Texas, 22
Thelwell, Michael, xi, 5, 12, 93–95, 108–17, 122n9, 133, 147
Thomas, Donald, 86–87n13
Thomas, Fitz, 80
Thomas, Henry, 71
Thomas, J. J., xv
Thomas-Hope, Elizabeth, 37–38, 52n25, 53n27–28, 56n40, 163n2, 211
top-down history, 4, 14n4, 34, 35
Toucouleur language, xviii
"Tradition and the West Indian Novel" (Harris), 8–9
translation, influence of, xviii
Transvaal War, 89n25
Tree of Life: A Novel of the Caribbean (Condé), 5, 12–13, 162–63, 169–90, 195n24

Trinidad: canal workers from, 65, 80; labor riots in, 122n13; popular songs of, 6
Trojan powder, 80–81
Tropic Death (Walrond), 5, 12, 147–49
Twentieth Century Jamaica (de Lisser), 201–2, 205
typhoid fever, 79

United States: backing of Panamá Railroad, 4; canal workers from, 25, 77, 78; control of Panamá territory, 21–22; foreign policy in Caribbean and Latin America, 19–20, 26; ICC workers as dedicated mavericks, 26; preoccupation with the Panamá Canal, 21–34, 52n22–23
USS *Nashville*, 24

vodou/vodoun, xxiin11, 9, 167n23

Walcott, Derek, xiv, 121n1, 122n15
Walrond, Eric, xi, 5, 12, 120, 131, 147–61, 200
Watkins-Owens, Irma, 86n11
Western, George, 14n4
The West Indian in Panama: Black Labor in Panama (Lewis), 14n4

West Indian workers, *x*, 2, 14n5, 16n11, 65, 89n26, *126*
"The Wharf Rats" (Walrond), 148–49, 151, 153, 161
Wheatley, Simeon T., 86–87n13, 88n22
Who Built the Panama Canal? (Pepperman), 26
"Window" (Senior), 5, 12, 89n24, 120, 131, 142–47, 162, 200
Winner, Charles A., 2
women: African-Caribbean identity of, 165n11; in the Canal Zone population, 198–210, 211n2, 213–14n14; categories and roles of, xix, 8, 11, 12; in Colón Men's mythographies, 117–20, 131–62, 167n24, 175–90, 200–210; imported by ICC, 50n15, 130, 198; isthmian migration of, 13, 66; as Panamá Woman, 122n11, 197–214; as workers in the Canal Zone, 130–31, 197–210
Woolf, Virginia, xii
work songs, 191–92n9
Wynter, Sylvia, xii, xiii

yellow fever, 15n9, 68, 79, 179, 194n19

Zami: A New Spelling of My Name: A Biomythography (Lorde), 8

About the Author

Rhonda D. Frederick is Assistant Professor of English and teaches Caribbean and African American literatures at Boston College. She earned a BA, MA, and PhD in English from the University of Pennsylvania. Her research interests include American literatures, particularly twentieth-century women's popular fiction; literatures of the African Diaspora; Caribbean and postcolonial studies; cultural studies; and narratives of migration. Completion of this book project was made possible through a research fellowship funded by the NEH/Schomburg Center for Research in Black Culture (Harlem, New York).